Refugees and Religion

Also Available from Bloomsbury

Figurations and Sensations of the Unseen in Judaism, Christianity and Islam,
edited by Birgit Meyer and Terje Stordalen
Religion and the Global City, edited by David Garbin and Anna Strhan
The Religious Heritage Complex, edited by Cyril Isnart and Nathalie Cerezales

Refugees and Religion

Ethnographic Studies of Global Trajectories

Edited by
Birgit Meyer and Peter van der Veer

BLOOMSBURY ACADEMIC
LONDON · NEW YORK · OXFORD · NEW DELHI · SYDNEY

BLOOMSBURY ACADEMIC
Bloomsbury Publishing Plc
50 Bedford Square, London, WC1B 3DP, UK
1385 Broadway, New York, NY 10018, USA
29 Earlsfort Terrace, Dublin 2, Ireland

BLOOMSBURY, BLOOMSBURY ACADEMIC and the Diana logo are trademarks of
Bloomsbury Publishing Plc

First published in Great Britain 2021
Paperback edition published 2022

Cover design: Ben Anslow
Cover image © Birgit Meyer, Twelve posters from the guerrilla art project
A Paper Monument for the Paperless by Domenique Himmelsbach de Vries

Typeset by Deanta Global Publishing Services, Chennai, India

To find out more about our authors and books visit www.bloomsbury.com
and sign up for our newsletters

Contents

Illustrations

Figures

Tables

Preface

This volume emerged from two workshops, one in December 2017 and a second in September 2018, both at Utrecht University. As organizers and editors, we saw an urgent need to reflect on religion as an often-neglected dimension of refugees' itineraries; in multiple ways, religion plays a role in the reasons that made people flee, during their flight, and in the societies they have fled to. While our concerns to embark on this project were triggered by the so-called European refugee crisis of 2015, we thought that the long history of religious refugees in Europe put some doubt on the use of the notion of "crisis" in public debates, which wrongly suggests that the accommodation of large numbers of refugees would be a new phenomenon that calls for exceptional measures. Moreover, the focus on Europe in these debates, as well as in scholarly works, seemed to ignore the global nature of the issues involved. Distinctions between "migrant" and "refugee," between force and free choice, and between identity and its enunciation in legal procedures involve paradoxes and contradictions. These were addressed in our discussions during the works and in the volume, which includes a selection of reworked versions of the papers presented in our workshops.

We are grateful to everyone who participated in the discussions. We were helped in logistics and organized conviviality by several students: Pieter van der Woude, Saskia Huijgen, and Rashmi Shetty, and the team members of the research project "Religious Matters in an Entangled World" (funded by the Netherlands Foundation for Scientific Research—NWO—and the Royal Netherlands Academy of Arts and Sciences—KNAW). The secretarial staff, Julia Müller and Jie Zhang in Göttingen and Jeanette Boere in Utrecht, lent their full support to various aspects of the project. We are grateful to the Max Planck Institute for the Study of Religious and Ethnic Diversity in Göttingen and the Department of Philosophy and Religious Studies at Utrecht University for their financial support of the meetings and of the publication in Open Access. At Bloomsbury, we were cordially and efficiently guided by Lalle Pursglove, Lucy Carroll, Lily McMahon, and Dhanuja Ravi.

The cover image was photographed by Birgit Meyer in Amsterdam. The posting of woodcut portraits of undocumented refugees throughout public space in- and outside the European borders is organized by the political-artistic project "A Paper Monument for the Paperless," initiated by Domenique Himmelsbach the Vries;* we are thankful to Rebecca Wandke for alerting us to the people behind these pictures. The issue of the dehumanizing portrayal of refugees persists. As we write this, the refugee camp Moria on the Greek island Lesbos has been destroyed by fire, leaving thousands of persons waiting longer and longer to enter the asylum procedure, which is their legal right. Clearly, five years after 2015, the European borders have been rendered even more closed. The opening or closing of borders for certain groups of refugees, as this volume shows, is a matter of politics. With this volume, we hope to contribute to broadening the horizon of the public and scholarly debates about the issues at stake.

Amsterdam/Nijmegen, September 2020
Birgit Meyer and Peter van der Veer

---

* www.Himmelsbach.nl—see here for possibilities to participate or to support the project.

Introduction

Refugees and Religion

Peter van der Veer

The image of Aylan Kurdi, a three-year-old Syrian-Kurdish refugee, washed ashore on a Turkish beach in 2015 was spread widely by global media and shocked its viewers. It gave a human face to the "refugee crisis" that emerged from the war in Syria, a war that is still going on in 2020. In 2015, Europe was confronted with more than a million asylum seekers who took the land route from Turkey and walked in the direction of Germany. The majority came from war-torn Syria and Iraq, but there were also large numbers from other sites of violent conflict, such as Afghanistan, Sudan, and Somalia, as well as asylum seekers from relatively nearby Albania and Kosovo, from several countries in Africa, from Pakistan, and from other countries. They were not welcome in Eastern Europe, but they themselves had set their eyes on Germany, the economic powerhouse of the European Union. The ruling political parties in Germany, Christian Democrats and Social Democrats, initially welcomed these asylum seekers. A phrase by Chancellor Merkel "We can do it" (*Wir schaffen das*), perhaps inspired by Barack Obama's "Yes we can," captured a moment of national pride in what was optimistically called a German "culture of welcoming" (*Willkommenskultur*).

The period of empathy and welcome was short-lived. Germany witnessed the ascent of a right-wing, anti-immigrant party, the Alternative für Deutschland (AFD), which won 13.5 percent of the national vote in the 2018 general elections, and has a very strong presence in Eastern Germany, the former communist German Democratic Republic. France saw the rise of Marie Le Pen's Rassemblement National (the National Rally Party). In Italy, the Lega Nord adopted a fiercely anti-immigrant political stance. In the Netherlands, Geert Wilders's party and the more recent one led by Thierry Baudet are also strongly anti-immigrant parties. Anti-immigrant sentiments dominated the anti-Brexit referendum and its aftermath in Britain. Eastern European countries have shown themselves to be staunchly anti-immigrant, and the previously tolerant

Scandinavian countries have also moved in that direction. Since many refugees are Muslim, the anti-immigrant positions are often combined with anti-Islam rhetoric that, for instance, has resulted in anti-burqa policies in the Netherlands and elsewhere, following the earlier anti-headscarf policies in France.

These European developments form the backdrop against which this volume was brought together. It proposes that the refugee issue today is of central significance not only in past and present Europe but also in politics globally. The refugee problematic continues to dominate politics not only in Europe and the Middle East but also in the rest of the world. For instance, anti-immigration policies also form the core of the nationalist politics of the Republican Party in the United States. However, while much global media attention is given to what happens in the United States and Europe, the majority of the refugees actually flee from one country in the Global South to another. In a number of cases in the Global South, the United Nations High Commissioner for Refugees (UNHCR) plays a role in the setting up and maintaining of refugee camps, while this supranational body does not play a role in the Global North, where national authorities handle refugee matters. Far from being an isolated crisis, the 2015 movement of refugees toward Western Europe should be considered as merely a moment in a long history of forced, partly forced, and relatively unforced movement of people in Europe and the rest of the world (Gattrell 2019). Moreover, it cannot be considered as completely different from other forms of mobility, such as labor migration. Refugees are looking not only for safety but also for a future for themselves and their children. This volume places the 2015 moment in a longer history of the creation of nation-states and borders that produce and stop spatial mobility.

While it is clear that refugee politics relate to the formation of nation-states with territorial sovereignty, the connection between religion and refugees is seldom analyzed (recent exceptions being: Horstmann and Jung 2015b; Mavelli and Wilson 2017; Schmiedel and Smith 2018). It is the purpose of this volume to draw attention to the importance of ritual purification and ethnic cleansing in the historical formation of nation-states, as well as to the problematic of conversion and assimilation in dealing with refugees. This volume presents a collection of historical and ethnographic case studies of refugees and religion in Germany, Britain, the Netherlands, the United States, Vietnam, India, Uganda, and Morocco in order to highlight both the diversity of human predicaments and their shared problematics. These studies also represent two different moments in recent history: the Cold War and its aftermath and the 2015 refugee moment, while being prefaced by a deep historical perspective on Europe's experiences with religion and refugees.

From the start, we have to make clear that the definitional distinction between refugee and migrant is hugely important in both a political and a legal sense, but that we need to analyze the definitional process in a dynamic and contextual manner. Refugee stands for "a person who is forcibly displaced." This sounds straightforward, but it is not. There are differences in the use of "force" and differences in kinds of displacement, all to be understood contextually. Forced displacements happen everywhere on a daily basis, but migrant workers who are kicked out of their dwellings in "slum-clearings" in India or China are not regarded as refugees, because they are forcibly displaced *within* a nation-state. On the other hand, some people, like the Uyghur in China are, on the contrary, forcibly kept in their place, while their passports are taken away as well as their means of communication with the outside world. Many would be refugees if they could only move out. Legally, the distinction between migrant and refugee is pertinent, but the boundaries between these categories are arbitrary and dynamic. One notices, for instance, an increase in asylum requests when immigration becomes more and more difficult. In one's lifetime, one can move between the status of refugee and migrant, of resident and citizen. Nevertheless, asylum is a protection of a foreigner under threat (Fassin and Kobelinsky 2012: 444), and it is the legibility and truthfulness of this threat that is being assessed in juridical procedures in nation-states. Fassin and Kobelinsky show that in these procedures a shift from trust to suspicion has occurred, and that in France the acceptance rate has fallen from nine in ten to one in ten from 1980 to 2010.

In his writings on the Postcolony, Achille Mbembe (2003: 1) has argued that "the ultimate expression of sovereignty resides, to a large degree, in the power and the capacity to dictate who may live and who must die." Mbembe's concern is "those figures of sovereignty whose central project is not the struggle for autonomy but *the generalized instrumentalization of human existence and the material destruction of human bodies and populations*" (2003: 14; emphasis in original). Mbembe takes his cue from Foucault's notion of biopower and Agamben's notion of "the state of exception." This perspective on sovereignty leads us away from exceptionalist understandings of communist states as authoritarian and therefore radically different from the ideal nation-state, which is conceptualized in liberal political theory as founded not on authoritarian rule but on the rational deliberations of citizens (Rawls 1971). It understands the nature of sovereignty itself as rooted in violence rather than in rational choice that leads to a collective will. That violence is based on religious notions of purity and danger (Douglas 1966).

It is primarily the nation-state that defines subjects and citizens through law and law enforcement, but one needs to realize that a wide range of political formations take the nation-form, despite being far less formalized and centralized than is assumed in political theory. Social actors deal with what one could call the legal fiction of the nation-state and its bounded territory. When one flees from Syria, for instance, one does not flee from a nation-state but from a Hobbesian War of All against All. Syrian refugees go over land and cross seas that are only partly under the control of nation-states with arbitrary, shifting borders. They come to what promises to be the iron cage of European bureaucracy but what is in fact a shifting configuration of arbitrary rules and overwhelmed bureaucrats. The chaos of all of this under the semblance of order cannot be overestimated. The idea that a citizen is protected by the state she belongs to is part of the legal fiction of the nation-state. Some citizens are, and some are not. Muslims in India, Uyghurs in China, and Jews in Europe's recent past, all are unprotected citizens. The language of racial and religious purity is pervasive in all these cases.

The boundary between those who belong and those who do not, is determined, largely, by shifting state discourses about the religious and ethnic foundations of the nation. The Spanish word *nacion* of course refers to birth, but, in turn, birth refers to religion. One is only truly born when baptized. In 1492, Columbus records in his logbook that he sees the boats of Muslims and Jews leaving the shores of Spain while he goes out to discover the New World. This is a major epistemic shift in the history of the modern world, in which the religious purification of the nation and the expansion of that nation's religion over the world is combined. It is precisely the unending work of purification that gives ample scope to the Inquisition spreading to areas like the Philippines and Mexico, where Spanish or Portuguese power is established. The ruling elites in China and Japan, where Iberian power was not established, successfully resisted Christian salvation. At the same time, they themselves were perfectly capable to follow the Iberian example by purifying their nations from Christianity.

Purity and danger are the main elements of a symbolic repertoire that one finds in a wide range of ritual purifications at the individual and group level. They are crucial symbols in the campaigns of ethnic and religious cleansing that accompany the formation of nations in Europe. The anthropologist Mary Douglas (1966) has defined impurity as "matter out of place." I propose to extend that to "people out of place," displaced persons. Migrants who "do not belong" are not merely regarded as "outsiders," but also as dirty and dangerous, threatening the purity of those "who belong." Migrants themselves may have similar notions about the host society as threatening their cultural and religious purity.

The Reformation stands out as the first period in European and possibly global history in which the religious refugee becomes a mass phenomenon. The Jewish and Muslim refugees of fifteenth-century Spain were followed by the sixteenth-century Anabaptists, who settled everywhere, including Russia, the seventeenth-century Puritan Pilgrim Fathers, who settled in the United States, and the Huguenots, who settled in Holland and elsewhere, and, basically, everyone else in the several wars of religion that followed the Reformation. The Reformation was not just a movement of intellectual and religious change. It was also Europe's first grand project in social purification. It was deeply about exile, expulsion, and refugees. Forced religious migration was a normal, familiar, and expected feature of public policy that was oriented to build a cohesive society. The formula of *cuius regio, eius religio* (people have to follow the religion of their rulers) was a principle meant to stop warfare between Protestants and Catholics by expelling religious minorities, and thus making religiously homogenous regions. At the end of the Thirty Years War, in 1648, the Peace of Westphalia, meant to deal with religious minorities, was the origin of the modern system of nation-states (see te Brake in this volume). According to Jose Casanova (2019a: 14–15) the confessionalization of nation-states resulted in a split between Northern Europe that became homogeneously Protestant, Southern Europe that became homogeneously Catholic, with Holland, Germany, and Switzerland as nonconfessional societies.

According to the 1930 Hague Convention on Nationality Laws, "it is for each State to determine under its own law who are its nationals." Michael Walzer (1983), a prominent political theorist, argues that political sovereignty is the absolute right of territorial bounded states to determine who belongs to the nation and who is an alien. Two principles, often in combination, are applied to determine citizenship: *ius soli* (where are you born?) and *ius sanguinis* (who are your parents?). In German: *Blut und Boden* (blood and land). Bureaucracies of identification are built around the accident of birth, showing the continuity between ethnicity and modern nationhood. It is therefore not surprising that the term "naturalization" is used for the process of acquiring citizenship. The worldwide inequalities in which children are born are, obviously, among the main causes for spatial mobility of those who aspire to social mobility or just want to escape poverty. In the endless debates about nature or nurture, it is never mentioned how much the simple fact of one's birth in a particular society determines one's life chances (Shachar 2009). Nevertheless, at first sight, the principles of *Blut und Boden* appear to be unavoidable. It seems perfectly reasonable to deny access to intruders whether this concerns your own house or the nation's territory. The problem, however, is not that one wants to keep outsiders out, but that one may also want to kick out those who are inside, as if they are not genuine members of the household or of the nation. These two desires are in fact connected. Borders are conceptualized as located at the edge of territory, but as an institutional practice of boundary making, they are located everywhere within and outside of the territory, sometimes occasioning ethnic and religious cleansing.

The Universal Declaration of Human Rights was proclaimed by the United Nations General Assembly in Paris on December 10, 1948. According to Article 14, everyone has the right to seek and to enjoy in other countries asylum from persecution. In 1951 the Geneva Convention, restricting itself to European refugees of the Second World War, codified the rights of refugees. In 1967 a protocol was added which removed this geographical and historical restriction and made the convention universally applicable.

The universality of the convention raises the intricate question of what is a human being. A human as a natural being needs to be distinguished from what is a citizen. A citizen has rights that are guaranteed by the sovereign nation-state that has made him or her a citizen. The individual who is the bearer of rights and obligations is produced at the same time as "we, the people" who are the subject of the nation-state. In that way the state is totalizing and individualizing at the same time. If indeed the idea of the sovereign individual goes together with that of the sovereign state, we need to determine what the appeal to "the international community" and its protection of human values means. Is there an "international community" that guarantees human rights in the same way as the nation-state guarantees the rights of citizens? We do not think so. There are different under-standings in different traditions in the world about what constitutes a human, and thus there are different communities carrying these divergent traditions. Even in the liberal tradition there are distinctions made between combatants and civilians, allies and enemies, children and adults. So, the question is which international community is envisaged in relation to which tradition of human rights. Is it the Muslim Umma or the Pax Christiana, or the Western democratic world? Moreover, who or what is the guarantor of these rights? The fact is that even if there would be an international community (a "family of man" so to say), it is the national sovereign state only that has the power to guarantee rights. This also implies that there has to be a narrative that authorizes particular claims and rejects others. That narrative needs to be in some way related to the narration of the nation.

For example, in the United States, the International Religious Freedom Act of 1998 says the following:

> The right to freedom of religion undergirds the very origin and existence of the United States. Many of our Nation's founders fled religious persecution abroad, cherishing in their hearts and minds the ideal of religious freedom. They established in law, as a fundamental right and as a pillar of our Nation, the right to freedom of religion. From its birth to this day, the United States has prized this legacy and honored this heritage by standing for religious freedom and offering refuge to those suffering religious persecution.

This act requires that the United States enforces religious freedom everywhere in the world. It is striking how the narrative of the emergence of the United States as a place of refuge to those who fled religious persecution is tied to the narrative of the United States as a guarantor of religious freedom globally. At the same time it is striking that this act has been implemented, for example, by requiring the State Department to report annually on religious persecution globally with an almost exclusive focus on the persecution of Christians, and not, for example, Muslims. This is just one example of the way the narration of the nation is tied to the narrative of who can be recognized by the state as a refugee. Different nations obviously have different narrations that need to be unpacked.

The other aspect of refugees and religion that this volume is dealing with is that of religious conversion and cultural assimilation. This is the flipside of ethnic cleansing and religious purification, since these are processes to force refugees to change their religion and culture into that of the host society or make it fit the secular framework of that society (Asad 2003). Many refugees are, in fact, already persecuted minorities in the countries of origin, like Jews in many countries in Europe, Syrian Christians, Muslim Burmese, and others. They had to flee to avoid being either killed or converted. In the receiving countries, they are again confronted with discourses and practices that are meant to make them change particular parts of their culture (see, for Syrian Orthodox, Heleen Murre-van den Berg in this volume). If they convert or assimilate that change is often considered "not sincere" and doubtful (see William Wheeler in this volume). One striking historical example is that of the Marranos in Spain, Jews who were forced to convert to Christianity in the sixteenth century but were suspected by the Inquisition to secretly continue to practice Judaism. In the twentieth century, race laws have replaced religious laws, but with similar effect. Jewish *Bildungsbürger*, totally assimilated in Germany and often converted to Christianity, were determined to be just hiding their essential Jewishness and were stripped from their citizenship. In 1943, Hanna Arendt writes about Jewish refugees who fled from Germany to France, England, or the United States. Despite the fact that they were not any longer considered fellow-citizens in Germany and had fled the country, the French, British, and American authorities immediately treated them as German citizens and put them in camps as "enemy aliens." Hanna Arendt describes with biting irony the absurd predicament of these Jewish refugees by quoting one Jewish leader who said: "We were good Germans in Germany, therefore we shall be good Frenchmen in France."

Europe and Refugees

In the first two chapters of this volume, the focus is on European history. Wayne te Brake and Peter van der Veer deal with the long history of religious wars and nation-state formation in Europe. They show the connection between the history of mobility in early modern Europe with that of religious purification. The Reformation resulted in a number of religious wars and forced migrations. Te Brake focuses on three important developments: the dislocation of refugees in the context of religious strife, the accommodation of newcomers into their places of refuge, and the survival of dissidents who were not able or willing to seek refuge elsewhere. Altogether, these three developments provide insights into the relationship between religious conflict and the production and accommodation of vulnerable religious migrants.

Van der Veer examines in detail the interconnected history of refugees and nation building in Germany from the early modern period until today. His focus is on the situation of those who fled for the Red Army at the end of the Second World War. Around seventeen million Europeans were on the move which was the cause for drafting the 1951 Geneva Convention for refugees. He also addresses some theoretical issues that are central to this volume, such as the nature of humanitarianism and the role of history in shaping humanitarian motivations. He proposes that ultimately an ethical position has to be based on political analysis and choice.

People on the Move from Vietnam

One of the most significant flows of refugees after the Second World War was from Vietnam, Laos, and Cambodia after the victory of North Vietnam in 1975. Americans had fought on the side of South Vietnam in a civil war against North

Vietnam that was supported by the Soviet Union and China. South Vietnamese tried to flee to the West after the North Vietnamese victory, while Chinese-Vietnamese were expelled around the Sino-Vietnamese war in 1979. Phi-Vân Nguyen brings us back to the 1954 exodus of Catholic refugees from North to South Vietnam after the communist victory against the French in the 1954 Battle of Dien Bien Phu, which resulted in the designation of the famous seventeenth parallel as the dividing line between the communist North and the capitalist South. In the 300 days that allowed civilians to opt for which zone they wanted to live in, more than 800,000 civilians, of which 80 percent were Catholics, left their home in the North for the South. Van Nguyen examines in detail the complexities and contradictions of Catholic politics that was involved in this first refugee crisis in Vietnam itself. In 1998, the French image of an apparition of the Virgin Mary in Vietnam, Our Lady of Lavang, was replaced with a Vietnamese image that has become very popular among refugee communities all over the world. Thien-Huong Ninh shows how this image has captured the transnational imaginations of Catholic Vietnamese communities. Janet Hoskins examines the development of Caodai and of Dau Mau trance dance in diasporic communities. While transnational Caodai networks concentrate in "little Saigons" in the United States, Canada, Australia, and France, the transnational Dao Mau networks concentrate on "little Hanois" in Eastern Europe. She shows the impact of forced migration on the theologies and ritual practices of these two forms of Vietnamese religion. She shows the interaction between experiences of mobility and their narrativization in ways that are comparable to what Alessandro Gusman finds in Kampala among Pentecostal Congolese refugees. Tam Ngo and Nga Mai explore yet another Vietnamese diasporic religious development, namely Buddhism in Berlin. They show that the opposition between North Vietnam and South Vietnam is a determining factor in the development of different kinds of Buddhism among the Vietnamese in Germany who were either boat refugees in former West Germany or contract laborers in former East Germany. These chapters on the Vietnamese show the different pathways of refugees and migrants that are intricately tied up with religious options.

People on the Move in and from Africa

The experiences of refugees in the spaces in which they are temporarily settled is immensely varied. Alessandro Gusman describes Urban Congolese refugees in the Ugandan capital Kampala. This is a mostly young population, because many of the elders have been killed. They try to live an ordinary life while hoping for a way to return to the Congo or leave for Europe. It is not international relief organizations but Pentecostal churches that offer them support. Such support is mainly of a religious nature. Gusman shows how the biblical narratives provided by Pentecostalism make it possible for refugees to make sense of their experience.

Johara Berriane describes West African migrants who are on their way to Europe, but are held up in Morocco because of the hardening of Europe's external borders. They bring a new element in the religious landscape of Muslim Morocco by introducing Pentecostal house churches. Berriane did ethnographic research among two Congolese and three Ivorian house churches and describes ways of placemaking in the in-between space between the country of origin and the European destination. She shows how people whose lives are unmoored and who have an unclear sense of what the future may bring for them find new roles and functions in the churches, engaging them in a religiously active life while waiting for a "deliverance."

A quite different urban context is that of Berlin. Abdoulaye Sounaye describes the predicament of West African Muslims, many of whom came to Germany after the collapse of the Gadhafi regime in Libya. In the face of mounting discrimination against Africans—both from within and from outside of the larger Muslim community in Berlin—they seek to create spaces for worship and community in which they feel safe and supported. This is strikingly different from the Vietnamese Buddhists in Berlin described by Mai and Ngo whose placemaking is dependent on internal Vietnamese dynamics rather than a response to discrimination by outsiders.

Political Spaces of Reception

Heleen Murre-van den Berg brings us from African refugees to Syrian Christians who have settled in Europe. She describes the predicament of Syriac Orthodox in Europe not so much in terms of placemaking, but in terms of text making. It is the subtle transformation of textual traditions that are perhaps less a sign of secularization within the European context than a conscious choice to downplay ethnic differences in relation to a shared religious identity. It is precisely in textual practices that one can see how the church's leadership tries to find a place in diasporic circumstances.

When one thinks of refugees, one thinks of camps in which they are gathered for transitional living. Alexander-Kenneth Nagel describes such a camp, Friedland near Göttingen in the German state of Lower Saxony, that has been a transit camp since the Second World War. Initially, the camp was meant for Germans from Eastern Europe, many of them fleeing for the Russian Red Army (see van der Veer in this volume). Even today, it is a transit camp for late emigrants (*Spätaussiedler*) as well as Jews from the former Soviet Union. Since the 1979s, however, other refugee groups, such as Chileans, Vietnamese, and recently many nationalities from the Middle East have come to stay in the camp. Nagel examines the religious configuration of the camp, materially built around Catholic and Protestant chapels, in the light of institutional secularism. The recent inflow of various kinds of Muslims and Christians from West and South Asia poses particular problems in both material and intentional sense for the officials of the camp who are Nagel's research subject.

A very different kind of camp is described in Salah Punathil's paper on the conflict between indigenous groups and Muslims in the Indian state of Assam. These are relief camps for Muslims who fled their villages during anti-Muslim pogroms. They were meant to be temporary but solidified into permanence to the extent that they themselves have become targets of large-scale violence. Punathil analyzes in detail the intricate history of Muslims in the area during colonialism, the Partition between India and Pakistan, and the 1971 emergence of Bangladesh. Within this tumultuous history, there is an often-neglected story of an indigenous group, the Bodos, who seek an independent homeland by attacking Muslim immigrants. Punathil shows that while the state is centrally involved in the refugee problematic, antagonist ethnic groups have their own agenda.

The role of the state in adjudicating citizenship, civil rights, refugee status, and religious rights is of central importance of much of the analysis in this volume. In the chapters by Nagel, and Wheeler, however, the state is disaggregated to the level of officials who have discretionary power. William Wheeler gives a detailed critical analysis of how British judges come to decisions about refugees who cite religious reasons for their claim to refugee status. He describes a secular culture of suspicion that leads judges to doubt the sincerity of religious conversion of the claimants. While Nagel's chapter deals with the ways in which the German state deals with religious diversity, Wheeler's chapter deals with some questions of authority and sincerity in the British judicial process that have always been central to religious conversion.

Part I

Politics of Religious Plurality
in Europe

War, Forced Migration, and the Politics of Religious Diversity

Wayne P. te Brake

Today we are acutely aware of the many ways that the flows of migration caused by the disruptions of civil and international war can roil the politics of both citizenship and religious diversity. From the Balkan Wars in the 1990s through the "terrorist" attacks on New York, Washington, D.C., Madrid, and London, and the ongoing civil wars in Afghanistan, Syria, and Yemen, the agents of violent political conflict have recurrently invoked religious identities to mark their enemies as well as their allies. In doing so, they have underscored the entanglement of religious differences with the forced migrations that their conflicts have occasioned. While such clusters of religious conflict are relatively rare historically, they are not unprecedented.

In the century and a half following Martin Luther's challenge to the Latin Christian Church in 1517, a variety of political actors who had ready access to violent means—kings, princes, magistrates, militia leaders, or warlords—responded to the "problems" associated with the transnational process of religious pluralization, which we often label "The Reformation," by deploying violence and unleashing the coordinated destruction of war. In my recent work on *Religious War and Religious Peace in Early Modern Europe* (2017), I identified six major clusters of religious war in the period 1529 to 1651 as well as six major episodes of forced migration between 1527 and the end of the seventeenth century.

This European historical record is valuable both because it is well documented and because we know how the stories end. My concern as a social and political historian has been to tell these stories of religious conflict and social disruption, correctly and dispassionately, paying close attention to getting the details right—that is, describing what actually happened during Europe's Age of Religious War and identifying, to the extent possible, the full range of historical actors who made it happen. At the same time, as a social scientist, I have tried to discern recurrent patterns and to explain how and why these patterns unfolded the way they did. To that end, I have identified a limited number of mechanisms that recurrently combined to move broader processes of historical change with a limited range of outcomes.[1] Here I will focus on demonstrating a rhetorical and analytic strategy for understanding recurrent historical phenomena.

While most of Europe's infamous religious wars ended with political compromises that validated religious diversity, decisive military victories, which were relatively few and generally short-lived, recurrently resulted in deep religious polarization and massive social dislocations, including forced migrations. This chapter reexamines Europe's bitter experience of religious war and forced migration, focusing on three recurrent developments: (1) the dislocation of refugees in the context of religious strife; (2) the accommodation of newcomers in their places of refuge; and (3) the survival of dissidents who were not able or willing to seek refuge elsewhere. Altogether, these three developments provide valuable insights into the recurrently fraught relationship

Table 1.1 The Principal Clusters of Religious War in Early Modern Europe

War	Inclusive Dates	Military Outcome or Peace Settlement
Kappel Wars (Swiss Confederation)	1529–31	National Peace (*Landfrieden*) of Kappel (1529), Second National Peace of Kappel (1531)
Schmalkaldic Wars (Holy Roman Empire)	1545–55	Peace of Nürnberg (1532), Augsburg Interim (1548), Treaty of Passau (1552), Religious Peace (*Religionsfriede*) of Augsburg (1555)
Civil/Religious Wars (France)	1562–1629	Separate Edicts ended each of the nine wars, starting with the Edict of Amboise (1563); the most successful was the Edict of Nantes (1598)
Eighty Years War (Low Countries)	1568–1648	The Pacification of Ghent (1576), Peace of Religion (1578), Twelve Year Truce (1609–21), and the (first) Treaty of Münster, which was part of the Peace of Westphalia (1648)
Thirty Years War (Holy Roman Empire)	1618–48	The Peace of Prague (1635); the Treaty of Osnabrück and the (second) Treaty of Münster, which were part of the Peace of Westphalia (1648)
British Civil Wars (Scotland, Ireland, and England)	1638–51	No formal settlement; war ended in England with the capture, trial, and execution of Charles I (1649); war ended in Ireland and Scotland with Cromwell's military campaigns (1649–51); monarchy restored in 1660

Source: Created by Wayne P. te Brake.

between religious conflict and the production/accommodation/survival of vulnerable religious populations.

First, let me introduce the broad outlines of the historical context.[2] Table 1.1 identifies the six principal clusters of religious war in the post-Reformation era and indicates how and when they ended.

To make a very long story short, let me suggest that the history of these wars has taught me that religious peace is always possible, even after the most destructive wars, though ending war can be very hard work. Negotiated *religious* settlements (as in the Swiss, German, and French cases) could be very helpful, but they quite readily failed if they were not accompanied by the demilitarization of the religious parties to the conflict. Negotiated *political* settlements (as in the Eighty Years War) and even *decisive military victories* (as in the British Monarchies) that did not entail religious agreements could also make religious peace possible, as long as they brought a durable end to the coordinated destruction of war. What these diverse settlements had in common, then, was something we might call *grudging consent*, in the sense that the forces in conflict agreed, reluctantly in all cases, that more war would be fruitless—that the ongoing coordinated destruction of war was the problem, not the solution to the problem of religious pluralization.

Table 1.2 Forced Migrations in Early Modern Europe

Original Location	Time frame	Refugee populations	Destinations
Swiss Confederation (Zürich, Bern, St. Gallen)	Sixteenth to eighteenth centuries	Anabaptists	Moravia, the Low Countries, North America
Southern Netherlands	Beginning in the 1560s, but especially after 1585	Anabaptists, Calvinists	Emden, Wesel, London, United Provinces
Bohemia	After 1620	Brethren, Utraquists, Lutherans, Calvinists	Saxony, Poland, Hungary, United Provinces, Sweden
Ireland (east of the Shannon River)	1650s	Catholics	Western province of Connaught
France	Beginning in the 1660s, but especially after 1685	Calvinists (Huguenots)	Switzerland, Rhineland Germany, the Dutch Republic, England, Ireland, North America
Salzburg (Prince-Bishopric)	The 1680s and the 1730s	Lutherans	Adjacent territories. Saxony, Prussian Lithuania, North America

Source: Created by Wayne P. te Brake.

Though I have not made a systematic study of forced migrations, I offer this summary of the principal flows of migration that I covered in my recent work (Table 1.2). This historical record, while less familiar to most of us, is nevertheless very instructive when juxtaposed with the more familiar record of approximately 130 years of episodic religious war.

Today we are likely to associate massive flows of religious refugees with dislocations and upheavals caused by civil and international warfare; this was also the case in the forced migrations within and from the Southern Netherlands, Bohemia, and Ireland (in the middle of my list). Each of these was predicated on the authoritarian claims of recently "victorious" rulers—the Spanish Habsburgs following their reconquest of the provinces and cities of the Southern Netherlands in the early phase of what eventually became an Eighty Years War; the Austrian Habsburgs following their victory at White Mountain in the first phase of what ended up being a Thirty Years War; and the British Commonwealth government following the defeat of the revolutionary Confederates in Ireland.

By contrast, the first example and the last two, in Switzerland, France, and Salzburg, are not immediately related to the dislocations of religious war. In the Swiss Confederation, the active persecution and the subsequent internal dislocation and eventual exodus of Anabaptists—more precisely, the Swiss Brethren—began in 1527, before the first of the two Kappel Wars, when the cities of Zürich, Bern, and St. Gallen concluded a "Concordat" that was intended to rid their territories of persons they considered dangerous radicals. In France, the exodus of Huguenots began following many decades of peaceful religious coexistence when the government of King Louis XIV began to misuse and eventually revoked the provisions of the Edict of Nantes. And the exodus from Salzburg began well after the Peace of Westphalia offered protection to religious minorities, when the prince-bishops expelled a small group of Lutheran "dissenters" from Tyrol in the 1680s and, then, some 20,000 Lutherans from the Pongau in 1731.

Learning from History

So how can this history of religious war and forced migration help us to think about the troubled relationship between refugees and religion today? To be sure, the history of post-Reformation Europe will not simply be repeated today in the Middle East, Africa, South Asia, or even Europe and North America. But there are important perceptual and analytic cues we can learn from this kind of broadly comparative history. Here I will focus on the principal actors and the dynamics of their interactions in relation to the production of religious refugees; the accommodation of religious newcomers into their places of refuge; and the survival of religious dissidents who could not seek refuge elsewhere. I will look at each of these in turn.

Even this brief review of the European historical context suggests who the principal actors were in the production of religious refugees: on the one hand, rulers, ranging from well-established authorities to rival claimants to political authority in revolutionary situations, who privileged one religious group over other alternatives in religiously diverse polities, and, on the other hand, "dissident" subjects—that is, people who chose religious beliefs, practices, or affiliations that were different from those privileged by their rulers. Figure 1.1

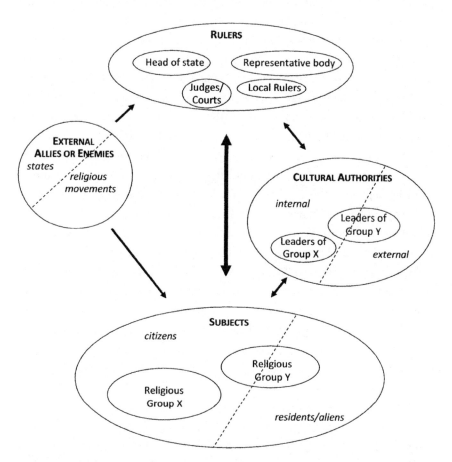

Figure 1.1 Principal actors in the history of religious conflict/coexistence. Created by Wayne P. te Brake.

shows how these actors fit into a larger array of political actors within complex political contexts.

Since religiously diverse rulers and subjects are not always in conflict, it is important to sort out the dynamics that lead toward conflict, violence, war, and, in exceptional cases, mass migrations. Because Europe's principal migrations were not always linked to the coordinated destruction of war, it is important to recognize what distinguished them from other religious conflicts. As I see it, what all of these cases had in common is that they were forceful expressions of *official religious intolerance* and, as such, they were the result of profoundly authoritarian political actions, in alliance with specific religious authorities, in situations where religious dissidents were powerless to counteract the (threat of) coercive force. In each case, rulers attempted to achieve religious "unity and purity" within their political domains by demanding conformity from all their subjects, under the threat of harm or expulsion (cf. Terpstra 2015).

If official intolerance was the sine qua non of the forced religious migration process and experience, it was hardly the whole story or the end of the story. Official intolerance necessarily forced religious dissidents, either explicitly or implicitly, to make choices. In some cases, like the Southern Netherlands and Bohemia, the triumphant rulers ordered their dissident subjects either to conform to the reestablished Catholic religion or to leave. In Ireland, Catholics east of the Shannon River were faced with the choice of either converting to Protestantism (under the Commonwealth there was no established version of Protestantism) or being deprived of their property and deported to Connaught, on the barren western periphery. In France, by contrast, the royal government pressured religious dissenters to conform to the established Catholic religion—in part, by annulling their marriages and by placing their children in the care of Catholic families!—but forbade them from leaving the kingdom. In all these cases, we have evidence that some "dissenters" did choose to conform to established religious practices, while many others chose to leave, even in France where this was expressly forbidden. In addition, I want to highlight a third alternative: the decision of many religious dissenters, under conditions of official repression, not to conform to the religious practices of the established religion and to remain "illegally" where they were. We will return to their experience in a moment.

The forced religious migrations in early modern Europe were smaller than the forced religious migrations we have seen in recent history—hundreds, thousands, and hundreds of thousands rather than millions of people—but they had an enormous impact on both the sending countries and the places where they found refuge. In the largest migrations—from the Southern Netherlands,

Bohemia, and France—the sending countries lost the human capital of relatively well-educated and commercially active populations, and in some places, like Antwerp, urban populations were reduced by half. Meanwhile, in the places of refuge, the experience of dislocation and the process of accommodating newcomers varied considerably in relation to religious differences among the migrants and the structures of political authority and patterns of religious diversity they encountered. In terms of the constellation of political actors I identified in Figure 1.1, the migration process effectively transformed the "external allies or enemies" on the left side of the figure into the rulers and local allies/competitors of the migrant groups in the places of refuge.

Let me begin with the patterns of religious coexistence and the structures of religious/political authority that the migrants encountered in the places of refuge. In my work on religious peace, I developed a new typology of religious coexistence that comprehends the broad variety of historical experience and incorporates the religious politics of rulers as well as relative visibility/salience of the religious identities of their diverse subjects in public life. Table 1.3 explicates briefly the terms I have used to describe the most common relationships.

Table 1.3 Types of Religious Coexistence in Early Modern Europe

Type	Characteristics	Examples
Confessional Parity	Multiple groups share responsibility for and access to the public domain	Shared churches in Germany, France, and the Low Countries; multi-confessional German cities; Swiss Thurgau
Political Integration	No dominant group; all are integrated into public life regardless of religious affiliation	Kingdom of France (under the Edict of Nantes); German imperial politics; Swiss confederal politics
Repression	Dominant group actively prohibits religious differences	Habsburg domains (Spain and Austria); France after 1685; Ireland; some constituents of the German Empire and Swiss Confederation
Confessional Privilege	Dominant group does not enforce uniformity; imposes restrictions/costs on diversity	Dutch Republic; Great Britain; some constituents of the German Empire and Swiss Confederation
Ad Hoc Tolerance	Specific exceptions are made to exclusionary rules	Jewish communities in London, Metz, Amsterdam and Hamburg; Jewish and Orthodox Christian communities in the Ottoman Empire; Merchant communities in commercial cities; Embassy chapels

Source: Created by Wayne P. te Brake.

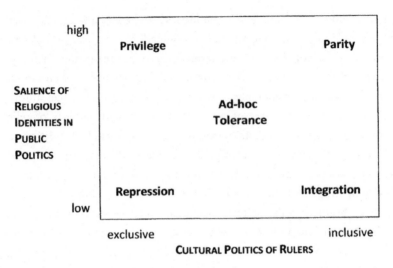

Figure 1.2 Variable patterns of religious coexistence. Created by Wayne P. te Brake.

Figure 1.2 represents this variation graphically.

What I offer, then, is a simple conceptual map of the variable patterns of religious peace I found in early modern Europe; though these terms are derived from European history, I believe they are also usefully descriptive of variations that are evident today.

So how can this help us to think about the process of accommodating religious newcomers in the places of refuge? At first blush, it might seem likely that officially inclusive regimes, located on the right side of Figure 1.2, might be most readily receptive of religious refugees. As it happens, however, the carefully negotiated compromises that recurrently make official inclusion possible can become rigid and resistant to religiously different newcomers, who might disrupt the compromises and threaten to alter delicate balances among competitive groups. By comparison, officially exclusive regimes that do not prosecute "dissenters" (in the upper left quadrant of my conceptual map) have proved to be capable of absorbing and accommodating large numbers of relatively diverse migrants, often by making ad hoc exceptions to otherwise operative rules of exclusion. Here the examples of the Dutch Republic and the German territory of Saxony are instructive.[3] Both of these regimes were officially exclusive—in the early sixteenth century, the Electors of Saxony broke with Rome and privileged the official Lutheran Church; at the end of the sixteenth century, during the Dutch Revolt against Spain, all of the provinces of the Dutch Republic recognized the Reformed (Calvinist) Church as the exclusive "public" church—but they both absorbed repeated waves of forced religious migration. Still, the experience of settlement in a place of refuge varied considerably, depending on both the nature of the host regime and the religious identities of the migrants.[4]

In the diverse Dutch territories that emerged as a loose independent confederation during the Eighty Years War, each province had the authority to regulate its own religious affairs, which gave local authorities considerable latitude to accommodate religious differences, but the Union of Utrecht, which served as the framework for their confederation, explicitly guaranteed freedom of religious conscience. Thus, from the mid-sixteenth century through the end of the seventeenth century, the Low Countries and eventually the Dutch Republic famously provided refuge to successive waves of both Anabaptist/ Mennonite and Calvinist migrants from Switzerland, the Southern Netherlands, Bohemia, and France. Each of these groups had long-standing allies who were willing to advocate for and assist in the resettlement of their coreligionists, but in general, it is safe to say that cities were more receptive to the outsiders than the countryside, and Calvinists were more readily accepted by the official "public" church than the Anabaptist/Mennonite refugees who, like their very numerous Dutch coreligionists, were expected to keep a low profile and to worship in spaces that did not resemble traditional churches.

By comparison, in the early sixteenth century, the Electors of Saxony had undertaken an exclusive "Lutheran" reformation, though the actual transformation of religious practices throughout the territory was a slow and incomplete process that left (largely invisible) remnants of Catholic worship. In the first quarter of the seventeenth century, however, this bastion of Lutheran orthodoxy received a flood of refugees from neighboring Bohemia as a result of the defeat of the Protestant-led Bohemian revolt against their staunchly Catholic Habsburg overlords. In very short order, the religious landscape of "orthodox" Lutheran Saxony underwent a dramatic transformation, and Saxony's rulers, both civil and religious authorities, were forced to accommodate a dizzying variety of Protestant "guests"—not just Lutherans, but Calvinists and the distinctively Bohemian "Brethren" and "Utraquists." After the Peace of Westphalia brought an end to the Thirty Years War, it became clear the non-Lutheran guests would not be leaving Saxony, much to the chagrin of the Lutheran authorities. Despite official objections from the exclusive established church, however, the dissenting guests were able to use the legal provisions of the Peace—in particular, the freedom of religious conscience—to secure a permanent and visible place in a significantly more diverse Saxony. Not surprisingly, the next wave of forced migrants to enter Saxony—the Lutheran dissenters of Salzburg—were more readily accommodated in this no-longer overwhelmingly Lutheran territory.

All in all, the experience of forced religious migration varied considerably, depending both on the religious identities of the migrants and on the existing patterns of religious affiliation within the places of refuge. From the refugees' point of view, having coreligionists who were willing/able to assist them was a great advantage, even when their local allies were "dissenters" within a regime of religious privilege. Still, even refugees whose faith was regarded as "foreign" or "heretical" were accommodated as "dissenters," who usually had to keep a low profile to avoid further trouble. In some cases, religious refugees eventually migrated even further from their homelands, like the French-speaking Calvinists (Huguenots), who fled to the German Rhineland and from there to the New World (e.g., South Carolina, New York, and Canada), and the Lutherans, who were expelled from Salzburg and ended up in the new English colony of Georgia.

But what is the experience of those who are not willing or able to flee the persecution of intolerant rulers? Here again, historical experience is instructive. What emerges clearly from my work on early modern Europe is that systematic repression was always a costly failure that inflicted enormous harm but never succeeded in eliminating religious diversity. In order to underscore the powerful agency of religious "dissenters," allow me to explicate what I see as the principal "subversive" mechanisms that enable survival under conditions of repression. While these are considerations that may not seem particularly germane to the questions of this volume on refugees, they are important for our understanding the problem of forced religious migrations in their full complexity. In addition, these dynamic mechanisms are important for understanding the "survival" of refugees who are not particularly welcomed, and sometimes considered dangerous, in the places where they seek refuge.

The most obvious of these survival mechanisms is *secrecy*. In situations of active repression of dissent, maintaining collective secrecy and worshiping clandestinely or privately is essential to the dissenting community's survival, but secrecy, even when an urgent necessity, is never absolute. As Benjamin Kaplan (2002) has shown, in a broad range of settings, the "privacy" of dissenting worship or devotion can be an elaborate fiction or a useful façade that is acceptable to both sides in order to keep up appearances and to maintain good order. Still, trying to be invisible is a recurrent feature of the experience of persecuted minorities that, over time, can become an essential element of dissident identities.

For individual dissenters, *dissimulation* or hiding under the false appearance of conformity can be a necessary means of not standing out and thus avoiding persecution. From the perspective of persecuting authorities, by the same token, dissimulation was perceived as a perennial and especially insidious threat to the privileged community's unity and purity. In the Southern Netherlands, members of the clandestine Calvinist Church not only hid their dissent under the nominal conformity of occasional attendance at the Mass but also presented their children for baptism, especially when a Calvinist pastor was not available. But the local priests were apparently not fooled to the extent that they identified these children as illegitimate in the parish registers.

Then there is *casuistry*, by which I mean to identify unauthorized adjustments to the strict demands of religious purity. In order to cope with the exigencies of persecution, dissenting communities frequently make ideological/theological adjustments in order to rationalize their failure to meet the strictest norms of public witness and ritual purity. I borrow the term "casuistry" from Marc Furner's (1998) careful reconstruction of Anabaptist survival in the Swiss Emmental to describe this largely defensive mechanism employed by clergy and laymen alike. The Catholics of Ireland, for example, developed or adapted a wide range of popular devotional practices, especially the ritual "patterns" that were associated with holy wells and certain pilgrimage sites, that looked profoundly suspect to the Counter-Reformation Church as well as the Protestant rulers of Ireland (Carroll 1999).

Clandestine communities of faith recurrently turned to *private education* in order to counteract official indoctrination and to pass on to future generations the essentials of a dissenting tradition. Women frequently played significant educational roles, not only within the household but also in the so-called hedge schools of the Irish Catholics. Likewise, "education in the Word of God" was explicitly stated as the core mission of formally trained pastors sent to the underground Flemish churches from the Reformed Classes of Zeeland in the Dutch Republic.

These four mechanisms recurrently alter the relations between dissenters or dissenting communities and the multiple claimants to political and cultural authority over them. But the "survival" of dissenting religious communities is never a solo performance, and any account of religious coexistence under circumstances of active persecution is likely to involve the kindness of strangers as well as neighbors—that is, of historical actors who stand outside the dissenting community as such. Here I should like to highlight three additional mechanisms that are recurrently evident in the histories of survival in early modern Europe.

Let me start with *indifference*. Policies of strict intolerance of religious diversity invariably require "good citizens" to avoid contact with and to report the deviant behavior of religious dissenters. Given the practical limits of secrecy or invisibility, simple indifference by outsiders to the religious differences that authorities condemn can be a powerful brake on repression (Schwartz 2008). By extension, the more explicit refusal of neighbors, friends, or even relatives to avoid contact with or report "others," often at their own peril, is a recurrent feature of the stories that sites of dissident memory, as well as official archives, reveal to us (Furner 1998).

In addition, no comprehensive regime of repression can be sustained or effective without the active participation of local officials, who are expected to enforce proscriptions from above. Yet, the history of Swiss Anabaptists and Irish Catholics is replete with local officials who either failed to follow orders or actively protected "their" dissidents, who might be friends, relatives, or neighbors (Power and Whelen 1990). In the Southern Netherlands, local officials recurrently subverted the "national" policy of strict religious uniformity by negotiating and/or accepting informal bargains that traded safety for Calvinists in the South for the "freedom" of Catholics across the border in the Dutch Republic. Repressive authorities frequently derided this kind of subversion or inaction as "*connivance*" with the forces of evil.

Over time, temporary compromises may become durable forms of religious coexistence, which may, in turn, be actively defended as essential attributes of the health and prosperity of the whole community (Kaplan 2007). This was not always the case, to be sure: familiarity does not always beget sympathy or understanding. In fact, durable forms of coexistence almost always beget durable forms of inequality, which might then become flash points for conflict under conditions of stress. Yet, when it did happen, the active defense of specific, local accommodations of religious difference may not rise to the level of a coherent philosophy or policy of *toleration*, but it surely did serve mightily to underwrite the assertion of official toleration by the end of the early modern period.

Thinking with History

As I suggested earlier, the history of post-Reformation Europe will not simply be repeated today; rather than looking for historical replication, then, we should practice thinking with history. By this I want to underscore the difference between a relatively static perception of where we are and a dynamic understanding of how we got to be where we are. With regard to the topic of this volume—refugees and religion—thinking with (European) history entails two kinds of *historical recognition*: recognition of the recurrent historical patterns— of forced migration or expulsion, of accommodation of (religious) refugees, and of dissident survival under repression—as well as recognition of the recurrent mechanisms and processes that gave birth to them.[5]

Let me illustrate what I mean by historical thinking, beginning with expulsions. Obviously, I can't begin to survey all the forced (religious) migrations in recent history. Peter van der Veer's contribution to this volume underscores the enormous complexity of the history and historical memory of expulsion and accommodation in just the case of Germany. Still, thinking with European history allows us to recognize broader comparative patterns in our current experience. Three very different examples come to mind: Bosnia, Syria, and Myanmar, where both the patterns and the politics of religious diversity vary considerably, much as they did historically.

Bosnia was, prior to its brutal civil war (1992–5), perhaps the most diverse component of the former Yugoslavia, with its significant communities of Croatian Catholics, Serbian Orthodox, and "Bosniak" Muslims, alongside the remnants of the formerly significant Sephardic migrants from Iberia; it's distinctive facts on the ground reflected the long history of *ad hoc tolerance* of Christians and Jews under the Ottoman Empire's *privileged* Sunni Islam. On the eve of the war, however, Bosnia's public politics were what I recognize as *integration* (in the lower right, inclusive quadrant of Figure 1.2),[6] in the sense that religious identities were not generally a salient feature of public politics in the officially secular Yugoslavian composite.

Syria was, prior to its devastating civil war (2011–ongoing), also a richly diverse polity, with significant communities of Christians and Jews, alongside its diverse Muslim majority, which pattern was also reflective of the long Ottoman history of *ad hoc toleration* of "People of the Book." On the eve of the current war, however, Syria's religious politics were particularly complex and messy, in the sense that within its diverse Muslim population, a politically dominant Alawite (Alevi Shi'a) minority enjoyed a *privileged* position over the (diverse) Sunni majority, while the Christian and Jewish populations continued to enjoy *ad hoc tolerance*.

Myanmar, by contrast, has a very different pattern of religious diversity, with a *privileged* Buddhist majority alongside smaller Christian, Muslim, Hindu, and folk-religious minorities. Its distinctive religious facts on the ground are reflective of Burma's very different history of foreign domination that was filtered through the experience of British colonialism since the mid-nineteenth century. After independence as Burma in 1948, the religious politics of Myanmar's military-dominated governments veered toward a newly minted Buddhist Nationalism, which exclusively and emphatically *privileges* its Buddhist core over its ethno-religious peripheries.

In all three cases, however, long-standing patterns of generally peaceful coexistence have been disrupted to the extent that they have produced large flows of religious refugees. What they have most clearly in common with early modern Europe is authoritarian intolerance—that is, political actors with ready access to coercive means have, in situations of rapid change or political uncertainty, exploited narratives or allegations of historical grievance to *polarize* previously peaceful relations among religious groups and to *demonize* their religious "enemies," thereby consolidating their own political/military advantages and precipitating refugee flows. As I found in early modern Europe and I believe Peter van der Veer has shown in recent German experience, the experience of forced (religious) migrations can be (re)produced in both wartime (Bosnia and Syria) and in relative peace (Myanmar).

Still, as European history shows, accounts of authoritarian intolerance (cf. Terpstra 2015) miss at least half of the story, because they ignore or underestimate the *agency* of the apparent "victims." These potent actors recurrently make consequential choices in difficult situations: choosing to "conform," to leave, or to "resist." These choices are consequential, today as much as in early modern history, in the sense that concerted efforts to compel conformity or even violent campaigns of annihilation have recurrently failed to recreate the "unity and purity" of some imagined past, whether in the "ethnically cleansed" Republika Srpska, the religiously "purified" Islamic State, or the militarily "pacified" Myanmar. In all these cases, recurrent mechanisms have combined to move the process of religious expulsion, with a limited range of outcomes.

Regarding the other end of the forced migration process, which is the focus of this volume, thinking historically can be equally illuminating— that is, in describing and accounting for the variant experience of (religious) accommodation in the places of refuge. Here I will focus on European examples, which I know best, though I think the analytic strategy would work well for non-European countries, as well. The key is to situate our observations of the present in the context of prior experiences of migration and accommodation. In considering the accommodation process, it is critically important, I think, to consider both historical legacies and the full cast of consequential actors. I will explore briefly the examples of the UK, France, and Germany, each of which represents a distinctive national "template" that descends from the early modern period.

In the UK, both England and Scotland have had established or *privileged* churches since the end of the seventeenth century, a national template that has enjoyed a long historical continuity. Although the connection between political and religious authority remains strong, the nature of the privilege has changed significantly over time, largely through the extension of *ad hoc tolerance* to a succession of religious groups: first, Protestant "dissenters," following the Glorious Revolution (1688); then, Catholics in the mid-nineteenth century; and in the course of the twentieth century, a broad range of religious "newcomers," including Muslims, Hindus, Sikhs, and Buddhists, especially from their (former) colonies. The preeminence of the Anglican Church in England and the Presbyterian Church in Scotland is still unmistakable, but this national template has recurrently proven to be capable of accommodating a wide range of religious diversity, as it did in the early modern period.

In France, by contrast, the politics of religious diversity have been disrupted recurrently by political upheavals, though there are nevertheless elements of long-term continuity in its national template. The French national experiment with *integration* emerged, much earlier than the British template, through a series of edicts of "pacification," beginning in 1563, by which the royal government guaranteed freedom of religious conscience and became the protector of both the established Gallican (French Catholic) Church and the national network of Huguenot (Calvinist) churches. Under the Edict of Nantes (1598), which was the most famous and enduring, the Huguenot population of France was granted equal political and civil rights, which dramatically reduced, in principle, the salience of religious identities in public politics, and in a secret agreement, the royal government even financed the Huguenot clergy, in compensation for the fact that Protestants still had to pay the tithe that supported the Catholic Church.

The first disruption of France's template came by royal decree in 1685, when Louis XIV revoked the Edict of Nantes, an act of profound authoritarian intolerance—*repression*—that occasioned one of Europe's largest forced migrations. Then, in the 1790s, the French revolutionary government disestablished the Gallican Church, seizing its enormous properties, and restoring, in effect, an even more rigorous version of the *integration* template. The Catholic Church was restored under both the empire (1811) and the monarchy (restored after 1815), and it enjoyed a position of *privilege* through the Second Republic, the Second Empire, and the early years of the Third Republic. Finally, the famous law of 1905 declared a formal separation between church and state (often referred to as the principle of *laïcité*, or secularism), which once again returned France, in principle, to a strict version of its *integration* template.

In Germany, a national template also emerged early, in the sixteenth century, and it, too, was recurrently disrupted by political upheavals. In this case, the *Religionsfriede* (Religious Peace) of Augsburg (1555) introduced *a parity* relationship among Holy Roman Empire's many rulers, who had been deeply polarized as defenders of "the old religion" and adherents of the "Augsburg Confession" (which was an early summation of Lutheran religious principles); it also endorsed parity between Catholics and Protestants in the Empire's many cities, large and small. This national template for religious peace was destroyed by the Thirty Years War, which precipitated another forced migration from Bohemia, but the *parity* template of the *Religionsfriede* was restored "in all its Points and Articles" in the Treaty of Osnabrück as part of the Peace of Westphalia (1648), which updated it to include provisions for the restoration of corporate religious diversity, where it had been disrupted by the war, and introduced the principle of freedom of individual religious conscience. This national agreement was rendered moot by the dissolution of the Empire in 1806, as smaller territorial jurisdictions regulated their own religious affairs. Germany's Catholic and "Evangelical" (as used in Germany, this term is generally inclusive of both Lutherans and Calvinists) communities were once again polarized nationally during the so-called *Kulturkampf* (Culture War) in the early years of the Second Empire (1871–1918), in which Bismarck promoted Evangelical *privilege* and sought to subordinate the Catholic Church.

Following the First World War, the Weimar Republic introduced a national *integration* template, guaranteeing religious freedom, but this was quickly undermined by the rise of Hitler and the establishment of the Third Empire. Under foreign occupation following the Second World War, Germany was divided between the officially secular German Democratic Republic (DDR) in the east (political *integration*) and the German Federal Republic (BRD), which reintroduced a form of religious *parity*. Under the federal constitution, all religious groups that are recognized and formally licensed are supported by a "church tax," which is a surcharge on the income tax of those affiliated with a recognized and licensed community of faith and collected by the government. Following the reunification of Germany in 1991, the BDR's *parity* template has been applied to the constituent states of the DDR as well. Still, the legacy of the division is reflected in the "facts" of religious diversity on the ground: in the six states of the DDR, the majority of the population is not affiliated with a religious community, while in the ten states of the original BRD, with the exception of Hamburg, the majority of the population is still affiliated with a Christian denomination, though that percentage is declining.

Each of these "national" templates—within which there is room for a great deal of local and regional variation—has been flexible enough, historically, to accommodate a wide range "newcomers." After sending out emigrants between the sixteenth and nineteenth centuries, each of these polities has, in the last century or more, absorbed a variety of immigrants, both "migrants" and "refugees" (to echo Peter van der Veer's distinction in this volume): from elsewhere in Europe, especially Eastern Europe; from (former) colonies around the world; and, most recently, from a variety of crisis situations, in the Middle East, Africa, and South Asia, in particular. But their structural differences do make a difference, presenting religious refugees variant sets of opportunities and challenges, just as they did in the early modern period.

The *privileged* religious template of the UK seems to offer religious refugees the paths of least resistance to safety and accommodation. There is, in principle, no requirement for religious refugees to declare a religious affiliation at all, inasmuch as more than one-fifth of population in the UK is unaffiliated with an organized community of faith; still, as William Wheeler's research shows (in this volume), the formal asylum process seems to reward both claims of religious "persecution" initially, and paradoxically, "genuine conversions" to Christianity, once asylum has been denied.[7] For non-Christian religious refugee communities, the UK's (Christian) *privilege* template also affords the prospect that "organized" communities of faith can be granted *ad hoc tolerance*, as various Christian "dissenters" and religious "others" have in the last several centuries, as long as they keep their heads down and avoid trouble. Such ad hoc accommodations of religious difference remain low-cost gestures for the places of refuge because their ad hoc increments do not fundamentally disrupt the privilege of the established churches.

In Germany, the *parity* template might seem, in principle, to be equally welcoming to religiously different newcomers; thus, individual refugees are afforded asylum and support on the grounds of religious persecution in their places of origin, although research presented in this volume underscores the challenges of the individual asylum process. But as is characteristic of parity regimes historically, the rules that govern official recognition/formal inclusion of communities of faith represent a relatively high bar regarding formal organization. Germany's initial experience of parity only included Lutherans and Catholics under the sixteenth-century *Religonsfriede*, and in the Peace of Westphalia formal recognition was expanded to include Reformed (Calvinist) Christians, almost as an afterthought (te Brake 2017: 264). The revival of the *parity* template after the Second World War included primarily the Catholic and the (now conjoined) Evangelical churches, though other Protestant communities (Brethren, Baptists, etc.) were included via the organizational network of "Free Evangelical" churches. Religious "others" appear to face greater challenges in achieving the benefits of formal inclusion, as communities of faith as opposed to individual refugees. Indeed, as outsiders, their communities may perceive religious *parity* as exclusionary *privilege*. For them, especially the large numbers of new Muslim refugees from the Middle East, sub-Saharan Africa, and South Asia, lacking formally recognized religious organizations, it is important to worship discreetly and to keep their heads down in order to avoid trouble.[8]

In France, the *integration* template, known generally as *laïcité*, would seem to be the most inclusive regime of all. Still, the formal disestablishment of the Catholic Church—both 225 years ago and, again, a century ago—failed to alter the obvious religious "facts on the ground." Indeed, France remains a majority-Catholic country, even if participation in its rituals or formal affiliation with the Catholic Church is no longer a salient feature in public life. Though the informal domination of its religious rituals (and holidays) has declined in recent decades, the cultural preeminence of the Catholic Church is still obvious, as evidenced by the "national" crisis that was occasioned by the tragic fire in the Cathedral Church of Notre Dame in Paris. For the new waves of (both Islamic and Jewish) religious refugees in the last decades, the inclusive promise of official *laïcité* is belied by the recent rise of popular anti-Semitism and Islamophobia, not only in France but throughout Europe.[9] Meanwhile, for larger communities of faith, formal recognition of their religious organizations, which can be hard to achieve, still has important legal and security implications, even if all groups are formally "disestablished." For them, too, French *integration*, like German *parity*, undoubtedly looks as exclusionary as, if not more exclusionary than, formal Christian *privilege* in the UK, especially when they are even prevented from wearing dress that expresses their religious devotion in public.[10]

Refugees and Religion, Then and Now

So, how does this kind of historical thinking improve our understanding of the more general problem of refugees and religion? To begin, I have proposed a vocabulary that allows us to compare the different patterns of religious coexistence ("facts on the ground") and the formal or legal structures of religious diversity ("national templates"), both geographically and historically. Figure 1.3, for example, plots the array of national templates in the contemporary examples I have discussed onto my conceptual map of historical variation.

Within these national frameworks for the management of religious diversity, which are more clearly prescriptive or aspirational than descriptive of the facts

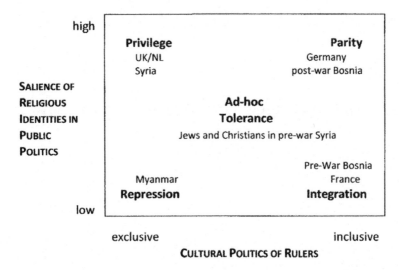

Figure 1.3 Variable templates of religious coexistence today. Created by Wayne P. te Brake.

of religious diversity on the ground, there is ample room for local and regional variation.

Recognizing local, regional, and national differences requires us, in turn, to attend to the powerful agency of religious "dissenters," "outsiders," and "newcomers"—this, in order to counteract the forceful pronouncements of those who claim political/religious authority and sometimes commit horrendous acts of authoritarian intolerance. Indeed, it is the subversive strategies that these religious actors deploy and the bargains that these political "subjects" make with their proximate "rulers" that account for the complex and messy patterns of religious diversity in the world today.

All in all, I have tried to demonstrate an analytic strategy—using the language of mechanisms and processes—that allows us not simply to observe where we are today—in this new era of exclusionary (religious) nationalism, following the refugee crisis of 2015—but also to account for how we got to be where we are today. Now, I freely admit that I can claim no special (political-scientific, sociological, or anthropological) expertise to give credence to my observations and analysis of where we are today. But that is precisely the point! Becoming critical observers of the challenges related to refugees and religion does not require expertise in all of their historical and contemporary dimensions. On the contrary, it only requires us to step outside our (academic or cultural) comfort zones in order to demonstrate the relevance of our special expertise to very big problems that are beyond the ken of any individual.

2

German Refugees and Refugees in Germany

Peter van der Veer

Introduction

Far from being an exceptional crisis, the 2015 movement of large groups of refugees into Germany is merely a moment in a long history of forced, partly forced, and relatively unforced movement of people in Europe and the rest of the world. The inescapable nature of global movements has led a number of leading social scientists, including the famous economist Thomas Piketty, to write an open letter to *The Guardian* (Thursday, June 28, 2018) in which they called for a science-based approach to policies on immigration rather than an approach based on electoral calculations. Unfortunately, policies on immigration have little to do with science, but everything with nationalism. The choice to publish this letter in *The Guardian* already makes the call a political one. *The Guardian* is a respectable, but in terms of readership relatively marginal, left-leaning newspaper in Britain, a country that has chosen to leave the European Union (EU) precisely because of nationalist perceptions of immigration, fueled by mass media controlled by Rupert Murdoch's News Corporation. The battle about immigration cannot be solved on straightforwardly empirical and scientific terms, but like any other major political issue on political grounds. For such politics, however, theoretical perspectives and historical awareness are crucial.

Refugee stands for "a person who is forcibly displaced." This sounds straightforward, but it is not. Conceptually, the distinction between migrant and refugee is pertinent, as a legal principle, but like all abstract principles, it runs into all kinds of difficulties in its application. To take only one random example, in Austria, in August 2018, an Afghan man who had asked for asylum on the grounds that he was homosexual and persecuted as such in Afghanistan was rejected because the judge did not think that he behaved like a homosexual or was clothed in a homosexual way. Directly relevant to this volume (see the contribution by

Wheeler) is the rejection of asylum seekers who have converted to Christianity and are refused asylum because they are judged to be fake Christians.[1]

Ultimately, much of our processual understanding of power and force, freedom and agency, property and citizenship depends on our theoretical perspectives. In my perspective, it is primarily the nation-state that defines subjects and citizens through law and law enforcement, but my understanding of the nation-state includes a wider variety of political formations ranging from fragile entities such as Libya and Afghanistan to supranational entities like the EU. Moreover, the recent history of Europe shows that what is understood today as established nation-states, such as Germany, Poland, and Russia, are very recent formations.

This chapter examines some aspects of the cultural history of refugees in Germany. Our focus in studying migration is often on migrants and their motivations and on the problems they face in their transition to another country. At the same time, it is crucial to see what the motivations are of those who are willing to receive refugees. Does history play a role in shaping these collective motivations? Historically, the German lands have been both producer and recipient of large numbers of refugees, both sending them out and receiving them. To what extent does that history play a role in the present and, if it does, what kind of role? Do people who are themselves refugees or children of refugees have more empathy for the plight of refugees than others? To what extent is empathy important in the political decision to accept refugees?

Moral Sentiments

The German novelist Jenny Erpenbeck (2015) has recently written a novel, entitled *Gehen, Ging, Gegangen* (in the English translation Go, Went, Gone). Richard, a retired professor of philology in Berlin, who, with his academic routine now disrupted, is unsure of what to do with the rest of his life. His wife of forty years is dead. He sleepwalks across the Alexanderplatz, oblivious of ten African refugees who have gone on a hunger strike to protest their dire situation as refugees. They refuse to give their names, but one of them has created a sign that reads "We become visible." That evening Richard watches a report on the hunger strike on the evening news and wonders how he could have just walked by without seeing the refugees. Something about the story catches his attention, and he thinks of his own story: as an infant his mother fled from Silesia to Germany, and mother and child nearly became separated. Like many, they lived through a postwar period of extreme need. At the same time, Richard is ashamed of his total ignorance about Africa. He begins to ask questions and conduct research: "Where is Burkina Faso? What is the capital of Ghana, Sierra Leone or Niger?"

But reading about Africa and the refugees is not enough for Richard: He composes a questionnaire and goes to a refugee shelter to meet with the men. He finds a receptive audience—the men are more than eager to tell their stories (no questionnaire required). In halting English or Italian they tell Richard about unbelievable horrors—losing everything—livelihood, home, family—from one day to the next, forced onto rickety boats in the Mediterranean Sea. Now they have nothing but time on their hands. Many have skills, but they are not allowed to work. Richard finds it ironic that the presence of the refugees has created thousands of part-time jobs for Germans but that the refugees themselves are not permitted to contribute their labor to the country where they are (temporary) guests. Richard gets to know several of the men—Raschid, Ithemba, Awad, Osaboro—quite well. Their stories are similar—varying only in the degree of horror.

Most of the novel is narrated in the third-person present tense from the perspective of Richard. Eventually, Richard is no longer a passive listener: he actively intervenes on behalf of the men. Why is Richard disrupting his quiet retirement to help these men? Is he simply a *Gutmensch*—a do-gooder acting on some Christian or humanitarian principle? Or is he atoning for something in his past? Richard is an East German who grew up as a refugee child in a land devastated from war. So he knows from experience that permanence is an illusion; none of us can be sure that we will be spared the fate of a refugee.

The American-Vietnamese novelist and theorist Viet Thanh Nguyen has recently written a book on war, memory, and identity, entitled *Nothing Ever Dies* (2016). Nguyen is concerned with the remembrance of the war in Vietnam as one in which American suffering was paramount and Vietnamese suffering is largely elided. This exemplifies what Nguyen terms "unjust memory," which "limit[s] empathy and compassion to those just like us" and "terminate[s] empathy and compassion for others" (2016: 267). Much of *Nothing Ever Dies* is a critique of such memories and a meditation on the difficulty of producing a "just memory" of the US war in Vietnam that "celebrates the humanity of all sides and acknowledges the inhumanity of all sides, including our own" (2016). Nguyen has also written an award-winning novel *The Sympathizer* (2015) dealing with the cultural production of memory and the ambivalences of agency and victimhood. The point that Erpenbeck and Nguyen in their different ways make is that for both the refugees and the receiving populations, the work of memory and history is essential to connect to the suffering of others.

In *The Theory of Moral Sentiments* (1759), Adam Smith observed that sensory experience alone could not spur us toward sympathetic engagement with others: "Though our brother is upon the rack, as long as we ourselves are at our ease, our senses will never inform us of what he suffers." For Smith, what made us moral beings was the imaginative capacity to "place ourselves in his situation . . . and become in some measure the same person with him, and thence form some idea of his sensations, and even feel something which, though weaker in degree, is not altogether unlike them." Empathy or "Einfühlung" is not a given, but structured according to narratives of connection. People all over the world broadly feel responsibility for their kin, and when they don't, this is seen as troubling and frowned upon. Depending on the nature of their kinship systems, this can extend from the nuclear family out toward a wider circle of kindred.

Fictive kinship—the inclusion of others in quasi-blood relations—can play a role in extending this feeling of responsibility. Forms of fictive kinship are based on commonplace of origin, ethnicity, or religion. However, the variety of forms of bonding is enormous, and the weakness or strength of ties beyond the family is relative. This is exactly what Benedict Anderson (1983) tried to express with his description of "the nation" as an "imagined community." What one considers to be "us" and what one considers to be "others" varies and is dynamic to the extent that one cannot easily take natural or primordial ties for granted as the basis of caring for others. It is also not simply the case that human beings feel a universal, "natural" responsibility when they see the suffering of others.

Moreover, it can also not be argued that "empathy" is required for social action to take place. Research in social psychology shows that "empathy," for example in cases of sudden disaster like earthquakes, is short-lived, depends on specific framing of the narrative of suffering, and does not extend easily beyond individual cases with which one can "empathize." In fact, people may feel all kinds of emotions, including a kind of elation that one is not suffering oneself or at least not to the extent that others are suffering. Such is suggested by Freud's famous argument in *Mourning and Melancholia* (1918) about the ambivalence we feel when someone close to us has died. Sad that the person is gone, and glad that one continues to live oneself. This shows that one cannot take universal and unequivocal emotions as the basis of an account of caring for others.

Caring for others outside the family is a product of collective social action and thus a matter of politics. A politician might, for example, argue that caring for others is in the national interest: Chancellor Merkel has denied that *Mitgefühl* (sympathy) was a motivation in her refugee politics and claimed that her position was in the interest of Germany and the EU. The boundary between those who belong and those who do not, between those for whom one has empathy and for whom one has not, depends on processes of state formation. This is largely determined by shifting state discourses about the religious and ethnic foundations of the nation.

State Formation and Religious Cleansing

A moment of particular interest in the European history of state formation and religious cleansing is the expulsion of Muslims and Jews after centuries of *convivencia* from the Catholic *nacion* of Spain (Nirenberg 2014). With the expansion of Spain and Portugal, this ideology of purification is spread to Latin America and the Philippines, with the methods of the Inquisition. When Iberian power is not established, like in China and Japan, the rulers in those places show themselves just as capable to purify their nations from Christianity. Japan is the clearest case when at the end of the sixteenth century after the crucifixion of twenty-six priests and converts 250,000 Christians were killed and Japanese were asked to register as Buddhists (Paramore 2009). Only pockets of surviving hidden Christians, like Marranos in Spain, stayed in Japan, constantly fearing to question about their beliefs.

The Reformation stands out as the first period in European and possibly global history in which the religious refugee becomes a mass phenomenon. After the Jews and the Muslims came the Puritans who exiled themselves to America, the Anabaptists, the Huguenots, and everyone else in the several wars of religion that followed the Reformation (see te Brake in this volume). As the historian Nicholas Terpstra (2015) argues, the Reformation was not just a movement for intellectual and religious change. It was also Europe's first grand project in social purification. It was deeply about exile, expulsion, and refugees. The forced migration of religious migrants was a normal, familiar, and expected feature of public policy that was oriented to build a cohesive society. The formula of *cuius regio, eius religio* (people have to follow the religion of their rulers) was a principle that legitimized a combination of migration and war. At the end of the Thirty Years War, the Peace of Westphalia in 1648 built a fragile international system to deal with the treatment of minorities. Nevertheless, the German lands continued to be sites of huge migration to Eastern Europe (including Russia) and the United States. Some forty-six million people of German descent live in the United States.

This is part of the deep history of modern nationalism. The idea of purification by expulsion became a legitimate aspect of statecraft, combining ethnic and religious cleansing. In the German case, Lutheran Protestantism became a dominant part of German nationalism in the nineteenth century, while the Catholics had to show their loyalty to the state (Lehmann 2007). However, one does not need religion for the cleansing of the nation. The two competing totalitarian ideologies of the twentieth century—Nazism and communism—were atheistic but very much into ethnic cleansing in which religion was a significant element, but race paramount. The collapse of the Habsburg Empire and Czarist Russia gave rise to an unprecedented unmixing of populations. Cleansing was both by expulsion and by extermination. From 1933 to 1945, Nazi and Soviet regimes murdered fourteen million people between Berlin and Moscow, not taking into account the war dead (Snyder 2010). These were all civilians, abandoned to state power which reminds us that the state protects some, but attacks others and that mass murder and massive forced migration is nothing new to Europe. The idea that European nation-states are stable democracies is a fiction that could only be maintained during the Cold War where geopolitical forces kept the West and the East under tight control. After the Fall of the Berlin Wall in 1989, this fiction was largely based on Germany's wish to be a stabilizing and unifying force in Europe and on the military hegemony of the United States. The global economic crisis of 2008 has shown the fragility of this fiction and continues to have a long-lasting fallout in the distrust that people have in liberal governments. So much for Fukuyama's *The End of History* (1992). Although German politicians have regularly declared that Germany is not an immigration country, in fact, that is exactly what Germany is already for a long time. In Germany, the main narrative frame that legitimates the right to settle in Germany as refugees, however, is nationalist. It is about ethnic Germans who live in Eastern Europe outside of contemporary German national borders. It is not about the forty-six million people of German descent who live in the United States, but about a combination of blood and territory (*Blut und Boden*) in Eastern Europe.

Recent German History

Automobilists using the Bundesautobahn 38 from Göttingen to Halle cannot fail to see a huge monument on a hill just outside of Friedland. It is a twenty-eight-meter-high Home-coming Monument of steel-like concrete slabs commemorating the Germans who died in the war or were pushed out of Eastern Europe (see Nagel in this volume). It was paid for by the Association of Returnees, Prisoners of War, and Relatives of Missing Persons of Germany

(Verband der Heimkehrer, and Kriegsgefangenen und Vermisstenangehörigen Deutschlands). The first stone was laid in 1965 by Konrad Adenauer, who had been between 1949 and 1963 West Germany's first chancellor and who had traveled to Moscow in 1955 to get 10,000 prisoners of war back to Germany, which after his death was seen by many as his greatest political achievement. In 1955, the Supreme Soviet of the USSR decided to release the deported Germans from their special settlements in Siberia and Kazachstan without however letting them return to their old areas near the Wolga (Eisfeld 2004). The return of the German war prisoners to Germany from Russian Labor Camps was followed for decades until today by the emigration of ethnic Germans from all over Eastern Europe to the Bundesrepublik. Among late emigrants (*Spätaussiedler*) are two recent German Nobel prizewinners, Hertha Müller for Literature (emigrated in 1987) and Stefan Hell for Chemistry (emigrated in 1978), who are both the so-called Banaterschwaben or Donauschwaben, an ethnic German population in Rumania.

The text on the monument calls for peace, freedom, human dignity, as well as reconciliation and the abandoning of hatred, which is probably why this monument is called a *Mahnmal*, since it is meant to admonish rather than merely remember. What is particularly noteworthy is its statistical enumeration and categorization of German victims of the war. Though the enumeration starts with referring to fifty million people that were killed in the entire world during the Second World War, it lays out in specific detail that fifteen million people were forced out of their Heimat east of the newly established Oder-Neisse Border and Bohemia, Eastern and Southeast Europe. And that more than two million people, mostly women and children, lost their life on the road killed by human hands or from exhaustion. Three-and-half million German soldiers were in thousands of Russian prison camps and were piecemeal released over more than a decade. More than a million Germans went missing and remained missing. And finally, it mentions that in 1956 the last transport arrived, but that in 1966 still not everyone was released.

An elderly gentleman whom I encountered at the monument told me that he was from the former DDR. He observed with anger in his voice that there was no mention of the guilt of Germans in causing all this bloodshed. This is a view one encounters more often in conversations with people from the former DDR that in the DDR they at least had the moral decency to understand these facts in terms of German guilt instead of in terms of victimhood. The prevailing view in the DDR was that in the BRD Germans saw themselves as victims. Moreover, since the BRD did not accept the borders of Germany, established after the war, it was revanchist.

Of course, Germans had turned the very areas from which the Germans were now expelled to killing fields of Jews, Poles, Russians, and others. What could not be acknowledged in the DDR was that Stalin had already begun the extermination of national minorities in the Soviet Union long before the rise of Hitler.

The Second World War turned almost seamlessly in the Cold War. The territorial division of Germany in a capitalist and a communist part (very much like North and South Vietnam or North and South Korea) ended only in 1991, while large areas that had been previously part of Germany remained forever part of Poland, Russia, and Czechoslovakia, after the BRD's acceptance of the Oder-Neisse border. Not only in terms of territory but also in terms of mentalities this history is continued as is witnessed until today in the continuous contradictions and discomforts in the relation between Ossies and Wessies (East and West Germans), exacerbated by large economic disparities. Clearly, not only Germans expulsed from the now Russian, Polish, or Czech areas were received in Western Germany, but also some 20 percent of the DDR population, about three and a half million people with especially skilled manpower, who left the DDR before the building of the Wall. Such migration from East to West picked up again after the Wall fell and has only recently abated.

Hitler's territorial ambition had been to bring all the Germans back into the realm (*Heim ins Reich*) largely by changing the borders that were established after the First World War, by moving ethnic Germans within these borders, and by moving non-Germans out or enslaving them, especially Poles, or exterminating them, especially Jews. This implied the "unmixing" of populations that had been living together for centuries in various demographic equations. If one formulates this ambition abstractly as that of creating a homogeneous nation-state with marginal groups of ethnically inferior laborers, one cannot help to note some similarities with political ambitions that are accepted even today in democratic systems. The brutality with which this ambition was achieved and the totalitarian use of the entire state system toward its ends are, however, exceptional, although there are clear similarities with Stalin's population policies in the same period. One is struck by the consistent emphasis by British politicians both after the First World War and after the Second World War that Germans should be removed from the areas in which they lived together with other nationalities (Münz and Ohliger 2003). Essentially, this is also what happened in the Partition of British India, in which Muslim Pakistan was separated from secular Hindu India. The Potsdam Conference of 1945 produced an agreement between the Soviets and the Western Allies to a massive transfer of ethnic Germans from Eastern Europe to divided Germany.

The breaking-up of the Habsburg Empire and the rise of ethnic nationalism in Eastern Europe can be seen as setting the stage for the radical population policies of the Nazis. One can perhaps say that the long-term result of such territorial ambitions has been the "unmixing" of Eastern Europe which has recently been further pursued in the falling apart of Yugoslavia and Czechoslovakia, and today is a major element in the Ukraine. At the end of the Second World War, the Soviet Union took part of Poland and pushed Poland to the West, which led to the expulsion of Germans from Eastern Prussia, Pomerania, and Silesia, which then were repopulated by Russians from other parts of the Soviet Union, and by Poles from Eastern Poland, while Germans from Bohemia and Moravia were pushed out to be replaced by Czechs. Ethnic cleansing was accompanied by toponymical cleansing: Königsberg became Kaliningrad, Breslau became Wroclaw, and Marienbad became Marianski Lazny. Who visits these areas today would have difficulty finding any evidence of the many centuries of German presence. In Poland, this has also been helped by the fact that the population of Polish territory that was annexed by the Soviet Union was moved to Silesia, where they had no historical roots and previous acquaintance with Germans. One can find similar movements of populations, for example from the Ukraine, in former East Prussia and in Czech Sudetenland resulting in local historical amnesia. The history of this huge ethnic cleansing of Germans in Eastern Europe has also not received much attention from historians outside of Germany (Evans 2012). However, not only Germans were on the move. The historian Peter Gattrell (2019) estimates that at the end of the war seventeen million people were on the move.

Given varying definitions of the German refugees like *Heimatvertriebene* or just *Vertriebene* or *Flüchtlinge*, one cannot come to a definite statistic about the German refugees in the first years after 1945, but in 1950 there were some twelve million refugees from Eastern Europe, around four million in the DDR and eight million in the BRD. This was around 20 percent of the total population with concentrations in Mecklenburg-Vorpommern, Niedersachsen, Bayern, Hessen, Sachsen-Anhalt, and Schleswig-Holstein. Obviously, with a large part of urban Germany in ruins, the refugees were often not very welcome, as a dirge that made the round in 1946–7 in Schwaben makes clear:

> Dear Lord in Heaven, see our need; we farmers have fat nor bread; Refugees eat themselves thick and fat and steal our last bed; we famish and suffer great pain, Dear Lord send that brood back home; Send them back to Czechoslovakia and free us from that brood. They have neither belief nor name, those threefold cursed, in eternity Amen. (Kossert 2008: 78)

In the BRD, the *Landsmannschaften* (hometown associations) came to play a very significant role in politics. In the DDR, however, there could only be a recognition of the expulsion of Germans by the Russians, Poles, and Czechs, all part of the communist brother people, in terms of the German guilt. Even the 50,000 *AntiFa-Umsiedler* from the Sudeten (who had been anti-fascist members of the communist and socialist parties and persecuted during the Nazi occupation of Czechoslovakia) were in fact expelled to the DDR, because in the end they were not regarded as fellow communists, but as Germans (van Hoorn 2003). In the DDR they felt that they were sitting between all chairs, since they were not allowed to form hometown associations, long publicly for their Heimat or be critical of what happened to them. At the local level they were regarded as intruders, and at the national level they were watched by the intelligence services.

What were the religious effects of this enormous forced migration of German speakers? Churches were almost the only institutions left after the war and trusted by the allied forces. Almost the first thing the churches did was to organize the search for expelled and lost Germans. They brought name cards from the many camps together and organized them according to place of origin (*Heimatortskarteien*). In 1999, more than twenty million people were registered through this system. In fact the churches replaced the state in an important function of locating and identifying citizens (Kösters 2005).

Another remarkable development was that with the influx of refugees the regional confessional boundaries were broken. Catholics moved to Protestant areas and vice versa. Even within one confessional community different traditions were introduced. The Germans in Eastern Europe were Pietist Lutheran or Mennonites or traditional pilgrimage-oriented Catholics. Germany had since the Thirty Years War always been characterized by strong geographic separation of confession which was significantly shaken up by the refugees. On the other hand, there was a strong pressure on the refugees to integrate in the existing churches of the area of immigration. This was often deeply resented and resisted by the refugees who wanted to keep their traditions (often the only thing of the Heimat that they had left) alive. This is, for instance, very clear in the Russian-German Free churches (*Russlanddeutsche Freikirchen*) in villages near Göttingen where the Russian-Germans till today continue to form very tight communities in which their church plays a central role. In short, the influx of refugees created a lively exchange of religious ideas that disrupted the traditional equations of the German countryside. They created a new, modern Germany that eventually also would become gradually secular.

A final religious element concerns dealing with the dead and the missed persons. When one visited German families in the 1960s, one would often encounter portraits of the missing or dead fathers, sons, or brothers who had been lost in the war. In an autobiographical book *Am Beispiel meines Bruders* (2003) (With the example of my brother), the novelist Uwe Timm tells about the shadow that was hanging over the household in which he grew up because of the death of his older brother as an SS soldier (and probably war criminal) in the war. The journalist Burkhard Bilger (2016) has reported on a spiritist in Berlin, named Gabriele Baring, who helped people to make peace with their dead. The therapist could sympathize with the plight of refugees, since her own father had lost a leg on the Russian front and her home town Hannover was largely destroyed. The spirit séances were a kind of Gestalt, a psychodrama in which patients reenacted traumatic memories through playing different roles in the family (*Familienaufstellung*). However, Baring's therapy, based on the very controversial theories and practices of Bert Hellinger, goes a step further by bringing the spirits of the dead. While the personal does not immediately reflect world history, there is something in the personal biography of several German generations, born before the war and being sent to the front as young adults and the generation that grew up immediately after the war in the hot war and in the cold war of a divided and truncated Germany that more than usual connects to Germany's traumatic history. The latter generation is not "Children of War" in the sense of having experienced the war but old enough to be traumatized by it. A major element in this is that Germans for generations have grown up with the wages of guilt (Buruma 1994). As the German comedian Mittermeier put it, "Three days a week we had Guilt; On Fridays, we had Shame." Germans were hardly allowed to mourn their dead, since they were almost constantly reminded of their guilt in supporting a regime that killed so many others.

The silencing of the past has received an alternative psychoanalytic interpretation by the Mitscherlichs (1967), who interpreted the German inability to mourn as an inability to deal with the traumatic loss of the father-figure, the beloved Führer. In their view it was therefore not the inability to mourn the many victims of the war and terror, but the inability to mourn the defeat of the Führer. This was such a shocking theory that the part about the trauma for the loss of Hitler was quickly erased by a more acceptable thesis about the inability to mourn the dead. It is indeed important to realize that many Germans had not only lost an assumed mass-psychological father-figure but also concretely mourned their dead and lost fathers.

Conclusion

Adam Smith's moral philosophy proposes that history and memory may indeed be important but only in so far as it is constitutive to the connections that bind people to the interested self. What kind of work do history and memory do? They can equally motivate people to accept refugees as to reject refugees, to deny them a place. Take, for example, Erika Steinbach, long-time president of the Association of German Refugees and MP for the CDU as well as Spokeswoman for Human Rights, who left the Parliament under protest against Merkel's refugee policies. In 2018, she was chosen as the president of the Erasmus Foundation, a think tank close to the AFD, the right-wing nationalist party that was one of the winners in the recent (2018) German elections. The Association for German Refugees stands for a conservative and sometimes reactionary German nationalism despite the fact that its members are refugees themselves. The debate about history and memory is crucially connected to the construction of the nation and thus to its relation with religion and refugees. In the late 1980s, this debate famously took the form of asking, to put it crudely, whether Hitler's Germany had been so much worse than Stalin's Soviet Union. Conservative historians, like Ernst Nolte, and leftist historians and philosophers, like Jürgen Habermas, found themselves at opposite ends of this *Historikerstreit* (dispute among historians). In the 2010s, it is the right-wing politicians of the Alternative für Deutschland that openly demand a more positive presentation of German history, and are very much opposed to accepting non-German refugees.

At the same time, Germans have been earlier very willing to accept Vietnamese refugees. Immediately after the Fall of Saigon in 1975 the West German government had declared a willingness to accept a contingent of refugees without submitting them to individual asylum procedures (this is when the term contingent, *Kontingent*, was coined), first 1,000, later expanded to 6,000, then to 10,000, and finally to 38,000. The government of Lower Saxony decided on its own without consultation with the Union government to bring 1,000 refugees out of camps in Thailand and Malaysia. Frankfurt also took the initiative to bring 258 refugees out of camps in Hong Kong, again without coordination with Bonn. When Germany had admitted 23,000 refugees from Southeast Asian camps in mid-1982, the German authorities restricted asylum to family reunion. All others had to prove personal persecution in Vietnam through a regular asylum procedure.

From 1979 onward, the journalist Rupert Neudeck started a campaign to rescue boat refugees which was called a ship for Vietnam. While some 10,000 refugees were saved by the Cap Anamur, a ship leased by Neudeck's committee, German political opinion gradually turned against it. The accusation was that the existence of the ship attracted people to try to escape by boat and that these were not political religious refugees, but economic migrants. An echo of this argument we hear today in relation to boat refugees in the Mediterranean Sea.

Why were Germans initially so eager to accept refugees? What was the narrativization of the plight of the Vietnamese that made this politically possible? First of all, the media and German humanitarian organizations primed the plight of the Vietnamese boat refugees and were able to get it recognized by the German public, which put considerable pressure on the political authorities to rescue them from the sea and from overcrowded refugee camps on the shores of Malaysia and Thailand. An interesting case is Lower Saxony, where the state government under Ernst Albrecht with considerable popular support took the initiative to invite 1,000 boat refugees to come. Albrecht made a straightforward comparison between the situation at the end of the Second World War when East European Germans were fleeing for communism and the situation in which Vietnamese were fleeing communism. After his death, there was a separate memorial service organized by the Vietnamese boat refugees, who wanted to show their gratitude for what he had done in their hour of need. Till the 1990s, Germany had a relative liberal asylum policy which can perhaps be seen as a form of atonement for having forced so many into exile during the Nazi years. The Germans had no direct stake in the war in Southeast Asia nor in its aftermath, but humanitarian arguments and solidarity with its allies led them to receive 40,000 refugees from the area. Public opinion was of course highly sensitized to the Vietnam War, which was the last direct confrontation between the so-called Free World and the communist world. Young people in the West had in majority been against the Western involvement, while the older generations had supported it. In Germany, this generational conflict was heightened by the Cold War relation between West Germany and East Germany. The boat refugees had fled communism and thus signified a justification of the Cold War, while opponents of the American role in the war could not easily be against accepting those who had fled in its aftermath. Crucial in the narrativization of humanitarian action is thus the Cold War context of Germany. This is further illustrated by the simultaneous recruitment of Vietnamese contract laborers by the DDR, the German Democratic Republic. In the mid-1970s, the DDR had signed treaties with Vietnam, Cuban, Angola, and Mozambique to bring contract laborers to work in the industry. These contracts were for four to five years. The treaty with Vietnam was signed in 1980, exactly at the time that West

Germany was accepting boat refugees. The largest number of contract laborers in the DDR was Vietnamese, amounting to 60,000 in 1989.

The narratives of the Cold War have been partly replaced by the "clash of civilizations," in which especially the incompatibility of Islam and modern Western civilization is highlighted (Huntington 1996). Such narratives are never entirely coherent or straightforward. They show ethical conflicts and ambivalences. At their core, however, is an ambivalence in caring for others which is perfectly underlined by the Indo-European linguistic relation between the words hospitality and hostility, as pointed out by the linguist Emile Benveniste (1969: 87–9). This is what seems to have happened in Germany from 2015 to 2018: a shift from hospitality to hostility which is the result of a massive political struggle about how to define the German nation. Ethics is perhaps less about transcendent values than about everyday politics that is supported by continuous struggle about interpretations of history.

Part II

People on the Move from Vietnam

3

Victims of Atheist Persecution

Transnational Catholic Solidarity and Refugee Protection in Cold War Asia

Phi-Vân Nguyen

Introduction

In 1954, the Geneva Conference ended the First Indochina War by dividing Vietnam into two temporary zones. Military troops had to regroup to the communist zone in the North or the noncommunist zone in the South. Civilians could also join the zone of their choice for 300 days. As a result, more than 800,000 civilians left the North to move to the noncommunist zone (Figure 3.1).

Many Western newspapers published the story of Vietnamese escaping communism. The French Catholic journal *Missi* sent its editor in chief to cover the story. Father Naïdenoff gave a vivid depiction of their ordeal. A photograph showed a man lying on the deck of a boat, with one hand on his forehead and the other one holding a crucifix to his chest (ECPAD 1955a). The accompanying caption read: "A poignant vision of faith. In the deepest sleep, they hold a crucifix which serves as an identity card in their exodus to freedom" (Naïdenoff 1955a). The importance of the Catholic faith in the exodus was paramount.

The Vietnamese Catholic community had grown since the first missionaries in the seventeenth century to almost two million. Although they made up only 10 percent of the Vietnamese population, 80 percent of the civilians moving South were Catholics (Bùi 1959; Nguyen 1995; Nguyen 2016). Others were Buddhists and Confucianists, and only 1,000 were Protestants. Donations from Catholics abroad reached such proportions that an Auxiliary Committee for the Resettlement was created to distribute them (Phạm 1955). Why was there a Catholic dimension to this migration? Why was one's religious affiliation important in this displacement and in the worldwide response to it?

Figure 3.1 A young man lies down on the deck of a boat transporting him from Phát Diệm to the regrouping point in Hai Phong, circa October 1954; photo by Établissement de communication et de production audiovisuelle de la Défense, https://www.ecpad. fr/presse/ (©Jean Lussan/ECPAD/Défense/NVN 54-166 R6).

Most studies have focused on the resettlement of these refugees (Hansen 2008, 2009b; Picard 2016). Instead, this chapter analyzes the relationship between their religion and refugee protection. It shows that refugee protection is best understood as a relationship that is intentional, dynamic, and dialectical. Catholic charity extended its support to other coreligionists across the globe because they considered they are part of the same family. But the dispatch of Catholic emergency relief overseas was neither automatic nor universal. The 1954 refugee crisis shows that missionaries and high members of the hierarchy, often former refugees themselves, channeled international Catholic aid into Vietnam for both religious and political reasons. This network did not appear in 1954, but years earlier in China and Korea, under the Japanese occupation and the civil wars. Religious authorities and missionaries fleeing communist rule sought both protection and new partners in their ongoing struggle against

Figure 3.2 Refugees disembark the French boat, *La Pertuisane*, in Haiphong and wait to be transported to Southern Vietnam, circa October 1954; photo by Établissement de communication et de production audiovisuelle de la Défense, https://www.ecpad.fr/presse/ (©René Adrien/ECPAD/Défense/NVN 54-158 R2).

expansion. This shows that humanitarian mobilization can serve political interests and that refugees are not only victims of persecution. They are also proactive actors seeking recognition and becoming the spokespersons of a common front (Figure 3.2).

Western Churches and Cold War Refugees

Refugee protection is not neutral. It also allows states to make gains in terms of scientific knowledge, trade networks, or military recruitment by selecting the refugees they protect. Even the 1951 Convention on the Status of Refugees let states pursue their own interests and use protection to denounce a political enemy (Goodwin-Gill 2008). Thus, refugee protection is an intervention that is both humanitarian and political. Humanitarian aid coming from religious networks emphasizes the ideals of solidarity among members of the same religious tradition, and charity toward others. Yet protecting refugees can serve both humanitarian and political objectives. This was obvious during the Cold War.

Contrary to the idea that the Vatican carried out a crusade against communism (Jacobs 2004; Manhattan 1984), Catholics did not follow the same policy toward communism (Chadwick 1993; Kent 2002; Lüthi 2020). In Asia, the Vatican's greatest concern was not communist expansion, but the risk of a schismatic church (Wiest 1999). What the Holy See feared was the creation of national churches, loyal to Beijing or Hanoi rather than to Rome (Naïdenoff 1956b). This was horrifying because of a demographic reality: proselytism had to take place in Asia and in Africa, where population growth was the fastest (The International Catholic Migration Commission and Foundation 1954). An article in *L'Actualité religieuse dans le monde* confirmed this: "In Asia, only 1% of Catholics," "Substantial progress in Africa," and "Europe in Decline" ("La situation religieuse" 1955). Keeping non-Western Catholics within the Roman Catholic Church was a matter of survival. So shortly after Chinese Communist victory, the Vatican issued *Ad sinarum gentes* in 1954, urging Chinese Catholics to remain faithful (Mungello 2015: 64).

Protecting vulnerable Catholic refugees overseas would have been the perfect opportunity to intervene in this matter. But Rome delegated this responsibility to national churches. Pope Pius XII's 1952 apostolic constitution, *Exsul Familia Nazarethana*, created institutions reflecting the needs of a more global Christian world. It also considered that the Vatican was not responsible for providing humanitarian relief. Since the eighth century, Pilgrim's Halls proliferated in Rome, welcoming Saxons, Franks, Frisians, Ethiopians, Hungarians, or Armenians. "This experience proves that the sacred ministry can be carried on more effectively among strangers and pilgrims if it is exercised by priests of their own nationality or at least who speak their language" (Pope Pius XII 1952). The Catholic faith was universal. But its networks of solidarity worked best within subcultural communities.

Refugees in Asia were high on the list of Western churches. Representatives of the Holy See and national Catholic relief associations met at the International Catholic Migration Congress in 1954, to discuss how Catholics engaged, supported, and received population movements. Papers on refugee crises discussed the situation in camps in Germany and Austria or the displaced population in Trieste. Yet a priest from the French Secours catholique also presented the exodus of the Northern Vietnamese Catholics, guided by their priests in the search of freedom of religion (de Rochcau 1954). Another paper reviewed the crisis in Hong Kong. Thousands of refugees, including 6,000 foreign Catholic missionaries, lived in horrible conditions (Donders 1954: 263). The final statements of the conference included one on refugees. It appealed to all Catholics to provide aid to Hong Kong or Macao and to "make known in their respective countries the courage and the faith of those hundreds of thousands of Catholics who have chosen to leave all their possessions in order to continue their lives as Christians" in Vietnam (Potulicki 1954: 390). Catholic solidarity extended its protection beyond international law. While the 1951 Convention only protected the population displaced by events happening in Europe before 1951, Catholic relief also reached out to non-Western refugees, especially those fleeing communism.

National churches did not contribute equally to the Vietnamese evacuees. Catholics in the UK, Germany, and Belgium raised funds for them. The French weekly *Missi* initially collected 900,000 francs. *Le Figaro* also raised thirty-seven million francs (Ély 1964: 225). Yet this paled compared to American Catholics who donated the equivalent of 700 million francs in the first year alone (Naïdenoff 1955a, 1956a). Of all national churches, the American National Catholic Welfare Conference (NCWC) was the most powerful.

After the Second World War, American Catholic aid went to diverse humanitarian crises. But relief to the victims of communist atrocities came as a priority. For the year 1957, only 30 percent of all the goods and gifts donated overseas went to Asia, of which only 13 percent came to Vietnam (Cardinal Spellman Funds 1957). In absolute terms, Vietnam was a small beneficiary, ranking after Poland, and just before Germany. But regarding the number of Catholics living in these countries, this aid was significant. There were only 5.6 million Catholics in Vietnam, compared to 35 million and 26.2 million, respectively, in Poland and Germany. Yet the amount allocated to Vietnamese Catholics was colossal. The dollar value per potential Catholic beneficiary for Vietnam ranked third in Asia, just after Japan and Formosa, two other places that, just like Vietnam, were both new lands of proselytism and bastions against communist expansion. The organization was not shy to support Washington's escapee program, which granted asylum and provided help to people fleeing communism (Catholic Relief Services 1954). Although many other populations received help, Catholics facing communist expansion was one of American Catholic' priority.

Then who decided which emergency situations were worthy of assistance? And who demanded to focus on certain situations over others? While American

Catholics donated for humanitarian reasons, political reasons, or both, a few individual activists kept the situation of the church in Asia at the forefront of American concerns. These activists came together into a Catholic arc of resistance against communist expansion, which originated in China.

The Birth of a Catholic Arc of Resistance

The generosity of Catholics from the United States and elsewhere in the Western world did not materialize in a vacuum. Key actors, such as missionaries and prominent members of the Catholic hierarchy, strove to attract and keep Cold War Asia among the Western churches' priorities.

Missionaries connected Catholics in China to international networks. They did not defend imperialist interests as many of them had in the previous century. Instead, they spread new ideas and practices which supported Chinese Catholics' nationalism, self-organization tactics, and a sense of resistance during the civil war. The Belgian missionary Vincent Lebbe was a pioneer in inspiring Chinese Catholic nationalism. He advocated for the creation of an entirely Chinese church served by Western missionaries (Gillet 2012; Young 2013: chapters 8–9). The missionaries he trained worked every day to free the Chinese church from imperialism and the domination of Western missionaries. This determination to make the church genuinely Chinese and independent from external interference inspired some of them, such as Raymond de Jaegher, to become just as opposed to communist rule. The Japanese imprisoned the missionary and released him in 1945. In Beijing, he organized a refugee shelter until communist authorities expelled him in 1951. He traveled to Belgium, then back to Asia, and raised awareness about "communist atrocities" in his memoirs, *The Enemy Within* (de Jaegher 1952, 1959a). He also formed the Free Pacific Association, whose purpose was to connect Chinese Catholics with overseas networks and unite all people of the Pacific area into one economic and moral stronghold against communism (de Jaegher 1959a, 1959b, 1221962).

American Jesuits created lay associations involved in propagating the faith or charity work, capable of sustaining the growth of Catholics as a grassroots movement even without the clergy members' initiative (Strong 2018: 285–94; Mungello 2015: 52). But this success put a target on their back (Mungello 2015: 59–62). Communist authorities imprisoned and then executed Father Zhang Boda, an American missionary of Chinese descent, for hindering the recruitment of soldiers for the Korean War. His death sparked violent confrontations between

Chinese Catholics and communist authorities (Clark 2017: 213; Mariani 2011: 59; Mungello 2015: 59–62).

Last, the Columban Fathers sent Irish missionaries who came with their lived experience in Ireland, which included resistance against British occupation in Ulster, particularly since the 1916 Easter Rising. While they opposed transferring responsibilities to local priests (Hoare 2006: 66), they still inspired a spirit of resistance and provided contacts overseas. The Legion of Mary, headed by an Irish Columban priest, mirrored the underground mobilization techniques of Chinese Communists (Mungello 2015: 58; Mariani 2011: 47–52). Just a few years after its creation in 1948, it mobilized over 2,000 youth at a time. As a result, it also became a target of communist repression (Mariani 2011: 61). Their periodical, *The Far East*, informed Irish and American Catholics of the state of the Chinese church. Columban father Patrick O'Connor became the chief news correspondent for the News Catholic Service Japan, China, Korea, and Vietnam in 1945. In 1948, the apostolic nuncio in China, Archbishop Riberi, requested that he create a news agency under the Catholic Central Bureau, the *Hua Ming News Service*, which suspended its activities the following year (Columban Fathers 2017: 109). His reporting proved capital in generating support overseas. In those three cases, missionaries inspired a fiercely independent church and connected it with the rest of the Christian world. Yet the most proactive agents in creating a transnational network of solidarity were not missionaries, but higher members of the Catholic hierarchy.

Monsignor Paul Yu Pin, the archbishop of Nankin, was a key architect in creating a solidarity network. In 1937, he had to remain in the United States, after the Japanese occupying China had offered a bounty for his capture. There, he visited dioceses and met congressional representatives in Washington, where he launched a periodical and created a cultural institute to raise awareness about the Japanese invasion (de Jaegher 1959a). His intention was obvious: Chinese Catholics had to find allies. The United States would be the most powerful of them all. The archbishop then returned to Chongqing, to the new headquarters of the Guomindang. During these years, he supported Korean independence fighters who sought refuge there (Choi 2016). When the Chinese Communist Party took power in 1949, the government expelled all the foreign missionary or recalcitrant members of the Catholic hierarchy. Paul Yu Pin went into exile again. He sought refuge in Taiwan, from where he continued to reach out to Catholic networks overseas.

His activism only matched American Cardinal Francis Spellman's passion for Asia and opposition to communism. During the Chinese civil war, Spellman visited the Nationalist government in Nankin, together with Monsignor Paul Yu Pin. There, he ordained fourteen Chinese priests, "some of whom, if things continue to deteriorate, may become martyrs," he reported to the archdiocese in New York (Cardinal Spellman Funds 1948: 2). After the Chinese nationalists evacuated to Taiwan, Spellman again caused a sensation by saying mass in the largest auditorium of the island. To continue this tradition, an official of the apostolic prefecture in Taipei imagined that only Paul Yu Pin could fill his shoes and lead the mass conversions (Cardinal Spellman Funds 1952).

The cardinal also served as a support in diplomatic offensives against communism, using the Vatican or the United Nations. When members of the Chinese church regrouped in Taiwan, Yu Pin and Chang Kaishek reached out to Spellman again. The cardinal lobbied the Vatican to ask why the papal nuncio to China, Antonion Riberi, was not transferred to Taiwan and whether Rome could send someone else to serve as an apostolic delegate (Cardinal Spellman Funds 1954a). This concerned the spiritual mission of the church. But it was clear that such a gesture was also an attempt to bring the Vatican to recognize Taiwan as the only government of China.

Korean nationalists also seized the cardinal for his support. In May 1951, the Republic of Korea claimed that communists were committing a religious genocide, by eliminating the religious leaders and depriving the 760,000 Protestants and Catholics from their religious ministers ("The Korean Dead" 1951). According to a press release, six bishops and around a hundred religious ministers had been imprisoned or killed. A mass grave of Catholic priests had been found in the province of So. Chungchong (Cardinal Spellman Funds 1951a). As the government was about to press charges of religious genocide at the UN Economic and Social Council, its permanent representative wrote a letter to Spellman, listing the countries meeting at the Economic and Social Council six weeks later, and asking him to do everything in his power to support their initiative (Cardinal Spellman Funds 1951b). Eventually, the Republic of Korea withdrew the charges, but its appeal to Spellman is revealing. His influence was such that he could lobby several governments to back up Seoul's diplomatic offensive.

Missionaries and certain members of the clergy not only exchanged information and vows about the propagation of the faith. Faced with communist expansion, some of them—often refugees themselves—also reached out to each other to take concrete measures against communist expansion. They used diplomatic channels to oppose communism or raised the awareness of Catholics elsewhere about the dangers of its expansion. Both refugees and protectors sought allies and a new battleground to fight communism. Many converged in Saigon in 1954.

Vietnam as a Rallying Point

Not all, but many Catholics in Vietnam also opposed communism. The major difference yet is that they initially fought together with the Việt Minh against the return of colonial rule in 1945 (Trần 1996; Keith 2012). It was only after the pope's excommunication of Italian Communists in 1948 and Chinese Communists' victory in 1949 that the Indochinese episcopacy declared that communism was contrary to the Christian doctrine and encouraged the faithful not to engage in any activity that may give an advantage to communism (Trần 1996: 93–5). While many Catholics disregarded this call and remained either supportive or neutral to the Democratic Republic of Vietnam, others, especially clergy members and the laity in the dioceses of Bùi Chu and Phát Diệm who had formed paramilitary troops to defend their administrative autonomy, clashed with communist cadres.

These Catholics also created associations connecting them to Catholics overseas. The Vietnamese chapter of the Legion of Mary, created in 1948, inspired a spirit of resistance to its members (Tổng giáo phận Hà Nội 2013). The association provided an important link to other parts of war-torn Asia. Their weekly publication, *Đạo Binh Đức Me* (The Legion of Mary), which started in 1952 in Hanoi, reported on the fate of other fellow Catholics. A feature piece in their first issue informed the readers in Hanoi of Chinese Catholics' experience of communist denunciation campaigns (Tình hình công giáo Trung Hoa 1952). Catholics in Korea, involved in a fierce civil war, enjoyed the same coverage (Hội thanh niên công giáo Triều Tiên 1952) (Tình hình giáo hội Cao Ly 1952). *Đạo Binh Đức Me* also published the letters the pope had sent to Catholics in the Soviet Union (Đức Giáo Hoàng Pio XII 1952). As they read the pages of the periodical, Vietnamese Catholics understood that they were not alone. They were fighting a global threat with their Chinese and Korean coreligionists.

Another important connection to Catholics abroad also came from the efforts of the Ngô family to reach out for help. In 1950, Ngô Đình Diệm, a political leader from one of the oldest Catholic families in Vietnam, went into exile with his brother, Ngô Đình Thục, the third Vietnamese priest ever to become a bishop (Miller 2013: 36–41). Just like Mgr. Paul Yu Pin in China, he was both seeking protection and looking for new allies. He left Vietnam because he learned he was on the Việt Minh's assassination list. Once overseas, he visited the Vatican, France, Belgium, and the United States. In the United States, he met Cardinal Spellman, and in Washington several congressmen who, years later, formed the Vietnam lobby (Morgan 1997). Despite this, there was still no major Catholic solidarity movement toward noncommunist Vietnam, until the refugee flow in 1954 provided the momentum to do so.

As the regroupment in Southern Vietnam progressed, the population displacement transitioned from a collateral damage into what the West saw as people fleeing communist persecution. Initially, the migration was only

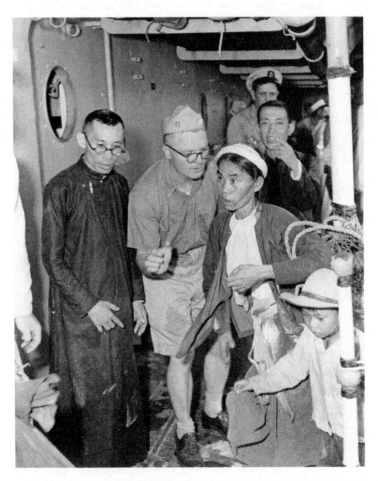

Figure 3.3 Navy Chaplain Lieutenant Francis J. Fitzpatrick and Vietnamese members of the clergy guide refugees transported by the US Navy during Operation "Passage to Freedom"; NARA/US NavyPhotograph/80-G-709243; photo by NARA/US Navy Photograph/80-G-709243, Operation "Passage to Freedom" 1954–1955/NARA/Naval History and Heritage Command, Washington, D.C.

partly Catholic. Refugees from the dioceses of Bùi Chu and Phát Diệm who had already arrived in Hanoi found transportation to the South. But airplanes also transported French civilians and equipment, together with civil servants, scientists, intellectuals, and entrepreneurs following their office or their business partners. It was only after parishes in Northern Central Vietnam experienced problems evacuating to the South that Catholics, more than any other Vietnamese civilians, came into focus (Figure 3.3).

Evidence of obstruction emerged from French ships patrolling the coast. As they traveled up the Đáy River, an increasing number of Catholic refugees reached the ship to request help (Broussole and Provençal 2013). At one point, villagers attempted to reach the sea during the low tide, walking out to a sandbank hoping that a French vessel would pass by before the return of the high tide (Naïdenoff 1955a). Obstructions became more obvious with an incident in Ba Làng, in the province of Thanh Hóa. According to a petition sent to the International Control Commission (ICC), created to oversee the ceasefire's implementation, 10,000 Catholics waited inside the church to move to the South. After Việt Minh cadres tried to dissuade them to leave, a company of the People's Army forced the entrance, captured 200 individuals, and dispersed 200 others (Service historique de l'armée de terre (SHAT) 1955a). Then, the communist authorities arrested five people and dispatched a military section, followed by two more. Tension escalated on February 13, when the army opened fire, claiming the lives of fourteen people (Naïdenoff 1955a). Now, the struggle of Vietnamese Catholics against communism also had its own martyrs. And the evacuation, which captured everyone's attention after the Geneva ceasefire, had become a Catholic exodus.

Transnational Solidarity in Action

When the evacuation period ended, the refugee flow was overwhelmingly Catholic. So was the humanitarian aid and the resettlement. Over twelve national Catholic relief associations sent aid to the refugees and supported their subsistence needs as well as the construction of 189 new churches across Southern Vietnam (Phạm Ngọc Chi 1955: 6). It would be misleading to believe that Catholic relief spontaneously went to Vietnam. The arc of resistance against communism which had emerged in China was instrumental in extending its mobilization to Southern Vietnam for humanitarian, diplomatic, and political purposes.

Cardinal Spellman's interest in the evacuation served as a magnet for the assistance of other important Catholic authorities. Diệm wrote to the cardinal on July 25 to request his support so that Spellman could "project an appeal for help to the free world, and above all to Christians of all denominations in America . . ." (Cardinal Spellman Funds 1954a). A week before calling for the help of the United States and all other friendly nations, the prime minister had already reached out to the archbishop of New York (Prados 2009: 113–14). Compared to all other Western governments and organizations, the archbishop was one of the most resourceful partners (Figure 3.4).

Spellman's visit also triggered a wave of support from other national churches. The Catholic hierarchy in France had not planned to dispatch any official representatives to visit the evacuees' camps. But General Ély urged the French church to send someone when he heard that the archbishop of New York

Figure 3.4 Archbishop Francis Spellman listens to a Catholic refugee during a mass he says in front of Notre Dame Cathedral, 1955; photo by Établissement de communication et de production audiovisuelle de la Défense, https://www.ecpad.fr/presse/ (©Tordjmann/ECPAD/Défense/SC 55-2 R31).

would come to visit. Saigon took Spellman's arrival as a major event. Officials came to cover his arrival at the airport; foreign correspondents followed his visits to refugee camps; around 70,000 people gathered in front of Notre Dame Cathedral to hear him give mass (ECPAD 1955b). The French did their best to generate the same interest for Monsignor Rhodain's trip, with less success. At least, he manifested the solidarity of French Catholics to the humanitarian crisis. So did Catholic dignitaries from Germany and Australia who came to visit refugee camps with Archbishop Paul Yu Pin, because Francis Spellman himself had come to Vietnam.

Cardinal Spellman was not the only important person to raise the awareness of Catholic churches in the West. In fact, his trips and the wave of visits from other dignitaries were one-time gestures. The interest of Western churches could wane. Other activists were central to keeping Vietnam at the forefront of their concerns. Father Patrick O'Connor continued his reporting as the Asian correspondent of the Catholic News Service. Now that the Chinese civil war and the Korean War were over, he focused on South Vietnam. It was his articles on the refugees that made the front pages of all 111 American diocesan newspapers (Jacobs 2004: 136). O'Connor was not just a veteran reporter of previous wars. He was also an important link that continued to feed stories of atrocities to the Catholic media in the United States. According to historian John T. Donovan (2004), O'Connor kept defending a staunchly anti-communist line even in the late 1960s, when the pope was calling for peace in Vietnam. Even humanitarian officers were veterans of battlefronts lost because of communist expansion. Monsignor Joseph Harnett, the director of the Catholic Relief Services, the largest NGOs involved in the Vietnamese evacuation and resettlement, previously worked in Trieste, where the population doubled with refugees fleeing communism, and in Korea, just before moving to Saigon (Kauffman 2005). He too became an important connection between Saigon, Catholics in Vietnam, and Catholics in the United States.

The transnational support received for refugee protection was also an opportunity for Saigon to gain support. For Ngô Đình Diệm, Catholic networks were instrumental for diplomatic relations. Ever since he became the prime minister in June 1954, he refused to take part in the Geneva Conference. After the signature of the ceasefire agreement, he refrained from doing anything that could come out as a recognition of its provisions. Diệm asked the French High Commissioner, General Paul Ély, to request local investigations on communist atrocities in Catholic parishes. He also wrote to Cardinal Spellman seeking American support. The prime minister explained that there were roughly

"25,000 Catholics waiting for French vessels on the sandbanks," proving once again how cruel and dangerous communist rule was. He also insisted on the peculiar situation which prevented him from seizing the ICC: "With respect to judicial aspects, it is not opportune for the National Government of Vietnam, which has not signed the Geneva Accords, to officially protest against its violation" (Cardinal Spellman Funds 1954b; TTLT2/PThT/An Ninh 1955). The Catholic Church was not only responsible for the spiritual lives of Catholics. It also served as a diplomatic pivot for Saigon.

Catholic authorities less inclined to support an all-out anti-communist policy also unwittingly supported Saigon's political campaign. The Vatican did not encourage the preservation of a distinct Catholic refugee identity (Nguyen 2016: 231). It also had to temper Saigon's anger when it appointed a politically moderate priest, Nguyễn Văn Bình, instead of the president's own brother (Cardinal Spellman Funds 1956b). Yet Rome had an interest in showing the Vietnamese Catholic refugee crisis as an evidence of both international Catholic solidarity and Catholic influence in the Third World. Years after the evacuation, Saigon used the Northern refugees as an opportunity to shine on the international stage. For example, South Vietnam could not participate to the 1958 Universal Exhibition in Brussels because both Hanoi and Saigon claimed they represented the country. Yet the Holy See dedicated a space in its pavilion to the 1954 Vietnamese refugees. Both Rome and Saigon used the refugees' successful resettlement for different reasons. But the Vatican was aware that by showcasing the Vietnamese refugees, it was also supporting Saigon's diplomatic struggle.

Catholic and governmental authorities were not the only ones taking advantage of this historical moment. Many Northern Vietnamese Catholic refugees previously involved in politics, the arts, or the paramilitary considered that the international support they received was a confirmation that they had to rewrite history. They formed selective memories of the First Indochina War and pushed for representations which implied that being a Catholic also involved an opposition to the spread of atheism in wartime Vietnam (Nguyen 2016).

Former refugees of the Chinese civil war also took advantage of the media focus, international support, and historical consciousness arising from the 1954 evacuation. Raymond de Jaegher, the missionary who had escaped both the Japanese invasion and communist rule in China, did not evacuate to Taiwan or return to Belgium, his home country. After creating the Free Pacific Association, he set foot in Saigon, where he became an active member of the Vietnamese chapter of the Asian People's Anti-Communist League (APACL). The organization was created at the Chin Hae Conference in Korea in June 1954 to regroup noncommunist countries in Asia into a joint cultural association (Tan 2019; Trần 2013). The English-language publication of the APACL's Vietnamese chapter, *Free Front*, reveals how this joint denunciation of communist atrocities operated. Raymond de Jaegher wrote at least a dozen articles on the communist threat to Malaysia, Burma, and India (de Jaegher, 1957, 1958a, 1958b, 1958c, 1958d). All of them suggested that communism was a threat to virtually every free nation across Asia. With the refugee crisis, religious authorities, missionaries, and political leaders extended the Catholic arc against communist expansion by injecting political objectives into a humanitarian crisis. This increasingly gave the impression that the Vietnamese church as whole—and not just a network of activists—was becoming a key player of anti-communist efforts.

Debating the Role of the Church in Asia

Not everyone agreed with the correlation between refugee protection, Catholic relief, and a global struggle against communism. The influence of key activists in channeling Christian generosity into their own *Weltanschauung* was so obvious that other Catholics became critical of the new face of the church in Asia.

The Christian Century, an ecumenical publication in the United States, criticized the expansionism of Roman Catholic aid in Taiwan (The Christian Century Editors 1958). According to the article, although there were two to three times more Protestants on the island, the NCWC had taken advantage of US surplus food to hold 84 percent of all relief goods imported, leaving the remaining 16 percent to the Church World Service and the Lutheran World Service.

The major problem with this imbalance was that Roman Catholic priests used relief goods as an incentive for newcomers to join the faith and for recent converts to remain with their church. A solution to this situation was to create ration cards, which would be distributed to the needy population of Taiwan. Protestant and Catholic agencies in Taipei agreed to evenly split the distribution of aid, regardless of which agency had imported it, so that no church would have greater material incentives if it used it to proselytize. But things did not go smoothly.

Priests rushed to get cards for their own members. When the proposition was made to split, not the cards but the time of distribution, with one agency distributing all the aid for a month, followed by another, the NCWC backpedaled, suggesting that this formula could only continue if its outlets were distributing 60 percent of the goods and Protestants were distributing 40 percent. Protestants refused this compromise and took it as further evidence of the "post-World War II and post-Korean War push by the Roman Catholic Church in the whole Pacific area, and in particular to the wide-ranging activities of Francis Cardinal Spellman, who is in charge of his church's relations with our military forces" (The Christian Century Editors 1958). Poverty relief was not neutral. The American Catholic Church's reluctance to share the burden with others gave the impression that Catholic aid was also a vehicle for proselytism and political influence.

Other dissident voices raised concern about Catholic relief assistance encouraging loyalty to Washington's foreign policy. British news correspondent Graham Greene had visited Vietnam several times to report on the Indochina War. When he came back in early 1955 to write a feature article on the partition of Vietnam, he was worried by the turn the Vietnamese church had taken (Hammer 1955: 28). In a series of three articles published in the *Sunday Times*, Greene, a Catholic convert himself, gave a dim picture of the Catholic Church in Vietnam.

According to Greene, one of South Vietnam's key problem was how the Catholic faith had transformed. Contrary to the claim that Catholicism had always been a tool of imperialism, Greene believed that the church had not always been a pawn of the West. But this was now becoming the case. According to him, Prime Minister Ngô Đình Diệm's Catholic faith was initially an advantage (Greene 1955a). He even saw similarities between him and Hồ Chí Minh, and between communism and Catholicism (Greene 1955c). Yet important transformations had made the Catholic faith increasingly unpopular.

Graham Greene conceded that Catholics had good reason to flee, as he quoted a doctor in the port of Haiphong claiming that there was a daily average of two atrocities committed, not by central authorities, but because of "the enthusiasm of local partisans or the results of private vendettas" (Greene 1955b). Yet the journalist was quick to recall that "atrocities can happen wherever there is hate, and hate is never confined to one side" (Greene 1955b). The Catholic civilians regrouping to the South were the greatest victim of this transformation of the Catholic Church as they had been abandoned by three "prince bishops with private armies," who had compromised themselves and "political priests" had whispered to their faithful that "God and the Virgin have gone south" (Greene 1955b). To him, Catholics had to pay the price for the priests' excessive involvement in the war.

American aid did not dissipate the impression that the Catholic faith had become a political tool. Countless ceremonies for the visits from Catholic officials such as Cardinal Spellman or Cardinal Gilroy, the archbishop of Canberra, gave the impression that the "Catholic Church is occidental and an ally of the United States" (Greene 1955a). The outpouring of aid for Vietnamese refugees did little to hide American self-interest: "This is not the unobtrusive, spontaneous acts of charity to which the poor are accustomed; the *tentatives de suicide*, the chicken bearing the badge of American aid demand a kind of payment—cooperation in the cold war" (Greene 1955b). Just as Ngô Đình Diệm had become "The Patriot Ruined by the West," in Greene's view, the Cold War had corrupted the Catholic faith (Greene 1955c).

Conclusion

The case of evacuation of Northern Vietnam in 1954 shows that although Catholics cherished the principles of solidarity among coreligionists and charity toward others, the way this generosity extended to population overseas reveals multiple interests and interventions from the local to the global level. We can draw three conclusions from this analysis.

First, an analysis of the Catholic transnational solidarity requires an understanding of the institutional structure of the Catholic Church, the political and economic power of national churches, and the role of key religious leaders or missionaries. Although Catholics responded to a clear hierarchy headed by a single authority in Rome, the Vatican did not centralize Catholic relief efforts across the globe. Instead, it was key Catholic leaders and missionaries which channeled the efforts of national churches into Vietnam, for humanitarian and political reasons.

Second, this case study showed that refugee protection served both humanitarian ideals and political objectives. This does not mean that a blind anti-communist sentiment guided every person contributing to the emergency relief. Yet, the main motivation behind the people channeling this generosity toward Asian churches was the containment of communist expansion, civil wars, and the fear of a schismatic church. The links to this chain not only connected Vietnamese to Americans. Foreign missionaries, Chinese, and Korean activists were also part of this network converging in Vietnam in 1954.

Last, refugee protection is a relationship that is dynamic and dialectical. States protect refugees for humanitarian and political interests. Yet refugees also use exile and international recognition to get support for their own cause. Both Paul Yu Pin and Ngô Đình Diệm, foreign missionaries in China, or Vietnamese refugees used their time in exile to regroup and find ways to continue their fight. These refugees sought protection. Yet they also raised awareness abroad and created new alliances to oppose communist expansion.

4

The Virgin Mary Became Asian

Diasporic Nationalism among Vietnamese Catholic Refugees in the United States and Germany

Thien-Huong Ninh

Introduction

From June 8 to 10, 2019, in Aschaffenburg, Germany, more than 6,000 Vietnamese Catholics gathered to pray to Our Lady of Lavang (Figure 4.3) at the Forty-third National Congress of Vietnamese Catholics in Germany. According to community leaders and regular attendees, the number of visitors to the annual event has grown dramatically since Our Lady of Lavang became the patron saint of Vietnamese Catholics in Germany in 2013. Unlike other representations of the Virgin Mary, Our Lady of Lavang is in the image of a Vietnamese woman wearing *áodài* (Vietnamese traditional costume) and holding baby Jesus. For nearly 100 years, she was represented as a European woman, modeled after Our Lady of Victories in Paris (Figure 4.1). However, in the mid-1990s, Vietnamese Catholics in the United States visually transformed Our Lady of Lavang into their ethnic image and received validation from the Catholic Church in their ancestral land, Vietnam. After receiving blessings from Pope John Paul II in Rome in 2002, six Vatican-blessed statues of the Vietnamese-looking Our Lady of Lavang were exported to six different countries across four continents. Vietnamese Catholics in Germany were selected as the guardian of the statue in Europe.

Today, the Vietnamese-looking Our Lady of Lavang has become popular throughout the world. It is the only Asian form of the Virgin Mary that has become global. Throughout Asia, within the walls of parishes and confines of loose parish networks, there are local ethnic forms of the Virgin Mary, but none has been catapulted to a global scale as Our Lady of Lavang.

Figure 4.1 Statue of Our Lady of Lavang representing the Virgin Mary as a European woman, modeled after Our Lady of Victories, in Lavang, Vietnam; photo by Thien-Huong Ninh.

This phenomenon of religious transnationalism and diasporic formation, concurrent with ethnic revitalization and nationalism, among Vietnamese refugees and their descendants is the focus of this chapter, particularly their communities in the United States and Germany. How and why do they look to Our Lady of Lavang as a modality to reconnect with each other, locally and globally? I argue that, through the Vietnamese-looking Our Lady of Lavang, Vietnamese Catholic refugees have elevated diasporic nationalism to a global level of religious sanctity. I illustrate that they have utilized Our Lady of Lavang in the image of a Vietnamese woman to recentralize their global religious community based on a common faith, ethnic culture, and political positionalities as refugees displaced from their homeland and excluded from full incorporation into their host societies. This ethnic image was visually created in the United States, sent to Vietnamese Catholics in Vietnam for validation, and then exported to the rest of the world, including Germany. I contend that Vietnamese Catholic refugees and their descendants uphold Our Lady of Lavang as an emblem of their deterritorialized nation in the diaspora, an imagined community that exists beyond the territorial boundaries of their dead homeland (South Vietnam) and new host societies.

Thus, the global circuit of this ethnic Virgin Mary does not simply draw upon religious and cultural repertoire of holy mother devotional practices in Vietnam, which was closed off from them for nearly twenty years due to the US trade embargo against the country between 1975 and 1995. Moreover, the globalization and Vietnamization of Our Lady of Lavang are simply not due to policies of multiculturalism within the Catholic Church and Western countries. These efforts represent a transnational project in which Vietnamese Catholic refugees strategize to create an alternative sacred space of refuge to contest, negotiate, and divert the conditions of social, cultural, and political marginalization.

I refer to "refugee" as an inclusive identification and an analytical framework, following the work of Espiritu (2014: 20–33). As a classification, it refers to individuals who are legally defined as such by resettling governments or international agencies as well as their descendants and individuals whose forced displacement has not been recognized by political and social institutions. While many (but not all) Vietnamese in the United States and Germany are either legally or voluntarily classified as refugees, studies have found that refugees' experiences and status do not end with resettlement but continue to linger in their lives (Nguyen 2012: 911–42; Nguyen-Vo 2005: 157–75; Espiritu 2002: 372–5). These vestiges are often passed down onto their descendants and shape their worldviews. Moreover, following van der Veer's works on narratives of nation, religion, and migration (2002; 1999; 1995), I employ refugee as an analytical framework to shine light on the multiplicities and asymmetries of power dynamics inherent in nation's knowledge production about refugees and nonrefugees. In doing so, I hope to re-represent, recover, and reconstruct "refugee" as a "socio-legal object of knowledge" (Espiritu 2014: 18–25), rather than as simply dispossessed, traumatized, and helpless victims. In turn, this analytical approach opens up empirical and theoretical spaces for uncovering the "lived religion" (Orsi 2010: 13–27) of Vietnamese Catholic refugees.

Background: Catholicism in Vietnam

During the seventeenth century, about a hundred years after the arrival of Portuguese Catholic missionaries, French Catholic missionaries successfully made gradual inroads into Vietnamese society by acculturating Catholicism into the local culture (Dutton 2016: Chapter 1; Keith 2012: 55–88; Phan 1991: 2–8). However, it was not until French rule (1887–1954) that Catholicism enjoyed full integration and acceptance into Vietnamese society. The Catholic Church flourished under the French colonial government in terms of wealth and authority. It built schools, churches, and medical centers, many of which remain standing today. However, its strength has deteriorated since 1954, when French colonial rule was replaced by Vietnamese communist control—first in Northern Vietnam and, by 1975, in Southern Vietnam (Chu 2008: 162–7).

Beginning in 1986, following policies of economic liberalization (*Đổi Mới*), the Vietnamese state slowly relaxed its control over religious practices (Fjelstad and Nguyen 2006: 9–11; Taylor 2004: 15–18; Taylor 2001: 23–30) and granted "qualified" religious freedom (Hansen 2009a: 185–92). As of 2014, the Catholic population in Vietnam is smaller only to that of Buddhist. There are approximately seven million Catholics in Vietnam (eight of the country's population of ninety million), and they are heavily concentrated in the Southern region of Vietnam (Home Office 2018).

The Religious and Symbolic Significance of Our Lady of Lavang

The history of Our Lady of Lavang is an inflection of the history of Vietnamese Catholics as religious martyrs and refugees constantly fleeing from religious persecution. According to an oral tradition, in 1798 the Virgin Mary appeared several times to a group of Vietnamese Catholics who were fleeing from anti-Catholic persecutions in Lavang.[1] She comforted them and said, "My children, have faith and be brave. I have heard your prayers. From now on, I will grant the wishes of all who come to me" (Tran 2009). Since then, Catholics and non-Catholics alike have sought refuge at the site of the apparition. Although the Vatican has not verified the historical accuracy of the apparition, Catholics and non-Catholics alike have continued to pray to Our Lady of Lavang. Except for a short hiatus due to war and violence during the 1970s, congresses have been held every two years to commemorate her apparition.

In 1901, when Vietnam was under French colonialism and Catholicism was much more tolerated, the first Our Lady of Lavang church was built and completed on the site where she had appeared according to faithful Catholics. At this historic event, the sitting French bishop placed a French-modeled statue of Our Lady of Victories (*Notre-Dame des Victoires*) to represent Our Lady of Lavang in the new church (Figure 4.1). The Virgin Mary is depicted standing and wearing a crown and a draped dress; her hands are positioned to the right holding a baby Jesus, who is also crowned and standing on top of a globe.

The Marian title "Our Lady of Victories" is old and tied to many names in the Christian world, most notably Our Lady of the Rosary (i.e., victory comes from the power of the Rosary). While the veneration of the Virgin Mary may represent Catholic conquest over and absorption of paganistic goddess-cults rooted in ancient Egyptian, Greek, and Roman cultures (Benko 2004: 5), the Marian imagery of Our Lady of Victories also embodies a distinctive French Catholic form and political conquests.

Many French Catholics believed that the Virgin Mary intervened in the miraculous victory of the French over the Greeks in Constantinople in 1204, which marked the siege and sack of Constantinople in the culmination of the Fourth Crusade. Since then, they often appealed to Our Lady of Victories in times of political crisis and threats from religious heresies (Santoro 2011: 570). Despite or perhaps because of the French Revolution, which challenged the influential role of the Catholic Church, Our Lady of Victories during the nineteenth century became "a symbol of the aspiration of the [French] Catholic Church to roll back the evil forces of the French revolution and to restore hierarchy, nobility, and authority" (Ashiwa and Wank 2009: 80–2). As France spread its colonial power overseas, different French regimes found the Catholic Church's religious authoritarianism useful in asserting and maintaining their power and dominance. Consequently, many statues and churches devoted to Our Lady of Victories can be found inside and outside of France. For nearly a century in Vietnam, this statue of a Western-looking Virgin Mary was associated with the apparition of Our Lady of Lavang. It was not until 1998 that Our Lady of Lavang was transformed and re-represented as a Vietnamese woman by the Vietnamese diaspora.

The Global Dispersion of Vietnamese Catholic Refugees and Local Marianism before 1998

Before 1975, there were approximately 300,000 Vietnamese living outside of Vietnam, mostly as students or official employees in France and the United States. Immediately after the Fall of Saigon in April 1975, millions of Vietnamese fled Vietnam either by plane, boat, or foot for fear of religious, political, and economic persecution. The refugee exodus subsided at the turn of the twenty-first century, but the overseas Vietnamese populations continued to grow with the continuing arrivals of family members sponsored by overseas Vietnamese refugees, migrant workers, and students from Vietnam.

Currently, there are Vietnamese in nearly forty countries in the Americas, Europe, Africa, Oceania, and Asia (outside of Vietnam). According to a 2016 estimate, the overseas Vietnamese population is as follows (excluding Russia and Eastern Europe):

Table 4.1 Overseas Vietnamese population (2016 *Yearbook of the Catholic Church of Vietnam*)

Year(s)	Total	Country						
		United States	Germany[a]	France	Australia	Canada	England	Other
1914–18	80,000			80,000				
1954–75	217,000	3,000		214,000				
1975	143,000	135,000		18,000				
1975–95	1,927,714	1,300,000	100,000	200,000	133,444	100,000	26,000	68,270
1995–2000	2,468,540	1,500,000	110,000	250,000	142,000	120,000	27,000	319,540
2012	4,000,000	2,200,000	250,000	300,000	300,000	250,000	40,000	660,000
2015	4,200,000							

[a]See Hüwelmeier 2014: 82.

Listed in the 2016 *Yearbook of the Catholic Church of Vietnam* (Niên Giám Giáo Hội Công Giáo Việt Nam), written and edited by the Confederation of Bishops of Vietnam, the total number of overseas Vietnamese priests is 1,096; and thousands of brothers and nuns are serving more than 300 Vietnamese congregations around the world.

Vietnamese Catholics in the United States

Compared with the percentage of Catholics in Vietnam (approximately 7 percent), Catholics make up approximately 30 percent of the Vietnamese population in the United States (Pew Forum on Research and Public Life 2012). The overrepresentation in the overseas Vietnamese population may be due to the fact that many had to flee Vietnam because of religious persecution. Moreover, a significant number of Vietnamese refugees converted to Catholicism during the processes of flight and resettlement, especially those resettled by Catholic relief agencies (Hoskins 2006: 191–209; Hoskins 2015: 32–40).

As they struggled to rebuild their lives in the United States, Vietnamese Catholics continued to pray to and venerate the Virgin Mary and, arguably, did so more fervently because of their traumatic experiences of coerced displacement and difficulty integrating into the United States as refugees (Dorais 2005: 172–5). For example, as a reflection of his devotion and gratitude to the Virgin Mary for safeguarding him during his boat exodus from Vietnam, well-known Vietnamese Catholic sculptor Nhan Van immediately created a statue of the Virgin Mary looking like a Vietnamese woman upon his arrival in the United States in the early 1980s. This was the first statue of its kind. Like himself, other Vietnamese Catholics most likely also worshipped the Virgin Mary but did not have devotion specifically to Our Lady of Lavang. Historical evidence has revealed that Vietnamese Catholics focused primarily on the European-looking Our Lady of Fatima in their yearning for the homeland. The popularity of Our Lady of Fatima—possibly more than Our Lady of Lavang—immediately after Vietnamese refugees arrived in the United States may be because of her greater universal appeal and official recognition from the Vatican. As echoed in Meyer's (2010) research in Ghana, "white" European representations of Christian figures in non-European contexts cannot be simply reduced to racial inferiority. They can possibly serve as a link to the world at large.

Vietnamese Catholics in Germany

Before 1975, there was only a small number (perhaps only a few hundred and about ten priests) of Vietnamese Catholics living in West Germany. With the large wave of Vietnamese refugees arriving after 1975, the number of Vietnamese Catholics in West Germany increased drastically. Between 1975 and 1976, Germany had about 2,000 Vietnamese, most of whom were students, including over 100 Catholics along with about ten priests and monks. By the end of 2014, there were approximately 16,000 Vietnamese Catholics in Germany. Most of them (at least 95 percent) lived in the former West German territory before the 1990s and account for more than 20 percent of the Vietnamese population. Vietnamese Catholic refugees have been scattered throughout West Germany, although there are significant population concentrations in certain large cities, including Berlin, Hamburg, Düsseldorf, Frankfurt, Munich, and Stuttgart.

The current Vietnamese Catholic refugee community in Germany also boasts a large representation in the religious vocation: thirty-eight priests (one-third of whom are ordained in Germany) and eleven brothers and thirty-one nuns belonging to various religious orders (including The Phát Diệm Cross, the Ursuline Order, the Dominican Order, the Dominican Order, and the Secular Order). While approximately two-thirds of Vietnamese Catholic priests are in charge of pastoral work of German parishes, the other eleven priests are responsible for both German parishes and the local Vietnamese Catholic community. There are Vietnamese masses at eighty sites. Although they are usually held on Sundays, they are sporadic (once a month or once to several times a year) due to the lack of Vietnamese-speaking priests.

While the German Catholic Church is divided into seven archdioceses and twenty dioceses, the activities of the Vietnamese Catholic communities are divided into eleven pastoral regions. Each region is under the care of a Vietnamese priest nominated by the local bishop. Depending on the local pastoral area, there are many spiritual, ministerial, and cultural activities, including summer camps for youths and adults, choir, prayer groups, and Vietnamese language classes. There are also organized associations, such as Cursillos, Catholic Mothers' Association (Hội Các Bà Mẹ Công Giáo), the Sacred Heart Alliance (Liên Minh Thánh Tâm), and the Society of God's Mercy (Hội Lòng Chúa Thương Xót.). Moreover, to maintain a community cohesion, there were many regularly distributed publications (e.g., newspapers, magazines, and newsletters), including *Âu Châu* that began in 1982 and had its last print in December 2014. Many publications have transitioned from print to online digital format, such as the popular website Danchua.eu.

According to my interviewees, there are two distinctive features of the Vietnamese Catholic community in Germany: (1) Their community is led by the laity and (2) they have one of only two national-level Vietnamese Catholic federations outside of Vietnam (the other federation is based in the United States).[2] This organization was established in 1976. It was named "Association of Vietnamese Catholics in Germany" and renamed to "Federation of Associations of Vietnamese Catholics in Germany" (FAVCG) in 1987.[3] It represents nearly 100 Associations of Vietnamese Catholics scattered throughout Germany. This umbrella organization is led by an executive committee, which is composed of four members of the laity of whom were elected for a two-year term by Vietnamese Catholics in Germany.

The federation organizes many activities, and the most popular event is the annual congress, which has been occurring since 1976. According to my Vietnamese interviewees in Germany, Vietnamese Catholic refugees are the only ethnic group in Europe that has its own Catholic congress (convention). The number of attendees at the event has grown steadily since its inception, from about fifty in its first year to nearly 6,000 in recent years. The congress concurs with Pentecost Sunday (usually in late May or early June) and usually spans over three days held at a school arena. It has attracted guests from all over Europe and other parts of the world, including the Bishop Mai Thanh Luong from Orange County, California, and other bishops from Vietnam. It has been held in different cities but most often in Königstein and, more recently, Aschaffenburg.

As in the United States, Marian devotion to the Virgin Mary among Vietnamese Catholic refugees in Germany did not emphasize Our Lady of Lavang before she became revisualized as a Vietnamese woman in 1998. There were many nearby popular Marian sites in Europe that had been attracting pilgrims throughout the world for decades and hundreds of years. Consequently, most of their Marian devotion was toward "European-looking" representations of the Virgin Mary, including taking regular pilgrimage trips to Our Lady of Altotting, Our Lady of Marnefried, Our Lady of Banneux in Belgium, Our Lady of Fatima in Portugal, Our Lady of Lourdes in France, and Our Lady of Czechoslovakia in Poland.

The Global Diasporic Circulation of Our Lady of Lavang, the Vietnamese Virgin Mary

The Vatican: The Recognition of Our Lady of Lavang

During the Marian Year of 1987, as the Vatican was considering petitions to canonize 117 Vietnamese Catholic martyrs,[4] Pope John Paul II formed the

Coordinating Office of the Apostolate for the Vietnamese in the Diaspora (*Văn Phòng Phối Kết Tông Đồ Mục Vụ Việt Nam Hải Ngoại*) to create an institutional bridge between the Vatican and the globally scattered Vietnamese refugee community.[5] The first director of the center was Monsignor Philippe Tran Van Hoai, a Vietnamese Catholic priest with a long history of working with Vietnamese refugees throughout the world.[6] In the spirit of the Marian Year, as the Catholic Church prepared for the turn of the millennium, Monsignor Tran undoubtedly informed the Holy Father about the 200th year of commemoration of Our Lady of Lavang's apparition in 1998, a major event for Vietnamese Catholics throughout the world. Born and raised in Central Vietnam not far from the Our Lady of Lavang sanctuary, Monsignor Tran had close historic and personal ties to Our Lady of Lavang. In 1959, he became the first priest to be ordained at Our Lady of Lavang church. His ordination ceremony occurred during the same year that the pilgrimage center was consecrated as a national shrine and became the most important Catholic religious center in Vietnam.

As a result of possible influences from Monsignor Tran and the Center of Pastoral Apostolate for Overseas Vietnamese, Pope John Paul II publicly discussed the significance of Our Lady of Lavang with Vietnamese Catholics on June 19, 1988 (Tran 2009). This was the first time in history that the pope had emphasized the importance of Our Lady of Lavang. The meeting occurred immediately after the canonization ceremony for the 117 Vietnamese martyrs in Rome. This was not surprising. As noted earlier, Our Lady of Lavang has been an important symbol of Vietnamese Catholic martyrdom since the early days of Catholicism in Vietnam, when Vietnamese Catholics sought refuge at Our Lady of Lavang's site of apparition in order to escape from anti-Catholic persecution. For Vietnamese Catholics, therefore, the canonization of Vietnamese martyrs must also occur in tandem with the recognition of Our Lady of Lavang.

By the early 1990s, Pope John Paul II referred to Our Lady of Lavang much more frequently in public addresses in anticipation of the celebration (Tran 1994: 299–323). One of his most popular presentations of Our Lady of Lavang was at the 1993 World Youth Day in Denver, which was attended by several thousand Vietnamese American Catholics. In his address, he commended "the whole Vietnamese Catholic community to the intercession of Our Lady of Lavang" and encouraged them to prepare for the bicentennial commemoration of Our Lady of Lavang's apparition in 1998 (Pope John Paul II 1993). He also blessed them for "an even brighter future for the new generations of Vietnamese." He said, "May they grow up with healthy pride in their national origin, the riches of their culture, the spiritual greatness of their forebears who stood firm in the face of trials of all kinds" (Pope John Paul II 1993).

The Vietnamization of Our Lady of Lavang in the United States

Within the context of economic globalization and religious tolerance after Vietnam reestablished diplomatic ties with the United States in 1995, a delegation of priests from Vietnam was able to visit their ethnic coreligionists in Orange County between 1996 and 1997. Well-known Vietnamese American sculptor Nhan Van volunteered to guide them. Since the 1970s, he had been very involved in the Orange County Vietnamese Catholic community. In 1978, he was a representative leader for the Vietnamese Catholic community in Orange County while it was trying to form a multi-parish umbrella leadership organization (Vietnamese Catholic Center 2013).

During the tour, Mr. Van showed the Vietnamese priests the Marian statues that he had created in the image of a Vietnamese woman. They were impressed and delighted by his works. This news reached the ears of the bishop of the Hue Archdiocese, which oversees the cathedral and pilgrimage center of Our Lady of Lavang. He was preparing for the 200th commemoration of the apparition of Our Lady of Lavang in 1998. It was an important event not just for Catholics in Vietnam but also around the world. Between 1996 and 1998, he had received many letters of blessings from Pope John Paul II in reference to the upcoming historic ceremony (Tran 1994: 299–323).

Consequently, the bishop of Hue Diocese and other church leaders in Vietnam decided to invite Van Nhan to create a Vietnamese statue of Our Lady of Lavang. His work depicts Our Lady of Lavangas a Virgin Mary dressed in a white Vietnamese traditional costume (*áodài*) under a blue decorative cloak, adorned by a Vietnamese golden headdress, and holding a statue of Vietnamese-looking baby Jesus on her left arm.[7] The blue and white colors of the statue symbolizes the traditional colors that symbolize the Virgin Mary.

On July 1, 1998, this statue received blessings by Pope John II in Rome to recognize the contributions of Vietnamese Catholics to the Catholic Church and faith (Tran 2009). At this celebrated event, the Holy Father also proclaimed Our Lady of Lavang as the patroness of the Catholic Church of Vietnam. Although this religious honor did not officially recognize the historical accuracy of the apparition of Our Lady of Lavang in 1798, it was a source of inspiration for Vietnamese Catholics throughout the world. For the first time in history, a Vietnamese icon of the Catholic faith was officially introduced to the global

Catholic community. On August 13, 1998, 200 years after her apparition, more than 200,000 attendees gathered in Lavang to worship Our Lady of Lavang in the representation of a Vietnamese woman.[8] This Vietnamese statue replaced the European-looking statue of Our Lady of Lavang (modeled after Our Lady of Victories) as the centerpiece in the Shrine of Our Lady of Lavang, on the grounds of the Basilica of Our Lady of Lavang in Lavang, Vietnam.[9]

Since Our Lady of Lavang's "ethnic" transformation, Vietnamese Catholics in the United States have increasingly popularized the symbolic coupling of the Virgin Mary and Vietnamese martyrs. Historically, for example, Vietnamese Catholic martyrs have often been depicted in paintings with an adult Jesus in the center. However, as the Vietnamese-looking Our Lady of Lavang became popular, she and the Vietnamese-looking baby Jesus "displaced" the adult European-looking Jesus as the central figure in many of these religious artworks.

Similarly, representations of Our Lady of Lavang are often displayed within steps near large panels depicting graphic scenes of the public execution of Vietnamese martyrs. The martyrs are usually portrayed as the most helpless person, with their limbs restrained and kneeling on the ground, and nearby them are tools of execution such as swords, saws, and metal chains. The visual pairing of Our Lady of Lavang and Vietnamese Catholic martyrs can be found at many important Vietnamese Catholic sites in the United States, including the Vietnamese Marian pilgrimage center in Carthage, Missouri, which attracts approximately 70,000 visitors each year, and at the Basilica of the National Shrine of the Immaculate Conception in Washington, D.C.

Our Lady of Lavang's popularity in the United States is also represented by the growing number of sites and parishes named after her. When the local bishop gave them permission to have a church with a Vietnamese name in 2001, Vietnamese Catholics in Orange County chose to name the church after Our Lady of Lavang. The decision was nearly unanimous and was much anticipated by the community that has played a central role in globalizing the representation of Our Lady of Lavang as a Vietnamese woman. The same community is currently raising $25 million to construct a monumental "Our Lady of Lavang Shrine" at Christ Cathedral, the seat of the Diocese of Orange.

Meanwhile, Vietnamese Catholics in Silicon Valley are building a $45 million parish dedicated to "Our Lady of Lavang." Similar to the case of the Our Lady of Lavang Catholic Church in Orange County, the naming of the church after Our Lady of Lavang was welcomed unanimously by local Vietnamese Catholics. They had wanted to have a church with a Vietnamese name since as early as the late 1970s. After their original church named St. Patrick Proto-Cathedral was heavily damaged by fire, they immediately mobilized to raise funds for the construction project. The new Our Lady of Lavang church is scheduled to be completed in 2021.

The Transplantation of Our Lady of Lavang to Germany

In late 1999, one year after the Vietnamese-looking representation of Our Lady of Lavang was declared as the new official image, two representatives of the FAVCG attended a meeting at the Vatican. The event was organized by the Coordinating Office of the Apostolate for the Vietnamese in the Diaspora (COAVD).[10] The purpose of the meeting was to prepare Vietnamese Catholics scattered throughout the world for the Holy Year in 2000, including World Youth Day XV. These representatives from Germany were the only two of the four members of the laity in attendance (the other two were from the United States and France). This reflects the observation that, as noted earlier, the Vietnamese Catholic community in Germany is distinguished by the relatively high level of involvement among the laity.

In 2002, following this meeting and continuing involvements, FAVCG was invited by COAVD to represent Vietnamese Catholics in Europe and receive a large Vietnamese statue of Our Lady of Lavang at an event in Santa Ana, California, which is in the heart of Little Saigon in Orange County (Figure 4.2). Mr. Tan Van Dinh (former president of FAVCG) and his wife from Germany represented FAVCG at the ceremony and have been the main guardians of the statue in Europe since then. Five other statues of Our Lady of Lavang were given to representatives of Vietnamese Catholics in other continents, including Australia (one statue), Asia (one statue), and North America (three statues, a greater number of statues due to the significantly larger Vietnamese Catholic populations in the United States and Canada). Although the Vatican had not verified the historical accuracy of the apparition of Our Lady of Lavang, all of these statues had been blessed by Pope John II in Rome to recognize and reaffirm the acceptance of the Virgin Mary in her Vietnamese image.

At this historic gathering, Father Dinh Duc Dao, the sitting director of COAVD, declared in his sermon:

> In the past, the Holy Mother appeared in Lavang during difficult times to comfort and soothe her suffering children, regardless of their faith. Today, we cannot easily go to Lavang to find the Holy Mother. However, we can pray to the Holy Mother to come to us, her children, who are scattered throughout the world. We can ask Our Lady of Lavang to comfort us and bring us together as

Figure 4.2 Representatives of Vietnamese Catholics in Europe—Tan Kim Dinh (former president of FAVCG) and his wife from Germany—posing in front of four statues of the Vatican-blessed Vietnamese-looking Our Lady of Lavang at a 2002 ceremony in Santa Ana, California; photo by Tan Kim Dinh.

a loving community devoted to God and committed to sharing his teachings to everyone around the world.

Throughout 2003, which was declared as the year of "Faith: Following the Proof of Faith of the Civil Community of Vietnam" by COAVD, the statue of the Vietnamese-looking Our Lady of Lavang traveled to nearly all major Vietnamese Catholic congregations in Europe. According to a representative of FAVCG, "Our Lady of Lavang has Vietnamese features that make her look like a mother for us, reminding us of our cultural roots and heritage that we cannot forget. Also, what is important is that she appeared in Lavang to help the poor and the suffering. Those are the important reasons why many Vietnamese Catholics in Germany and throughout Europe feel much closer to her than other representations of the Virgin Mary. We can go to her and pray to her. We know that she would protect us, as she did when Vietnamese flocked to her for protection from religious persecution in Vietnam."

Ten years after the Vietnamese statue of Our Lady of Lavang arrived on German soil, on November 11, 2013, FAVCG proclaimed Our Lady of Lavang

Figure 4.3 Vietnamese Catholics surrounding and praying to a statue of Our Lady of Lavang (one of the replicas depicted in Figure 4.2) at the Forty-third National Congress of Vietnamese Catholics in Aschaffenburg, Germany (June 8 to 12, 2019); photo by Thien-Huong Ninh.

as the *first* patron saint of the Vietnamese Catholic community in Germany. Moreover, FAVCG chose to name the Monday following Pentecost Sunday, the closing day of the annual congress of the Vietnamese Catholic community in Germany, "Happy Our Lady of Lavang Day" (Ngày Hiền Mẫu Lavang; Figure 4.3). The day is devoted to venerating Our Lady of Lavang, including an elaborate procession and traditional flower-offering dances.

Although there was some initial hesitation to accept the new Vietnamese ethnic image of Our Lady of Lavang (Nguyen 2017), this depiction has spread to many countries, including the Philippines where local Catholics embrace her as patroness of Puerto Princesa and Palawan and, most recently in October 2018, in Abu Ghosh, Israel. Beyond her visual image as a Vietnamese woman, Our Lady of Lavang is important to many overseas Vietnamese because she represents their history of coerced displacement and global dispersion. This is clearly evidenced by the integration of the symbolically significant stars in her representations. In 2002, at the twenty-sixth Marian Convention in Lavang, Vietnam, the original Vietnamese-looking Our Lady of Lavang in Vietnam was slightly modified. The newer version depicts Our Lady of Lavang's headdress decorated with twelve stars. Vietnamese Catholics in Vietnam and abroad have interpreted these stars to represent the ones that Vietnamese boat refugees used to guide themselves to their new homes. In the Chapel of Our Lady of Lavang at the Basilica of the National Shrine of the Immaculate Conception in Washington, D.C., which was completed in 2005, the stars are decorated throughout the sanctuary as sacred reminders of the Vietnamese people's global dispersion.

Despite their geographical separation from each other, the Vietnamese-looking Our Lady of Lavang represents and facilitates the diasporic reconnection between Vietnamese Catholics around the world, including those in Vietnam. In 2010, a stone engraved with *Cộng Đồng Hải Ngoại* (Overseas Diocese) was placed at the Our Lady of Lavang pilgrimage center during the opening ceremony of the Holy Year. It recognizes overseas Vietnamese Catholics as the twenty-seventh diocese of the Catholic Church in Vietnam. The stone was later buried on the construction ground of a new church at the pilgrimage center, symbolizing the significance of overseas Vietnamese Catholics as a foundation of the Vietnamese Catholic Church in Vietnam and beyond. Meanwhile, a brick from the Basilica of Our Lady of Lavang in Vietnam has been on display on the compound of Christ Cathedral in Orange County, California, where a $25-million shrine for Our Lady of Lavang is being constructed (anticipated date of completion is the end of 2020).

Today, statues of Our Lady of Lavang have become a popular diplomatic gift from one Vietnamese Catholic community to another in a different country, as I have observed in Germany, Taiwan, Japan, Belgium, the Netherlands, and France. In an email exchange, the former and last president of COAVD further affirmed that "Our Lady of Lavang . . . symbolizes overseas Vietnamese Catholics' connections to each other and to the Catholic Church in Vietnam." This transnational mediation through the Virgin Mary has also been observed by other studies of immigrants in the United States (Tweed 1997: 108–30; Horsfall 2000: 381–3; Castañeda-Liles 2018: 146–66).

Conclusion

Our Lady of Lavang is the crucible of faith for many Vietnamese Catholics and has become the symbol of the Vietnamese Catholic Church inside and outside of Vietnam. Throughout the history of Catholicism in Vietnam, Our Lady of

Lavang has been popularly known as "mother of refugees," the one to whom Vietnamese Catholic faithful would call upon for protection from religious persecutions, stability in times of forced displacement and uprootedness, and solace amid political trials and tribulations that marred Vietnam's twentieth-century society. Following the Fall of Saigon in 1975, Vietnamese Catholic refugees were forced to flee their homeland and became dispersed throughout the world. They sought Our Lady of Lavang even more vigorously during their escape journeys from Vietnam, resettlement in their new home, and cross-border reconnection to each other.

Thus, while holy mother veneration is a significant part of religious and cultural traditions in Vietnamese Catholicism, I argue that Vietnamese refugees and their overseas-reared descendants have innovatively adapted Marian devotional practices to their local settings and consequently recentralized their globally fragmented religious community. In particular, Vietnamese American Catholics have transformed the image of Our Lady of Lavang into a Vietnamese woman and exported this image to other parts of the world, including Germany. Through their shared devotion to Our Lady of Lavang, these geographically disparate Vietnamese Catholic communities have been able to rebuild relations with each other and reconstitute themselves as a nation in the diaspora.

While Our Lady of Lavang represents an ethnically and culturally specific form of Marianism similar to other "ethnic" versions, as has been studied by Robert Orsi (2010) and Thomas Tweed (1997), she is also particularly unique in that she does not simply reflect her followers' relations with their host societies and homeland. Our Lady of Lavang embodies the home—a deterritorialized and imagined space of belonging—that her followers have sought, yearned for, and created in a religious space that is distinctive from both their host societies and homeland.

The Vietnamization and global popularization of Our Lady of Lavang was rooted in sociopolitical mobilization by Vietnamese Catholics outside of Vietnam. Although the Federation of Asian Bishops promoted religious indigenization and localization as early as 1974 (Rosales and Arévalo 1997: 10–34), Vietnamese Catholics were isolated from this transition as their country had been drawn into a war and their church was politically divided between North and South Vietnam. Moreover, because Our Lady of Lavang's ethnic transformation was initiated outside of Vietnam, it was not influenced by various religious traditions of female veneration that are local to Vietnam, such as the practices of Mother Goddess mediumship and Kuan-yin devotion. Nevertheless, it is arguable that the Vietnamization of Our Lady Lavang into a more "familiar" form may have created bridges with Vietnamese of other religious backgrounds, including Buddhism (Truitt 2017: 83–107), Caodaism (Ninh 2013: 53–67; see also Hoskins in this volume), and the Mother Goddess religion (Nguyen 2017; Fjelstad and Nguyen 2011: 75–83; Endres 2011: 35–41; Salemink 2015: 231–46).

The nation is a ghostly matter for Vietnamese (Kwon 2008: 12–15; Tai 2001: 8–13). This is particularly so for Vietnamese Catholics who were forced to flee Vietnam as religious and political refugees (Nguyen 2018: 65–103; Huynh and Nguyen 2009: 34–40). They cannot claim Vietnam, nor their host societies in the United States and Germany, as homes.

Vietnam is the gravesite of their dead country (the Republic of South Vietnam), one that they have not and cannot properly bury or forget. For Vietnamese Catholics, South Vietnam under the Republic of South Vietnam government was a national haven where their religious practices flourished. More than 70 percent of Catholics from Northern Vietnam fled to the south in 1954 to escape political, economic, and religious persecution (Hansen 2009a: 185–92). The "death" of the Republic of South Vietnam and their inability to properly mourn for it in the aftermath has created a near-apocalyptic experience that continues to haunt them. As refugees in the United States and Germany, many Vietnamese Catholics have not been able to return to present-day Vietnam to reclaim the ghostly remnants of their past and to commemorate their dead nation. The lingering tension between the Vietnamese government and overseas Vietnamese Catholics is vividly exemplified by the delayed renovation of the Our Lady of Lavang pilgrimage center within the past ten years. The Vietnamese government supports the project as a means to attract generous monetary contributions from overseas Vietnamese Catholics. However, many Vietnamese politicians remain wary and guarded of the potential subversive influences that such support may foment.

Meanwhile, the United States and Germany have not fully integrated Vietnamese Catholics as citizens, nor have the Catholic churches in these countries fully accepted them. Even though religious diversity and freedom are fundamental rights in these Western countries, religion has become the proxy through which Vietnamese refugees are marginalized to the fringes of society as ethnic and racial minorities. As Catholics in the United States, for example, Vietnamese have been racialized in American society as ethnically unrepresentative of Catholicism or not being "truly Catholic" because they are Asians practicing a "Western" religion (Ninh 2017: 140–67). These processes of racialization have essentialized ethnicity and religion for the Vietnamese faithful, misconstruing the fundamental religious tenets and historical legacy of universalism in Catholicism, which welcomes followers across different ethnic backgrounds.

From this positionality of "in-between-ness, in-both-ness, and in-beyond-ness" in relation to Vietnam and their host countries (Fernandez 2003: 265), Vietnamese Catholics in the United States and Germany have evoked Our Lady of Lavang to reimagine their deterritorialized nation. Neither the country of resettlement or the homeland constitutes their sole place of belonging. Instead, it is from this point of the plurality of vision, seeing these worlds as occurring together "contrapuntally" (Said 1984: 172), that they have reenvisioned their nation of belonging in contemporary global society.

Refugees in the Land of Awes

Vietnamese Arrivals and Departures

Janet Alison Hoskins

Spiritual journeys that take groups of people to new territories, seeking some form of scripture or message, are as familiar in the famous Chinese religious adventure novel *Journey to the West* as they are in the Hollywood fantasy of the *Wizard of Oz*. The theological implications of migration and especially the forced displacement of refugees have rarely been explored, although religion has recently been theorized as providing a "watch and a compass" for migrants who come to "cross and dwell" in new spaces (Tweed 2006). Religious ritual and scripture can serve to provide a narrative that explains the reasons for this displacement. Particular ritual techniques structure and anticipate changes in consciousness. And these changes—expressed in texts or bodily movements— have implications for how these refugee communities can build and sustain themselves. The Vietnamese living overseas provide a particularly compelling example of this process, since from 1975 to 1990 large numbers of them left their homeland as refugees, but an almost equally large number also left as contract workers and students, and the different trajectories of these different groups, one traveling to the capitalist west and the other to the socialist east, provide an especially rich comparative case.

The refugee story is usually told as a story of suffering, displacement, "the loss of the country," and persecution for those once associated with the Saigon regime, who lost their jobs, their homes, their businesses, and often their freedom by being sent to reeducation camps. The sense of desperation led people to escape in very dangerous boats, where they often drowned, were attacked by pirates, or perished from thirst and starvation. This legacy of "the boat people" is, however, often countered by stories of Vietnamese migrants to Europe—"the truck people" or "the box people"—who also endured dangerous trips through frozen forests and snowy hills, hidden together in poorly heated and ventilated vans. The tragic deaths of thirty-nine young Vietnamese migrants who suffocated in a truck in Essex, Southeastern England, in October 2019 brought their sufferings into the headlines. In the last leg of a perilous 6,000-mile trek across Asia and into Europe, these young people were among an estimated 18,000 Vietnamese illegal migrants who paid smugglers to sneak them across many different borders in the hopes of finding a better life (Mueller, *New York Times* 2019, Freidingerova 2019). Precarious journeys to a mythical "land of awes" (inspired by visions of the hostland as similar to the legendary Oz) fused the migrant's travails with an exaggerated sense of hope and possibility.

Vietnam has also been the birthplace of several distinctive indigenous religions, practiced according to a survey by Pew Charitable Trust by about 45 percent of the population. While most people think of Vietnam as a Buddhist country with a Catholic minority, only about 16 percent of the population identifies as Buddhist, with 8 percent identifying as Catholic.[1] Almost all Vietnamese families practice ancestor worship, even those who do not have any formal religious affiliation. In Southern Vietnam, Caodaism is the most popular indigenous religion, with over 1,300 temples and about 12 percent of the population (Hoskins 2015). In Northern Vietnam, spirit mediums who "serve the spirits of the Mother Goddesses of the land" (Đạo Mẫu) perform increasingly public rituals at their homes, temples, and heritage sites, but are officially classified as a form of "intangible cultural heritage" rather than a religion (Nguyen Thi Hien 2016; Fjelstad and Nguyen 2011; Salemink 2013, 2018). Mother Goddess temples are now transnational, and found in Vietnamese communities in California, Germany, Poland, Russia, and the Czech Republic. A comparison of the varying responses of two "migrating indigenous religions" allows us to focus on the role of narrative in guiding responses to migration.

Both Caodaism and Đạo Mẫu could be seen as having a theological narrative and ritual practice which emphasizes a form of movement: for Caodaism, this is the idea of a sacred journey "to the west," involving both a search for new doctrines and the biblical notion of exodus (since Caodaism blends Christian elements with an East Asian pantheon). For Đạo Mẫu, this movement takes the form of trance dances, a bodily practice in which "Vietnam comes to dance inside us," and spirits from the homeland are made present through the experience of spirit possession. Different narratives of departures and arrivals are used by Vietnamese refugees who practice Caodaism (primarily in the United States, Canada, and Australia, but also France) and Vietnamese migrants who practice Đạo Mẫu in the former socialist areas of Russia, the Czech Republic, Poland, and

Eastern Germany. The mobilities of refugees and migrants have also produced different notions of debt, with refugees seeing their perilous boat escapes as linked to a debt to the hostland which gave them "freedom" and refuge, while migrants who were part of state-sponsored labor programs have a debt to the homeland, paid in remittances and patriotic ceremonies at temples in Eastern Europe.

Caodaism: Cosmopolitan Syncretism and Anti-Colonial Resistance

Caodaism (also called Đạo Cao Đài)[2] is a new religious movement formed by a group of colonized intellectuals in 1926 when Saigon was the capital of the French colony of Cochinchina, the most thoroughly colonized and modernized part of French Indochina. Its new vision of the world has usually been interpreted as a response to the great dislocations of colonial conquest, what one its most prominent leaders called the "bouleversement total," or complete reversal of traditional values and meanings (Hoskins 2015). At a series of séances conducted initially to seek literary inspiration and guidance, three young men who worked in the colonial tax office made contact with a powerful spirit who eventually revealed that he was the Jade Emperor, come to found a new religion in Vietnam, using the new name Cao Đài ("the highest tower," a term also used to designate Jehovah, and so one that establishes Jesus as the son of the Jade Emperor).

The revelation that the Jade Emperor was the same figure as the Christian Jehovah allowed the traditional Vietnamese fusion of Buddhism, Taoism, and Confucianism to be resynthesized as a masculine monotheism which could absorb Christianity, Judaism, and Islam into its more encompassing East Asian pantheon. The personal contact with a fatherly, affectionate divinity was continued through séance transmissions of scripture, and what came to be called the Religious Constitution and New Religious Laws of Caodaism. Formed by a committee of prominent citizens rather than any single human founder, Caodaism gathered several million followers in its first decades and aspired to be both the "national religion" of Vietnam and a global faith of unity which could bring about religious reconciliation in other countries as well.

The pantheon represented on the pediment suspended from the ceiling of the Great Temple in Tây Ninh has five levels (Figure 5.1), which are the five levels of spiritual attainment outlined in Caodai religious doctrine. At the top is Buddha, who has attained enlightenment and become fused with divinity, and he stands

Figure 5.1 The Caodai pantheon represents five levels of spiritual attainment, represented by Buddha (fusion with the divine), Confucius (the way of sages) and Lao Tzu (the way of the immortals), Jesus (the way of saints), and Khương Tử Nha (the veneration of local spirits). Photograph on the California temple in Garden Grove; photo by Janet Alison Hoskins.

for the "way of Buddhism" or Đạo Phật. On his right side stands Confucius and on his left Lao Tzu. Confucius stands for the "way of the sages," or Đạo Nhơn, often called Confucianism, and Lao Tzu stands for the "way of the Immortals," or Đạo Tiên, often translated as Taoism. At the next level, we find the Tang dynasty poet Li Bai (Lý Thái Bạch in Vietnamese), who is the "invisible Pope" of Caodaism and its master of ceremonies, flanked by the female Boddhisattva Quan Âm and the East Asian God of War Quan Công. They are also all part of the "way of the immortals." Below them is Jesus Christ, who stands for the "way of the saints," or Đạo Thanh, and this level includes not only Christian saints but also Jewish and Muslim figures, and Vietnamese military heroes like the thirteenth-century Trần Húng Đạo. Below him is the figure of an old man called Khương Tử Nha, who is associated with the veneration of local spirits called Đạo Thần.

The divinities who can come down in Caodai séances, however, are much more numerous than these eight figures, who become nine when we add the overarching figure of Cao Đài, the Jade Emperor himself (depicted by the naturalistic Left Eye at the top). In fact, many of the most common conversation partners of Caodai séances are deceased Caodai leaders, especially the Interim Pope Lê Văn Trung (1870–1934) and the Head Spirit Medium or Hộ Pháp Phạm Công Tắc (1890–1957). They come down in séances to advise religious leaders on administrative decisions, and to help them move forward under difficult situations. The spirit writing received in formal séances is an "elevated discourse" which is distinguished by its high literary quality and beautiful verse.

A number of Christian themes were reinterpreted in the context of colonial resistance: The Vietnamese were seen as "God's chosen people" because they were a virtuous and hard-working people but had had to bear the brutal European colonial yoke more directly than any other people in the East Asian civilizational sphere (Hoskins 2012). Christ was a prophet who fought for the independence of his people against an imperial power based in Rome, but since he died young and tragically, he never acquired the full wisdom of the much older Asian sages. His "way of the saints" sits one level below the "way of the Taoist immortals," which itself is also placed below the "way of Buddhist enlightenment."[3] Elements of Catholic religious rankings—a pope, both female and male cardinals, bishops, and archbishops, a "Vatican" sacred city—were fused with titles earlier used in Confucian rituals to erect an elaborate new administrative hierarchy. Caodaists asked the secular French state to show the same respect for their sacred city in Tây Ninh as they did for the Catholic Vatican in Rome.

At a time when anti-colonial activism was growing, Caodaism emerged as religious organization that sought to create a spiritual sense of the nation to support struggles for political independence and decolonization. One of its first goals was to give the Vietnamese people a new sense of purpose under divine leadership and to unify the disparate elements of Vietnamese daily devotionalism—saint worship, veneration of local spirits and ancestors, Buddhist and Taoist forms of meditation—into a syncretistic whole.

Caodaists accept the religious adventure novel *Journey to the West* (*Tây Du Ký* in Vietnamese) as part of their scriptures, since it deals with the relationship of Buddhism, Taoism, and Confucianism. Familiar to the younger generation through Chinese kung fu films, this classic text was a frequent point of reference for the Caodai leader Phạm Công Tắc, who compared himself both to Tripitaka (Tam Tạng, the Buddhist monk who journeys to India seeking scriptures) and to the Monkey Saint (Tề Thiên Đại Thánh). There are even spirit messages in the unofficial canon of Caodai said to come directly from the Monkey Saint. The journey of Vietnamese refugees "to the west," while often compared to a biblical exodus, is also sometimes also seen as a Buddhist journey seeking new teachings, or new skills in science and industry, which can later be brought back to the homeland.

While embracing this Chinese literary tradition, Caodaism infused it with elements of Vietnamese history and a specifically anti-colonial message, prophesying that the "third age of universal redemption" would come at the same time as the collapse of the great European colonial empires in Asia. A new set of scriptures were revealed through spirit writing with a phoenix-headed basket, held by spirit mediums who received, transcribed, and interpreted these new messages as the basis of a new theology of unity. The elitist, literary, and cosmopolitan aspirations of Caodaism contrast strongly with the spirit possession religion of Đạo Mẫu ("the way of the Mother Goddess"), which developed in Northern Vietnam and is closer to shamanism in most of its manifestations.

Đạo Mẫu Spirit Possession: Spirits of Nature and the Imperial Past

The mediums of Đạo Mẫu are primarily female, and include many street peddlers, businesswomen who sell snacks, clothing, or trinkets on the streets of the city, but aspire to expand to become small-scale entrepreneurs. In the past, many were not even literate since their bodies shake with the power of imperial family members without speech. Sitting in front of a mirror placed in front of an ancestral altar, their heads are draped with a red veil while sacred music is played, and they make a hand gesture to signal the spirit coming to possess them so their assistants can dress them in the appropriate costume and the singers can accompany their dances with verses praising the right spirit (Figure 5.2). Beginning with the highest-ranking lords and alternating male and female spirits, they are possessed by roughly a dozen warriors, scholar-officials, ladies of the court, spoiled princes, and highland princesses, until finally they finish with the spirit of a playful, often naughty young boy.

The pantheon of thirty-odd spirits all come from imperial times, including members of the Trần dynasty and the thirteenth-century military hero Trần Hưng Đạo, who kept the Mongols from invading Vietnam. Most are unspecified figures from Vietnamese history who are known mainly through the order in which they are incarnated ("fourth mandarin," "fifth prince," "sixth princess") and a series of personality traits—wisdom, opium addiction, flirtatiousness—which link them to those mediums who have a "spirit root" that calls them to "serve" these particular entities. The trance dancers of Đạo Mẫu say that

Figure 5.2 Đạo Mẫu spirit medium standing in front of a mirror awaiting spirit possession, in Huntington Beach, California; photo by Janet Alison Hoskins.

"Vietnam dances within them," and that they feel empowered and energized by feeling these great spirits of the past descend into their bodies and move with grace, skill, and precision in stylized dances (Hoskins 2014b).[4]

While Caodai literary spirit mediums seek wisdom and advice from their interlocutors, the trance dancers expect to get help with concrete personal problems—illness, financial issues, and the loss of love or good fortune. Caodaists note that the spirits who come down to Đạo Mẫu spirit mediums are largely inarticulate: "They dance and sway but they cannot speak, or else they simply yell and simper, without any clear message that can be understood." It is the experience of being possessed and energized by these powerful spirits that the follows of the Mother Goddess seek, rather than teachings or moral guidance.

As a researcher, I was repeatedly told that going to ceremonies would make me more beautiful and youthful, and would enhance my chances to snare a new husband or reconcile with an older one. Since mediums are usually most attracted to spirits of the opposite sex, the experience of performing offers a form of physical excitement and tension release which is in many cases a substitute for experiences of intimacy not shared with human partners. Having a "spirit husband" or "spirit wife" may even preclude marriage, or offer consolation for a marriage which has gone bad. Female spirit mediums are notoriously flashy, flirtatious, and bossy, while male spirit mediums enjoy dressing as women so much that many of them are perceived as transgender (Norton 2003; Endres 2008). In the dark days of Marxist authoritarian rule (1975–95), these colorful and highly commercial displays were severely repressed by the government, but today these ceremonies are held quite openly.

Vietnamese folklorists and anthropologists (Ngô Đức Thịnh 2010; Nguyễn Thị Hiền 2002; Pham Quynh Phuong 2009) have struggled to raise the status of what used to be called "the Four Palaces cult" to that of a "religion" (*đạo*) on a par with Buddhism, Confucianism and Daoism (*đạo Phật, đạo Nho, đạo Lão*), so that it could be "accepted as equal to other imported religions and given legitimacy" (Phuong 2009: 181). In 2004, when a new government ordinance concerning religion was released recognizing the worship of Vietnamese saints, heroes, and ancestors as "patriotic," their victory was celebrated. It reversed an earlier 1975 ordinance ("Instruction on the Implementation of New Ways of Life in Weddings, Funerals, Death Anniversaries and Festivals"), which explicitly forbade "the consulting of fortune-tellers, the reading of horoscopes, the practice of physiognomy, the conjuring up of a dead person's soul, spirit possession, the casting of lots, the production of amulets, the worshipping of ghosts, the burning of incense, the buying and selling of joss-paper objects, and the use of magic to cure diseases" (Dror 2005: 172). I have witnessed all of these practices in temples in California, as well as in Vietnam, but several California Đạo Mẫu followers I spoke with could not believe that all of these practices were once again "legal."

The frankly sexual, acquisitive, and athletic displays of Đạo Mẫu evoke a distant past to recharge the present with possibility: People serve the spirits to find favor with them and gain the supernatural resources to become more successful in their daily lives. Their nostalgic evocation of the splendor of the imperial court fills them with the power to entice new lovers, pull in new clients or buyers, and rise out of money troubles. Worldly accomplishments are seen as indexes of a harmonious relationship established with potent spirits, who will continue to bestow gifts of good fortune as long as they are propitiated with annual or semiannual ceremonies on their feast days.

Differences and Tensions between These Two Indigenous Religions

Caodaists describe the spirits incarnated by the predominantly female Đạo Mẫu mediums as "low ranking spirits," which they also consider more dangerous and volatile. Getting spiritual advice from a Taoist philosopher or a great literary figure is seen as appropriate for elite practitioners, and these spirits do not need to be flattered, placated, and "rewarded" with lavish sacrificial meals like the more capricious spirits summoned in Đạo Mẫu rituals. The two pantheons do occasionally overlap, however, but only at their borders: The spirit of Vietnam's most famous national hero, Trần Húng Đạo, is summoned by both groups. But Trần Húng Đạo sits at the top of the Đạo Mẫu pantheon and can be summoned only on his feast day, which comes shortly after the beginning of the new lunar year. He sits at the third level of the Caodai pantheon, among the "saints and heroes" (which include Jesus Christ), but below both the immortal philosophers like Confucius and Lao Tzu and the Buddha, who have attained enlightenment.

Early Caodaists did not want to be associated with this tradition. In 1926, in the midst of the great excitement generated by the "Opening up of the Way" at Gò Kén pagoda, two people had spontaneously fallen into trance, possessed by the spirits of Quan Âm and the Monkey King from *Journey to the West*. This was seen as inappropriate to the solemn ceremonial character of the occasion, and the two were quickly controlled and led away. In conversations in California, the Caodai historian Đỗ Vạn Lý (Hoskins 2011) speculated to me: "I think the French were behind all this monkey business. They wanted to be able to dismiss Caodaism as some form of shamanism or popular superstition. They did not want to take our movement seriously, so they probably got their own agents to misbehave in that way." While I do not necessarily share his proclivity for conspiracy theories in understanding this outbreak of uncontrolled religious inspiration, I find the logic of this argument fascinating. It goes to the heart of division between a literary, elite tradition of spirit writing and a more popular, theatrical one of trance and dancing while possessed.

Both Caodai literary séances and Đạo Mẫu trance dances have been described as "revivals of tradition," but the ways in which they have reappeared in the world of the twenty-first century are very different. Caodaists worship the Supreme

Being under the sign of the Left Eye, anatomically closer to the heart and thus tied to a vision filtered through the lens of morality, ethics, and introspection. They oppose their "Asian" perspective to the "Western" perspective of the right eye, featured on the US one-dollar bill and associated with visions of domination, industrial power, and conquest. Their literary interlocutors look down at the world from the "White Cloud Lodge" of the Asian sages and share their insights only with those people who have enough elite culture to appreciate their verses.

Đạo Mẫu dancers see their own faces turning into the faces of the royal figures they incarnate at ceremonies, and while they are usually unable to speak during their trances, their bodies respond to the music and the words of the praise songs to trace beautiful gestures in front of an appreciative human audience. They get immediate benefits from their participation in these performances, being "ennobled" themselves by performing skillfully as noble personages. Their bodies are the instruments that they use to serve the spirits and to reap the rewards of this devotion. The world of the here and now, of sensory delights and invigorating energy, is where they seek their fulfillment.

The Different Geographies of Caodaism and Đạo Mẫu in the Diaspora

Diasporic Đạo Mẫu temples are scattered, episodic, and animated by charismatic mediums who draw their followers from all Vietnamese who identify with ancestor worship practices in a livelier performative format. Diasporic Caodaism is led by several rival mission organizations, riven by political differences about whether to realign themselves with religious leaders "contaminated by communists" in the homeland. Both are part of remittance networks to rebuild temples in Vietnam, and both now feature transnational leaders who move between diasporic locations and Vietnamese cities where the resurgence of popular religion has become increasingly evident. The spirit mediums of Đạo Mẫu dance out a vision of the power of the past in bodily movement, while Caodai dignitaries and disciples chant scriptures and seek new séance messages from a phoenix bird whose beak traces teachings about the new millennium.

There are over a hundred Caodai temples in the United States, Canada, and Australia, which have the largest Vietnamese refugee populations, but only a few in Europe, since Caodaism is associated with southern refugees rather than northern migrants. The Église Caodai was founded in 1983 in the Parisian suburb of Alfortville and has held worship services continuously for almost

Figure 5.3 Đạo Mẫu Temple in Erfurt, Eastern Germany, with Mother Goddess altars, the yin/yang symbol, and the celestial snake spirit worshipped on both sides of Buddhist figures; photo by Janet Alison Hoskins.

forty years (Hoskins 2015: 138; Jammes 2014: 326–9). There was also a smaller temple in Vitry-sur-Seine that held spiritist séances in the 1990s, studied by the French anthropologist Jérémy Jammes (Jammes 2014: 29–31). The Vietnamese population in France is politically diverse, including some very anti-communist refugees, some strong supporters of the Hanoi government, and many others who are relatively secular and neutral. There are spirit mediums in the Paris region who practice a form of Đạo Mẫu, and there is also a Đạo Mẫu temple in Southern France near Nice, but nothing as well organized and ritually dense as Đạo Mẫu temples in Erfurt, Germany, Warsaw, Poland, or Moscow, Russia (Figure 5.3).

Indigenous Religions and the State: Persecution and Efforts at Normalization

Both of these practices have suffered from government censure: Caodaism had a history of political engagement which included both fighting against the French (as allies of the Japanese) and later collaborating with them for a "nonviolent process of decolonization," modeled on Gandhi's ideas of protest (Hoskins 2015: 67–96). While Caodaists tried to present their religion as neutral, arguing that they aspired to "peaceful co-existence" with northern Marxists, they were considered "reactionary and counter revolutionary" by the Vietnamese government after 1975, so religious activities were almost completely suppressed (Hoskins 2015: 172–85; Blagov 2001). Most Caodai temples were effectively closed down from 1975 to 1995, but in the Renovation era, they were reopened and renovated (usually with funding from overseas Vietnamese), and are now filled with worshippers. While the elaborate administrative hierarchy of Caodai dignitaries survived a quarter century of state repression, literary spirit séances are still forbidden in today's Vietnam.

Since 1954 in the North and 1975 in the South, Đạo Mẫu had been condemned as a "superstitious practice," both wasteful and delusional (Fjelstad and Nguyễn 2011; Norton 2009; Endres 2011). However, the lively dance performances dedicated to the Mother Goddesses have been resurrected as folklore. On December 1, 2016, Đạo Mẫu ceremonies were officially recognized by UNESCO as an "intangible heritage" of Vietnamese culture. This recognition was a victory of sorts for the Vietnamese anthropologists and folklorists who have championed this ritual practice and wanted to retrieve it from the wastebasket of "superstition" where it had been cast (Ngô Đức Thịnh 2010; Fjelstad and Nguyễn 2006, 2011; Nguyễn Thị Hiền 2015; 2016; Pham Quynh Phuong 2009). But there are also dangers to this kind of official recognition, as Oscar Salemink has noted (2018). When a practice is officially "heritagized," it no longer remains the property of the local people who turned to spirit mediums to seek healing, better business, and a more harmonious family life and becomes subject to government regulation as a "spectacle of the past," with outside experts testifying to its value as a part of traditional culture. There are now many state-sanctioned performances of rituals devoted to the Mother Goddess, newly valorized as part of the "indigenous foundations" of Vietnamese culture.

Vietnamese contract workers and students from Northern Vietnam, who settled in the former socialist nations of East Germany, the Czech Republic, Poland, and Russia, now participate in the revival of popular religion which swept through Vietnam in the early twenty-first century. These communities are very concerned to maintain a good relationship with the Hanoi government, because they continue to travel there and send remittances to family members in Vietnam. The wealthier ones often also invest in restaurants, resorts, factories and businesses in their homeland, and perform "rituals of patriotism" like celebrating Ho Chi Minh's birthday and Vietnam's national day. The colorful pageantry of Đạo Mẫu, once seen as wasteful and superstitious, is now welcomed into some of these rituals of patriotism. The commemoration of the Hùng Kings (the legendary first kings of Vietnam) is a ritual of patriotism which draws on the same imperial costumes and finery as Đạo Mẫu performances (Dror 2016). Since 1994, this has been developed into a national holiday in Vietnam (Jellema 2007), and since 2010 it has also been commemorated, with the support of the Vietnamese embassy, by Vietnamese communities in the former socialist world. In Russia, Poland, Germany, and the Czech Republic, the embassy also organizes Tết Festivals to celebrate the lunar new year—although in Warsaw there are also dissident pro-democracy Vietnamese groups which sponsor a separate Tết Festival in the style of the anti-communist communities of "Little Saigon" (Szymanska-Matusiewicz 2015: 58–61).

The internally divided Vietnamese communities of France and Germany also have separate Tết Festivals in different parts of Paris and Berlin, and there are even competing Buddhist festivals like Buddha's birthday and the Hungry Ghost Festival (Vu Lan) which are held in in refugee-associated pagodas (whose members identify as part of a "stateless diaspora") or in government-affiliated pagodas (whose members identify as a "state-linked diaspora"). Two rival Vietnamese Buddhist associations—one linked to the official government Buddhist sangha (Phật Giáo Việt Nam), whose slogan is "religion, nation, socialism," and the other linked to the dissident United Buddhist Church of Vietnam (Giáo Hội Việt Nam Thống Nhất)—have separate monks, nuns, and pagodas, although their congregations are sometimes mixed.

Religious traditions such as ancestor worship, Buddhism, and the imperial legacies of Đạo Mẫu are seen as a shared patrimony, but in practice the performance of these rituals is polarized. The rituals of migrant associations in Eastern Europe remain tied to the Vietnamese state, while those of refugee associations in France and Germany remain opposed to it. As Grazyna Szymanska-Matusiewicz has argued in a study of Vietnamese migrant associations in Poland,

> as long as Vietnamese migrants in Poland perpetuate the model of an "enclave economy," the Vietnamese state—through its official institutions such as the embassy and unofficial zones of influence such as migrant organizations—will continue to shape the politics and the political orientation of the migrant associations, even as these diasporic institutions attempt to secure more autonomy for carving out new space for Vietnamese civil society abroad. (2019: 69)

Consequences for the Future: Debts to the Hostland versus Debts to the Homeland

Vietnamese refugees left their homeland to travel to Nước Mỹ, which literally means "the beautiful country," and for many of them, it may have seemed a fabled land like Vulture Peak in India or the Emerald City of Oz. While not literally in search of magic gifts or sacred scriptures, they did hope to achieve a dream of freedom or a better life. That dream often proved elusive, and "the gift of freedom" came to seem illusory, something that required years of paying back a debt to the hostland and sacrificing a new generation that would grow up without understanding the culture of their parents (M. Nguyen 2012).

When I speak of "refugees in the land of awes," I am referring to the mystified, sanctified idea of a land of refuge and freedom that was almost inevitably disappointing. Refugees are often told they "should be grateful for having been saved," and the rescue missions sent to collect orphans or boat people are cited as proof that the American war was justified because so many people fled after the Fall of Saigon. Ignoring the role of military intervention in making these populations vulnerable, this creates a "we-win-even-when-we lose" narrative in which capitalism lost the war but "wins the peace" and sacrifices on the losing side find validation (Espiritu 2014).

Mimi Nguyen argues that the gift of freedom—first through war, and second through refuge—precludes the subjects of freedom from escaping those colonial histories that deemed them "unfree." To receive the gift of freedom then is to be indebted to empire, perhaps without end. "As a process that does not have as its end completion, but instead continually stages postponement or deferral, the gift of freedom is a thing, force, gaze and event that refers both to the wars that promised it and those that must follow after" (M. Nguyen 2012: 188). She explains how this gift feeds a never-ending sense of debt:

> Debt points toward a different social order, keeping us in contact with alternate collectivities of others who bear that trace of human freedom that fall apart, or seizes hold, in its giving. Put another way, we may join an audience of all those who have heard this song of freedom and empire before, and therein lie other passages to an unknowable future. (2012: 189)

Within Caodaism, discourses about coming to a "land of religious freedom" are re-inscribed in prophecies of the global expansion of the religion after 1975.

Unlike most immigrants, refugees have gone through a process of extrusion from a place of origin, have usually renounced their citizenship of birth, and come to see their new homeland as their "only future." For Vietnamese, this was particularly true in the period 1975–95, before relations between the United States and Vietnam were restored. In the twenty-first century, a great many former refugees have returned to visit Vietnam, and many have invested in family businesses there and even applied for dual citizenship. So what was once seen as a one-way journey is no longer unidirectional and absolute.[5]

The new phenomenon of "refugees writing back" is characteristic of the second and the 1.5 generation, who now offer a critical perspective on earlier narratives that saw them as pathetic victims, without agency, dependent upon the mercy of foreign states. The biting sarcasm of Viet Thanh Nguyen's novel *The Sympathizer*, the trenchant criticism of Yen Le Espiritu's *Body Counts*, and the ironic distance of Mimi Nguyen's *The Gift of Freedom* all testify to the ways in which former refugees have come to reclaim their own dignity and decisiveness. Viet Thanh Nguyen has proposed describing what used to be called "the boat people" as "oceanic refugees," noting that even the founding fathers of the United States traveled to the continent by boat (V. T. Nguyen 2017). Another Vietnamese American scholar has described the process of adjusting to a new way of life in Little Saigon as "becoming Refugee American" (P. T. Nguyen 2017).

How do the different orientations of Caodaists and Đạo Mẫu followers situate them for the future? Both groups seem likely to grow as more Vietnamese travel overseas, establish businesses in other countries, and seek international training. Caodaism during the colonial era was identified to some extent as a "religion of the educated," led by former land-holding families in the Mekong Delta and Tây Ninh. Although many of these families suffered tremendous losses after 1975 and endured dangerous escapes sometimes following years of incarceration, they now have international networks which make them likely to receive remittances from North America, Australia, or Europe. They can also use these family and religion-based networks to send children overseas for training or university educations, and they are well placed to draw on external resources to rebuild family businesses.

Đạo Mẫu followers are stereotyped as small-scale entrepreneurs, vendors, and traders, and many people in these categories traveled as workers to Eastern Europe in the 1980s as part of efforts within the "socialist world" to help Vietnam recover from the war. Now these ritual practices have resurfaced in Vietnamese enclaves in the Czech Republic, Poland, and Russia, as well as the reunited nation of Germany. Small Buddhist prayer houses and temples in Prague, the Czech Republic, deliberately recreate the atmosphere of a Vietnamese village, featuring a small bamboo altar "like the ones used by naïve peasants" (*bàn thờ nhà quê*).

Evocations of the homeland (*quê hương*) are tied to performances of folk songs and traditional dances, rather than the more Westernized love ballads so popular in "Little Saigons" (Hoskins and Nguyen 2020).

These "transported peasants" were also skilled in transnational trade and commerce because of their experiences in sending goods back to Vietnam. In Prague, a Czech anthropologist explained that "it was the Vietnamese transnational traders who taught the Polish people how to be capitalists." Shortages of clothing, household goods, and fresh foods during the transitional years when former socialist nations opened up to market forces created an opening for Vietnamese traders to use their networks to get wholesale goods and sell them, first on the streets and later in ramshackle settlements along the German border. Forced to become street vendors because the factories where they once worked had been closed, they became an important part of an underground economy focused on cigarettes, liquor, and other sometimes semi-legal commodities.[6] The uncertain world of petty commerce has an elective affinity (in Max Weber's sense) for people who worship the capricious pantheon of Đạo Mẫu spirits who may bestow gifts of prosperity, so it is not surprising that such practices came to find a new home in the ethnic enclaves grouped around wholesale markets in cities like Berlin, Warsaw and Prague (Hüwelmeier 2015, 2017a, 2017b).

The "Little Hanois" of Central and Eastern Europe are now characterized by prominent merchants from Northern Vietnam who may seek out the advice of a spirit medium, fortune-teller, or psychic when they want to make an important business decision. These ritual practices have opened up new gulfs between the forms of Buddhism favored by former socialist workers and those favored by refugees from the South. Critical former refugees in Berlin describe the rise of these ritual practices as showing "the communist fondness for magic," asserting that Marxist materialism manifests itself in religious practices such as praying to win the lottery, to lure clients from rival vendors, and to make their businesses more prosperous. These were contrasted with more contemplative practices of meditation, scripture study, and social work associated with Buddhist centers in Hue and Ho Chi Minh City. As a former southern refugee woman interviewed in Berlin said: "I see religion as the center of morality, the moral way of life, not a place where you seek material benefits or you become rich." Many practices at the temples in Eastern Berlin she described as "silly superstitions" (*ngu ngốc mê tín dị đoan*), which she condemned from the perspective of elite forms of religious practice like Zen Buddhism and Caodaism.

The former socialist countries of Europe also hosted students and intellectuals who were sent to East Germany, Czechoslovakia, Poland, and Russia to go to universities. Leading the "privileged yet precarious" life of nomadic scholars (Bayly 2007: 13), they were educated in Russian, German or Polish, and often stayed on after they graduated, working first as managers for groups of contract workers and later in professions like currency transfer. While most of them described themselves as secular revolutionaries in the 1980s and 1990s, many later helped to establish cultural performances of patriotism which featured Đạo Mẫu music and dancing in the twenty-first century. For refugees in the United States, Canada, and Australia, Vietnamese temples were often the first locations for cultural gatherings in the 1980s. For migrant workers in Eastern Europe, they did not come to play that role until about two decades later, in the 2000s.

Both communities have a mixture of intellectuals and workers, ritual devotionalists, and secularists, but they are distinguished by their differing relationship to the Vietnamese state. While Vietnam now has a market economy, it is an economy still heavily controlled by the state, and so any overseas Vietnamese person who wants to continue to travel to the homeland and invest in business there has to be aware of which "cultural celebrations" are sanctioned by the Vietnamese government and which ones are affiliated with dissident groups. Caodaism had a history of opposing the Communist Party, and while it tries to present itself as neutral, it is still in the process of "normalizing" within Vietnam, and Caodai temples do not participate in state-sponsored cultural festivals. Đạo Mẫu, on the other hand, has become an important part of public celebrations in Vietnam, so it is now welcomed into state-sponsored performances, and its spirit mediums (like the one who runs a large temple in Erfurt, Germany) proudly fly the flag of Hanoi near the image of the Buddha (Figure 5.4).

In countries like Germany, many of the most assertive Vietnamese capitalists are former communists from the North, who now own successful businesses which cater to the migrant community. Southern refugees (many of them educated professionals) are more integrated into German society, but choose to participate in Vietnamese festivals and religious holidays because they fear that their children will lose knowledge of their own language and culture.[7] Refugee organizations like "Thank You Germany"[8] reenact the idea of the "debt of freedom,"[9] while the livelier folk performances of the homeland associations (*hội đồng hương*) made up of former workers show the idea of a "debt to the homeland," also always present in religious charities and social services directed to send assistance back to their region of origin. While I had initially expected to see pagodas and temples as offering a terrain for reconciliation between former Cold War enemies, my recent fieldwork did not find much evidence for this reconciliation. Instead, I saw the "land of awes" now settled by Vietnamese

Figure 5.4 The spirit medium prays besides celebrations of Buddha's birthday, the Hanoi flag, and Đạo Mẫu offerings in Erfurt; photo by Janet Alison Hoskins.

refugees and workers as far from a magical land where all wishes were granted but rather a terrain still deeply divided in religious and political terms.

Acknowledgments

My field research on Caodaism in California and Vietnam goes back to 2004, and I started looking at Đạo Mẫu in 2008 (working Thiên-Hương Ninh, and funded by the National Science Administration grant no. 0752511). In 2018, I did several months of research in Europe in Paris, Prague, Berlin, and Moscow with my Vietnamese colleague Nguyễn Thị Hiền, funded by the Global Religion Research Initiative, administered by Northwestern University. I am grateful to both of them for their assistance with the field research and its interpretation.

In Search of a Vietnamese
Buddhist Space in Germany

Tam T. T. Ngo and Nga T. Mai

Introduction

This chapter attempts to capture the contesting and contradictory migration categories by examining the different Vietnamese migrant groups in Germany. Vietnamese boat refugees, Vietnamese contract laborers, and other Vietnamese migrants are regularly distinguished from one another on the ground of their political background, migration routes, and integration experience. This distinguishing encapsulates the division that has begun from Vietnam as the war and historical legacies. The main argument is that all these people have left Vietnam, but have not left it behind. Vietnam, as the country of origin, still looms large not only in an imaginative sense but also in a direct political sense. One could call this the enigma of arrival, that one never fully arrives and that many of the troubles that make one move to another country keep following the migrant. This enigma of arrival is addressed by Buddhism both in a religious and in a political sense. Buddhism in Germany has become a major site of contesting people's relation to Vietnam. This chapter starts with a description of how the Vietnamese came to Germany. It then goes on to discuss the political history of two Buddhist temples in Berlin. Finally, it examines how Buddhism addresses the spiritual needs of the different kinds of Vietnamese migrants.

Vietnamese in Germany

The two large groups of Vietnamese that have been received in Germany are the boat refugees of 1978 and the subsequent years in the German Federal Republic (hereafter GFR) and the contract laborers in the same period arriving in the communist German Democratic Republic (hereafter GDR). On April 30, 1975, Saigon fell, and in 1976 North- and South Vietnam were officially united as the Socialist Republic of Vietnam. When the Americans left South Vietnam, they evacuated some 130,000 Vietnamese to the United States (Espiritu 2014: 24). The communist regime targeted first the former South Vietnamese military and civil authorities and put them into reeducation camps that contained up to a million people. Subsequently, small businesses were disowned, and their owners put in reeducation camps in order to create a socialist plan economy. Among them were many Vietnamese people of Chinese descent. During 1978 and 1979, about 250,000 Chinese-Vietnamese in North Vietnam began to flee to China with permission (Osborne 1980), but in fact, they were pushed by the Vietnamese authorities, because the relations between China and Vietnam had deteriorated quickly after the victory of North Vietnam and especially after the invasion of Pol Pot's Cambodia by Vietnamese troops.

Soon other groups also started to flee Vietnam: students, shopkeepers, former South Vietnamese officials, and intellectuals; prominently also Catholics and Buddhists who feared the religious persecution by the communists (see Nguyen, this volume). Many of them fled by land to Cambodia and Thailand or by sea to Indonesia, Malaysia, Singapore, and the Philippines; the number of asylees registered in Southeast Asian countries reached 209,000 by July 1979 (Stein 1979). In July 1979, a refugee conference was called in Geneva and decided to speed up the adoption of refugees in the so-called third countries. The number of refugees to be distributed was determined as 260,000 for 1979 and 1980. The United States, Australia, Canada, France, and, with lesser numbers, the GFR and Britain were the main recipients. The governments of Indonesia and the Philippines declared a willingness to act as regional centers for redistribution over third countries (Robinson 1998).

Immediately after the Fall of Saigon, the GFR government had declared a willingness to accept a contingent of refugees without submitting them to individual asylum procedures: first, a thousand, which later expanded to 6,000, then to 10,000, and, finally, to 38,000 (Wolf 2007: 6). The government of Lower Saxony decided on its own without consultation with the federal government to bring 1,000 refugees out of camps in Thailand and Malaysia. The Vietnamese boat refugees who were brought to the Federal Republic of Germany in 1979 did not have to apply for asylum when they were taken out of refugee camps in Southeast Asia or from boats crossing the South China Sea. For this purpose, a specific legal status was developed, that of the *Kontingentflüchtling*, which made it possible to accept refugees as a group rather than as individuals. Also, the *Kontingentflüchtling* obtained asylum without going through a regular procedure requested by the Federal Republic. It also allowed for distribution over the regional states of the GFR. All family members of those who had been accepted as *Kontingentflüchtling* were also included in this status.

At the same time, the GDR began to recruit Vietnamese contract laborers. In the mid-1970s, the GDR had signed treaties with Vietnam, Cuban, Angola, and Mozambique to bring contract laborers to work in the industry. These contracts ranged from four to five years. The treaty with Vietnam was signed in 1980, exactly at the time that the GFR was accepting boat refugees. Since then, the largest number of contract laborers in the GDR was Vietnamese, amounting to more than 60,000 in 1989 (Weiss 2005; Hüwelmeier 2017). Besides contract labors, the GDR also received Vietnamese for educational purposes. Between 1973 and 1978, the GDR had a program for teaching children of political cadres that reached 10,000 Vietnamese children. These flows of humans and supports were part of the socialist development program that had had a modest beginning in the 1950s and was part of a Cold War mirror program of Western development aid. Contrary to a widespread understanding among Vietnamese themselves, Vietnam paid its war debts to the GDR not by the contract labor, but rather by agricultural products (Raendchen 2000).

With the fall of the Communist regime in the GDR and the East-West reunification, a new situation emerged, in which the Vietnamese *Kontingentflüchtlinge* in the GFR, who had come in the early 1980s, still applied for family reunion, albeit obviously in diminishing numbers, while new refugees had to go through the regular asylum procedures. At the same time, the consensus was that Vietnamese contract laborers should, in principle, be sent back to Vietnam after having concluded their five-year contract. In practice, the collapsing economy in the GDR at that time could not even provide jobs for the ongoing contracts. Seventy percent of Vietnamese workers were unemployed (Hillmann 2005). Contract workers were encouraged to return to their homeland with 3,000 Deutsch Mark as compensation. During the transition to a unified political system, legal status for the contract workers of the GDR was a complicated question. In the meantime, the Vietnamese government reluctantly took back its citizens who had a firsthand experience of the revolution leading to the loss of communism in Europe and who did not sign on a return application (Weiss 2005). After negotiations, the German and the Vietnamese governments came to an agreement in which the former paid development aid of 100 million Deutsche Mark in 1995 and another 100 million in 1996. In return, the Vietnamese government declared a willingness to take back 20,000 people. All of this, of course, boils down to a negotiation between the states of Vietnam and Germany in the aftermath of the Cold War, signaling the possibility of new economic relations. The German government took it for granted that returnees, all of them contract workers, would not face persecution back home. As of December 31, 1990, about 21,000 contract workers remained in unified Germany (Weiss 2005: 80). The Vietnamese who remained in Germany found themselves living in legal limbo. Many of them applied for asylum with the hope that they would prolong their residency in the GFR (Weiss 2005). There is no information about asylum applicants and the political and religious motivations of their claim. Among those who returned to Vietnam, some were regretful about their decision (Hillmann 2005), and some found ways to go back to Germany years later (Weiss 2005).

In this chapter, we propose to see the "Vietnamese migration" as a total phenomenon in which people who suffered from the devastation of their country after several decades of war did everything they could to leave for more promising regions of the world. This "total phenomenon" approach, deriving from the notion of "total social fact" of Marcel Mauss (1990), means that, on the one hand, Vietnamese migration is seen as the single case study, and on the other hand, this single case requires an examination of the historical and social context of the interrelated world in which it is situated. The imposed difference between Vietnamese boat refugees and Vietnamese contract laborers is contested by Vietnamese migrants themselves. Who they are depends on the way their choices and actions are narrativized in conflicting versions of nationalism within the context of international relations.

The relation between the Northern Vietnamese contract workers and Southern Vietnamese boat refugees is but one of many examples that show how state policies, both German and Vietnamese, failed to capture the dynamic realities. Although being aware of each other's existence, members of the two groups only had their first encounter after the fall of the Berlin Wall. Starting with social and commercial exchanges, the relation between many former boat refugees and contract workers soon became intimate. We don't have the exact statistics since the ethnicity of citizens is not recorded, but we have observed that marriage between North and South Vietnamese is common in Germany. Due to the state policy that divided them into small groups and assigned them to various localities in Germany, the dominance of ethnic endogamy among the first generation, and the political difficulty of connecting with the home country, Vietnamese refugees had a serious problem in finding marriage partners from their own ethnic background in Germany. The flow of especially male Vietnamese former contract workers from East to West Germany following the fall of the Berlin Wall provided a solution to this problem. In Göttingen alone, we encountered almost a dozen families with partners from both groups. Marriage is the most intimate way to national unification among the Vietnamese population in Germany.

Religion is another area in which the two groups sought unification and reconciliation, but not always with success. Religions that Vietnamese boat refugees and contract workers claim to follow are significantly different. While the later mostly claim to be nonreligious, the former identify themselves as Catholic or Buddhist followers (Baumann 2000; Hüwelmeier 2011). Although claiming to be nonreligious, the religious practices of former Vietnamese contract workers are far more diverse. Throughout our fieldwork, we have seen people practicing folk religions (the worship of Mother Goddess, Hùng kings, or other national heroes), ancestor worship, Buddhism, Pentecostalism, and Catholicism. The popular claim of nonreligious identity among Vietnamese contract workers resonates with the statistical data taken for the population in Vietnam, which reflects the tricky division between institutionalized religions and everyday beliefs (Salemink 2007). There is a clash between followers of different religions. However, in the scope of this research, we center on the political division playing out in Buddhism.[1]

In the following, we discuss the history and relation between the Linh Thứu Temple in West Berlin, established by Southern Vietnamese, and the Phổ Đà Temple, established by Vietnamese traders who were former contract workers in the Đồng Xuân bazaar. Traders in Đồng Xuân came from diverse nationalities and practiced various religions, including Christianity, Buddhism, Vietnamese folk beliefs, Islam, and Sikhism (Hüwelmeier 2016). However, we want to focus on Buddhism in this chapter. The relation and competition between these two temples, as we will show, is just one of many examples about how the legacy of the Cold War and its unfolding in its most important center (Berlin City) is experienced by an ethnic community like the Vietnamese.

While the dynamic relation between former boat refugees and former contract laborers remains important, it is significant that since the 1990s other groups of Vietnamese migrants have joined the community as students, tourists, family members, or undocumented migrants. This does not change the importance of the North-South opposition, but it does affect the nature of the overall relations in subtle ways. Not everyone is burdened with the same history.

Two Temples

In this part, we first discuss the establishment of different Buddhist temples in Berlin. This establishment resonates with the irreconcilable split between the former Vietnamese boat refugees and contract workers. The political division playing out in the religious field in Germany is nothing but the continuation of the political and religious tension during the Vietnam War, which is subsequently reviewed.

In Berlin today, there are nearly a dozen Buddhist temples, several of which serve exclusively the religious needs of more than 20,000 Vietnamese migrants in the city. Linh Thứu Pagoda in Spandau, West Berlin, is the oldest among these ethnic-religious institutions. It has been legally recognized by the Berlin municipal government for more than two decades and has been celebrated as a space of refuge for Vietnamese in distress. In the 1980s, a group of boat refugees met in a small apartment in Spandau district to meditate and pray for the Buddha under the instruction of Venerable Phương Trượng, a Buddhist monk based in Hannover. Sometimes when the number of attendants in these prayer sessions rose over the capacity of the apartment, the group would borrow a room at the Theravada Buddhist Temple run by Sri Lankan monks in the neighboring district, Frohnau. The collapse of the Berlin Wall in 1989 was perceived as a critical historical turn to the development of this Buddhist community. After the Wall came down, there were active efforts to extend this space of refuge to the former contract workers, who had come mostly from North Vietnam to the GDR and lost their legal residence status in the newly unified Germany. Members of the community organized charity and support for North Vietnamese crossing the Wall to West Berlin. Seeing themselves as refugees who a decade ago risked their life to leave Vietnam in search of freedom, Buddhist boat refugees of Berlin saw the Vietnamese contract workers as refugees fleeing the exploitative and controlling communist East Germany. Now the boat refugees had the power to help and to shelter these people in distress: a perfect Buddhist merit-earning act. In the words of Mr. Luong, a former boat refugee from South Vietnam, under the benevolent shadow of Buddha there was no more North-South, Communist-Republican enemy, there was only the warmth of the Viet blood that they shared (see Figure 6.1).

The participation of North Vietnamese contract workers boosted the growth of this Buddhist community. Throughout the 1990s, under the leadership of Nun Diệu Phước, the community purchased a large plot of land and built a new temple. In 2006, Linh Thứu Pagoda was completed. Architecturally, the main hall of the pagoda is a modern interpretation of the One Pillar Pagoda in Hanoi, perhaps the most famous religious architecture of North Vietnam. This reflects both the idea that the temple leadership wants to promote, namely Buddhism as the essence of Vietnamese identity, and the nostalgia of many North contract workers who had financed the construction of the temple.

Figure 6.1 Linh Thứu Pagoda on a quiet day, 2017; photo by Nga T. Mai.

These efforts to include the North Vietnamese contract workers also reflect a desire to promote Buddhism as a reconciliatory force between the past and the future, and the North and the South Vietnamese. This idea can be found in many publications by Vietnamese Buddhist authorities in Germany. It is also expressed in popular writings, one of the best examples of which is a short story that received an award in 2006 in a writing competition organized by Viên Giác Temple in Hannover (to which Linh Thứu Pagoda organizationally belongs). Hien, the protagonist, was a young contract worker from North Vietnam who found himself in an impossible situation after the Berlin Wall collapsed. Jobless and without hope to return to Vietnam, Hien went into the illegal cigarette trade and lived in constant anxiety, fearing for his life from gang violence to German police raids. In one distressful encounter with German police, instead of being arrested, Hien was convinced by a young and kind police officer to give up the illegal trade. The police officer also helped Hien to set up his life as a shopkeeper, and the two became friends. The police officer was a Buddhist and brought Hien to Viên Giác Temple, where he met Van, and soon the two fell in love. Van came from a Vietnamese boat refugee family. Van's father liked Hien instantly when Hien was introduced to the family. But when Hien recognized his own father in a photo taken with Van's father in the Mekong Delta in the late 1960s, the mood changed. It turned out, contrary to what Hien initially assumed, that his father was not a friend of Van's father. Instead, to Van's father, Hien's father was a terrible communist cadre, who would not hesitate to shoot at people who refused to fight for the communist side. Van's father was one of these people, in a battle that they could not win. His best friend was killed by Hien's father. This discovery of Hien's family history put a halt to the plan for the future of Van and Hien. However, thanks to the advice of Venerable Thích Như Điển, Van's father eventually agreed not to punish Hien for his father's bad deeds and let bygones be bygones. Moreover, Hien's father had already paid for his crime with being disenchanted with communism and going mad at his late age. Hien and Van's marriage received the blessing of Van's father as well as that of the Venerable Thích Như Điển. After marriage, thanks to Van's excellent command of German language and knowledge about German bureaucracy as well as Hien's large networks of friends of former contract workers, the couple could set up a trade center for the Vietnamese community in Leipzig. Eventually, the couple's ambition was to set up a Buddhist temple in Leipzig for their own community.

This short story is a narrative told about Buddhism's power to heal wounds and soothe the pain for Vietnamese refugees (Van's parents and their refugee community). Buddhism is idealized as a reconciliatory force to bring two former enemies together so that they can embrace each other again in ethnic sanguinity and love. Such ideal, however, is far from being realized in various Vietnamese communities in Germany, especially among the North and South Vietnamese Buddhists in Berlin. The effort to include North Vietnamese former contract workers into the Linh Thứu Buddhist family soon ran against a number of obstacles. On a daily basis, the cultural differences, sometimes very subtle, led to disagreement and resentment between the two groups (Su 2017). In the words of Mrs. My, a boat refugee and one of the core members of the Linh Thứu Buddhist family, "North Vietnamese got it all wrong when it comes to worship the Buddha. They come here [Linh Thứu Pagoda] still out of *tham, sân, si* (delusion, greed, and aversion). They don't care about being enlightened by the Buddha." The fact that Mrs. My assembled her wealth by trading with North Vietnamese entrepreneurs and organizing several rotating credit associations (*tổ hụi*) in which she charged a hefty fee for safeguarding and circulating the cash earned from backbreaking informal labor by former contract workers did not prevent her from criticizing North Vietnamese. She listed a number of improprieties of Vietnamese Buddhists from the North, such as dressing inappropriately when coming to the temples, addressing monks and nuns inappropriately, speaking harshly and loudly, and bringing inappropriate offerings (such as meat and cigarettes) to the temple, etc. In her view, these shortcomings resulted from the decades of indoctrination by the atheist communist government. It was her job and that of others in the Buddhist family to carry out the Buddha teaching to be benevolent and forgiving and to patiently guide the northern brothers to find the true path to the enlightenment.

It is commonly agreed among Vietnamese, north or south alike, that the Southern Vietnamese accent was better than the Northern one in prayers. Ms. Thuong, a widow of a North Vietnamese former contract worker, told us that when she heard a Buddhist chanting by South Vietnamese voice, it touched her heart. It was as if the soft and gentle sound of the accent always brought her right away into the calm, the serene, and the benevolent realm of the Buddha. On the other hand, she would need a few more minutes to reach such meditative stage should the sutra be chanted by a North Vietnamese accent, which in her word always sounded so *trần tục và giả tạo* (vulgar and fake). The distinction in the perception of North or South Vietnamese voice and sound in Buddhist prayers is directly connected to the recent history of North-South Vietnamese separation. For three decades, North Vietnamese under the warring socialist regime were forbidden to explore certain areas of their "sensory regime" (Meyer and Moors 2016). Revolutionary songs, militant slogans, or somber preach of ideology were allowed, whereas sentimental songs, poetic speeches, and romantic music were banned. The South, on the contrary, witnessed a boom of sentimental bolero music in addition to an exuberant musical and theater scene that featured classic and modern sagas celebrating loves and personal feelings. For a short while following the unification of the country, Northern authorities condemned it as "yellow" music—the music was seen as *sến, ủy mị* (sad, emotional). Soon, however, the wave of sentimental sound swept over the whole North to the extent that it is observed that the North may win the war, but it is the South that wins the heart of all Vietnamese people.[2] For North Vietnamese now, the accent of the South helps them to overcome the cold distances between communities, between individuals, and even between their inner and outer selves.

In the spiritual realm, a parallel process took place. Before 1975, while Buddhism was entirely under state control in the North and was made into a political tool for mass mobilization, Southern Buddhists enjoyed greater autonomy. The conflict between Buddhists and the Catholic regime of Ngô Đình Diệm[3] not only clearly demonstrated the wider social and political influence of Buddhism (in comparison with Catholicism) but also lent South Vietnamese Buddhism a greater air of independence and purity from the influence of political ideologies and state control. With the revival of Buddhism in the North since the 1990s, South Buddhist practices, meditation, and teachings have been seen as the most authentic and pure form of Vietnamese Buddhism. The chant of a monk from South Vietnam makes a sutra more intimate and powerful. Many Vietnamese Buddhists in Berlin concurred to the fact that they liked to attend prayer and meditation led by South Vietnamese monks.

However, the sound alone would not convince North Vietnamese Buddhists to be fully a part of the Linh Thứu Buddhist family. Toward the end of the 2000s, many traders in Lichtenberg district in East Berlin met to form their own. In 2007, with the active leadership and sponsorship of Ms. Trịnh Thị Mùi, the owner of the Asia Pacific Center, one of the two largest Vietnamese trading bazaars in Berlin, a temple called Phổ Đà was inaugurated within the grounds of the Bazaar. Buddhist and Guanyin statues were selected and sent from Vietnam to Berlin by supportive members of Vietnam Buddhist Sangha, the official Buddhist organization in Vietnam. Sixty sets of lay Buddhist robes were brought over from Vietnam so that the temple's members could dress more uniformly and solemnly. In the following years, two monks, one from Vietnam and one from Paris, were invited to take residence in the temple to lead this growing Buddhist community (see Figure 6.2).

Since 2011, a group of Buddhists traders in Đồng Xuân Center, another giant Vietnamese Bazaar, bigger and faster-growing than the Asia Pacific Center, announced the establishment of yet another separate Buddhist Association,

Figure 6.2 The gate to Phổ Đà Temple next to the entrance of the Asia Pacific Center (a bazaar owned by a Vietnamese former contract worker), 2018; photo by Nga T. Mai.

with their own temple, also (confusingly) called Phổ Đà. This Phổ Đà Temple, however, existed only virtually between 2011 and 2013. A Vietnamese New Year celebration that took place in the office building of the Đồng Xuân Center in January 2012 also included an elaborated requiem (a Buddhist ritual to appease the souls of the dead and to pray for peace) and a "bathing the Buddha ritual" conducted by two monks who came from Vietnam. Mr. Nguyễn Văn Hiền, the owner of Đồng Xuân Center, and his family were given the honor to pour the first scoop of water over the baby Buddha with his finger pointing upward. This Buddha had been bestowed upon the community by a delegation of monks from the headquarter of the Vietnam Buddhist Sangha on an official visit in the year before. However, since the group did not have a physical temple structure, the Buddha was stored in a closet inside the administrative office of the market on the first floor of the outer building. In the afternoon before the requiem took place, one of us (Tam Ngo) was talking to the monks in this office. At the moment before the Buddha should be taken out, dusted off, and brought to the altar set up downstairs in the meeting hall, Tam was asked by Ms. Van, the head of the association, to wait outside. Later, she was told by Ms. Van that the monks had instructed her to do so because a "researcher from a German religious institute" should not see a "not-so-sacred moment," namely a dusting of the Buddha. Tam told Ms. Van that on the contrary she found that that was a very sacred moment, as it shows a magical transformation of an object (a statue being stored and covered in dust) to a powerful religious symbol, an embodiment of the Buddha no less, by a simple act of cleaning off some dust on him. And for Tam, as a researcher, it was fascinating and important to gain insights into this moment by witnessing it. Ms. Van looked rather puzzled at Tam's explanation and shied away from any further discussion on the matter. Later, Tam learned from other members of the Phổ Đà Temple that, like Ms. Van, they found having to store the Buddha statue inside a closet was an act of "extreme reluctance" (*bần cùng bất đắc dĩ*) and showed the poor material condition of their earnest attempt to honor the Buddha, something they preferred not to be confronted with, even by themselves. This Đồng Xuân's Phổ Đà Temple existed as an underground as it has neither legal status (as being registered as a religious institution or association) nor a physical space (such as a temple building), as the Buddha had to live a mobile life in various locations inside the huge Đồng Xuân market. In 2013, the group purchased a large piece of land (3,000 square meters, on Dorfstraße 28, Berlin) and renovated an old building existing on the land into a temple. Since then, there have been two Vietnamese temples, which were just a few kilometers from each other, and both were called Phổ Đà. During the establishment of the second Phổ Đà Temple, internal conflict ripped the Đồng Xuân Buddhist community apart, with one fraction wanting to remain operating inside the bazaar and the other fraction wanting to invest in the expansion of infrastructure outside the bazaar. To avoid confusion, in October 2013, the monk in charge of the Dorfstraße Phổ Đà Temple changed its name to Từ Ân Temple.

In spring 2016, we visited the Venerable Thích Đức Thiện, the head of the international relations department of the Vietnam Buddhist Sangha, in Hanoi. The monk spoke enthusiastically about the wealth and the importance of the Vietnamese community in Germany which hosted him on several visits in the previous years. He was not so forthcoming, however, when asked about any plan for the Vietnamese community in Berlin specifically. Two months later, the *nguoiviet.de*, the community online newspaper, published several articles announcing the official visit of Thích Đức Thiện and members of the Vietnamese embassy in Đồng Xuân Center, prior to the Vesak Day to break the ground for the construction of a new Buddhist temple, on a plot of land even bigger than that of Từ Ân Temple. This temple was envisioned to be the headquarter of the Vietnam Buddhist Sangha in Germany.[4] But until it is built, the Vietnamese embassy actively utilizes both Từ Ân and Phổ Đà as venues for political and cultural events directly connected to the agenda of the Vietnamese government in gaining access and control of Vietnamese immigrants (mostly former contract workers).

The decision by North Vietnamese Buddhists to set up their own temples separate from the Linh Thứu Pagoda has many explanations. While some informants mentioned the 30 kilometer distance from Lichtenberg district, where most North Vietnamese Buddhist lived and worked, to Linh Thứu, others reasoned the irreconcilable cultural difference between the two groups. Some North Vietnamese informants straightforwardly condemned South Vietnamese refugees they encountered at the Linh Thứu Pagoda as arrogant and hostile, calling the contract workers behind their back as *phi nhân*, a term that was coined by South Vietnamese refugees to call contract workers who were brought to the GDR mostly by airplane (*phi cơ*) as opposing to themselves *thuyền nhân* (boat refugees). However, the term *phi nhân* is mainly for its pejoratively meaning referring "a person without any humanity" as some South Vietnamese anti-communist activists saw all North Vietnamese contract workers as inhuman agents of an inhuman regime. We argue that the most important reason why many North Vietnamese refrained from participating in Linh Thứu Pagoda was political. After some years of disorientation, many North Vietnamese former contract workers became successful entrepreneurs in Berlin. Having a good political connection with the communist government of Vietnam became desirable. Linh Thứu Pagoda was founded by the refugees and organizationally belonged to the Unified Vietnam Buddhist Sangha, which is not recognized by the Vietnamese government (and treated as an underground sect in Vietnam). To a lesser extent, as the concentration of North Vietnamese in East Berlin grew, a desire developed to have their own Buddhist temple, which could be used as a venue for the community's cultural activities. To a greater extent, the support of the Vietnamese government, from indirect to direct by sending various members of the Vietnam Buddhist Sangha, the official Buddhist organization in Vietnam, to come to conduct Buddhist service and take control of these temples escalated the political rift and conflict between the East Berlin-North Vietnamese and West Berlin-South Vietnamese Buddhist communities.

The relations, conflicts, and schism in the Vietnamese Buddhist communities in Berlin reflect the ongoing legacy of the Cold War and its unfolding in the city of Berlin. During the Vietnam War (between 1955 and 1975), South Vietnamese Buddhist authorities were predominantly members of the Unified Buddhist Church of Vietnam (UBCV), established in 1964, partly to take a position against the suppression of Buddhism of the Catholic Ngô Đình Diệm regime. In 1975, after the takeover of the South, the North Vietnamese government targeted the UBCV, in the general plan to dissolve all religious and secular associations of the South, forcing an absolute unification with the North. Thích Huyền Quang, the patriarch of UBCV, and Venerable Thích Quảng Độ, the head of UBCV's Viện Hóa Đạo (Institute for the Dissemination of the Dharma), had from the beginning already refused to collaborate with the communist government. Instead, in 1977, the Patriarch Thích Huyền Quang sent a letter to then premier Phạm Văn Đồng detailing all the crimes and corruption of communist leaders in various locations in the South. This led to Thích Huyền Quang's arrest and subsequent years of detention and then house arrest. In 1981, the Vietnamese government established the Vietnam Buddhist Sangha (VBS), an organization allegedly representing all branches, temples, and Buddhist schools in the country, directly under the control of the Fatherland Front. The leadership of UBCV refused to become part of the VBS, and ever since it was deemed not only illegal (unrecognized) but also an anti-communist and anti-state religious association. Before he passed away in 2008, Most Venerable Patriarch Thích Huyền Quang named Venerable Thích Quảng Độ his successor, the Most Venerable Patriarch of UBCV. Like his predecessor, Thích Quảng Độ remains a fervent opponent of communist rule. He became known worldwide as an advocate of human rights and democracy.

Most Buddhist temples in the West see themselves as members of the UBCV, and many take the same political position as that of Thích Quảng Độ. However, toward the end of the 2000s, a desire to return and reconnect with Vietnam grew among both leaders and followers of many oversea UBCV temples. A number of Buddhist authorities in Overseas UBCV actively organized a round trip to Vietnam with charity activities and visits to original temples (*tổ đình*), and started dialogues with the Vietnamese government. This willingness for dialogue was perceived by Thích Quảng Độ and his disciples as an act of betrayal. This led to a separation in the UBCV. In a press release on August 24, 2008, the Paris-based spokesperson of UBCV, Võ Văn Ái, announced Thích Quảng Độ's decision to renounce UBCV with three of its branches in Canada, Australia, New Zealand, and Europe. Buddhist members of the South Vietnamese refugee community in Germany are embedded, organizationally and theologically, in the larger network of European UBCV. After the decision of Venerable Thích Quảng Độ, most of the temples attended by South Vietnamese refugees in Germany were excommunicated from the Vietnam-based UBCV.

The Linh Thứu Pagoda in Berlin, led by Nun Diệu Phước, who is a member of the European UBCV, was accordingly disowned by Thích Quảng Độ. In 2010, the leadership of Linh Thứu was accused of abusing the name UBCV to call for donations. This accusation was made by members of a fervent anti-communist group in Berlin, who run the online forum Thongtinberlin.de. To answer their accusation, the Parisian-based spokesperson of UBCV stated that while the UBCV has excommunicated the European branch, Linh Thứu Pagoda had never been officially registered as a member of the UBCV, thus, indeed, using of the title UBCV for their charity activities or to propagating the Dharma was a violation of the law.

An Alternative Buddhist Space in the Heart

To avoid being caught in this rivalry, a growing number of Vietnamese Buddhists, mostly consisting of former female contract workers and semi-documented female migrants, have been in search again for a new Buddhist space in which they do not have to confront the question of political ideologies nor social belongings. Recently, many of these women found their answer in the online Light and Sound Meditation movement, led by the obscure Master Ruma, or Venerable Trần Tâm, a Vietnamese refugee who converted to Tantric Buddhism a decade ago and is now leading a global follower and owning a chain of vegan restaurants in Thailand and Cambodia. We will illustrate this by highlighting just one extended case from the category of recent migrants to Germany.

Mai came from an ordinary peasant family in central Vietnam. She was married at the age of nineteen and moved in with her husband. The marriage was followed by the birth of their two children. In 1987, when she was pregnant with her second child, her husband died from a disease. Being left on her own, she took her two children with her to the neighboring province southward in search for economic opportunities. She opened a street-side shop selling tea, beverages, and groceries to earn a living. There, she found it very difficult to live as a single woman and a single mother in a society where women were seen as men's property. She recalled one of many similar accidents which led to the event of the third pregnancy:

> I was teased and harassed in those days because the men knew I was a widow. Some even lurked around my house and whistled. By that time, Xiu's father [Xiu is Mai's youngest daughter] worked on his construction project in Quảng Bình and lived near my place. He liked me, although he was married. He was good to me. One day, a man sneaked into my house. He [Xiu's father] was there outside and saw what happened; he came back and chased the man away. I thought he was a nice person. When I got pregnant with Xiu, he promised to get divorced. I did not want that to happen; then, I left him.

In 2004, Mai deserted the place where she had lived since her husband's death, brought her three children to Hanoi, rented them a house in a suburb of the city, and left them by themselves in the city with some money. She got on a flight heading to the Czech Republic, from where she traveled to Germany—her desired destination. When she left, her oldest son was about twenty years old, and the youngest daughter was just ten. She spent 500 million Vietnamese Dong (about €20,000) by mortgaging her parents' piece of land on the smugglers. For many years until now, Mai could not resolve her resentment and feeling of hurt toward her relatives for leaving her and her children unsupportive and forsaken.

Since arriving in Germany, Mai has untiringly worked any job that has been given. She always shared her living space with other Vietnamese fellows. She worked as a domestic helper in Vietnamese families, caring for children and household chores. There was a very limited choice if one clandestine migrant, like her, wanted to make money. This babysitting job was always in high demand since hiring a countrywoman without legal status was the cheapest option at hand. In the meantime, migrants easily accepted the live-in requirement and twenty-four-hour standby service. For taking the job offer, Mai would earn her children decent lives and a shelter to sleep. Without contract and subtle job agreements, she constantly moved from one family to another.

On some occasions, Mai found refuge in a small pagoda in Brandenburg, a neighboring state of Berlin, where she supported the staff voluntarily in their daily works. The refuge in the Buddha's welcoming arms was significant for her and many other Vietnamese who could not avail themselves to the German state's support. Historically, Linh Thứu Pagoda had achieved its reputation in putting the war aside and giving a helping hand to the disoriented Vietnamese after the collapse of the Communist Block. Now, to the undocumented migrants, Buddhist space has gained its name as a place of refuge. This role, though, is not an established one compared to the "sanctuary communities" (Marfleet 2011) from the Christian tradition. For undocumented Vietnamese migrants like Mai, a religious place provides them a place to stay, daily meals, and a closer social and language environment to their origin. More importantly, this refuge does not require from them proof of persecution and the horrendously bureaucratic application.

Throughout the years, Buddhism has played an increasingly significant role in consoling Mai's life and influencing her worldview. Her perspective toward her joys and suffering was embedded in her religious beliefs. Mai explained to us as to why many times she could not find anything better than a babysitting job. This no-other-choice situation was her karmic debt that she paid for her parents, who lost their baby before Mai was born. Often citing the law of cause and effect, she always found the answer to the important question "why" as in "why did it happen to me?" In this way, Buddhism provides her an explanation for the existence of inequality.

For the last three years, Mai became an ardent disciple of Master Ruma. For her, this conversion does not strongly contradict her previous religious belief. Indeed, this conversion was like a breath of fresh air brought in together with her new social status and a new feeling of belonging. Master Ruma, or Venerable Trần Tâm, was born in 1972 in Vietnam to a Buddhist family. At the age of twelve, he flew to the United States. There he was adopted into a Catholic family. This family background had an impact on his religious practices later. He established a Buddhist sect, called Pháp môn Diệu Âm (Light and Sound Meditation), followed by mostly Vietnamese migrants in the States, Europe, and Southeast Asia. Pháp môn Diệu Âm promotes meditation and vegetarianism as the way to enlightenment and the Knowledge of Truth. Master Ruma claims himself to be a living Buddha with the divine power to guide and lead people to the self-liberation and the internal existence. In his autobiography, he emphasizes his own move from a happy family man and his marriage in California to establish a huge Buddhist faction in Thailand, Lao, and Cambodia and to expand his outreach to Europe. Through feeling light and sound during meditation, with the help of Master Ruma, practitioners can experience the grace of *Thượng Đế* (Heavenly Ruler or the Highest Deity, or God) and Buddha.[5] Over the years, the Buddhist sect of Master Ruma has been growing in numbers. The establishment of the Meditation Center in Cambodia is evidence of this growing. To facilitate his disciples' meditation, Master Ruma recorded his voice in CDs distributed to people at a voluntary cost. To Vietnamese authorities, Master Ruma and his sect is seen as heresy and following his practices means disturbing the social and public order.[6] Official Buddhists in Vietnam consider him a fraud and his religious doctrine harmful to Buddhism. Mai, among the increased number of followers in Berlin, became the core members of Master Ruma's group. Being aware of the controversial position of Master Ruma and his belief, she defended her conversion and said, "all streams flow to the sea. All religions aim at one goal. What is important is how you transform yourself, rather than which religion you choose. As soon as you follow the Master [Master Ruma], you don't worship, venerate [as in ancestor worship], and consecrate any more."

What can we learn from the conversion from conventional Buddhism to Master Ruma's Light and Sound Meditation in the case of Mai? First, Vietnamese Buddhism lacked the systematized consistency in its religious practices (Soucy 2012). Thus, in Vietnam, Buddhism shared many features of folk beliefs or spirituals. Although Master Ruma and his faction adopted different practices and religious ideologies from various Buddhist factions and Catholicism, his core languages and beliefs still borrowed mostly from Buddhism. Mai's conversion can be understood in this context. Changing to Light and Sound Meditation is choosing a different Buddhist leader and seeking a different way to happiness and protection. Second, and more importantly, her alienation from conventional Buddhism of the Vietnamese diaspora in Germany reveals the political tension manifested in religious life between boat refugees and contract workers and the emerging need of new Vietnamese migrants in their search of a religious space. Mai, with her new legal and social status, actively engaged in the new religious movement of the Light and Sound Meditation, felt estranged from the established Buddhist communities of West and East Berlin. Her migration history, her political stance, and her economic background do not fit into both. This discrepancy led Mai to find herself in the alignment with Master Ruma's personal history and teaching. Master Ruma was himself a migrant who often raised questions about the self and proclaimed to find Dhamar through meditation and vegetarianism. His teaching places great emphasis on the struggles of migrants, love for Vietnam, health, and emotional self. Confronting and belonging to a political ideology is not part of the path to find a self and the Enlightenment. His beliefs and practices face obstacles for recognition, similar to the obstacles that new migrants faced in their search for a social place.

Conclusion

This chapter has argued that the country left by various types of Vietnamese still looms large in their minds and daily concerns. The legacy of the American war and later the Chinese war is still the most important element in relations among the Vietnamese in Germany. Vietnamese former refugees are often much better off than North Vietnamese former contract laborers, but slowly this is changing with the expanding opportunities for trading with Vietnam. The ones who are truly disadvantaged are the illegal migrants who have come to Germany as a fabled land of opportunity long after the reunification of Vietnam. All these divisions and tensions are reflected in Vietnamese Buddhism in Germany. Buddhism is not a neutral, transcendent belief system, but historically a major player in Vietnamese politics. It is inevitable that the Vietnamese government tries to use Buddhism to control the diaspora. It is just as inevitable that South Vietnamese boat refugees resent this. At the same time, some Vietnamese attempt to escape this political game. For the search of a Buddhist space of each Vietnamese group, Buddhism evidences its dynamics and adaptability to accommodate diverse needs across space and time. To show this, we have ended with giving a case study of an individual for whom Buddhism offers a way to cope with an incredibly fraught and difficult migrant situation.

Part III

People on the Move in and from Africa

"Are We an Elected People?"

Religion and the Everyday Experience of Young Congolese Refugees in Kampala

Alessandro Gusman

Preface

While I was working on this chapter in late August 2018, the Italian media were busy telling the story of the "Diciotti," a boat of the Italian navy that had been kept in the harbor of Catania, Sicily, for several days with 177 people on board, mostly Eritrean asylum seekers. The Italian government refused to let them disembark, arguing that other countries of the European Union (EU) should take a number of the asylum seekers. Matteo Salvini, the interior minister at the time, was particularly vocal in asking the EU for a shared solution, while a number of organizations held a demonstration in the harbor asking to let the asylum seekers free. The event was highly spectacularized by the Italian media, with images of the people stuck on the boat, of their weak bodies, and of testimonies from doctors and volunteers who went on board to check the conditions of the people on the boat.

There was in that period—and there still is—a general overexposure of the so-called refugee crisis in the Italian media; yet, in the case of the "Diciotti" ship, data show that the number of asylum seekers who had arrived in the country from the beginning of 2018 till August had decreased by around 80 percent, if compared to the previous year. Almost everyone in Italy knows about this and other stories, and yet very little is known about the everyday life asylum seekers and refugees live after they disembark in Italy.

When speaking of refugees, the focus in the media (and often in scholarly work) is on "crisis," "emergency," thus on extraordinary situations and conditions of people fleeing from wars, famines, persecutions. Despite this, displaced people often live for extended periods in the country where they find refuge, waiting for resettlement to a third country, or to go back to their home country. What about the ordinariness of their lives and of their everyday experience in these transit countries?

Starting from eight months of fieldwork carried out in Kampala from 2013 to 2015, this chapter focuses on the everyday experiences of Congolese refugees living in the urban areas of the capital city of Uganda, specifically in the neighborhood of Katwe, and on the role religion plays in daily circumstances. With this focus, it aims at showing how refugees try to carry out a life project in the new context, and to what extent religion contributes in conferring a sense of "ordinariness" to the long period of transition in Kampala waiting to be resettled. It does so by highlighting the complex interactions they establish with the religious domain, striving to build a frame to explain their condition of "people on the move" and their suffering and maneuvering this sphere in order to gain a reputation within the Congolese community in Kampala and experience social mobility in a general context of poverty and stuckness. Negotiating the official narratives produced by Congolese churches in town, refugees often react to and translate these narratives in a highly creative (and at times critical) way in the everydayness of their urban lives.

The Context: Congolese Refugees in Katwe (Kampala)

The phenomenon of refugees living in African urban contexts (also referred to as "urban refugees") is still understudied. Some 75,000 asylum seekers and refugees were living in Kampala, the capital city of Uganda, at the end of August 2018.[1] Around 40,000 of them were Congolese, mostly from the Kivu region in the Democratic Republic of Congo (DRC), an area that has been devastated by conflicts and violence for the last three decades.

The number of urban refugees—people who decide to live in town rather than in the UNHCR camps—is increasing in Uganda as well as in other African countries.[2] The Ugandan "Refugee Bill" (2006, applied in 2009) has been regarded as an exception in the African context, as it recognizes the right of refugees to live anywhere in the country, to move freely, and to work; yet, at the same time, it states that they do not receive any assistance outside of refugee camps (Kreibaum 2016).[3] The Refugee Bill received criticism because it is still insufficient to guarantee protection and assistance for those who live in urban contexts (Bernstein and Okello 2007). This is even more significant considering that the period of "temporary protection" in Uganda has become longer and longer, so that many people are experiencing "protracted refugee situations" (five years or more waiting for resettlement).

Following these recent changes in the legislation, and because of the prolonged period of staying in Uganda waiting for resettlement, a growing number of Congolese decide to leave refugee camps and move to town in search for employment and better educational opportunities for their children (Omata 2012).

The UNHCR gives refugees three options: an assisted voluntary return to their home country, integration in the host country, and resettlement to a third country. With some exceptions, the Congolese refugees I met in Kampala did not plan to stay in Uganda; some of them were willing to go back to the DRC, although only few were finally able to do it, because of the persistent violence in the Kivu region. The majority were instead waiting for resettlement to a European or North American country, and complained about the excessive length and the opacity of these processes; some had already been living in Uganda for ten years or more.

This was mostly a young population, navigating the urban life with little aid from the Ugandan state or from international organizations. In this situation of extreme physical and existential uncertainty, religion becomes for many refugees a resource for meaning-making, to explain their condition and to locate their everyday life of suffering and waiting in Kampala within a meaningful frame. Thus, religious congregations, and mainly the Églises de Réveil,[4] are a space to find solace from everyday suffering and to share experiences and emotions with others (Gusman 2020).

Pentecostal churches are often the first place Congolese address to find a place to stay at their arrival in Kampala (it is not unusual to be hosted at a church for some weeks or months); these churches offer first aid and the possibility to build new social networks. The lack of welfare from the Ugandan state and from international organizations creates the condition for churches to become service providers, too. Many of my Congolese interlocutors in Kampala converted to Pentecostalism (mostly from Catholicism) after having been hosted or helped by Pentecostal congregations during the first months in town.

In the new context, Congolese refugees often build "kinship-like" relationships with people they have just met. It is not infrequent for those who arrive alone to be "adopted" by a family of refugees, and to live with them for a period, waiting to settle in the new context, or even for several years. This was, for instance, the case for Héritier, who came from a Muslim family and converted to Pentecostalism after becoming part of his "new family" whom he met in Kampala. In contexts of migration and forced displacement, fictive kinship often helps people to reproduce family relationships. Churches play an important role in this process of reconstructing social and intimate relationships after the arrival in Uganda, as people stay together on the basis of a common faith, instead of a common lineage. Moreover, priests and pastors can become surrogate parent figures, especially for young people who are hosted at church or who find in the congregation a sort of extended family in the absence of relatives (Morgan 2019). Once they arrive in Kampala, Congolese look for relatives or friends to receive initial assistance and to find a place to sleep. When they do not know anyone in town, as is often the case, they rely on the "protective networks" organized by religious organizations (Sommers 2001), which help them settle in town by providing information on how to live and move in the urban context and on how to apply for the refugee status.

Although Congolese refugees live in different areas of Kampala, the highest density is in Katwe, one of the poorest neighborhoods of the capital city. Until the 1970s, this area was almost unpopulated and covered by swamps. Its growth in the last decades has been due mainly to the arrival of migrants from the rural areas and of refugees from neighboring countries.

In September 2013, I mapped the presence of fourteen Églises de Réveil in Katwe, which I call "refugees churches" as the quasi-totality of their audience is composed by Congolese and other francophone refugees from neighboring countries; all of these congregations—with one exception—had been founded in Kampala by Congolese pastors after 2000. Considering the broader context of Kampala, in November 2014, the Communauté chrétienne congolaise en Ouganda comprised fifty-five Congolese churches and seventy churches in total in the country. However, this figure seems to be largely incomplete as, according to the leader of the association, there were at the time around 150 Églises de Réveil in Kampala alone.

The size of these congregations is usually small (30 to 300 members), and fluctuating, as Congolese move frequently from one church to another. Church buildings are in simple and perishable materials, such as wood and metal sheeting.

Religion and Everyday Experience

The idea of this chapter grew out of a sense of dissatisfaction I felt during fieldwork for some widespread representations about refugees' trajectories and about the place of religion in their everyday life. Despite the significant body of work on the religion-migration link, the role of religion in displacement contexts has not been extensively explored in literature. Refugee studies generally focus on livelihood strategies and economic and demographic aspects, leaving the religious side—and thus processes of meaning-making—apart.

Some of these representations clashed against the empirical data of my research, as they seemed not to consider the dimension of "life as it is lived," the everyday experience of refugees in the transit country.

Observers' attention, when it comes to refugees, has often been caught by the extraordinary, the newsworthy, the "crisis," rather than by the daily life people live, its routines and its challenges. This is not limited to the analysis of displacement contexts, but a more general tendency within social sciences, part of what Sherry Ortner (2016) has defined as the turn to a "dark anthropology." The ordinary has been in part abandoned as if it were not interesting, compared to the "spectacular" and the extraordinary (Highmore 2010; Rakodi 2014: 84). Yet, a focus on the everyday is part and parcel of the ethnographic practice, as the approach to the field includes experience-near encounters with common people in their daily occupations. It is thus not surprising that in recent years there has been an increasing attention to the everyday and to the ordinary in anthropology (Lambek 2010; Schielke 2010; Schielke and Debevec 2012; Mattingly 2013; Das 2015).

In the case of refugees, this focus on people's ordinary life allows—I argue—to nuance the image of refugees as passive and vulnerable subjects who need help and to analyze how they are busy building their lives with new meanings and routines in transit contexts. This makes it possible to look at refugees' cultural creativity and to the strategies they employ to engage with structural powers in their everyday lives (De Certeau 1984).

Moreover, studies on the role of religion in displacement contexts have mostly focused on churches as actors of social welfare and as resources in an emergency (Fiddian-Qasmiyeh 2011; Lauterbach 2014), leaving aside their place in the construction of a frame through which refugees try to make sense of their suffering.

Taking these considerations as a starting point, I felt it was necessary for me to rethink some of the approaches I had used until that moment. This implied two interrelated shifts: first of all, I needed to focus more on the ordinariness of the life of the Congolese people I was working with in Kampala. During the first months of fieldwork, the time I spent with them had been mostly marked by routines, common daily activities, dull and exciting moments, sharing of meals, and other ordinary activities. The existence these "urban refugees" carried on in Kampala seemed to me not so "extra-ordinary," nor something one could define as "emergency," as most of them had been living in town for several years, struggling to find a way to survive, a house to live, and places in which to build a sense of "home" and of belonging in their exile (Russell 2011).

As the focus of my research was the place of religion in refugees' lives, I had to analyze not only the role Christian churches and religious organizations played in providing refugees a shelter at their arrival in town, a help with the bureaucratic procedures at the Office of the Prime Minister in charge of their dossiers, and with other practical and material needs. There was, I was beginning to realize, much more to explore by focusing on "lived" or "everyday religion," thus acknowledging that religious sentiments are rooted in the lifeworlds of individuals and groups (Streib, Dinter, and Söderblom 2008) and the work of social agents as narrators and interpreters of their own experiences and stories (Orsi 2010).

This does not mean to set lived religion against religious institutions,[5] but rather to analyze how the two dimensions, the existential and the institutional, are related and contribute together in giving shape to the everyday of Congolese refugees in Kampala.

For many of my Congolese interlocutors in Kampala—as surely in other contexts—religion seemed to provide not only (spiritual) means for coping with their situation but also a sense of normality in their lives; it is exactly this ordinariness that is often undervalued in scholarly works on refugees. Refugees' situation is often thought and described in terms of its "extraordinariness" and as an "emergency"; yet, for people who have been living in Kampala for years (not unusually five or more), there is also the need to carry out an "ordinary" life, although amid the harshness of the situation they live as refugees. The frequent references to the need to surrender to "God's will," to be patient and wait for one's turn (to be resettled, mainly), and to Uganda as a land of passage before reaching the "Promised Land" may be seen as a way to neutralize social criticism toward the national and international institutions; yet, they are also an instrument to shift the refugees' disproportionate suffering from a social to a spiritual level. Religion thus becomes a resource to face suffering, as it provides refugees with a meta-historical narrative and with habituated actions[6] that create a stable horizon, helping reducing uncertainty in believers' everyday lives.

With this approach based on everyday religion, I aim at analyzing the interactions between religion and other social spheres from the perspective of common believers, who in daily life negotiate, doubt, rely on, and strategically use their faith. This implies to give up on the need for coherence between religious "grand schemes" and the "ordinary lives" people live (Schielke and Debevec 2012); contradictions and ambiguities have not to be discarded as problematic, but rather considered as constitutive of the "grand schemes" themselves. Official narratives do of course have a role as a guide for believers in the everyday actions in the world and the way they see and think about it, but they play this part within a precise context; they are in fact "informed by the lifeworld they are embedded in" (Schielke and Debevec 2012: 2). This is why religious practices are unsystematic, complex, and plural in the everyday.

An ethnographic focus on everyday religion shows how believers use, negotiate and rearrange beliefs, norms, and the ordering of life religious institutions set, in order to navigate their daily existence and to make sense of their condition. Hence the need for attention to the small scale of everyday practices, actions, and strategies; these dimensions are intrinsically central to the ethnographic practice, and yet sometimes they seem to be nonessential in scholarly approaches that focus on refugees' exceptionality and do not consider the everyday lives they live in contexts of refuge.

Against this background, the aim of this chapter is to analyze the role of Pentecostal religion in the everyday life of my Congolese interlocutors in Kampala. Rather than focusing on beliefs expressed during church services, the point is to highlight the complex and often ambiguous relationships between the "grand schemes" of Pentecostal discourse (i.e., the representation of a moral subject and of a "good Christian" who is patient and fully relies on God's will) and the everyday practices and ordinary lives people live as refugees in Kampala. This approach is influenced by recent developments in anthropological theory around the notions of ordinary or everyday ethics (Lambek 2010; Das 2015) and of lived religion.

Theorists of "ordinary ethics" have more or less explicitly tried to keep the institutional religious side out of the ethical domain (Lambek 2012), arguing that ethics is "relatively tacit, grounded in agreement rather than rule" (Lambek 2010: 2). In partial contrast with this approach, Joel Robbins has expressed the concern that obscuring the contribution of religion to ethics is a potential blind spot of most of the studies on ordinary ethics (Robbins 2016: 3). He claims for a focus on transcendent religious values, especially as they are expressed through rituals, as constitutive of believers' ethical sensibilities they apply in everyday practices. While I agree with his concerns over the marginal role played by religion in the growing body of work on everyday ethics in anthropology—and I suggest this is mainly due to a way of thinking about religion as a transmitted set of ideas as opposed to everyday practices—I object to his view that everyday ethics finds its foundation in "transcendent religious values." Rather than thinking about these values as constitutive of everyday ethics, I argue for an understanding of religion as lived experience, in which the main focus is on "what people do with religious idioms, how they use them, what they make of themselves and their worlds with them, and how, in turn, men, women, and children are fundamentally shaped by the worlds they are making as they make these worlds" (Orsi 2003: 172). I thus share Birgit Meyer's and Dick Houtman's critique of the mentalistic understanding of religion, grounded in the Protestant tradition, and share the idea that "religion becomes palpable through people, their practices and use of things" (2012: 7).

In order to enlighten the role of meaning-making religion plays in contexts of refuge, the next section focuses on the way the adhesion to the Pentecostal movement frames the experience of being a refugee. Through the identification with the story of the people of Israel, Congolese refugees find continuity in their discontinuous experience, a parallelism with the "elected people," thus being able to rebuild a moral world based on the assumption of a future redemption from their present situation.

Pentecostal Narratives, Sense-making, and the Ordinariness of Refugees' Experience

In this section, I explore narratives adopted in religious discourses in order to reflect upon and explain the refugees' situation, and how refugees use these discourses in their everyday living in order to build a frame from which to explain their past and present condition.

Most of the Congolese refugees and asylum seekers I met in Kampala lived in a state of extreme uncertainty, also due to the lack of protection and assistance from the Ugandan state and the UNHCR. This creates a situation in which legal uncertainty and physical insecurity are part and parcel of their everyday experience.

Given this situation, religious idioms become a resource for them in the effort to situate their condition within a meaningful framework. The Pentecostal discourse is transformed, in order to become an instrument to describe the condition of being a refugee: the uncertainty, the sense of being suspended in time, and the need to find a "community of trust" (Lyytinen 2017) that are central to their experience.

One of the most common narratives Congolese refugees refer to is the story of the people of Israel and the crossing of the desert. Here, the indeterminate process of waiting in the transit country is represented as similar to the long way Jews had to walk in order to reach the "Promised Land" (the country of resettlement). In this narrative, a "good Christian" needs to be patient and to put his life in the hands of God, aware that the promise to reach a new land will be fulfilled, one day or another.

It is through this parallel with the people of Israel that Congolese refugees in Kampala try to make sense of suffering as part of God's plans for them. Several times my interlocutors mentioned in our conversations the following biblical saying: "Happy are those who are persecuted because they do what God requires." From this perspective, afflictions can thus be converted into a way to elevate oneself, the instrument through which to become the "elected people." Stories of those who had already been resettled to Europe (mainly Norway, Denmark, and Sweden) or North America—and who are in touch with refugees in Kampala through Facebook and other social media—with their testimonies of the "new and prosperous life" they started in the resettlement country, nourished the idea that the challenges refugees faced in the past, and were still facing in Uganda, were necessary steps toward the "Promised Land." As one of my interlocutors put it, his past life in the DRC was no less than "captivity," as he saw no hopes for his country of origin to go out of the wars that have been devastating it for decades; his long staying in Kampala (six years) was instead the period of redemption, to become "a new person" and be able to finally reach his final destination.

It is interesting to notice here that flexibility of Pentecostal language makes it possible to adapt it to express immobility, as in the case of Congolese refugees who are waiting for resettlement. With the emphasis on deliverance and the break with a sinful past (individual or collective), this powerful interpretative narrative defines this experience of immobility, a situation Congolese refugees often explain in terms of spiritual "blocages" attributed to witchcraft (Gusman 2018). Through this idiom, suffering is transferred from the personal and social level to a spiritual one, as a part of the wider problem of the presence of evil in the world. Hence, the refugees' situation has to be seen within a moral system in which suffering is due to the action of evil spiritual forces and in which Pentecostalism offers a temporary frame according to which people are on the move to the promised land, but not there yet.

Undoubtedly, this kind of narratives influences the way Pentecostal Congolese conceive their lives in Kampala and the "protracted refugee situation" many of them experience, and the way they act in daily contexts. Yet, this should not lead to the conclusion that believers are passive receivers of the discourses Pentecostal churches produce and disseminate. On the contrary, in their everyday activities, Congolese refugees reworked these narratives in order to adapt them to different contexts and situations. As Ruth Marshall stated, the Pentecostal theology is "less a set of doctrines or dogmas than an ensemble of practices, the political valence of which depends on the ways in which in any given context they become operationalized as a pragmatic, strategic, concerted campaign" (Marshall 2016: 94). This definition is close to my notion of religion as lived experience, in which the focus is on the way people use and elaborate religious idioms and beliefs.

The ethnographic approach provides a deeper perspective on the way people interact with and negotiate these narratives in their everyday lives outside the church. In these contexts, the young Congolese refugees I worked with made frequent references to their faith and to the moral and spiritual help it provided to face uncertainties, doubts, and challenges. To provide an example of this role of faith in everyday contexts, I will focus briefly on prayer. While most of my interlocutors during church services prayed in a highly emotional and intense way, asking God for help and for a "miracle," following some of them in their daily work, routines, and duties I noticed how the presence of prayer was constant, yet very different from what I had observed in church. When it accompanied everyday activities, prayer became quiet and constant, a form of self-discipline, both for the mind and for the body, as, for instance, in situations when one had been walking for a long distance to sell merchandise at the market, or when people pray while fasting.

Furthermore, it was in these situations that I noticed the way my interlocutors negotiated with and transformed the narratives I had heard in the Églises de Réveil in town. On the one hand, they regularly repeated that one needs to be patient and to rely on God, as "he always has a solution for us," which is one of the most recurrent topics in Congolese "refugees churches" in Kampala. On the other hand, in the way they acted and talked, they showed a constant and complex interaction with the values preached at church. This was clear in several situations, when they disclosed sometimes that it is hard to be patient and wait, especially when one is tired, angry, or worried. In one of these situations, Erick— one of the young Congolese I was going around with—resorted to his brilliant irony to ask for my help: "It's already night and I have sold only one belt in the whole day. I have been waiting for God's help for all the day, but he forgot to answer to my prayers; could you maybe lend me 10.000 USh?"

Faith as a Guide in Everyday Situations

Erick, together with his friend Héritier, was one of the key persons to help me understand the role of Pentecostal faith in the everyday lives of young Congolese refugees in Kampala. Erick had arrived in Uganda in 2011 from Bukavu, where his parents were both killed. He was twenty-one at the time, and in Kampala he had to become the breadwinner for his family, looking after his five younger brothers and sisters.

At the arrival in town, Erick did not know anyone, so he was advised to go to a Congolese church in Katwe with his brothers and sisters, and there they were hosted for the first three months. Some members of the congregation also helped them with the documents to request the refugee status, and to find a small house of two rooms, where they moved and where they were still living when I met them.

The first time I met Erick, he was at a clinic, recovering from a serious gastroenteritis, and with a bill of something more than $200 to pay. His friends took up a collection and put together part of the sum, but were still short of $30. That was when one of the Congolese I was working with took me to the clinic. I paid the remaining sum, and Erick received the treatments he still needed. The following day he was released from the clinic.

It was on this occasion that Erick revealed his faith, saying, "I knew God would find a solution to my problem, and you are that solution." That sentence made me a bit nervous, to be honest. I did not reply to it; yet, from my perspective, the reason why I got to the clinic and paid part of the bill was that one of his friends asked me for help. The rhetoric of God's help seemed to me somehow out of place, in that context. I was wrong, as I did not recognize the role of the religious frame that informed that way of speaking, and more or less consciously I confined that kind of discourse to the church setting.

After that day, I heard Erick and other Congolese repeat that same (or similar) sentence many other times, in different situations. "God has a solution for my problems" and "I rely on God, he always has a solution" were recurrent expressions for my Congolese interlocutors, to defuse everyday difficulties.

After Erick left the clinic, we started to meet frequently, at least two to three times a week, most often at the seat of the small association, he and other Congolese had founded in Kampala. It was at that time that I started spending more and more time outside churches and organizations, to share daily routines with mainly four young Congolese refugees. It was through this different positioning that I began to realize the life they were living in Kampala was an "ordinary" life, despite its harshness: a life not only of everyday efforts and labors to make a living, of uncertainties, and of doubts but also of periods of calm, talks with friends, clothes to wash, and meals to cook. The challenges they had to face were not much related to their "extraordinary" condition as refugees; the main difficulties they encountered in their urban lives were not so different from those of many Ugandans residing in the slum of Katwe. Despite the image of a constant emergency and the widespread imaginary around refugees, the Congolese I met in Kampala struggled to live an ordinary life and to build an everyday routine, in order to make it possible to organize their life during the long stay in Kampala. Their faith—through the constant presence of prayer and of Christian music in their daily routines; the help in reconstructing social relationship in Kampala with the common belonging to a church; and the frame it provided to understand their condition of refugee—played an important role in the construction of this ordinariness, instead of their being in transit in Kampala (yet, as we have seen, usually a prolonged period of transition) and "out of structure" in the context of refuge, with little institutional assistance and officially waiting for resettlement.

So, part of this ordinariness, for born-again people, was the place Christian faith and prayer had in everyday life. During the three months he spent at a Congolese church after his arrival in Kampala, Erick converted to Pentecostalism (in the DRC he was a Catholic) and received the baptism. During our conversations, he told me several times that in the beginning his conversion was, at least in part, instrumental. With this, he did not mean he converted because he was hosted in a Pentecostal church, but rather since he thought becoming born-again was a way to obtain a miracle, as he seemed to have no other hopes to find a way out from his situation.

> I felt I was too young and weak to take on the responsibility of my brothers and sisters; I was so lost, alone, I was worried and distressed about how to find a survival in this place. I did not know what to do, and I felt that the only solution was to receive a miracle from God, so I started praying, praying and praying, for many hours a day, without even having a break to eat something. And in my prayers, I was always asking God to help me, to send me a sign. I was angry, because he did listen to my requests; but he was the only one who could do it.

Erick said that with time he started to develop a new awareness that the role religion played in his life was a different one: after two months in the church, he felt that faith was becoming a help to orientate and settle in the new context, and not to lose himself in the harshness of the circumstances he was living:

> Many people lose themselves, here. 90% of the Congolese in Kampala haven't a good life, so many just start doing bad things (prostitution, robberies, . . .). In Congo, although I came from a Catholic family I was a "big pagan" but, since I arrived here, God is the guide in my life. At the beginning I felt bad when people told me "God helps you." I looked at my life and I felt like they were mocking

me, but then I realized that God was doing a lot in my life, not miracles or big things (like getting a visa to travel abroad) but helping me to survive and in my daily choices.

Instead of a request for miracles, according to Erick, prayer became a moral and spiritual guide, and a sort of protection in his life. This is in line with the results of the research Eveliina Lyytinen carried out among Congolese in Kampala, which shows that a large majority of Congolese refugees relied on the support found in Christian churches—mainly Pentecostal—and that they consider the assistance provided by Pentecostal churches more in terms of spiritual protection than of material help (Lyytinen 2017: 999).

As in the answer Pam—one of her interviewees—gives to Nancy Tatom Ammerman, I would say that for most of the Congolese who were part of my research, faith can ground them "when things seem to be spinning out of control" (2013: 1). With this, I mean that faith for Congolese born-again refugees is a lens through which to look at everyday events and difficulties, build relationships with people, and think and (re)imagine their present, past, and future life. This perspective contributes to create a self-discipline in their lives and participates in the construction of the believer's subjectivity, made explicit through prayers practices at church, but also through daily practices at work, at home and elsewhere.

Yet, self-disciplining does not mean that moral dictates are absolute, and that following their guidance is to submit oneself to a moral regime. As recent developments in the directions of an analysis of "ordinary ethics" in anthropology suggest, analysis based on this kind of Foucauldian assumptions may entail the risk of missing some key elements of moral practice, as they do not account for "the vagaries of everyday life and the difficulties of discerning what might constitute the most morally appropriate action in the singular circumstances life presents. It is insufficient for examining how people face changing worlds or situations in which it is unclear what kind of self one ought to become" (Mattingly 2013: 304). Since Durkheim, anthropologists have tended to give too much emphasis on morality as social obligations imposed upon individuals. Yet, describing people's behavior in terms of a mechanical self-reproduction of social structures takes the anthropologist far from the complexities of judgments and actions the researcher experiences through the ethnographic approach, with its focus on the first-person perspective of the subject, and on life as it is lived by particular people. From this point of view, "ethical life" (Keane 2014) has to be found in the interstices of everyday activities and practices, rather than in abstract social norms. This "action-centred approach to ethics" (Lambek 2010:

16) suggests that making judgments in everyday life is a much more complex affair than following a set of norms.

A widespread Pentecostal narrative advocates that following the norms of Pentecostal faith leads to predictable effects (salvation, prosperity, health, and wealth); however, these effects are located in an undetermined future. In daily circumstances, this predictability is made much less certain due to the intricacies and the multifaceted nature of social life; thus, in real life, religious "grand schemes" are always negotiated by subjects, in their effort to live a "good life."

In the case of Congolese born-again refugees in Kampala, what the Pentecostal narrative offers to believers is a moral guidance and sense-making frame through which they interpret their condition. This leads them in the effort to be patient and endure their misfortunes. Yet, in daily contexts, they often negotiate, interpret, and sometimes criticize this guidance and frame, in order to adapt it to their condition.

Religion in the Construction of Leadership in the Refugees' Community

Another way in which Congolese born-again establish a complex relationship with the religious sphere is by maneuvering it in order to gain a reputation within the Congolese community in town.

As already mentioned, Congolese Pentecostal churches in Kampala are also spaces to build social relationships and construct social networks that can be of help in enriching one's social capital. The Congolese community in Kampala is a "deparentalized" one, in which most of the old people were killed or remained in the DRC, and in which the gerontocratic system does not work any longer. Churches thus become also an instrument of social mobility for some young Congolese who find there a space of leadership among the community of refugees. Although some of these churches do not survive for more than a few years, others are well established. In this final section of the chapter, I analyze the way some Congolese pastors have been able to make the most of the opportunities this specific social conditions generate.

Literature on religion in migration contexts often underlines the extent to which belonging to religious groups can be considered as a coping mechanism for migrants, providing a sort of "home away from home" (Adogame 1998). This view, however, appears to be too narrow, as it assumes that religion has a merely protective role and a tendency to lock people within a closed circle.

Although this of course at times happens, it is important to investigate also the way Pentecostal messages may become a stimulus to entrepreneurship, even in situations in which economic resources are limited, as in the case of the large majority of Congolese refugees in Kampala.

Pentecostal discourses often are about the way believers should organize to manage one's life in order to be able to start a business; here, religious messages become instructions on how to follow biblical values to develop the capacity to run one's affairs in ways that pleases God (Van Dijk 2009: 106). This is evident in many cases in which Congolese in Kampala start a small business (a hairdressing salon, a tailoring shop, a commerce of small jewelry, etc.) with the material and spiritual support of the congregation they belong to, as in the story of Hortense, a tailor who was living alone in Kampala with her three children. After some months since her arrival in town, Hortense was looking for ways to start a tailoring shop, but she had no means to do it. Thanks to her faith, she explained, "God helped me, connecting me with generous people at the church, who bought a sewing machine for me and gave me some money to pay the rent of the shop for the first three months. This is how I started my new life."

This inclination becomes even more manifest in cases where Congolese Pentecostals decide to start their own Église de Réveil in Kampala. A number of studies have already investigated the correlation between the growth of the Pentecostal movement and the capitalist (or neoliberal) expansion in the African continent. Central to the interpretation of this link has been the concept of "occult economies" (Comaroff and Comaroff 1999), which positions the rise of Pentecostalism—and mainly of the so-called prosperity gospel—as part of a wider response to the economic crises and inquietudes generated by the insertion in a global capitalist economy. Yet, more recent studies in part distanced themselves from this interpretation, examining local entanglements between the economic sphere and Pentecostal practice, thus highlighting different and more complex ways of defining "prosperity" (Haynes 2012). Again, the ethnographic in-depthness allows for a more nuanced representation of how actual practices do not conform to "grand schemes" (here, the mainline narrative on prosperity within the Pentecostal movement), and rather they transform and adapt these schemes to local situations.

The Ugandan media often portraits the success of the Pentecostal movement in the country through the reference to some few successful figures of "rock star" pastors, with Pastor Robert Kayanja—founder of the Miracle Center and today leader of that veritable religious enterprise called "Kayanja Ministries"—as a major example of this religious entrepreneurship.

In opposition to this widespread image, the Congolese churches and pastors I am dealing with in this contribution are part of a constellation of small and medium-sized churches that form the large majority of the more than 1,000 Pentecostal churches in Kampala (Figure 7.1).

In the situation of existential uncertainty and of socioeconomic fragility that marks the lives of the majority of the Congolese living in Kampala, ideas of "success" and "prosperity" take on a different meaning, as people often react to socioeconomic harshness by looking for networks of trust and of mutual help to start small commercial activities, rather than for a neoliberal momentum toward individualism which is part of a sometimes simplified scholarly interpretation of the prosperity gospel.

In this context, the "success" of pastors' religious entrepreneurship has to be conceived in terms of their role of leadership and of the building of a reputation within the Congolese community, rather than from the model of the car they drive or of the size of their house. The stories of some of these Congolese pastors in Kampala show how individuals—especially under circumstances of intense social and economic change—can manipulate the religious field in order to build their leadership within a group.

Figure 7.1 One of the numerous Congolese Pentecostal churches in Kampala; photo by Alessandro Gusman.

Pastor Shadrac arrived in Uganda from Bukavu in 2008, fleeing the conflict after his mother had been killed. When we met in Kampala in 2013, he was the main pastor of a small Congolese church in Katwe, started in 2009 by another Congolese pastor, who had resettled in the United States in 2012 and left him the leadership of the church. The congregation was at that time a small one, of around 50 members; one year later, under Shadrac's leadership, it had grown to around 120. Yet, since the first time we met, he expressed the will to start his own church and "to train men of God."

Following his view, in 2014 Shadrac left the older church to start working on his own church. Indeed, the inauguration of "The Shelter: New Generation of Pentecostal Churches" took place almost one year later, although the building had been completed in 2017 only. The new congregation had around 60 members, while today it is a medium-sized congregation of almost 200 believers.

What is interesting in Shadrac's story is that his "success" (again, more in terms of reputation and leadership than of material wealth) has been due mainly to his ability to act within the Congolese religious field in Kampala to start a new religious project, investing not only his own time and work but also his economic resources, as he sold his old car, a Prado, to collect money for the new building. He thus took an entrepreneurial risk, leaving a church that had grown under his leadership, but that was not "his" church, to realize his vision. In doing this, Shadrac—like other Congolese pastors in Kampala—made use of his charisma, mainly his ability in preaching, but at the same time, he took advantage of a situation in which the gerontocratic system crashed as a consequence of the war in Congo. Moreover, the resettlement of the former pastor of the Rehoboth Church helped him to "make a career" more quickly: the lack of senior pastors and the resettlement of some of them create favorable conditions for young pastors to assume a position of leadership in the Congolese Pentecostal community.

Through his religious entrepreneurship, Shadrac had the opportunity to "become someone," and experienced a quick—albeit moderate—upward social mobility, if compared with the common condition of poverty and marginalization Congolese live with in Kampala.

Conclusion

Instead of focusing on the extraordinariness of refugees' condition, and on religion as an instrument to cope with the displacement experience, this chapter analyzed the role religious discourses and practices have in the everyday life of Congolese Pentecostals who chose to live in the urban context of Kampala.

Most of them live in "protracted refugee situations." Hence the need to organize one's own life in Kampala in a medium-term perspective, trying to navigate amid economic constraints, poor housing conditions, and other daily challenges. In such circumstances, religion can provide a frame to explain the condition of being refugee, narratives that can serve as spiritual guides in daily practices, and also instruments to gain a reputation and to obtain a certain degree of social mobility.

It is from a scrutiny of these everyday contexts and practices that I derived the idea of the need to focus more on lived or everyday religion, rather than on the institutional religious level. In the perspective of the young Congolese Pentecostals I worked with in Kampala, faith is not so much a sequence of norms to follow, but rather a way of looking at things and events, and of relating to other people in everyday life. An ethnographic approach to everyday religious practices and discourses shows how Congolese refugees rely on the official narratives produced by Congolese churches in Kampala and, at the same time, how they negotiate and reformulate them on a daily basis in order to build a meaningful frame through which to reflect on their own experience as refugees and to adapt their narratives to the present situation. As I have shown, this provides refugees with a sense of ordinariness, thus helping them to carry out their everyday lives in a condition of high uncertainty.

"Conquering New Territory for Jesus?"

The Transience and Local Presence of African Pentecostal Migrants in Morocco[1]

Johara Berriane

Introduction

Access to mobility has become increasingly unequal. Apart from preventing people from moving (Carling 2002), changes in international border controls and restrictive immigration policies contribute to "fragmenting the journeys" of individuals who then become trapped in transit countries (Collyer 2007) at the outer borders of traditional receiving regions such as Europe and North America. This has been the case for many West and Central African migrants heading for Europe who, due to the increased hardening of the EU's external borders (Vacchiano 2013), have been blocked in Morocco since the end of the 1990s. Whereas some have decided to settle there permanently (Mourji et al. 2016; Madrisotti 2018), integrating themselves into specific niches of the urban economy since the end of the 1990s (Kettani and Péraldi 2011), others still see their stay in Morocco as a stepping-stone on their journey, even though this stay may turn out to be permanent (Berriane 2018). Despite their comparatively small number, African migrant communities are becoming more visible in the urban space and presenting local society with novel cultural and social practices.[2]

One of the fields in which this new presence is observable is Morocco's Christianity. Following independence in 1956, the Christian churches built during colonial times served only a very limited number of European worshippers, with Christianity primarily perceived as the religion of the French and Spanish colonizers (Baida and Féroldi 1995). With the arrival first of sub-Saharan African Christian migrants, these mainline churches were not only reactivated but also found themselves in competition with semiprivate churches founded by migrants in working-class districts of the main cities (Coyault 2014; Bava 2016). These latter religious spaces belong primarily to the Pentecostal Charismatic movement, a form of Christianity characterized by its "missionary aim [with] explicitly global aspiration" (Vásquez and Knott 2014: 344) "in which believers receive the gift of the Holy Spirit and have ecstatic experiences such as speaking in tongues, healing and prophesying" (Robbins 2004: 117). They are mainly founded and used by migrants from countries such as the Democratic Republic of Congo (DRC), Nigeria, Cameroon, and Ivory Coast, and are all located in semiprivate spaces. Their members call them house churches or ministries.[3]

The establishment and spatial expansion of these Christian places have contributed to the pluralization of Morocco's religious landscape and local society's confrontation with new religious forms and practices. Notwithstanding the existence of Moroccan Christians, who have become more vocal via online channels and virtual social networks, Christianity is still seen as the religion of foreigners. The Moroccan state recognizes the mainline Catholic and Protestant churches inherited from the colonial era as places of worship for foreigners and controls and monitors them. Apart from the small minority of Moroccan Jews, who are recognized and protected, Moroccan citizens are officially Muslim, with Sunni Islam the state religion by constitution. Moroccan law does not allow Moroccan Muslims to convert, condemning Shia Islam and combating Christian proselytism. Within the Muslim sphere, the state is increasingly attempting to control the entire religious debate by prohibiting and co-opting every dissident religious voice, particularly those emerging from radical forms of Salafi Islam (Zeghal 2005: 244). At the same time, the state promotes a Moroccan Islam based on Sufi culture and tolerance in order to project an image of Morocco as a moderate Islamic country (Berriane 2016).

This chapter explores how, in this "urban spatial regime" (Vásquez and Dewind 2014: 258) shaped by control of any divergent religious expression and recent migratory changes, African Christian migrants are able to establish places of worship at Morocco's urban margins. It focuses on the local effects of this religious presence and placemaking and considers how such spaces and the religious practices they involve enable their congregants to build a safe and supportive space and develop new or existing identities (Baker 2013), and how the missionary dimension of Pentecostal movements translates into this context where Christian mission is prohibited. The chapter shows that the Pentecostal house churches are mainly shaped by their members' transience and aspiration to move on, while at the same time the religious practices and theology involved allow the congregants to reevaluate their stay in Morocco and to become locally present. The first section describes how Morocco's migratory context impacts on migrants' transient belonging in the Pentecostal house churches. The second section explores how these ritual spaces and the Pentecostal theologies that they mobilize help the migrants to reevaluate their failed migration and forge new identities while they are unable to move on from Morocco. The third and final part discusses how these migrant congregations and their leaders negotiate their local presence in a Moroccan society in which religious and cultural pluralism have only recently reemerged.

This chapter is based on ethnographic research at five different house churches—two founded by migrants from DRC and three by migrants from Ivory Coast—founded between 2010 and 2015 in Rabat (two), Casablanca (two), and Salé (one), which I visited regularly over four periods of fieldwork: during October 2015–January 2016, June 2016, October 2016, and September–November 2017.[4]

Spaces of Transient Belonging at Europe's Southern Frontier

It is 10.30 am. I meet Pastor Paul in front of the vegetable market. His church is in one of the narrow streets of small shops and workshops in a poor neighbourhood in the eastern part of Rabat. After a few minutes' walk we enter in the courtyard of a house, and Pastor Paul rings a bell next to the ground floor entrance. A woman opens the door and brings us in; she is, I learn later, in charge of protocol. We arrive in the garage of the house. It is fitted with a red carpet and a red curtain covers the front wall. White plastic chairs are arranged in rows in front of a small platform where a transparent desk serves as an altar. The woman of the protocol invites me to sit in the front row. Two big armchairs upholstered in turquoise and gold fabric have been placed to the right of the altar. On the other side, three young men are testing their instruments—a drum set, a djembe and an electric organ—and microphones. The moderator is on the stage, calling loudly to the Lord as she walks around the stage. Another woman is walking back and forth at the back of the room, praying aloud. It is 10:30 and there are only five congregants there, but the moderator asks the three men to start singing, regularly interrupting their songs with her prayers. The room slowly fills with people, and by 11.30 there are 40 people in the church. Pastor Paul, who had disappeared when we arrived, enters and starts his sermon. (Fieldnotes, Rabat, 15.11. 2015)

This Sunday service could have been anywhere in the world where DRC Congolese have settled and created a religious space. However, unlike other Congolese transnational "religious territories" (Garbin 2014: 365), this church is the outcome not of a planned permanent settlement but of the involuntary immobility of its founders. It is one of the many Pentecostal churches founded by African Christian migrants when the country became a site for the implementation of Europe's border policy. Whereas the Moroccan state at first refused to cooperate with the EU on migration, since the early 2000s, in exchange for privileged partnership with the EU the country has implemented certain operational, administrative, and legal adjustments and passed a new law (law 02-03) in 2003, to address undocumented migration, increasing the power of the military and the police to tackle those whose stay had suddenly become illegal (Perrin 2009: 248). These measures, among others, have led to the more permanent settlement of African migrants who redeployed from the Moroccan north region to the country's main cities such as Rabat or Casablanca.

During this period, the first Pentecostal Charismatic church in Rabat was founded by DRC migrants who, after many attempts to cross the fences separating Morocco from the Spanish enclaves Ceuta and Melilla, settled in the city, where they hoped to be less exposed to police control (interview 24, DRC, male, Rabat, 24.10.2017). In 2005, this church was replaced by another in the same district (interview 24, DRC, male, Rabat, 24.10.2017). These first churches essentially operated as places that offered both somewhere to live and spiritual and social support for stranded migrants. At this time, these Charismatic Christian churches were regarded by the state as migrant-smuggling organizations, which resulted in numerous police inspections and the expulsion of migrants, as a former church leader recalled (interview 12, DRC, male, Rabat, 13.01.2016). However, when these first churches disappeared, new ones took their place, and ten years later a survey found around thirty churches representing different Christian faiths where primarily DRC and Republic of Congo Congolese, Nigerian, Ivorian, and Cameroonian migrants gather (Coyault 2014: 19–20). They begin with a few people meeting in a living room, who then move on to rent a place entirely dedicated to church activities and decorated to emphasize its distinctiveness. These places of worship are situated in districts where African migrants have settled more or less permanently over the last twenty-five years. In Rabat, former migrants also run hostels, typically referred to as "foyers," in the same districts where transiting migrants stay until they are able to continue their journey (Timéra 2009: 182).[5] In the last five years, African migrants have also started to move to the outskirts of Rabat and the neighboring city of Salé, where they have also created spaces for worship.

This spatial expansion of the Christian landscape at Morocco's urban margins is probably also an outcome of the more stable settling of the African migrant population in Morocco's main cities, favored by a new shift in national migration policy. In late 2013, the Moroccan state launched a migration policy which gave around 50,000 immigrants, primarily from African countries and Syria, residency and access to public health care, education, and the formal job market. These measures were implemented to demonstrate Morocco's respect for human rights to the African states that have become relevant to its economic and political interests, and are simultaneously an outcome of Moroccan-EU cooperation.

Whereas the legal and political situation of many African migrants in Morocco has recently changed, the house churches are still mainly shaped by people on the move.[6] Today, the congregations are migrants for whom Morocco was the main destination, and others who initially came to emigrate to Europe and have been able to gain residency and make an income in Morocco or are still waiting for an opportunity to continue to Europe. However, although the worshippers' migration and life projects have become more diversified, most still share the aspiration to move northwards, despite the possibility that they will never realize this. The lack of job opportunities in Morocco, which also causes many Moroccan citizens to aspire to emigrate, influences the transience of the church's membership as well as the supportive role of the congregations. There is a small number of economic niches where African migrants can find employment, such as international call centers for those who have at least completed high school, housekeeping, construction, and trading (Kettani and Péraldi 2011; Madrisotti 2018). With access to residency, many engage in trade between Morocco and sub-Saharan cities. However, the majority are still unemployed. Only twelve of the seventy-eight members of a church I visited in Rabat were employed, with two working at an international call center, one as an NGO animator, and nine as housekeepers for Moroccan families (interview 23, Ivorian, male, Rabat, 26.10.2017). The others are still reliant on funds sent by their families and the solidarity of Morocco's migrant churches. For example, an Ivorian lady who arrived in Marrakech in early 2017 to work as a housekeeper found refuge in an Ivorian church in Salé, where I met her in November 2017, after her employer discovered that she was pregnant and terminated her employment. Pastor Paul recalled several times when African migrants stranded in Rabat had sought his help. The small church office is furnished with a thin mattress that is occasionally used by stranded migrants (interview 17, DRC, male, Rabat, 20.10.2016).

My informants among the church leaders often insisted that the size of their congregation changes consistently according to the migration flow and opportunities for their members to cross the border. Church leaders face "a rotation of people" (interview 26, Ivorian, male, Rabat, 26.10.2017). Even though emigration to Europe has become more difficult and the borders are now controlled more tightly, some are still able to move on via a longer or more dangerous route (Vacchiano 2013). There are regular assaults on migrants at the fences separating Morocco from the Spanish enclaves of Melilla and Ceuta during which some manage to get into Spain while others are injured or lose their lives (interview 24, DRC, male, Rabat, 31.10.2017). Some congregants, as well as other African migrants and Moroccans with financial means, fly to Istanbul and then take the Balkan route to Western Europe, a path that has also become a way into Europe, especially during the so-called refugee crises of summer 2015 (interview 19, DRC, male, Rabat, 26.10.2016). In his 2014 investigation, Coyault (2014: 92) found that every house church has a person called (in French) a *connexion* who is responsible for connecting migrants with the networks of smugglers who organize emigration to Europe. The church leaders I interviewed, however, tended to deny that they had a direct role in their members' emigration and insisted rather on their spiritual support for their journey. For example, one part of Pastor Jerome's work is sending Bible passages to members of his congregation who have left "to help them succeed in their journey to Europe" (interview 19, DRC, male, Rabat, 26.10.2016).

This transience affects the house churches' financial situation as they cannot rely on regular tithes from their members. However, the departure and successful emigration of church members can play a crucial role in their churches' existence. For example, Pastor Paul was able to make contact with a Pentecostal church based in the United States and run by a Nigerian pastor with the help of his Congolese mentor, who entrusted the church to him prior to leaving for France. Today, Paul's church is financially supported by the church in the United States and has become its North African branch. In May 2016, the Nigerian supporter based in the United States traveled to Morocco to organize a five-day seminar on leadership and to consecrate Paul as a reverend. Paul also emphasized the importance of church members' emigration for the maintenance of his church, not only as a place but also as a transnational network:

> The members rotate because new people arrive and others leave; there are those who are passing and want to continue to Europe and others who are here. If worshippers (*fidèles*) leave, they are going to Europe, they can send us 50 Euro or 10 Euro [. . .] there are worshippers who leave and we stay in touch, and there are others [who have left and] don't even call, but there are others who are loyal, it's already family, so they leave [and call to say] "I arrived well, I am fine,

but if I find a job, if God blesses me, I will send you something for the church."
(Interview 2, DRC, male, Rabat 19.10.2015)

Apart from former church members' financial support, the departure of congregants enables church members to connect with Christian communities in their European and North American destinations. As I show elsewhere, these transnational ties are consolidated through the circulation of Pentecostal preachers from Europe and Africa (Berriane 2020). The transient membership of these churches is further influenced by the fact that for most of the church leaders, the establishment of parishes in Morocco is seen as only a stage in their journey that will lead on to other places, preferably in Europe. Nine of the seventeen leaders still intend to move northward. Finally, the temporal membership is also the result of church members and leaders who, when they find permanent work in Morocco, usually withdraw from church activities. This was the case for Theodore, who had been an evangelist at a Congolese church in Rabat's J5 district. After finding work at an international call center, getting married, and becoming a father, he completely withdrew from his church (interview 16, DRC, male, Tamesna, 30.06.2016).

The house churches are therefore still spaces for mooring and solidarity for migrant populations on the move or in a transitory life phase which, while it can last a few years, is rarely permanent. Although some church leaders and members are able to secure a steady income, these churches are forged by their members' temporary presence rather than by their permanence. When members move on, the spaces for worship that they initially founded are used and shaped by newcomers, who later entrust them to new Christian immigrants before withdrawing themselves. These religious spaces therefore offer resources (Timéra 2009) for migrant populations who, like many northbound migrants in Morocco, cannot rely on strong social networks. Although there were already some small African migrant communities and networks before the arrival of "transit migrants" in Morocco (Timéra 2009), scholars have demonstrated that most African migrants rely solely on the "transient social ties" (Schapendonk 2012: 36) that they build during their journey across North Africa. Such ties function as bridges in their process of migration but are changeable in the dynamic context of migration trajectories (Schapendonk 2012: 36). Informed by logics of itinerancy, these associational forms are ephemeral: moments of social engagement may be immediately followed by the individual migrant's withdrawal to pursue his or her route and project alone (Escoffier 2008; Alioua 2009). Even though the migratory pattern of church members has been changing recently, the house churches can be seen as an outcome of these "circumstantial solidarities" (Bredeloup 2013a). They are primarily mooring spaces for migrants who need spiritual support and social relations in moments of in-between, and the temporal membership and transnational connections that members create contribute to their maintenance. This transient and temporal dimension also reverberates in the religious practices that primarily shape the temporal association of people with similar migratory aspirations.

Becoming and Deliverance in the Migrant House Churches

Whereas the Pentecostal house churches in Morocco are created by and for African migrants in transitory space-time and offer a social network and circumstantial solidarities, religious practices in these spaces also have a performative and transformative function for the worshippers, many of whom see their emigration as a means of emancipation from their former life. The trans-Saharan journey of many African migrants, and the migration of young Africans in general, has been analyzed as a means of emancipation, breaking away from family obligations and duties to engage in a new life of adventure and freedom, becoming "actors in stories of their own making" (Bredeloup 2013b). As this section will show, this notion of liberation from the past and of personal fulfillment also is evident in both the Pentecostal migrant house churches' theology and religious practices and the religious reinterpretation of the migrants' stay and struggle in Morocco.

For those who cannot move on or who feel blocked, the Pentecostal migrant churches, like other religious spaces in other settings, are safe, supportive spaces where they can build a sense of home, identity, and belonging (Sheringham and Wilkins 2018) sheltered by the "emotionally nurturing benefits" (Baker 2013) of their church membership. Members' individual involvement can lead to their acquiring important roles. The churches are generally highly hierarchical with mainly male leaders holding most of the authority, although women in particular use the church to compensate for their limited social life in Morocco and are involved in different areas of its organization.[7] It was striking to see how despite or maybe because of their unofficial status the organization of these religious spaces includes several departments including music, deliverance,[8] social action, women, youth, protocol, and evangelization, offering many functions and roles to their members, who are all expected to participate in the congregation's formation and prosperity. As I show elsewhere, this social engagement may be coupled with bureaucratic activity and serves to develop a sense of belonging and religious citizenship among church members (Berriane, forthcoming).

Besides the social and emotional dimension of religious involvement, the Moroccan stay can also be transformative for church members and leaders. The role of conversion and baptism as a ritual of rupture and a complete break from the personal and collective past (Meyer 1998) is particularly relevant in this setting. Due to Pentecostal Christians' belief that anyone inspired by Spirit can found or run a church regardless of educational qualifications (Robbins 2004: 124), the house churches are spaces of engagement for people who feel the need or are inspired to give their stay in Morocco a religious meaning. The leading or founding of a church has become a mechanism through which many church leaders manage to settle and live in Morocco. The church leaders I interviewed tended to emphasize the religious aim of their migration and their function as pastor, apostle, or evangelist as a spiritual gift or divine grace they have received. However, most had received the revelation that they should found a ministry or lead a church during their journey to or stay in Morocco. Pastor Paul, whose initial plan was to seek a life in Europe and who had twice failed to cross the Morocco-Spain border, had not been a pastor or religiously involved before his emigration. In Rabat, he had stayed with a Congolese pastor who, before leaving Morocco for France, ordained him as a pastor (interview 2, DRC, male, Rabat, 19.10.2015). Their forced immobility in Morocco pushed other spiritually inspired Christian migrants to give a new meaning to their stay by founding churches to spread the word of Jesus (interview 10, male, Rabat, DRC, 18.12.2015) and "bring the Gospel of Jesus Christ to life in this country where the Gospel was dead" (interview 2, DRC, male, Rabat, 24.10.2014). Some pastors expressed the desire to gather the souls of Moroccans, but they were all aware that the law does not allow them convert locals. Their evangelist activities are therefore mainly directed toward African migrants, usually from their own country and rarely with a Muslim background, but who, according to church leaders, have "never heard about Jesus before" (interview 26, Ivorian, male, Rabat, 26.01.2017) and who are converted and baptized in Morocco.

This proselytizing and conversion activity is also understood as part of the church leaders' "deliverance" work. The belief in deliverance was very widespread among my informants. Many understand their struggle in Morocco and especially their forced immobility as the result of occult forces that somebody, usually a family member, brings about via animist religious practices, sometimes also called witchcraft (interview 3, Ivorian, female, Casablanca, 22.11.2015).

According to the Ivorian congregant Simon, who had attempted to cross the fences around the Spanish enclave Ceuta three times, he was stuck in Morocco mainly due to his family's adherence to traditional African religion. In his eyes, the need for a "ministry of deliverance for Africans" is particularly great: "We can't pray with the white people because unlike us, they don't have to fight against this legacy: their ancestors were already Christians, not like ours" (interview 29, Ivorian, male, Rabat, 29.11.2017). Another Ivorian church requests new members to complete a questionnaire, called *fiche de cure d'âme* (sheet for the cure of the soul), in which they must state, among other things, whether their parents were fetishists, made sacrifices, and/or had moral diseases. Filling in this form is understood as the first step toward deliverance from blocks experienced in life and during migration (interview 20, Ivorian, female, Casablanca, 1.10.17). These practices refer to the widespread Pentecostal belief that the struggles the believer encounters are the result of not only one's own past and current actions but also one's ancestral past: sins committed by parents and grandparents (Meyer 1998: 323). From this perspective, emigration to Europe can therefore only be realized if the worshipper can break this curse and be delivered from the spiritual blocks to their emigration (see also Van Dijk 2002).

Religious worship also tends to focus on migrants' emigration aspirations and struggles. Sermons particularly address mobility, the restriction of which is understood as a spiritual test that must be passed. The Sunday services I attended in Congolese and Ivorian migrant churches had same time sequences: praising through hymns, worship through collective and individual prayer, the sermon, the testimonies, the offerings, and the announcement of the week's activities. The prayers and hymns sung at services represent a religious space-time that highlights the participants' shared waiting and suffering and calls for strength. In the Ivorian churches, dancing was encouraged during the hymns of praise to welcome and celebrate God's presence, as it also was at a service I attended in a small Ivorian church in Salé:

> Twenty worshippers gather this morning in this living room, among whom twelve are women. The service, as in other Ivorian churches, is composed of three phases: first the worshippers are encouraged to pray and dance to glorify God, purify the space and liberate it from the presence of the enemy, Satan. In the second phase, worshippers are encouraged to speak out in public and share their testimony. Three worshippers express their feeling of God's presence in their lives and how it makes them feel empowered and strengthened. One tells how he has the feeling that God is with him and loves him and gives him joy. Others recall specific events that have happened to them that they see as God's

action: one woman tells the assembly how she was able to find a place to live in Rabat that she can afford; a young man recounts how he has been hired by an international call centre, even though he did not work very well during the probationary phase. Another woman tells about a near miss in her car that was a sign of God's presence in her life. After these testimonies the worshippers dance and pray aloud, asking the Lord to take the floor and take control of the sermon and inviting the preacher to speak. The preacher is Tina, a young woman who is wearing a Moroccan caftan; she asks her followers to open their Bibles (some have books, others follow on their smartphones) and read Genesis 26, verses 12–25. Today's sermon is about Isaac, who had to abandon his home and his well and start life in a new place. He is presented as a model to follow. The preacher exhorts the congregation to "be strong: the fact that you're facing difficult times does not mean that God has abandoned you. Even though God is silent, He is here and looking to see if you are coming to Him." She continues: "Probably you ask yourself 'Will I be able to go home with something in my hands? Will people one day talk about me? Am I going to be in Canada or the US one day?' But don't be in a hurry, because unlike you, Isaac didn't have the Holy Spirit to console him, he didn't have the Bible to comfort him. God will bless you, but you must be patient and pray, you have to pray for God's consolation." Later Tina recalls Job, "who lost everything and later received double," and says to her congregation "Your actual situation is not your final situation because here we are not at home, we are at the front; we don't have family here, so don't lose your zeal for coming to church and don't lose heart, because God is with you." (Fieldnotes, Salé, 26.11.2017)

Emigration to Europe or North America was one of the main topics of the sermons I attended, with the preachers typically advising the congregation to pray and fast regularly and to maintain their belief in the force of the Holy Spirit and the Bible, which would help them to achieve their goals. Migration is therefore positively valued, with Isaac seen as a model to follow to achieve the social and economic capital that the congregants aspire to. The sermons and public prayers all addressed finding a job, housing, and financial means in Morocco, and hopes of a Western Union cash transfer arriving soon. At the same time, the struggles encountered in Morocco are understood as a spiritual test to overcome. At every sermon I attended, the church leaders constantly referred to following the model of Job, who, although he lost everything else, never lost his belief in God. This account suggests that the house church members' difficulties were a test from God, who has allowed the Devil to act in their lives as he did with Job. The testimonies at the gatherings were also important as they functioned to strengthen members' Christian faith. Describing God's work in their lives is a further means of translating and mediating God's presence and blessing in the congregation (interview 16, DRC, male, 30.06.2016).

This "sensational" (Meyer 2009) collective worship enables the congregants to experience a transformation. Collective worship involves "embodied performances" (Vásquez and Knott 2014) with a formative function for the believers. A female member of Pastor Paul's house church compared her experience of the divine in her church to that of the Protestant mainline church:

> Here it's not difficult to keep up with the service. The worship service is different: here it's more eventful, and in the Protestant church there's the liturgy, it's ta-ta ta-ta when you have to sing, then everybody has to be quiet and when you have to pray its only one person who gets up—that's the difference. Apart from that, the prayers especially are similar to our prayers [and] there are some things that are a little soft with the Protestants. I mean the pastors of the local parishes are usually cold; when the pastor is cold you feel this coldness in the church. If the pastor is hot you also feel it and you see the difference. Here we are in a revival church, it is this revival that you feel, you feel God's Spirit moving among the assembly: that's Jesus' will. (Interview 5, Republic Congo, female, Rabat, 13.12.2015)

The notion of movement is prevalent here. Although it takes place in another realm, the forced geographical immobility that many church members are experiencing seems to be replaced here by a religiously experienced mobility enabled by the powerful energy or "heat" generated by the religious worship. Besides the more spontaneous and energetic religious worship in the Pentecostal church, the worshippers' "sensory engagement with the divine" (Meyer 2009: 13) has a performative and transformative effect. The dancing, singing, and loud praises evoke a sacralization of the space-time of the worship that enables a religious presence and the congregation's local participation. This production of sacred spaces goes beyond the confined space of the house church, as the following section will show.

Local Encounters in the Moroccan City

As mentioned, Christianity in Morocco is mainly understood as the religion of foreigners. Morocco's policy toward Christianity, such as the migration policy launched in 2014, is primarily linked to the country's foreign interests and the kingdom's attempt to appear to the world as a tolerant and welcoming country that protects the rights of foreigners. However, while Morocco recognizes the existence of foreign Christians in the country, it does not recognize the newly established Pentecostal migrant house churches.[9] From early 2000 to 2014, these churches were regularly subjected to police raids, with undocumented members deported across the Moroccan-Algerian border (interview 27, DRC, male, Rabat, 31.10.2017). Today, due to changes in the migration policy and many congregants' access to a residency permit, expulsions are no longer witnessed. However, the churches' location in residential neighborhoods and the loud prayers and singing during services cause conflict with neighbors, which must be managed. Local authorities have to find a balance between protecting immigrants' religious rights, addressing the complaints of house churches' neighbors, and keeping the Christian religious groups' out of the public eye and preventing them proselytizing. These religious communities are therefore primarily seen as belonging to the officially recognized churches established during the colonial era, such as the Catholic Church and the *Eglise Evangélique au Maroc*, which the Moroccan authorities frequently ask to intervene and persuade their "followers" to stop disturbing their neighbors.[10]

The imposed invisibility and confinement is particularly problematic for Pentecostal churches, whose prosperity and success depend on their capacity to conquer and occupy space (De Witte 2008). As it will be demonstrated now, migrant churches participate in the local soundscape, and their leaders engage in social activism to circumvent their church's imposed public invisibility and spatial confinement. These strategies have evolved remarkably during the last ten years in the new migratory context.

First, the use of sound and music during services despite the disturbance and conflict this produces can be understood as a means of expanding the church's influence beyond its confined and invisible place of worship and asserting its existence in the neighborhood. On a Sunday afternoon in late October 2016, the Congolese evangelist Jerome invited me to attend a religious gathering. It was the last session of a three-day seminar that he had organized. When I arrived in the street where the church stands, I could already hear the drum and electric bass guitar and hymns being sung in Lingala.[11] Whereas there was no visible indication of the existence of a church in the street—a common feature of all the migrant churches I visited—the music and loud praising of God clearly suggested that a religious meeting was taking place. During the service, the moderators and preachers explicitly encouraged dancing and loud prayers to chase out evil and prepare for the divine presence (Fieldnotes, Casablanca, 1.10.2017), suggesting that these corporeal sound practices were also a means to sacralize the space beyond the walls of the room where worship was taking place.

The Pentecostal Charismatic movement's constant need to conquer and occupy space is expressed here as sound practices that "transgress spatial boundaries and mediate between public and private, presence and absence, visibility and invisibility" (De Witte 2008: 692). This temporal expansion of the religious space is a means of affecting local spaces through sound and participating in Morocco's "audible city" (De Witte 2008): it seems to provide a way for Pentecostal migrant churches to announce their presence.

Paradoxically, the conflict caused by this audible presence can also be understood as a way for Christian migrants to participate locally and claim their right to the city. Their audible "presence making" (Larkin 2014) has become even more pervasive since 2014. Although their sound practices led to conflict and local police summonsing the church leaders, after stopping for a few weeks, the churches were usually able to resume their activities. Since the change in the country's migration policy, church leaders have become more confident, aware of the legal protection that, according to Roger, regularized migrants have since been enjoying:

> Since 2014 things have changed, many things have changed. The persecution and the pressure of the neighbors has decreased considerably because of the regularization operation that the King has launched. It has created more peace—when the King launched the operation he created a climate of rapprochement and it has changed the mentality of the population. Moroccans have understood that the King is trying to get closer and they tell themselves that now [the migrants] have their residency. Before they didn't have it so they could depend on that, but now they have residency that means that if [a migrant] is right he can even make complaints against us: now the game has changed. (Interview 26, Ivorian male, Rabat, 26.10.2017)

The fact that the house churches do not have permission to exist as a church could be used to prohibit their activity, but the Moroccan authorities evoke other, more secular arguments to manage the issue such as "disturbance produced on Sunday morning when the neighbours want to have a rest" or Morocco's prohibition of gatherings of more than ten people without permission (interview 2, DRC, male, Rabat, 19.10.2015). For example, the governor of the city asked a church leader facing resistance from the inhabitants of a social housing estate of Salé, where he had established his first church, to enter into a dialogue with his neighbors "to explain the importance of the church to them directly" (interview 2, DRC, male, Rabat, 19.10.2015). The fact that the authorities do not base their argument on religion when banning congregations gathering in private echoes the requirement to protect minorities' religious rights. It can be seen as a sign of a certain respect for Christians and other "people of the Book" in the national context, where religion plays an important political and social role. At the same time, we can assume that the conflicts involved—although they have led to temporary banning of worship—have been a way for the churches to become locally visible and to claim their right to exist.

Finally, church leaders also gain publicity via their role as social activists. Under its new migration policy, the Moroccan state and national civil society have to manage the integration of new established migrant communities and need interlocutors for these groups. Among these, African church leaders have become important partners due to their active involvement in the social and political mobilization of migrants that has made the migration issue in Morocco more visible both locally and internationally.[12] Church leaders have started to found associations and therefore become more public. Of the church leaders I interviewed, four had decided to found a local association, and the others told me that they intended to adopt a similar approach. Although such associations are primarily founded to gain legal status and permission to organize gatherings, they are more than a mere facade for church activities: they are a means of making their charitable and cultural dimension public through the churches' organization of sports activities and concerts.

With the new migration policy, the humanitarian market and services for regularized migrants have increasingly developed in Morocco, and many Moroccan and international organizations and public agencies are involved in the field today offering traineeships, microcredit, and other services to migrants. Through their association with these organizations, the church leaders have become important interlocutors for them, enabling them to organize food distribution, donations of clothing, and information sessions on health and legal issues. Moroccan associations and local authorities even seem to favor working with church leaders, as I observed during a meeting organized by the Congolese pastor Louis's association to inform African migrants about their rights and access to employment. The Moroccan co-organizers, from the Moroccan Human Rights Council (CNDH) and the public employment agency, insisted to me that due to Louis's religious authority he would "make a better work." (interview with members of the national human rights council CNDH, Mohammedia, 25.11.2017). The integration narrative was also incorporated by the church leaders and recurred frequently in the interviews, showing how church leaders were able to legitimize their religious activity in this mainly Muslim setting. The church leaders constantly insisted on their role "as spiritual guides guiding the migrants" (interview 19, DRC, male, Rabat, 26.10. 2016), "to teach them how to have good relationships with their neighbors" (interview 3, Ivorian female, Casablanca, 22.11.2015), "to show them how to respect morality, [...] to respect the law and live in harmony" (interview 2, male, Rabat, DRC, 19.10.2015), and to become "good citizens" who "respect Moroccan norms, their religion, and work for good cohabitation" (interview 12, DRC, male, Rabat, 13.01.2016).

The local encounter that the churches create is therefore mainly shaped by the different actors involved adopting "techniques of inattention," in the sense of "attending enough to know that one does not have to attend" (Larkin 2014: 1007). Although the Moroccan authorities are fully aware that house churches have no official status, the fact that their members do not try to make themselves publicly visible and/or evangelize to the local residents makes it unnecessary to pay too much attention to their activities. Although locals feel disturbed by the noise produced by churches in their neighborhoods, their complaints have no effect, and as a result, they attend less to this disturbance. Finally, the church members have developed strategies for ignoring their neighbors' complaints since such complaints now threaten their safety and their church's existence less, and continue to attempt to impose their religious practices and identity and their right to be. These techniques paradoxically enable the church leaders and migrant congregations to be locally more present and to participate—even though via conflict—in the Moroccan city.

Conclusion

This chapter has demonstrated how the making of religious spaces and the engagement that unfolds within them has become a means for many spiritually inspired migrants including both house church leaders and worshippers to reevaluate their ruptured emigration to Europe and give new meaning to their period of stay in Morocco. The existence of Charismatic house churches is not only a mechanism for Christian African migrants to settle in Morocco and claim a local presence but also an outcome and means of circulation. Whereas the very existence of these religious spaces is linked to the blocks and ruptures that many West and Central African migrants experience during their journey toward Europe, their religious practices are forged by transience, circulation, and movement. This reveals perfectly how religious placemaking is both the outcome of the stabilization of a migrant group in one place and a significant supporter of circulation. The churches are places for migrants to not only become locally grounded but also move on, although in this age of unequal access to mobility such movement is often temporally stopped, hindered, or redirected to other destinations. From this perspective, these religious places can be seen as "gateway nodes" (Vásquez and Knott 2014: 344) where Christian African Charismatics can live and temporarily ground themselves and also connect with transnational Pentecostal networks.

The church leaders' relative success in maintaining their churches and becoming locally publicly present raises further questions about their actual and future impact on Morocco's cities. Today, Morocco's attempts to promote itself as an inclusive and tolerant country influence its management of the unofficial migrant house churches. However, the religious aim of the church gathering, even though it produces "noise," is treated with more respect than before, leading to less attention from locals. This acceptance is, however, conditioned by the migrant churches' public invisibility and the church leaders' adoption of secular roles in public, shedding light on the intermingling and overlapping of secular and religious norms in this context in which religious pluralism has only recently reemerged.

Ritual Space and Religion

Young West African Muslims in Berlin, Germany

Abdoulaye Sounaye

How do refugees/migrants live and practice their religion in their new environment? And where do they find space for ritual practices such as prayer, wedding, and naming ceremonies, breaking the fast, etc., especially when they are in a double minority situation? How does their new environment in return affect their practices and perceptions of religion and religiosity, in times of dramatic change? Embracing religion and making it a reason to join specific groups and communities could be part of the experience of both forced and voluntary displacement. How do we account for such experiences when migrants and refugees attempt to make a living, secure residence and social status?

Following the so-called refugee crisis that resulted from the Syrian and Libyan wars, statements from state institutions in Germany have emphasized integration as a way to *make space* and, at the same time, *place* and accept refugees. Accommodation and spatial organization, as Alexander-Kenneth Nagel's chapter in this volume alerts us, have been part of this process. The pronouncements have consistently used *integration* to underline the humanitarian policy of the government and push for openness of the German society. This policy line translated into concrete measures such as *Willkommensklassen* and *Integrationsklassen* that are courses intended to facilitate refugees' transition into German society. How does religion become a factor in this process? What are those expected to integrate or be integrated doing to make space and place for themselves?

This chapter focuses on young Muslims from West Africa who found themselves in Berlin after the collapse of the Libyan state in 2011. Having arrived as migrant workers before the country's civil war, many of these young people were trapped and forced to cross the Mediterranean Sea to seek refuge in Europe.

Once in their new environment, what spaces were available to them for religious practice? How did they use those spaces? What strategies of appropriation did they use to make a space of their own in a city known for its secularism, leftism, and humanitarianism, but yet to experience such a "flow" of migrants from West Africa?

Accounts of religion in contexts of displacement and migration have pointed to the ways in which the experience of changing place, moving, and settling in a new environment could affect practices and perceptions of religion (Vecchio 2016; Bass 2014; Grodź, Smith, and Adogame 2014; Olupona and Gemignani 2007; Adogame 2005). As I will show, ritual spaces such as mosques serve not only a religious purpose but also a social inscription agenda in a city where West African Muslims struggle to avoid marginalization, vulnerability, exclusion, and outright discrimination, even among their coreligionists. In conversations, my interlocutors have used the "Turkish model" to refer to the ways in which Berliners from Turkish background have managed to find and create a set of social and religious infrastructures that allow them to secure a space of their own.

As several studies on religion and African migrants to the West have shown, displacement can have a significant impact on religious communities, perceptions, and practice. In return, religion often contributes to social inscription, that is, a process through which individuals, groups, and communities attempt to have a life of their own as they discover and navigate their new environment (Nieswand 2010; Olupona and Gemignani 2007; Grodź, Smith, and Adogame 2014; Adogame 2005; Gaibazzi, Dünnwald, and Bellagamba 2017; Gutekunst et al. 2016).

Those I refer to in this chapter as my interlocutors are young migrants and refugees from West Africa, mostly in their twenties and thirties with whom I had regular conversations from 2014 through 2018 at gatherings in their apartments, in cafes, in mosques, during Muslim festivals, or in parks across Berlin. They found in religion an important resource to rely on as they face the predicaments of living in Berlin and negotiate the terms of their social conditions, in particular (im)mobility, vulnerability, and residence status.

A Quick Note of Context: Beyond the Economy

The study of migration and displacement in Africa-EU connections suddenly regained steam, as Libya collapsed and Jihadi movements arose in the Maghreb and the Sahel-Sahara regions. This development has prompted a number of observations and arguments intended to shed light on a multilayered phenomenon. The new trend of EU-bound migration has not only affected policies intended to continue and reinforce the externalization of EU frontiers both physical and imagined but also illustrated how social, political, and economic dynamics entangle Europe and Africa (Pries 2018; Beauchemin 2018; Gaibazzi, Dünnwald, and Bellagamba 2017).

In this context, political discourses on migration have raised concerns over what some called the "death of Europe" as a consequence of an "uncontrollable flow" of young Africans (Murray 2018). The "African scramble for Europe" and the "Africanization of Europe theory" (Smith 2019) are two variants of a discourse that is used to alarm against both a so-called refugee crisis and a migration trend that is primarily viewed as a menace. As the Africanization theory suggests, the "flow" of young Africans threatens to make Europe African and therefore unsettle a peaceful and balanced continent. Earlier works on migration from Africa to Europe have already pointed to this fear of "an African invasion of illegal migrants," as Beauchemin puts it. Indeed, while the idea of an "invasion" may simply be a myth (Haas 2008a), it has nevertheless drawn controversy, fear (Murray 2018), and policies that affect now not only migration as a process but how African migrants are perceived and treated (Beauchemin 2018; Grodź, Smith, and Adogame 2014; Schinkel 2017; Bass 2014; Acoroni 2016). Images of young men jumping over the fences of the enclaves of Melilla and Ceuta and police forces countering them have contributed to reinforce this fear (Haas 2008b) and justify, in the eyes of many, not only "Fortress Europe" but also its underlying policies.

Berlin was rocked in 2012 when a group of young West Africans and their local support network challenged these policies in what is known as the Oranienplatz movement, a struggle against German and European immigration policies (Fontanari 2018; Mudu and Chattopadhyay 2018; Swiffen and Nichols 2017; Monforte 2014). On that occasion, civil society organizations, refugee groups, and religious organizations joined forces to fight for residence status and "humane conditions to refugees and migrants," among whom many of my interlocutors.

Clearly, the repercussions of the Africanization and invasion narratives extend beyond the economic realm and affect the perception of refugees, asylum seekers, and migrants, and what social space they are entitled to in Europe today. While my discussion focuses on Berlin, it must be said that across Germany voices have consistently attempted to influence state policies and public opinion[1] for the "right and appropriate measures" to treat humanely refugees or to counter "migration flows" and "sharianisation," as the Patriotische Europäer gegen die Islamisierung des Abendlandes (*Patriotic Europeans Against the Islamisation of the Occident*), Pegida, would put it. The Islam debate, as one may put it, has a long history in Germany, like in most of Europe. It has become more public while taking passionate and emotional turns, fueling both a nationalism and an islamophobia that fear a growing Muslim presence or even dominance (Sarrazin 2018, 2012), and worry about how migrants "prey on the country's diminishing welfare benefits" (Solibakke 2012: 219).

Living in Berlin, refugees, asylum seekers, and migrants from West Africa were caught in the middle of this heated debate which, in many ways, has created categories of bad refugees/migrants (those that "cannot learn German and do not change") and good refugees/migrants (those that "integrate and respect German laws").[2] Being black and Muslim makes them a prime target of the rising and nationalist discourse of Pegida, according to which they are "bad."

Although these debates tend to focus on the economy to a large extent, they have also regularly emphasized securitization of migration (Mavelli and Wilson 2017) in times of refugee crisis and jihadi threat. This adds a surveillance component to the critical issue of managing immigration (Gaibazzi, Dünnwald, and Bellagamba 2017). Reinforcing checkpoints at borders, systematic fingerprinting, and creating common databases, in order to control the mobility of migrants, are all parts of a state instrumentation that reduces immigration policies to a security concern. "Protecting" and "securing our borders" are phrases that one regularly hears among state officials, security officers, as well as concerned ordinary citizens.

My attempt at analyzing the case of West African Muslims in Berlin opens a window onto the modes through which refugees/migrants become qualified as a social problem not only because they need assistance but also because they socially inscribe themselves in a sociopolitical environment as they make their social space. Churches as well as mosques in Berlin have proved central to this process in the last five years, especially for many migrants and refugees who get disconnected, are left with little or no resources, and feel robbed of their lives.

Like in many other contexts in Europe, during the recent refugee crisis, religious organizations and institutions have played a major role in assisting refugees and migrants to rebuild their lives (cf. Horstmann and Jung 2015a). Mosques, churches, and other civil society organizations have been particularly active in providing assistance to refugees during that time. The religious segment of the city, in particular, was among the most involved in relaying the motto once very perceptible across Berlin: *Refugees Are Welcome*. The search for ritual space in that context and the initiatives it leads to are part of a self-representation (Frederiks 2014; Grodź and Smith 2014) process that has become central to refugees' and migrants' perception of their own agency. It is also central to the ways in which they search for and define a place of their own (Mandel 1996).

Placemaking, as a way people insert themselves into a particular social setting, and making one's own place, as a way to exercise agency and transform one's conditions in that setting, are two necessary conditions for human life. Many would actually argue that they are at the foundation of *humane* existence. Refugee and migrant experiences in Berlin are shaped by this twin-process as they feel not only robbed of their lives but also profoundly immobilized and incapacitated by both the structures set to accommodate them and the negative discourses pertaining to them.

This is so especially as young West Africans strive to make a space and a *life of their own*. Having a choice, deciding where to perform ritual and how, that is, under what conditions, were key concerns for my interlocutors. For many of them, Berlin proved not the end, but the culmination of an ordeal. In fact, as Mo (Conversation at Café Kotti, Berlin. May 14, 2017) put it, from braving state borders in West Africa, to defying the Sahara harsh conditions and surviving the "slave-like conditions in Libya," their journey has been one of *wahala*, a Hausa concept that captures the lost hopes of youth and the distress of the disenfranchised in general.

Being a Muslim in Muslim Berlin

When Mohamed, one of my interlocutors who spent seven years in Khadafi's Libya, landed in Berlin after he transited via Lampedusa and Italy, he was told not to worry. As there were many Muslims and mosques in Berlin, it wouldn't be a problem for him to integrate. Indeed, and although they account only for around 10 percent of the overall population, Muslims form a dynamic and active demographic group that shapes life in this city known for its libertarian norms and lifestyles (Bendixsen 2013; Ewing 2008). Berliners pride themselves on being open, tolerant, and welcoming. Berlin's popular neighborhoods, such as Neukölln, Kreuzberg, Friedrichshain, Mitte, and Prenzlauer Berg, host various nationalities, and people with different political orientations and economic backgrounds.

This diversity and the possibilities of interactions and community organizing Berlin offers have made it a prime political arena and a hub of cultural, artistic creativity, especially among young people. Among migrants and refugees from Africa too, Berlin became popular, especially with the recent flow that followed the Syrian and the Libyan crises. Many Berliners contributed a great deal in invigorating the "Refugees are welcome" and the Oranienplatz[3] movements which rose to push for pro-immigration policies, but also promote the opening up of the German society.

Public opinion and the initiatives taken by groups and civil society in Berlin contributed to inflect public policy, but they also gave the city a reputation of hospitality, especially among West Africans. Unlike many cities in Europe and even in Germany, Berlin was perceived by many as "a bright spot" and multicultural enough to be the "next destination." "Lorsqu'on était en Italie, on a beaucoup entendu parler de l'Allemagne, mais surtout de Berlin. Après avoir passé trois mois à travailler dans une municipalité, finalement, mes amis et moi, nous avons pris la route et nous sommes venus à Berlin" (Mo, conversation 14-5-2017). In those terms, Berlin appeared as a promise. This rush to Berlin, as one may call it, coincided with a policy change in Italy— the first European land after the Mediterranean Sea—which allowed asylum seekers in the country to migrate up north to seek regularization and better fortune. Several of my interlocutors "received 500 or 1,000 euros," and were told to "try up north because Italy doesn't have enough to take care of everyone" (Idriss, Conversation at Café Kotti, Berlin. June 7, 2017). That journey led many to Berlin, where they eventually joined forces with groups who were already established and organizing for refugee rights and protection.

Strictly speaking, there is no quarter of the city known as Muslim Berlin, although some quarters will have more Muslims than others, as is the case in most cities in Germany. The concept of Muslim Berlin refers here to the institutions, groups, and organizations spread across the city which have sought to keep, promote, and nurture a Muslim identity. And for that reason, they have concurred to create an environment conducive to Islamic practices and Muslim lifestyle.[4] With this picture in mind, one could easily draw the conclusion that Muslin Berlin is diverse, multiethnic, and multinational, and encompasses numerous groups, organizations, and institutions, from the Turkish Islamic organizations and German Islam Conference (*Deutsche Islamkonferenz*) to the African mosque and the Ahmadiyya (Wunn and Mohaghegh 2007). Furthermore, and as one may also guess, it is fragmented and informed by many theological orientations, from the Habashi[5] group to the Salafi and the Shia. One could even equate it to a micro-Muslim world. Indeed, in many ways, as I have realized, it forms a microcosm which has its own dynamics, politics, and prejudices.

The particularity of the young people I focus on is that they are a minority within a minority group (Schader 2017)—a group of Muslims within a Muslim community which is already demographically a minority in Berlin. For many, being black in Muslim Berlin comes with challenges such as xenophobic sentiments which take discriminatory forms. Scholars have used the trope of visibility/invisibility to characterize the conditions of West Africans, in particular Muslims, in Europe (Ter Taar 1998). The case I discuss echoes such conditions, although one has to note that the protest movement of 2012 and the Syria refugee experience have affected significantly the ways in which sub-Saharan Africans are perceived and organize themselves.

In many ways, my interlocutors are all but invisible. But not every visibility is welcome, as they would say. While visibility becomes an ally which helps them both raise awareness about their dire conditions and keep the hope of getting legal residence, they have also experienced visibility as an issue while they try to settle and be part of the complexion of the city. In our conversations, they have regularly expressed unease and concerns over the publicity the so-called refugee crisis has brought to them: "On parle trop de nous," said Issa, a young man from Burkina. "Dès qu'on vient dans un lieu, on nous voit et regarde" (Moussa, Conversation at Umar Mosque, Berlin. February 17, 2018). In this situation, their minority condition ends up exposing them in public life, in their interactions with other Muslims, but also with immigration services. With this administration in particular, their visibility ends up burdening their interlocutors and those official structures from which they seek assistance.

Adding the fact that most of them are newcomers to Berlin, navigating these conditions has proven challenging, especially when they felt discriminated and victim of unfair treatment. Among my interlocutors, their experiences go from outright discrimination to pouring support. "I expected Muslims to be more open and welcoming. What I received was less than what I expected; I was better treated by Christian organizations and churches. I really thought our Muslim fellows would be welcoming us in their mosques. On the contrary, some didn't even want to pray next to us" (Idriss, Conversation at African Mosque. April 21, 2018). As Idriss explains, many of them decided to come to Berlin because they had heard that Berlin is more welcoming and home to a large Muslim community: "on avait entendu que Berlin était ouverte et accueillante, et qu'il y avait une grande communauté musulmane dans la ville. On avait quitté l'Italie pour cela."

Safia, a Ghanaian woman who came to Berlin in 2014, relates her experience in a mosque: "As you know, women do not pray with men; so I joined the women's corner in the mosque, but I felt unwelcome. I felt some women did not want to pray next to me. In the end, I was praying alone" (Safia, Conversation in

Wedding, Berlin. September 22, 2017). Although there are more West African men than women, a numerical reality that may favor their acceptance among Muslims, men face similar issues and often narrate their relationship to other Muslims on a critical tone as they also feel feared, unwelcomed, and marginalized, and are not even "getting the treatment one Muslim could expect from other Muslims" (Habu, Conversation at Café Kotti, Berlin. October 17, 2019). One of my male interlocutors who has been living in Berlin for more than thirty years observed that "we are all Muslims, but no Turkish or Arab woman would marry a Sub-Saharan African" (Sale, Conversation at Umar Mosque, Berlin. October 19, 2019). Experiences of this kind lead Mohamed to question the Umma: "On nous parle de la Ummah musulmane, mais nous n'avons pas vu cela. Au contraire, nous avons eu beaucoup plus de solidarité de la part des Églises et des Chrétiens" (Mohamed, Conversation at Umar Mosque, Berlin. August 12, 2018).

This perspective on the Umma could amount to a critique of Islam and non-West African Muslims, in particular Muslim Berlin and the treatment it offers other coreligionaries. In fact, many have also reported mistreatment in Libya, a Muslim majority country where they spent time prior to their crossing the Mediterranean, yet they seem to be more critical of Berlin's context.

Searching for a Ritual Space, Constituting a Social Space

My interlocutors have regularly articulated a claim of belonging which is based on commonality of religion, but also produces expectations to be welcomed and well treated as part of the Umma. As we shall see, the search for a ritual space is intricately linked to that of a social space. A mosque, for example, is not just a space for daily prayers and Dhikr.[6] For many, praying in the Omar Khattab[7] mosque is also part of a practice that constitutes a social space, especially in a migration/refugee context. On the one hand, the mosque has profiled itself as an institution devoted to serve migrants and refugees, offering them a prayer community; on the other hand, my interlocutors have often used the mosque as a rallying point. The Friday congregational prayer, for example, determines the time and the venue of many of their activities, in particular group meetings which are generally held after the prayer and in Café Kotti, a few minutes' walk from the mosque.

Not all of them, however, go to Omar Khattab Mosque. Besides the reputation of the mosque being under watch by German security services,[8] several Ghanaians, for example, prefer to travel to Khadija Mosque in Pankow, the main Ahmadi ritual space in Berlin. Tidjaniiya followers have also expressed similar attitudes. Thus, affiliations and sectarianism are important factors that shape the search for both ritual and social spaces.[9] Issa, a Sunni Muslim who found himself once in the Tempelhof Shia mosque, felt unease and eventually decided not to return there. Many have, however, downplayed theological cleavages and sectarianism. As they adapt to the situation and relax on these cleavages, at the same time, they rethink their theological affiliations and religious concepts they have taken for granted. In fact, I have rarely heard arguments along religious lines or leanings among my interlocutors. Though they know their differences and somewhat cultivate them, along, for example, national and generational lines, they have silenced arguments and have sought to establish a communal space, an initiative that further transpired as a claim to the city (cf. Sacks 2013; Chattopadhyay 2005). Community organizing, NGO initiatives in collaboration with Berlin-based humanitarian activists, and participation in public events such as demonstrations and debates and fund-raising contributed to this claim. In this context, too, the Oranienplatz refugee protest camp became an inspiring model of how groups and organizations claim space and status[10] (see Figure 9.1 a, b, c, and d).

Figure 9.1 (a) Omar Mosque from the street. (b) Screen carrying French translation of the sermon. (c) Fellows praying inside the Omar Khattab Mosque. (d) Fellows greeting each other after Eid prayers; all photos by Abdoulaye Sounaye.

The First African Mosque in Berlin (FAM)

Like in many cities in Europe, in Berlin, too, Muslims from West Africa sought to gather, organize, and set up their own social and religious infrastructures. The Murid case in Italy (Kaag 2008; Marabello and Riccio 2018; Riccio and Uberti 2013), the Tidjaniyya in France (Accoroni 2011; Cottin 2007), and most recently, the Izala in Hamburg[11] are illustrations of these trends and social entrepreneurship. Migrants or refugees, West Africans who ended up in Europe carry various religion-related initiatives not only personally but also as groups or communities. Settled enough in Germany and Berlin and having reached a critical mass of people to perform a congregational prayer, a group led by Muqaddam Masoud Hassan established in the mid-2000s the first initiative for a mosque intended to cater for Muslims from West Africa. The initiative was primarily for English-speaking West Africa, that is, Ghana, Liberia, Sierra Leone, and Gambia. In Masoud's own words, the goal was to assemble Muslims from West Africa and offer them "a venue of their own" (Masoud, Conversation at African Mosque, Berlin. October 21, 2017), especially as their number increased following the Libyan civil war.

The FAM was then thought as an attempt at providing a self-representative group and space for people who have constantly faced the challenges of being both displaced and feeling out of place in Berlin. The FAM is a culmination of a process of carving a communal space, of self-representation, and of being part of Berlin, and therefore claiming the right to be different. As an intervention, it is a way West Africans have found to insert themselves into the activist and political culture of Berlin. Therefore, their search for a communal space is to be interpreted as a step further in their claiming a right to the city (cf. Lefebvre 1991).

The FAM is also referred to as the African Mosque, the First Black African Mosque,[12] stressing its *Africanity* and blackness, so to speak. Being a social space, as most mosques, the FAM has also provided social services, from wedding and naming ceremonies to hosting migrants, especially at the peak of the refugee crisis in 2014–15 in Germany. In a wedding video Nasrul Faida posted on YouTube, the ceremony follows several steps, from the introduction of the bride and the groom to the verbal agreement that would open to the recitation that consecrates and legalizes the marriage. In a typical West African manner, cola nuts are distributed, and elders offer advice to the newly married. And as is customary, the bride is not present; only her representatives are asked for their agreement. Particularly with Ghanaians and Sierra Leoneans, for example, FAM has played a major social role. Each prayer—and especially at *Eid*[13] time—is an opportunity to socialize. Ramadan has also turned out to be a major moment of gathering and congregational prayer. *Iftar* usually attracts not only West Africans but also friends from various parts of the Muslim world.[14] FAM has also served to celebrate Independence Days, as one can see in a YouTube video.[15]

As already pointed out, the idea of an African mosque emerged as part of the politics of belonging (cf. Yuval-Davis 2006) that made "some feel uncomfortable," especially when they join some Turkish mosques, as one of my interlocutors noted. Other Muslim groups and communities such as Ahmadi, Alevi, and Habashi have all their own mosques. While this trend can be read as the sign of a dynamic and differentiated Islamic sphere in Berlin, setting up their own mosque allows West Africans also to be socially creative, assert their identity, and institutionalize their presence in an increasingly changing context. Being organized pays off in the sense that it provided many interlocutors with a platform to voice their concerns and a social space. The FAM was then intended to serve West Africans find their place, carve a space for themselves, claim a presence in the city, and, at the same time, distance themselves from others, in particular those considered to be troublemakers and radicalized. In fact, in their Khutbah (Friday sermon), imams at FAM have persistently called Muslims to "abide by the laws of the country" and show the tolerant side of "African Islam" (Masoud, Conversation, Neukölln, Berlin. January 17, 2019).

Over the years, the discourse of being African, tolerant, and a law-abiding Berliner has been further emphasized, especially at the peak of the refugee crisis. In their own words, it "was crucial to show that we are not part of ISIS[16] as some have become in France"[17] (Ali, Conversation at Umar Mosque, Berlin. July 13, 2017). Indeed, as many have lived in, studied in, and traveled through Libya, they felt "suspected of having become radicalized, and potentially supportive of Islamic terrorism" (Ali, Conversation at Umar Mosque, Berlin. July 13, 2017). German security services themselves have shown concern over youth's radicalization that happens within mosques and, for that reason, have had several mosques under watch, as a mosque manager pointed out.

In more sociological terms, what the FAM allows is a social inscription (Schiller and Caglar 2010; Smith 2005) in an environment where many feel the need to carve a space both religious and social as a way to survive. The consequence is that while the community of Muslims in Berlin increases, ritual spaces also diversify to accommodate practices sometimes uncommon among Muslims in Berlin. For example, the FAM was initially thought of as a Tidjaniyya[18] initiative providing a space for wazifa, the group's devotional prayer, which was not welcome in other mosques of the city. "We don't do the Tidjaniyya wazifa," as an official of the Omar Khattab Mosque pointed out. In this specific case, officially, the mosque management feared that the sectarian practice would alienate the majority of the mosque community; but it is also known that the wazifa prayer is controversial and rejected by most rigorous and Salafi views.

Both the FAM initiative and the desire to erect an African mosque contribute to what Metcalf has referred to as "the making of the Muslim space" (Metcalf 1996). For my interlocutors, however, this process has to be qualified: it is an inscription in a social context where religion has slowly become an important dimension of their lives, experiences, and identities. Already Muslim, many were not particularly concerned with their Muslimness before they arrive in Berlin. But they engage Islam now in a particular way and with a new awareness, finding in Muslimness and in being part of a mosque community, for example, a key component of their lives.

In Berlin, this "turn to Islam" is not exclusive to West Africans. As Bendixsen notes, youth with Turkish background have also turned to Islam to assert a presence in Berlin. They articulate a discourse that emphasizes their background as Muslims, yet in a particular sociocultural and generational context. They are not necessarily following the practices and the institutions set up by their parents; they experience different living conditions, and moral and political references, and imagine other ways of being Muslim in Berlin.

In the case of West Africans, however, and perhaps more than for the Berliners with Turkish background, space translates into a critical resource, in particular because the marginalization they face is not only political, economic, and social (Bendixsen 2013); it is also religious, as many have pointed out. While many aspects of the daily practices of the FAM community could be understood as a reinvention and *emplacement*[19] of homeland practices, we must note the differentiated character of this resort to Islam and Muslim space making (cf. Read 2012; Englund 2002), in particular in a migration or refugee context. For most of my interlocutors, the primary preoccupation is one of social inscription in a context they try to figure out and navigate the political, economic, and social conditions of their lives. Space and placemaking[20] in this instance are not only part of the politics of belonging, tools of differentiation, and social inscription. As Miriam Schader has shown, religion is a powerful political resource and carries an emancipatory potential among West Africans in Europe (Schader 2017). Thus, the preoccupation with setting up the FAM is not so much about a defense of Islam as one may see it in many West African activists with whom religiosity and politics of religion are shaped along that line. Here, the move is intended to create the conditions for particular expressions, practices, and identities (Grodź, Smith, and Adogame 2014) that struggle to be accepted and established elsewhere. Perhaps more than anything, what the FAM initiative shows is the significance of infrastructure open to identities and religiosities.

The FAM provides a structure for collective action readily convertible into a political resource for a group that arguably includes the most vulnerable in Berlin. With no degree or qualification, economic integration has proved hard for many. Even when they have managed to secure a resident status that would allow them to escape the anxiety of deportation, finding a network and accessing social services may be a challenge. Here again, the FAM has offered a prime opportunity for both ritual practice and networking, similar to the case of the migrant foyers in France (Grodź, Smith, and Adogame 2014) with the only difference that FAM intends to build on "circuits of faith" (Farquhar 2016) while emphasizing Islam, being Muslim from West Africa in Berlin (Figure 9.2 a and b).

My examination of the religion, refugee and migration nexus here is not intended to speak in a comprehensive manner about West African Muslims in Berlin. Based on a so far limited fieldwork, I wanted to show how these young people have organized themselves in the context of the so-called refugee crisis. Those I have encountered in Berlin have regularly brought up their experience of migrating to Libya for job opportunities, and once they have been exposed to the civil war to Europe, though they had no plans for such a move. Political and social contingencies ushered to Europe new categories of migrants, some of whom, even before the collapse of Libya and the ensuing political chaos, have experienced migration. Many young men from Northern Niger and Mali, for example, would travel to Libya essentially for seasonal economic migration. But I have also encountered those who ended up in Libya in the search for further

Figure 9.2a and b Socializing after Eid prayer; photo by Abdoulaye Sounaye.

Islamic learning. In this context, too, migration (fitta) is a common practice that shapes the training and the reputation of the young Muslim scholar. As Heiss (2015) demonstrates, for example, migration is part of becoming a man in many Muslim contexts in Africa. It is inextricably linked to social mobility and therefore constitutes one important dimension in youth's aspirations to make a good living and "reussir,"[21] as many would put in French.

From Mosques to Umma

In the process of making a place of their own, my interlocutors both experience and participate in the Umma, expanding the diversity of the Muslim groups and communities in Berlin, as their participation in the FAM, Omar Mosque, and search for ritual space in general show. They have evoked this concept in various conversations, emphasizing their desire to fit in and their expectations of solidarity, especially from fellow Muslims. However, their rethinking of the Umma beyond these expectations of a free and welcoming entity illustrates the ways in which they reconceptualize not only their being Muslims but also the Umma as a concept of global Muslim community. Expectations to be welcomed could be natural for these subjects who have taken for granted the reality of the Umma. Both political and religious, and at times appropriated and mobilized for group solidarity or to counter policies and ideologies portrayed as anti-Islamic or anti-Muslim, the Umma is also in many contexts experienced as a disappointing reality. In fact, many have expressed similar feelings as they reflect and narrate their experiences of "abuse and mistreatment in Libya" (Mo 2018).

While the FAM could be read as a critique of the Umma and how it fails to materialize effectively at least in the way my interlocutors expected it, the initiative could also be understood as a move to show another face of the Umma and being Muslim, especially in displacement situation. The same could be said about the Africanness or blackness of churches where religion gets entangled with nationality or ethnicity, illustrating the ways in which other identity markers provide foundation for religion. The now all too familiar concepts of African Islam (Østebø 2015; Rosander and Westerlund 1997; Monteil 1964), African Christianity (Wilhite 2017; Klinken 2013; Kalu 2007; Gifford 1998), European Islam (Buturovic 2006; Nielsen 1999), or even German Islam (Özyürek 2014; Luis 2018) are indications of those connections, but also of the significance of religion and religiosity in minority, refugee, migration, or diaspora contexts. At this juncture, it is important to note that these concepts have also been problematic, especially when African Christianity and African Islam have been used with a derogatory meaning, pointing to the "impurity" and the "syncretism" of their practices. In my conversations in Berlin, I have also come across views on German Islam, especially when the concept is used to promote culturally differentiated and law-abiding Muslim practices in Germany, as opposed to a Jihadi Islam which is primarily portrayed as intolerant and violent and for that matter, un-German, so to speak.

Muslim migrants and refugees from West Africa have several opportunities to pray, perform rituals and celebrate festivals. They feel unwelcome in many mosques. FAM is in part a response to this experience. But FAM helps them also to find a proper ritual space and a social space to deal with vulnerability, marginalization, and discrimination in a context where migration, Africa and young men prompt anxieties across Europe. And as one may see, these anxieties have also resulted in a discourse that emphasizes the need to protect Europe and keep it undisturbed. Thus, the religion of the migrant can be an issue, especially in light of the narratives and claims of Islamization and Africanization of Europe which make social inscription even more challenging in the face of the juridical state and its power structures. This is part of the predicaments of my interlocutors.

What lies then behind such an idea of the Umma? What implications do these experiences of disappointment have for the ways of being Muslim and finding *one's space*? What would be the impact of my interlocutors, twice a minority—Muslims and blacks—on the ways of being Muslim in Berlin? These are key questions that arise from the discussion presented in this chapter. But it suffices here to note how displacement and encounter inspire (re)appropriations of religion and, at the same time, deconstruct and relativize key concepts such as the Umma. Obviously, these (re)appropriations prove an opportunity to fuel this concept.

The idea of being part of and constituting a collective is central to my interlocutors. Yet, West Africans are not a homogenous group. Not only are they diverse, but they have also as of late begun to experience frictions. I have witnessed among my interlocutors several exchanges that remind of the classical Sufi-Salafi argument over the Mawlid, the celebration of the birthday of the Prophet Muhammad, or whether one should pray with the arms along the body or crossed over the chest, two contentious issues among Muslim in West Africa. Furthermore, an argument arose a year ago over the funding of some activities and the idea of another organization.

A key question to ask, however, is how the next steps of their being in Berlin will shape the spaces they *make* and the practices they now promote. What other social inscriptions will emerge as they get used to Berlin, acquire legal residence, develop relationships beyond their regions, and get out of their status of "sans papiers"? What alternative placemaking should one expect? Which significance would ritual space and practice carry or maintain?

Conclusion

While it is manifest that religiosity has become a factor in the social inscription of refugees and migrants from West Africa in Berlin, to unpack the extent to which this condition is specific to Muslims, analyzing at least the case of their Christian counterparts is needed. In fact, the need for social inscription in Berlin is by no means exclusive to Muslims. On the contrary, as Nieswand (2010) shows, Charismatic Christians from West Africa have also used this strategy to find space and congregate in Berlin. Though they transit via German-dominated churches, in the end, they form their Bible reading groups and even churches that place them in a vibrant religious landscape and give an African touch to religion similar to that of the FAM.

As I have shown, the search for a ritual space is intricately linked to that of a social space. It is part of the process of self-representation and constituting a collective which in turn is also related to having one's own space. It is not surprising that religion becomes a powerful resource and a modality of asserting one's agency in one's own life. Thus, focusing on religion is not only relevant but necessary to understand and problematize the refugee/migration condition. The search for a space among migrants and refugees in Berlin in the last five years has demonstrated just that. In the case of my interlocutors, it is even part of being African with all the rethinking and renegotiation of one's own religiosity and the political implications this might have.

The case I contribute to the broader conversation on religion, refugees and migration has sought to bring to light the experience of being Muslim of many young West Africans as they struggle to inscribe themselves in the Berlin religious, social, and political landscape. Starting with the idea of analyzing how these migrants and refugees find ritual space, I also show that the ritual, the social and the political are all entangled. Finding a space and making a place could be highly political as one seeks to escape marginalization and vulnerability. Grouping, community organizing and acquiring visibility, as two other "African" initiatives in Berlin have demonstrated,[22] are effective strategies to make one's own place in Berlin.

As noted earlier, what my interlocutors have referred to as the Turkish model, has inspired, for example, the *Afrikanischer Muslimkreis* (AMK, African Muslim Circle), an organization that provides social services and raises awareness against discrimination while it contributes to educational programs in Cameroon. Alarmed by the increasing level of intolerance vis-à-vis refugees and migrants from African background, and the growing number of discrimination cases against sub-Saharan Africans, AMK has engaged in sensitizing and offering a space for socialization to many from sub-Saharan Africa. Similar to the FAM, but trying to appeal to more secular constituencies, AMK builds on Islam to make a space for sub-Saharan Africans.

A further analysis could investigate how Africa, Africanity, or Africanness get performed in this process. What calls, claims and political agendas lie behind the designation FAM? What baggage does this intervention in a Muslim minority context carry? What parallels could we draw with other and similar initiatives that sought to offer a space for migrants and refugees in a context where new categories such as European Islam or German Islam make their way into not only political but also academic arenas. How would these categories relate to those we use and which have sedimented in our renderings of religion and religiosity?

In the aftermath of the so-called refugee crisis of 2014–15, Berlin became a vibrant arena for young migrants and refugees from West Africa who found in religiosity a way to claim space in the city. It is important to note how in this case religion has mediated the agency of these young people and helped them set the conditions for reconstructing their lives, at the same time that they faced the challenges of socioeconomic integration, legal status, and debasing stereotypes. Their initiatives demonstrate the significance of religiosity for the whole experience of being displaced, but also for the attempts at reconstructing one's life. The process has opened new horizons for being Muslim, West African, and migrant/refugee in Berlin; it has also raised new concerns and prompted new debates.

Part IV

Political Spaces of Reception

Texts, Language, and Religion in the Making of Syriac Orthodox Communities in Europe

Heleen Murre-van den Berg

Introduction

Since the 1970s, Oriental Orthodox Christians from the Middle East and Africa have settled in Europe, fleeing societal pressures and war-related violence. These include the Armenian, Coptic, Syriac/Aramean, Assyrian, Ethiopian, and Eritrean churches. One of the prominent aspects of contemporary religious practice of these transnational Oriental communities is their strong emphasis on the writing and publishing of texts. These include traditional religious texts (from liturgy to history), retranslated and recontextualized texts, and completely new texts. As part of a larger project on the transformation of Orthodox Christianity in Europe, the current chapter zooms in on the Syriac Orthodox Church. It will discuss its successful online and offline bookshop and publishing house located in the Mor Ephrem Monastery, in the eastern part of the Netherlands. To bring into focus what exactly this bookshop does in relation to earlier practices among these churches, this contribution discusses the contents of this particular collection against the background of similar collections from other churches, two from the past, and one from the present.

Unlike *Oriental* Christians, *Eastern* Orthodox Christians (such as Russian, Serbian, Rumanian, and Greek Orthodox) have long been part of the European imagination, even if they have often been excluded from Europe's self-image as modern and secularized, as in the two rather different discussions initiated by Samuel Huntington's *Clash of Civilizations* (1996) and Charles Taylor's *A Secular Age* (2007). If Eastern Orthodoxy's ideological inclusion in Europe is considered contentious by many, this is even more the case for the so-called "Oriental" Orthodox Christians. Originally a term devised by church historians in order to distinguish this group as *non-* or *pre-*Chalcedonian from those who accepted the imperially backed decisions of the Council of Chalcedon in 451 on the two natures of Christ, the term has increasingly been used in scholarship (Hämmerli and Mayer 2014; Ross et al. 2018; Teule and Brüning 2018) as well as by the churches themselves. In recent ecumenical encounters such as the Roman Catholic-sponsored *Pro Oriente Consultations* in Vienna (Kirchschläger and Stirnemann 1991–9), the term "Oriental" became a proudly worn badge of distinction, indexing not only their origins in separate institutional, ritual, and theological traditions but also their origins outside Europe, in the Middle East, and in Africa. Conversely, the Syriac, Coptic, and Ethiopian churches have emphasized the epithet "Orthodox" in their official names, aligning themselves with the Eastern Orthodox from the Byzantine traditions rather than with Catholics or Protestants.

The first group of migrants from the Oriental churches arrived in Europe in the 1920s, after the genocide on Armenian, Syriac/Aramean, and Assyrian/ Chaldean Churches in Anatolia in 1915. Survivors found new homes in the Middle East (Syria, Lebanon), Russia, and the United States, whereas others established new homes in France. Syriac Orthodox Christians arrived in Europe from the 1960s onward, fleeing Turkey during the Turkish-Kurdish conflict in Eastern Anatolia (1978–1990s) when they were mistrusted and subject to anti-Christian violence from both sides. Smaller groups of Syriac Christians left the region for Europe in relation to the Lebanese Civil War (1975–90), opposition crackdowns in Syria in the 1980s, and the violence in Syria and Iraq from 2005 onward.

Almost all European countries have taken in Syriac Orthodox Christians, with highest numbers in Germany, Sweden, and the Netherlands (Atto 2011; Birol 2016). The Dutch community is thought to have originated from a few men who came as labor migrants in the early 1970s. When the violence in Eastern Turkey was also directed against the Christians, larger numbers came as refugees and settled, before and after being granted refugee status, mostly in Twente, in and around the city of Enschede. Although it took some time before asylum was granted, in general the Syriac Christians were welcomed and were supported especially by Protestant and Roman Catholic churches and organizations that recognized them as fellow Christians. In the village of Glane, close to Enschede, a diocese was established in 1977. In 1981, the Syriac Orthodox Church acquired a former Catholic monastery which became the center of the "Central European" diocese, led by Archbishop Julius Cicek. With the growth of the European community, the diocese was split up, and by the time the current Archbishop

Mor Polycarpos Augin Aydin was consecrated in 2005, the archdiocese was responsible for the Netherlands only. Over the past forty years, the European dioceses acquired church buildings and monasteries and have set up a European hierarchy that owes allegiance to the head of the church, Patriarch Mor Ignatius Aphrem (in office since 2014), officially located in Damascus (though spending much time abroad), seeing themselves mostly as diasporas relating to the center in the homelands (Romeny et al. 2009; Atto 2011; Knott and McLoughlin 2010). Most European countries do not keep track of the precise numbers of Oriental Christians in general or of any of the churches in particular; a rough guess on the basis of self-reporting brings the total number of Oriental Christians in Europe to around two million people (cf. Pew Report 2017; Hämmerli and Mayer 2014; Leustean 2014; Schmoller 2018), with the Syriac Orthodox numbering around 200,000 people, of which about 25,000 are in the Netherlands. The population of Oriental Christians is dwarfed by an estimated eighty-two million Eastern Orthodox in Europe (excluding Russia, another ca. 100 million), the vast majority of which lives in countries with Orthodox majorities in Central, Southern, and Eastern Europe.

The fragmentation and fragility of the transnational Oriental churches have motivated them to put great efforts in transmitting their literary heritage to the new generations born in the diaspora, further developing time-worn practices that connect the past to the present. In the Netherlands, Archbishop Julius Cicek set up a publishing house, under the name of Bar Hebraeus Verlag (now also: Bar Ebroyo Press) after one of their great medieval authors. The corpus of this publishing house, accessible via the electronic bookshop Mor Ephrem (named after their most famous fourth-century poet and exegete), shows how the total corpus encompasses a wide range of genres, including liturgy, theology, saints' lives, history, and grammar. All of these genres come in different forms, some serving the clergy and the learned lay, others to bringing to children and laypeople the liturgy, history, and language of the church. Notably, the Mor Ephrem Bookshop (MEB) is part of a wider literary movement that can be traced among Copts, Armenians, Ethiopians, and Armenians in Europe. To study this wider movement among the European Oriental churches, I took the MEB as a pilot study. Over twenty years, many of its publications made their way into my personal library and have been used for various aspects of my research. While the "bookshop" as such is decidedly modest—in fact, it is little more than a side room in the Mor Ephrem Monastery with lots of books stacked along the walls—the accompanying website enables those who come to browse it to easily order the books. In a few clicks, one can expand one's Syriac library with publications that vary from photographic reprints of handwritten manuscripts to recent publications by Syriac Orthodox and Western authors.

The current chapter explores the further "literarization" of religious practice in Orthodox Christian communities, understanding these textual practices as indicators of how the religious leadership (which is the major driving force behind these publications in their roles of authors and publishers and which includes both clergy and lay) sees the future of their community in the European context. Over the last century, both Eastern and Oriental Orthodox Christians went through enormous changes, going from mostly locally organized ecclesial structures to global and transnational communities. As such, they are part not only of what increasingly is recognized as a distinct "global Orthodoxy" (Roudometof 2014; Leustean 2014) but also of global Christian dynamics more generally.

The Name Debate

One of the ongoing debates in the global Syriac Orthodox community is that over the names that they would like to go by, especially in the languages of the diaspora and especially in contexts where a focus on religion and religious denomination do not seem appropriate (Atto 2011). In the Aramaic language of the liturgy (usually referred to as "Classical Syriac") and the spoken modern Aramaic vernacular of the majority of the Syriac Orthodox from Turkey (referred to as *Turoyo* or *Surayt*), the regular term is *Suryoye*, or, in Arabic *Suryani*, the equivalent of "Syriacs/ns," or *Syrisch(e)*, in English, Dutch, and German. From the late nineteenth century onward, local nationalists felt the need for additional terms which allowed them to separate ethnic from religious identities. The oldest of these is "Assyrian," which was introduced by nationalists of the Church of the East (Becker 2015). This church, usually called "East Syriac" by scholars after "Nestorian" fell out of use, shares the Syriac (Aramean) literary tradition with the Syriac Orthodox Church and uses the same ancient Bible translation (Peshitta) and the same Classical Syriac language in its liturgy. Many of its adherents speak a modern Aramaic language (*Sureth*), closely related to the *Surayt* of the Syriac Orthodox. However, dogmatic, political, and geographical boundaries dating back to the third to sixth centuries have made for two separate churches with distinct histories, the first dominant in Western Mesopotamia (Turkey, Syria); the other in Eastern Mesopotamia (Iraq, Iran) (Murre-van den Berg 2007).

Early nationalists in Urmia wanted to get away from the term "Nestorian," which at that point was used mostly with pejorative connotations, as well as from "Syriac," which was felt not to be specific enough. With the remains of the Assyrian empires being excavated in Northern Mesopotamia, it made sense to take this name as the label for a new type of ethnic and national identification. The term, which was in use to indicate Christians of the Mosul region (*Athur*, in Aramaic), slowly became the overarching term to bring together Aramaic-speaking Christians from both the Syriac Orthodox Church and the Church of the East. This type of "Assyrian nationalism," however, found supporters mostly in the Church of the East which in the twentieth century made "Assyrian" (*Athuraya*) part of its official name. Among the Syriac Orthodox, the ethnic epithet "Assyrian" always remained contested—with some using it alongside "Syriac," others being strong advocates of it, and yet others actively fighting it.

Over the last few decades, opponents to the usage of "Assyrian" as an ethnic indicator in the Syriac Orthodox Church have successfully introduced the term "Aramean" as an ethnic term. The proponents of the term "Aramean" often were critical of the more secularist and leftist leanings of many of those using the term "Assyrian." More importantly, the term "Aramean" was added to "Syrian" or "Syriac Orthodox" in order to respond to the European context that seemed to demand ethnic rather than religious markers. The initial European term "Turkish Christians" (i.e., Christians from Turkey) was strongly rejected by the community itself because of the implication that they were of Turkish descent. Within the community, mostly the emic Aramaic term *Suryoye* is used, which therefore has also gained some currency in academic and governmental publications in the Netherlands. However, because *Suryoye* in most European languages translates to "Syrians," which implies a unique relationship with the Arab Syrian state, most did not find this a satisfying term. On the other hand, using "Syriac Orthodox" to refer to this group, as I do in this chapter, prioritizes ecclesial over ethnic identity and preemptively closes the shared Aramean/ Syriac/Assyrian heritage to the variety of groups that may identify with it. The epithet Aramean opens this up, by separating religious from ethnic identity, allowing those who are not members of the Syriac Orthodox Church to identify with it—even if the vast majority of Aramean activists keep emphasizing their unique links to the Syriac Orthodox Church. Over the past decades, the term "Aramean" has gained considerable weight, not only over "Assyrian" (which never held a majority position within the Syriac Orthodox Church) but also over the term "Syriac," which until today, however, is the term used by most clergy and laity and which reflects all the ambiguities of an "ethnic-like" ecclesial

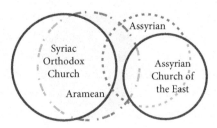

Figure 10.1 Interplay and overlap of ethnic and ecclesial identifications; created by Heleen Murre-van den Berg.

community (Bakker Kellogg 2019; Brubaker 2015; Murre-van den Berg 2013b) (see Figure 10.1).

Texts, Collections, and Textual Practices

When I started to study the setup and contents of the MEB, the collection reminded me of collections that I had come across in my earlier research, even if most of these are from East Syriac (i.e., Assyrian Church of the East) rather than West Syriac (i.e., Syriac Orthodox) circles. While most of the actual texts are different, the genres are very similar and can easily be compared, thus helping to delineate the developments of the last fifty years against the background of migration and new forms of self-understanding in a European context. Unfortunately, so far no studies are available that discuss similar pre-1900 Syriac Orthodox collections. However, considering the close and long-term connections between both major church traditions, I take the collections from within the Church of the East as a valid starting point to contrastively analyze the contemporary collection of the Syriac Orthodox Church in the Netherlands and beyond.[1]

The oldest is the collection of the monastery of the Church of the East in Jerusalem. In the seventeenth and eighteenth centuries, the Church of the East maintained an active presence in the Holy City, with a small monastic community in the monastery and church of Mart Maryam in what today is the Muslim quarter of the Old City (Brock 2006–7). Sometime between October 1717 and September 1718, Priest Kanun—the monk in charge—made a list of the holdings of the monastic library. This inventory has been preserved (the oldest such inventory in Church of the East circles; see Rücker 1931), and about half of the manuscripts are still to be found in Jerusalem. The inventory lists 100 items, and includes the essential items of a monastic East Syriac library of the time—

serving the church in its ritual functions first and foremost, and, second, the monks in their spiritual and scholarly needs (Murre-van den Berg 2015a).

The second East Syriac collection is the manuscript collection of the American Protestant mission in Urmia, on the basis of the catalogue that was made by William Shedd, an American missionary, and Oshana Sarau, an archdeacon who worked for the East Syriac Patriarch Mar Shimon Ruwil XVIII, in 1898 (Sarau 1898; Murre-van den Berg 1999). Going by its contents as well as by the preface of the catalogue, the primary function of this collection was educational and scholarly. It intended to provide study materials for the Assyrians in the missionary schools as well as to collect manuscripts for the wider American and European scholarly community. Its collectors—both American missionaries and local Assyrians—focused on the Classical Syriac heritage, mostly from the Church of the East, but including items from Catholic or Syriac Orthodox origins.

The third collection is that of *Atour Publications* (AP). Like that of the MEB collection, it is online and ongoing but has its basis in East Syriac "Assyrian" literature in its widest sense. AP is the work of an American-Assyrian scholar, David G. Malick, who is committed to collecting and printing old (copyright-free) and new books relevant to the Assyrian Church of the East in the widest sense, "specializing in reprinting valuable books and periodicals concerning Assyrian language, literature, history and culture." Different from the three other collections, this is a private enterprise which is not connected to one of the churches and their hierarchies, or to an educational-missionary enterprise like the Urmia collection. Like the MEB, it features about 150 items. Like AP, the MEB commits itself to providing cheap copies of old and new texts. Where AP for the older Syriac texts employs older, out-of-copyright editions and translations alongside privately produced contemporary writings, MEB offers a mixture of similar cheap reprints of earlier publications and contemporary productions with publications based on photocopied handwritten materials—thus combining the tradition of manuscript writing with the technical possibilities of mass production and distribution. Whereas at first sight it seems a long shot to compare two contemporary collections with the older ones, similarities in types of actors and aims (ecclesial and scholarly), and the overlap of genres and the common basis in the Classical Syriac heritage allow us to identify a number of new developments in the contemporary Syriac Orthodox Church. These developments are closely related to concepts of learning and textual transmission and can be related to the new transnational European context of a vulnerable migrant community.

Tradition and Continuity

In many ways, the Syriac Orthodox MEB collection is characterized by continuity
with the past. Like in Orthodox churches everywhere, the historically tested
formulations of faith in the language of the church constitute the solid base
of the heritage that is being transmitted. The Syriac Orthodox, therefore, like
other Orthodox churches, put much effort in upholding their ancient liturgical,
linguistic, and literary traditions as the primary means to establish and reestablish
themselves in a new context. In the MEB collection, like in the three other
collections introduced earlier, the liturgical texts in the Classical Syriac language,
the texts that one needs to execute the daily and weekly liturgies, form the core
of the collection. The full gamut of liturgical texts is available, often in large-
volume and beautifully executed editions, ranging from the Gospel lectionaries
and Anaphora's for the weekly Eucharistic service, the liturgies for Baptism and
Weddings, to the important hymnal collections, subsumed in the *Beth Gazzo*,
of which also an audio edition is on offer.[2] In comparison, the contemporary
liturgical collection of Atour Press is less wide ranging. This is understandable
because it is not a church press as such, but nevertheless it sells the three basic
liturgical texts of the Assyrian Church of the East, the Eucharistic and Baptismal
liturgies, and the daily prayers, complemented by a hymnal in the modern
language which includes translations of older hymns as well as contemporary
compositions.[3] In all four collections, the Bible is present in a variety of formats,
testifying to its importance in past and present iterations of the faith.

In the MEB collection, the subcategory of "Religious Books" takes up an
important traditional genre. The term refers to monasticism, monastic life, and
mysticism more generally, in line with older definitions of the term "religious
life" in both East and West. Indeed, a selection of highlights from the traditional
monastic literature dominates this category. These include Gregory bar Ebroyo's
thirteenth-century *Book of the Dove*, treatises by Isaac of Nineveh, a well-known
East Syriac mystic author from the seventh century, and a selection of the *Sayings
of the Desert Fathers*, a traditional early Eastern Christian text available in many
ancient and modern languages.

Finally, in continuance of its strong presence in the older collections, the genre
of hagiography is well represented in the contemporary collections. In MEB, a
separate category entitled "Biographies of the Saints" includes thirteen items, all
on individual saints, some of which are well known also in other denominations,
such as St. Mary and St. George. Others are specifically West Syriac, like St.
Jacob of Nisibis, Queen Theodora, and Mor Gabriel. These traditional texts are

Figure 10.2 *The Life of St. Jacob of Nisibis*—book cover; photo by Heleen Murre-van den Berg.

published in attractively formatted single-story booklets, with Classical Syriac, a modern translation, and an audio CD (see Figure 10.2). In line with its general policies, the AP collection restricts itself to reprints regarding this genre, most importantly that of Paul Bedjan's seven-volume edition of the Classical Syriac versions of the Saints' Lives (Bedjan 1890–7).

New Genres, New Readerships, New Languages

However, there is one major difference when comparing these traditional texts in the modern collections against the background of earlier practices of producing and collecting texts. According to a broad survey of manuscript collections of the Church of the East, liturgical texts usually made up more than half of the average monastic or parish collection (Murre-van den Berg 2015a). The East Syriac Jerusalem collection, with about 60 percent of liturgical manuscripts, conforms neatly to this model. This has completely changed in the modern collections, which show much lower percentages of liturgical texts: in the Urmia collection of the late nineteenth century it is no more than 13 percent, in AP it is around 2 percent, and in MEB, the focus of this investigation, it is 7 percent of the total collection.[4] As argued in the previous section, there is no reason to believe that the interest in liturgy and religious literature more generally has declined. Indeed, a quick survey of the collections makes clear that the main reason for the lower percentages of liturgical books is the fact that other genres have become more numerous, thereby diminishing the relative rather than absolute importance of liturgical manuscripts.[5] So what are the major innovations that we see in the modern collections, especially in that of the Syriac Orthodox?

One of these expansive genres is that of the Bible. The first shift is that to the continuous Bible text in one or two volumes, first noted in the nineteenth-century Urmia collection. This is closely connected to the rise of printed rather than (the bulkier) handwritten volumes, which always came either as lectionaries or as the five-part Peshitta. In the two contemporary collections, AP offers a reprint of the Urmia Bible in Classical Syriac and Literary Urmia Aramaic (Murre-van den Berg 1999), whereas MEB sells a 1979 reprint by the United Bible Societies of the Classical Syriac-printed Bible edition by Samuel Lee (London 1823). More importantly, the MEB has on offer various editions of the Gospel lectionary, in Classical Syriac, Arabic, and Turkish. These combine traditional liturgical ecclesiastical usage and context with the sensibilities of the contemporary multilingual context and the increasing weight that is put to "understanding what you read."

This focus on "understanding what you read" is further underlined by a Turkish translation of the continuous New Testament available in the MEB, but even more so by a completely new genre in comparison to the three other collections, namely editions that are geared specifically toward children, such as the Classical Syriac translation of a graphic novel about the life of Jesus that has been widely used in mostly Evangelical circles and is available in many languages.[6] Also primarily focused at children and young people are the catechisms, in Syriac as well as in Dutch, under the title *Yulfono Mshihoyo* ("Christian Teaching"). The most important one was written by a patriarch from the early twentieth century, Mor Aphrem Barsoum (in office 1933–57).

Catechisms in Syriac are first attested in the seventeenth century, when under influence of Roman Catholic missionaries also Orthodox churches embraced this way of teaching the fundamentals of the faith to the lay.[7] The fact that these texts are increasingly also translated into Dutch underlines the fact that these catechisms are meant to help children and young people to learn from texts, rather than orally from the priests. Vice versa, these editions confirm that many of these young people, who grew up in the Netherlands, prefer to read Dutch rather than the vernacular Aramaic, Classical Syriac, or Arabic.

The linguistic issue comes to the fore even more prominently in another genre that has seen many changes and expansion in the modern period. Those not at home in the literature of Orthodox churches might be surprised to learn that in an ecclesial bookshop like the MEB, grammars and dictionaries are well represented. In this, the MEB collection follows traditional patterns in which grammatical scholarship played an important role. This is to be explained from the fact that in the Orthodox churches the usage of specific traditional languages for church ritual tended to go hand in hand with sustained forms of multilingualism and literary exchange, both within each church and between various Orthodox churches. This made translations from one language to another an ongoing concern, from the earliest period in which Greek was the major language in Christian circles with Syriac, Armenian, Ethiopian, Georgian, and Arabic to be added to it—up to contemporary transnational and multilingual times. Over the centuries, therefore, monastic libraries tended to include dictionaries and grammars, some of which date back to the Abbasid period in which linguistic scholarship flourished (Murre-van den Berg 2015a).

At first sight, the MEB library focuses on the classical liturgical language rather than the vernacular, though mostly by way of modern grammatical and lexical works. This corresponds to the fact that the modern Aramaic vernacular language that is spoken in many of the Syriac Orthodox communities, called *Turoyo* or *Surayt*, does not have a stable status as a standardized language.[8] All dictionaries in the MEB collection, therefore, concern themselves with Classical Syriac: the learned all-Classical Syriac dictionary produced by Thomas Audo in Urmia in 1896 in the East Syriac script,[9] a simple Classical Syriac lexicon explaining basic words with pictures produced in the Netherlands, and two versions of the Classical Syriac dictionary produced by Aziz Bulut, Sabo Hanna, and Bishop Julius Cicek, in its Dutch-Syriac/Syriac-Dutch version, and in its German/Syriac version. The MEB collection also features a range of Classical Syriac grammar books for children that are used in Sunday and summer schools to teach the children the language of the liturgy. All of this underlines the importance, in the eyes of the church leadership, of Classical Syriac as the language of the church.

However, this exclusive focus on the liturgical language—which is spoken and understood easily only by a few of the learned clergy—appears to be shifting. Recently, a Dutch-Syriac version of the Sunday liturgy was published in a beautiful small churchgoing edition, suggesting that "understanding what you read" is at least as important as cherishing the liturgical language of the church community (see Figure 10.3 a and b). Increasingly, also, the modern vernacular language is being embraced as a potential communal and religious language. The MEB collection includes a children's book (in both Latin and Syriac script, and accompanied by a German translation; see Figure 10.4 a and b), a popular grammar book by Murat Can to learn the modern language: *Toxu yelfina Surayt / Laten we Surayt leren*, and a learned grammar of the modern language. Some of these books use the Syriac script, while others use transcription in the Latin alphabet, indicating the desire of those in charge to propagate the knowledge of the modern vernacular to young and older readers with all possible means and methods.

While one is inclined to interpret this as a modern vernacular turn, moving away from the exclusive attention to the classical language, a comparative look at the four collections makes clear that Classical Syriac, despite being the dominant language of the liturgy, always had to share pride of place with other languages, such as Arabic, Turkish, and the modern vernacular (Murre-van den Berg 2015a; Mengozzi 2011). The MEB list, in line with its emphasis on grammar, dictionaries, and teaching materials of Classical Syriac, tends to

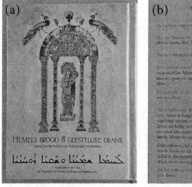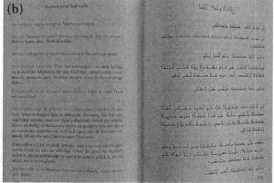

Figure 10.3a and b Bilingual prayer book, Dutch-Syriac; photo by Heleen Murre-van den Berg.

Figure 10.4a and b Eliyo and Maria Aydin, *Die Grossmutter und der Fuchs / I-Qashtowu-Ta ʾlo* (Bar Hebraeus Verlag, 2012); photo by Heleen Murre-van den Berg.

prioritize Classical Syriac, with a few German or Dutch items, alongside the already-mentioned Bible translations into Turkish and Arabic. As important, however, is the fact that despite the efforts to promote both Classical Syriac and the vernacular languages in the modern collections, the mere fact that the websites of both MEB and AP are in English indicates that the publishers assume that ultimately the Syriac/Aramaic languages are not understood well enough to function as a common language. It is English rather than Syriac that is the language that allows as wide a public as possible regarding what the online bookshops have on offer; it is children and their lay parents as much as priests and monks who are supposed to read, learn, and teach.

Thus, there are important differences between the older and contemporary collections. The most fundamental change concerns the fact that nonclergy, men, women, and children are seen not only as listeners but as readers and participants in the religious-literary enterprise. While this (re)inclusion of the lay into the orbit of the literary public started in the nineteenth century (as reflected in the Urmia collection), it considerably broadened in the twentieth century, first in the Middle East and later, more profoundly, in the diaspora communities. Both the children's books and catechisms in the MEB and the range of languages that are used to print and publish testify to the desire to include nonclergy and nonscholars into transnational debates that are seen as essential by the clerical and sociopolitical elites. While further study of print runs and reading practices is needed to assess to what extent and how these publications are being appropriated by the lay, the publications as such testify to the commitment to these themes by the mostly clerical actors. Their main focus indeed remains the transmission of tradition, but judging from their publications, the actors believe that transmission can succeed only when the community as a whole is involved, not only in living the tradition in pious imitation but in appropriating it via reading, understanding, and reformulating this tradition for themselves.

Iconography

Another major difference with earlier textual practices concerns the increasing importance of images. Compared to the Eastern Orthodox churches, the Oriental churches give icons a less theologically central and less visually prominent role. While in the past this led to a near-aniconic religious practice, today the absence of a theology of icons allows for a rather free and eclectic use of religious imagery, in church buildings and in manuscripts, books, and digital publications. This is the case, for example, in an English-language children's Bible which was translated into Classical Syriac and which includes the drawings of the English original. Different from the translation of the graphic novel discussed earlier, in this case the cover has been Syriacized, using a well-known Syriac icon of Christ's Entrance into Jerusalem rather than one of the images that are used in the running text (Figure 10.5 a and b). This iconographic hybridization not only visualizes the wide-ranging borrowings that go on but also underlines the shift discussed earlier, expanding the traditional readership of the Bible from monks to laypeople especially children, mixing global aesthetics as to what is fitting for children with traditional Syriac biblical imagery. Another type of hybridization and global aesthetics concerns the increasing use of photographs, of monasteries and churches, of Syriac monks in traditional monastic attire adorning spiritual literature (in which the monks feature as examples for laypeople), and finally that of a Jesus look-alike that reminds one of similar images used in Evangelical circles that is found on several editions of the most popular catechism.

More than in the domain of the texts, borrowing of images seems to be guided by few explicit rules, with images originating in Catholic and Protestant sources added to those originating in Oriental and Eastern Orthodox churches. This iconographic hybridization suggests that there are strong religious and

Figure 10.5a and b Children's Bible in Classical Syriac; photo by Heleen Murre-van den Berg.

aesthetic affinities (among the Christian churches and especially among the Orthodox churches) that make such borrowings popular and effective, despite the persistent dogmatic and cultural differences between them (Mengozzi 2020). This, in turn, indicates that the contemporary development of these textual and iconography practices does not happen in a vacuum, but is influenced by what happens in other churches, even if these practices as such are aimed at preserving their distinct ecclesial and linguistic heritage. This case study suggests that mutual influencing takes place at a number of intertwined levels, transnationally within each of these Oriental churches, among these Oriental churches themselves, among Eastern and Oriental Orthodox, and among European and Global Christianity more broadly. This was already suggested in the works of Hämmerli and Mayer (2014) and Leustean (2014) which sketch the contours of an emerging European Orthodoxy consisting of a plurality of Eastern and Oriental churches that sees itself not only as representatives of distinct, often ethnically or nationally defined, churches but as part of a wider European or Global Orthodoxy that positions itself as different from Protestantism, Roman Catholicism, and secularism.

Hagiography and History

An interesting aspect of the use of photographs or naturalistic images in these productions is that they tend to naturalize and historicize texts that earlier were not illustrated at all. Or, if they were, these consisted of icon-type illustrations, that is, highly stylized images that conform to strict iconographic norms as to the basic elements of the image, resulting usually in images that are timeless and universal, rather than contextually and historically grounded. The *Life of the Holy Jacob of Nisibis*, for example, a church father and saint that lived in the fourth century, is illustrated by a photograph of the well-preserved ruins of the Church of St. Jacob in Nisibis, where tradition tells that he lived (Figure 10.2), whereas an introduction and a considerable number of notes further contextualize and historicize the ancient Syriac text.

This historicizing tendency comes across very clearly when comparing what is comprised in the category of "history" between the older and contemporary collections. In the older collections, the historic genre had been somewhat neglected. This trend, however, has completely been reversed in both modern collections, MEB as much as AP, with "History Books" being the largest subcategory of the MEB (thirty-four items). This category includes modern copies of the medieval Syriac Orthodox works of Mikho'il Rabo (Michael the Great) and Bar ʿEbroyo, but most of the works are modern, including historical works written and published in the 1920s to 1950s in the Middle East, like the *History of the Syriac dioceses* and the *Berule bdhire*—"Scattered Pearls: History of Syriac scholarship and literature"—by Patriarch Aphrem Barsoum.[10] It also includes works written by Western scholars and published elsewhere, such as the widely distributed three-volume work *Margonito Gnizto* (*The Hidden Pearl*).[11] AP features the more modest but equally impressing *Literary History of the Assyrians* by Pera Sarmas and the so far unexplored work by David Giwargis Malik, *History of Assyria*.[12]

A specific subgenre under "History" is memoirs and narratives about the genocide of 1915. It is here that the historic genre starts to overlap with the hagiographical. Historical accounts, when dealing with steadfast faith in the face of persecution, tend toward the hagiographical and the hagiographical—in the recent or the less recent past—being interpreted firmly as part of the group's history, with the martyrs of the faith as the founding fathers and mothers of monasteries, churches, and the community itself (Murre-van den Berg 2015b). The republishing and rereading of the works of the medieval chronographers add to this pattern by underlining the longue durée, situating the Syriac churches in the wider Christian and general history of the times with explicit and implicit references to the special history of the Syriac Christian people that always suffered from discrimination and persecution. Against the background of new groups of Syriac Orthodox coming in from the Middle East fleeing the advances of ISIS in their region, and of the transnational community following these events closely via social media and satellite TV, the prominence of past stories of persecution and martyrdom interacts with and models those that are newly lived and written in the contemporary world.

Global Orthodoxy and Ethical Issues

Those who are at home in discussions among Eastern Orthodox communities might be surprised that, different from what happens, for example, in Russian Orthodox or Roman Catholic circles, the publications in MEB appear to *not* include explicit debates on ethical issues, such as abortion, same-sex marriage and *lgbt* rights (Suslov 2016). This does not mean that the texts are neutral in this respect: the Saints' Lives, for example, are imbued with references to the Christian way of life, espousing the so-called traditional values even if family life is usually not the major topic of these stories. This suggests that if and when these debates over contemporary ethical issues take place within the Syriac Orthodox community, it would be in the more or less private circles of family and church rather than in publications that are advertised in MEB. It seems, therefore, that church leaders tend to be careful not to complicate the nuanced and careful debates that take place within these communities, in which constraints from the dominant liberal discourses in the host country have to be squared with the demands from Orthodox practices in the home countries. To what extent the Oriental churches, especially when compared to the fairly explicit and outspoken traditional stances of the Eastern Orthodox churches from Central and Eastern Europe, will seek to steer a middle course, or will move toward the sometimes-belligerent anti-modern perspectives of some of the Eastern Orthodox, remains to be seen.

Discussions over these ethical issues tie in with one of the major frustrations of the members of the Oriental churches. Syriac Orthodox Christians in the Netherlands find that they are often categorized in the same group as Muslims, as part of this "other," non-Dutch, and nonwhite group that looks, talks, and moves differently from the majority white population. From the perspective of the Syriac Orthodox, however, they are fully part of Dutch majority society, because of their Christian religion, their acceptance of the secular state, and their modern (i.e., non-Islamic) gender norms. This suggests that the Syriac Orthodox accept a combination of ethicalized and racialized conceptions of Dutch citizenship (Baumann 2010). At the same time, however, this is not exactly the case with regard to their ethical norms, which, when taken in the traditional way (which often is not stated explicitly), may be as different from majority secular Dutch society as those of the perceived Muslim other. The careful way in which the texts seem to circumvent these questions suggests that for now the Syriac Orthodox leadership intends to steer away from an antagonist position, even when in private some may espouse and perhaps even try to enforce traditional norms and values.

Concluding Remarks

It is time to return to the question which was posed by this volume, as to what extent the developments as described earlier are related to the refugee situation of the Syriac Orthodox, in past and present. On the one hand, many of these developments are part of wider changes within Orthodox Christianity, Christianity, and perhaps religions in general. Whether one labels it "modernization" or "westernization," or perhaps even "secularization," there can be no doubt that many religions, which for the majority of its adherents tended to emphasize participation and embodied practice over and above learning, understanding, and believing (the work of the learned elites), over the past two centuries have adopted and propagated some kind of intellectualism for the masses. Every believer today needs to be fully aware of the consequences of their religion, and needs to be able to explain to others what it entails and why things are done the way they are. The move of the Syriac Orthodox to the West (voluntary and involuntary) did not cause this development; it merely accelerated it.

However, the way this process takes form, in Europe and other places of the Syriac Orthodox diaspora, is predicated on their specific refugee situation. The most important aspect is the ongoing precariousness and fragility of these communities. Different from many other migrants, there is no state to back them up and safeguard their religious-communal heritage: it is up to those who left to safer shores to do so. Worries over continuity and preservation, which plague migrant communities everywhere, take on an existential shade if the group is that small and has so few power bases around the world. Texts (in addition to buildings and organizations) are a manageable way—fitting their particular history and fitting modern European society—to preserve their past and build their future. However, marginality and precariousness have not ended with migration, and perhaps lead the community to be more careful than others in stating their particular position in European society, in order not to risk their hard-won safety and acceptance. At the same time, the fact that there is no state power to back the church gives the church a flexibility to deal with these European challenges in a way that other Oriental and Eastern churches—which have to reckon with strong powers back home—do not have.

Many of the explicit debates in and about the Syriac Orthodox Church are about ethnicity. The publications of the bookshop indicate that the church leadership tends to downplay the ethnic issue. While there is lot about language, there is nothing that prioritizes ethnicity. This may be interpreted as a deliberate choice to avoid clerical involvement in the political struggles between the "Aramean" and "Assyrian" parties, each of which has its power base in secular nationalist organizations. More importantly, one may conclude that from the perspective of church leaders organizing as a distinct ethnic group is not necessarily the best way forward in European society, even if it brings certain perks as to recognition in the secular Dutch context. As Sarah Bakker Kellogg (2019) has shown, for the Syriac Orthodox, the feeling of kinship, of "groupness," is closely tied to the church as community in which "religion" is functionally equivalent to "ethnicity," rather than an addition to it, and thus not something that in a secular context can be neatly separated from "religion." Perhaps we can interpret the focus in the MEB collection on religious content as a way to overcome the threatening dichotomy between the religious and ethnic aspects of Syriac Orthodox communal identity. The collection prioritizes religion, in its specific Syriac Orthodox form and its ecumenical and generic "Christian" way simultaneously, just like it stimulates Syriac/Aramaic language learning and communal participation while at the same time acknowledging the usage of Turkish, Arabic, German, Dutch, and English by productions that make use of these languages. While this may strike some as inconsistent and unsatisfactory, it might in fact reflect and therefore acknowledge and own the community's liminal and creative position at the center of a new European citizenship.

Between Hope and Fear

Migrant "Illegality" and Camp Life in Assam, India

Salah Punathil

Introduction

On August 31, 2019, 1.9 million people in northeast India's state of Assam were identified as illegal migrants from Bangladesh after government officials published the National Register of Citizens (NRC).[1] Although the exact religious demographics of this population are not yet officially available, Bengali-speaking Muslims constitute a significant number. On December 11, 2019, a few months after the NRC's publication, the Indian Parliament passed the Citizenship (Amendment) Act (CAA), which guarantees citizenship to illegal migrants from Bangladesh, Pakistan, and Afghanistan who are persecuted on religious grounds. This includes Hindus, Sikhs, Parsis, Jains, Buddhists, and Christian minorities, but not Muslims. Soon after, protests erupted across the country.[2] The central government's plan to expand the NRC nationwide and the implementation of the CAA are seen as part of a common agenda that will heavily disadvantage the Muslim minority in India. It is evident from Assam, where the NRC is already being implemented, that the future of the Muslim population, who constitute a substantial number of those excluded from the NRC list, is going to be worse than that of the Hindus. Detention, the threat of deportation, and other human rights violations are looming for a large section of the Muslims in Assam. This chapter goes beyond the immediate humanitarian question of the "stateless" populations in the wake of these amplified state interventions—including threat of detention and deportation of Muslims—to examine the longer history of violence against migrant Muslims, with a special emphasis on camps and camp life in Assam.

While refugees are seen as "unwanted" and regarded as "stateless" in most societies today, the experience of migrants varies, depending on the sociopolitical and economic conditions of the particular territories where they find refuge. Due to the "refugee crisis" in the West over the past few years, there is widespread attention to this in the literature on migration. The academic discussions in such Western-centric scholarship mostly revolve around the questions of accommodation, assimilation and potential policies to tackle the "crises" of migration (e.g., Morris 2000; Waters and Jimenez 2005; De Genova 2017). There is also considerable attention to the suffering of refugees, as discrimination, stereotyping, and various forms of violence are increasing in their lives in the West (Fassin 2007; Ticktin 2011). The camp life of migrants is increasingly visible today as they are pushed into enclosed spatial settings in hostile circumstances. The emergent scholarships on camps offer interesting insights into how these spaces assume the norms of modern nation-states (Malkki 1996; Khalili 2004; Peteet 2005; Sanyal 2010). By taking the case of Bengali-speaking Muslims in Assam, this chapter analyzes the camp life and violence against migrants in a South Asian context.

The Context

Bengali-speaking Muslims in Assam are migrants or descendants of migrants from what is now Bangladesh.[3] Though the history of this migration stretches back to the early colonial period, large-scale influxes of migrants in the latter half of the twentieth century led to intense conflicts. Bengali-speaking Muslims have suffered militant attacks and massacres at the hands of various ethnic groups since the late 1970s. Initially, they were the target of a "subnationalist" movement. The most heinous of all the violence against them was the Nellie Massacre of 1983, which left more than 2,000 Muslims dead and a large but uncounted number homeless, who moved to different parts of the state to find refuge (Kimura 2013). Fifty-three camps were set up for them across the state, and many refused to go back to their home villages (Kimura 2008). Since the 1990s, the Bodo tribe's movement for a separate state within Assam has accentuated the crisis, targeting Muslims with attacks and killings until very recently.[4] In response, camps were set up as Muslims were displaced from their lands on a massive scale, especially in areas where they constituted a minority. Assam's Bodo Territorial Area Districts (BTAD) now has several camps for Muslims, both old and new. They are isolated places with overcrowded shelters and limited infrastructure. While all of them were originally set up as relief camps by the state, the state no longer protects them, and the inhabitants have been left to fend on their own. These camps were established as relief efforts for a temporary purpose, but life inside them and their durability as spatially segregated units raise pertinent questions about the specificity of such camps in a South Asian context.[5]

The Idea of Camps and the South Asian Reality

In the Western context, camps represent the most significant sites of segregation, violence, and social suffering. Agamben (1998: 15) traces the paradox of sovereignty in the modern nation-state by examining the concentration camps and extermination camps set up for Jews by the Nazi regime as the extreme expression of the camp. While Agamben's theory is highly influenced by Foucault's (1990) notion of "biopolitics," the politics of governing and regulating an entire population, he proposes the more critical view of "thanatopolitics"— how the politics of a sovereign power leads it to kill people, and to explain how systematic state machinery tortures and murders human beings in camp-like situations (Agamben 1998: 121). The violent articulation of migrant "illegality" is one of the major ways in which camps have once again gained significance. To understand the horrific experiences of migrants now, we must frame "migrant illegality" as a more serious concern than the fact of illegal migration (De Genova 2002, 2013). The "illegality" of a population constructed through various discursive forms in today's world leads to overpowering denunciations, humiliation, and the "rightslessness" of such "unwanted" groups. While acknowledging the universality of confining migrants in camps, we must see camps and life inside them from a historical and contextual viewpoint, for a more nuanced understanding of the politics of violence and suffering.

Sovereign power, the camp life of migrants, and violence are increasingly significant in the present time. However, Agamben's idea of the camp, clearly a response to the Nazi extermination camps, has limits in the South Asian context. This chapter thus moves beyond Agamben to examine specificities of camp life characterized by the conditions in postcolonial South Asia. The camp's multivalent potential as an analytical category is reflected in prominent works of the past. Apart from Agamben, Foucault (1990) and Hannah Arendt (1958) have been influential in envisioning camps in modern nation-states from the perspectives of "biopolitics" (Gupta 2012) and "humanitarianism"

(Fassin 2007). Didier Fassin, in his study of migrants in France, demonstrates the need to move beyond Agamben's view. He argues (Fassin 2007: 367) that even under a discriminatory regime not all migrants are reduced to "bare life" or *zoë*, the fact of merely being alive, in opposition to *bios*, or full life including political rights, as Agamben (1998: 15) claims. For example, someone with biological defects or a severe illness such as AIDS can be given French citizenship on humanitarian grounds. Here illness offers a possibility for migrants to claim political life. Fassin argues that France's new immigration policies prove exactly the opposite of what Agamben says, as they not only break the distinction between *zoë* and *bios* but also show the increasing confusion of migrant life, in which one's status can transform from one to the other or even to something more complex, contingent, on political circumstances. This confusion and dynamism inform the camp life I describe in this chapter too. Miriam Ticktin, in her study on "sans-papiers'"(2011), migrants "without papers" in France, perceives camps in a completely different way, identifying temporary settings such as waiting centers, holding centers, and prisons for illegal migrants as new manifestations of the camp, where the sovereign power inflicts suffering upon migrants. From its original, singular form, the camp has become multifarious. Ilana Feldman's (2015) work on Palestinian refugee camps provides interesting insights on different forms of camps, characterized by their social, material, geographical, and political conditions and varying degrees of legitimacy in the official discourse on refugee status. She also questions the view of camps as mere humanitarian spaces removed from political articulations.

Achille Mbembe (2003), though drawing heavily on Agamben, provides again different examples of camps and violence. While Agamben locates sovereign power and violence in the Nazi concentration camp, Mbembe draws attention to the camp in the form of plantations, slavery, penal settlements, and the whole array of colonial economic structures that rested upon the sovereign violence of the colonizer in African societies. As he writes, "The ultimate expression of sovereignty resides, to a large degree, in the power and the capacity to dictate who may live and who must die" (Mbembe 2003: 11). What makes Mbembe's work significant in the present-day South Asian context is his emphasis on the militant ethnic groups that have assumed sovereign power and inflict deadly violence on their enemies in the turbulent postcolonial era.[6] In Assam's postcolonial context, too, it is not the state, which has always inflicted direct physical violence, but rather ethnic groups that are waging war on the weak in the pursuit of sovereign power.

Throughout South Asian history, populations have always moved across regions. However, the creation of national borders, as is the case everywhere in the world, gave birth to the category of "illegal migrants," even if their movements and relations across those borders predated the formation of nation-states. Anthropologists have thoroughly critiqued statist analyses of migration, which are largely based on demographic surveys and view migrant populations as objects of policymaking and surveillance (Malkki 1996; De Genova 2013). Several ethnographic studies have also challenged the positivist model that reaffirms the territorial and judicial boundaries of nation-states, by exploring the lived experiences of migrants, especially in the recent context of increasing numbers of forced migrants, stateless people, and refugees (Schendel and Abraham 2005; Samaddar 2016).

It is clear, in both the Western and the non-Western context, that the image of the camp has shifted, from a simple spatial unit to a model of modern life (Peteet 2005; Vajpeyi 2007; Sanyal 2010; Datta 2016). For Ananya Vajpeyi, to properly understand political life in contemporary India, "we [must] devote as much attention to the camp as we do to the nation, to the refugee as we do to the citizen and to the state of exception as we do to the rule of law" (2007: 6). The pertinent question here is what makes the South Asian experience of camps distinctive. The approach toward camps in South Asia must rely on descriptions of migrant lives within them (Datta 2016). Again, camps in South Asian contexts are complex and varied; riots, displacement, and forced migration have given rise to relief camps, refugee camps, and rehabilitation camps. The persons confined to these sites experience the paradoxical situation of relief and suffering, inclusion, and exclusion, hope of life and fear of death. The notion of the camp as a space of exception can be pushed when we look at the complex ways in which the camp has operated in the South Asian context (Vajpeyi 2007; Datta 2016). Hence, the task of this chapter is to extend (and modify) Agamben's theory of the camp against the horizon of camps in South Asia.

Historicizing Migration in Assam's Colonial Context

Colonial history and the history of partition are crucial to understanding the plight of Muslims in Assam today, as the nationality of those who speak Bengali is highly contested. Assam's west, including the present-day Kokrajhar and Goalpara districts, was part of Bengal until 1774 and was annexed by the British much before the rest of the state. During the colonial period, feudalism and poverty severely affected what is now Bangladesh (Hussain 1993). Overpopulation, a poor natural resource base, frequent floods, and a nondiverse economy (due to overreliance on jute and rice) have also historically plagued this region (Hussain 1993). The resulting instability has led to large-scale migrations into neighboring areas. Assam was the preferred destination, just across the Brahmaputra river from Eastern Bengal and with similar geography. After the British annexed Assam in 1826, they encouraged this migration as part of plans to plunder and exploit the new territory (Hussain 1993; Baruah 2007). Significantly, the Eastern Bengal migrants mostly settled in geographically vulnerable places, like low-lying, flood-prone plains (Baruah 2007), but the frequent erosion of riverbanks in these areas forced them to seek new homes elsewhere in India. In their new local communities, this large population of internal migrants is today seen as "Bangladeshis," despite belonging to or descending from a group that had settled in Assam in the colonial period. Again between 1920 and 1940, migration contributed to a substantial increase of the Muslim population in the state (Hussain 1993).

While increasing Muslim population led to intense political debates and occasional violence, Bengali Hindus have also faced ethnic tensions since the colonial period (Weiner 1983; Guha 2014). Since modern education came later to Assam than to Bengal, Bengali Hindus, who were generally well educated, dominated its administrative, bureaucratic, and economic spheres and thus enjoyed higher status. Moreover, the British perception of the Assamese language as a dialect of Bengali and Bengali cultural hegemony had serious repercussions after independence (Hussain 1993; Baruah 2007).

The Postcolonial Situation

Homeland movements by various tribes and other ethnic groups have prompted the Indian government to carve several states out of Assam for them, yet the most striking and continuing crisis in Assam derives from its ethnic tension and violence, especially directed against the Muslims who came from what was then East Bengal. Assam witnessed more anti-immigration and subnationalist politics in the 1970s and 1980s, manifested most extremely in the United Liberation Front of Assam's separatist militancy, and in the 1990s, when the Bodo tribes sought separate statehood.

In the 1960s, Bengali Hindus and Marwaris, an ethnic group that migrated from North Indian regions and constitutes a successful business community, were the prime targets of what is called the Assam agitation or the Assam movement. The Assamese middle classes were struggling against the Bengali Hindus because the latter still dominated them not merely economically and politically but culturally too. For example, the official language of Assam continued to be "Bengali" even after independence. This led to a language movement and subsequently to the Assam movement, initiated by the All Assam Students' Union. The Assam agitation initially did not target Muslims, because they were largely poor peasants and did not pose any threat to the state's economy or culture. Indeed, they were sympathetic to the Assamese language movement, learning the language and trying to assimilate to Assamese culture to a great extent (Hussain 1993; Goswami 2008). However, the situation changed after Bangladesh declared its independence. At that time, the movement began to claim that a large number of migrants from there, especially Bengali-speaking Muslims, had come to India after 1971.

The Saga of Ethnic Assertions and Violence

The most devastating outcome of the Assam movement was the Nellie Massacre of 1983, which took place in Assam's Nagaon district at the height of the agitation. The immediate background was an Assam state assembly election that a vast section of the population boycotted in protest of the unresolved "Bangladesh migration" crisis—the specific claim being that "foreigners" were included in the election rolls. In this incident, more than 2,000 Muslim peasants were killed in several villages on a single day by the local Tiwa tribes with the help of Assamese Hindus. Unofficial figures suggest that the number of deaths are far higher than this. Although this massacre is often read as a culmination of long-term hatred directed at "immigrant encroachers" in Assam, scholars have demonstrated the significant role of Hindu religious organizations' in inciting it (Dasgupta and Guha 1985; Guhain 1985). Targeted violence against Muslims across Assam has thus been a product of both Assamese subnationalism and Hindu religious nationalism. The most shocking aspect of the Nellie Massacre is the impunity of those responsible: not a single person was ever punished for it.

There has been a shift in the perpetrators of violence, although Assamese subnationalist assertion continues to be a major source of threat to Muslim life. The militant outfits of Bodo plain tribes in the BTAD have been committing large-scale atrocities against Muslims since the 1990s, along with major attacks against Adivasis such as Santhals and occasional violence against Hindu

Assamese. The larger context is the violent turn of marginalized Bodo tribes' long-term movement for a separate state. The Bodos are an indigenous tribal group, one of the earliest to settle in Assam. They practice shifting cultivation, so the East Bengal migrants who settled on the Brahmaputra's north bank in Assam's western-most district in the colonial period and took up commercial agriculture came into conflict with them (Goswami 2008). Although the Bodos were in this region first, prominent Muslim leaders in colonial Assam and organizational support for Muslims in the political sphere helped the East Bengal migrants to settle there.

The Bodo movement started as a response to discrimination and negligence at the hands of caste Assamese. Although Bodos joined the Assam movement and shared the political platform of fighting against "immigrants," more and more felt increasingly marginalized from the Assamese Hindu society. Their movement intensified in the early 1990s with the realization that the state offered no protection for their lands, livelihoods, or cultural diversity. They have also been politically underrepresented and vulnerable to economic exploitation. Peaceful protests were ignored by the government and soon gave way to militant assertion. Though Bodo militants targeted the state and Assamese Hindus and Koch Rajbongshis[7] in the beginning, they later turned against the BTAD's Muslim population.[8] The Bodos' first ethnic cleansing campaign began after the signing of the Bodo Accord of 1993, between the Government of India, the Government of Assam, the All Bodo Students' Union, and the Bodo Peoples' Action Committee, which created the Bodoland Autonomous Council (BAC) to administer contiguous villages with more than 50 percent Bodo population. Because many villages that were claimed as eligible for the BAC area did not have an adequate Bodo percentage, Muslims who were already tagged as illegal migrants became easy targets for militants. Over the past three decades, Bodo organizations have participated in a series of negotiations with the state to reformulate the policies on Bodo autonomy, but violence has continued to erupt.

The violent experiences of Bengali-speaking Muslims in Assam perfectly illustrate Mbembe's (2003) observation that the politics of killing is no longer confined to sovereign powers; instead, armed ethnic groups are increasingly involved in the elimination of "threat populations," acting for or with the state. As Von Holdt notes in his study on collective violence in postcolonial South Africa (2013), because the state does not have a monopoly on symbolic or physical violence, that of ethnic groups can become legitimate, especially when their enemies are "unwanted" populations produced by the sovereign power. Likewise, in India it is not always the state but rather ethnic projects of power and control over territories that inflict massive violence on these groups' perceived enemies.

The existing discourse of migrant "illegality" gave rise to a consensus among Bodos that Muslims had encroached upon their land and were now a hindrance to their political goals. Migrant "illegality" also promises impunity for assailants, a clear lesson of the Nellie Massacre. In the more recent violent episodes of 2012 and 2014, Muslims again suffered massive militant attacks and displacement, but these times Bodos in some BTAD villages were targeted too. The Khagrabari Massacre of 2014, when militants killed thirty-eight Muslims on a single day, stands as the most heinous of the more recent attacks. Significantly, even though this violence was not a consequence of communalized ethnic hatred, migrants' religious identity as Muslims was a convenient justification for its production and legitimization.

Old Muslim Camps in Assam and the Chain of Violence

After various attacks on Muslims from the early 1990s to the recent past, camps were established for them in Assam. These camps persist to the present day, revealing a normalization of violence and suffering in Muslim life. The first ones were set up following a massive attack by Bodo militants from October 7 to 11, 1993, throughout Bodo-dominated districts such as Kokrajhar, Bongaigaon, and Chirang, which affected 3,658 families, a total of 18,000 people (Goswami 2008). This assault encompassed mass killings, injuries and destruction of houses and provoked large-scale flight, even to places very far away. The camps, such as Sanlartari, Nagalbhanga, Bengtal, Bangaldoba, Hapachara, Sidalsati, Tapatari, Salabila, and Goroimari, to name a few, are still in use.

Hapachara, in Bongaigaon's Bijni subdivision, is one such camp, where inhabitants have lived for almost thirty years. Shockingly, there are around 1,118 families still there (Azad 2015: 47). The camp was first established in a different place, but after Bodo militants killed two inhabitants just outside the camp in 1994, it was relocated to the present area. This was not an isolated incident: also in 1994, Bodo militants attacked a Muslim relief camp in Bashbari, then in Barpeta (and now in Baksa) district, killing nearly 100 inmates (Azad 2015: 49). Relief camps set up by the state to provide basic security and protect the fundamental right to live have obviously miserably failed to protect Muslims. Many have informed me during my fieldwork that the government provided gratuitous relief (GR), mostly in the form of rice, lentils, and oil, regularly for a few years. However, this was a temporary arrangement which was gradually discontinued, and now the state offers neither rehabilitation nor proper support and care. Thus, the camp has become a permanent settlement, whose inhabitants must develop their own autonomous means of survival and struggle. The camp dwellers narrate the story of their misery: they suffer from poverty and disease, and their children have no access to proper education. Once ethnic militancy has enacted physical violence against Muslims, the state confines them to camps, exposing them to structural violence.

Salabila is another camp, located in Assam's Chirang district. Its inhabitants are also victims of the widespread Bodo attacks of 1993. They have been displaced several times. When a flood eroded the soil of their original camp, they built a temporary camp near a highway and finally moved to the current location in 2007. During my fieldwork, I have learned that private individuals own the land where some camps have been set up to replace government-established camps that had to be evacuated for security reasons. In such instances, the inhabitants pay a sum of money to the landowner every month. This is another distinctive feature of camp life in Assam: private individuals supplant the state in controlling the grounds and those confined to them. This somewhat reflects the situation in Palestine: as Feldman's (2015) study illustrates, camps there have become permanent settlements, which leads to their having autonomous characters; she mentions how houses are rebuilt, altered, and even sold as a regularized part of camp life.

Protest and the State's Passive Response

Camp dwellers protest against discrimination by the state in a number of ways. Inmates have told me of their involvement in organized protests in the state capital, Guwahati, and the national capital, Delhi, for compensation and rehabilitation. Muslim political organizations such as the All India United Democratic Front have supported these protests by inhabitants of Hapachara, Bordubi, Garogaon, Salabila, Bangaldoba, and other camps; the government reacted by visiting camps to look into possible interventions. However, inhabitants dismissed this attention as very passive and ineffective. They say that the officials arrived to make a survey with no advance warning, so many people who were working in different parts of the country as migrant laborers were excluded and hence deprived of the monthly ration of free rice and money. Inmates also told me that the officials asked those who received a financial grant from the government to leave the camp, as the state assumes that they can sustain themselves with this money. In reality, it is hardly enough to buy land on which to settle in another place. Interestingly, I found the inmates who received this compensation living in a slightly better-off camp in the same area. There is not much difference between the two, and this kind of "rehabilitation" does not mean movement or real mobility for this population.

Inmates from Salabila told me that they too had gone to protest in Delhi, while living in the camp near a highway, where they did not feel secure. In response, the government agreed to resettle them, but they resisted the proposed plan because they anticipated land erosion in the locality to which they were supposed to move. Later, however, officials forcefully pushed the camp dwellers from the highway to that place, where they still live.

The Sense of Home inside the Camp

What is the image of home among camp dwellers and how do they picture their future? For many, the camp has become a permanent home. Multiple factors prevent them from returning to their villages, despite their desire to escape such a miserable life. In some cases, floods have destroyed their homes. Most Bengali-speaking Muslim migrants settled on flood-prone river islands, locally known as *chars*. In Assam, these are distributed along the Brahmaputra's entire course, from Sadiya in the east to Dhubri in the west, in twenty-three subdivisions across fourteen districts. The majority of Bengali-speaking Muslims in Assam live in char areas, where they suffer from poverty, illiteracy, ill health, and poor infrastructure. State development policies systematically exclude and neglect this population, rendering it the most vulnerable in the region. Moreover, the prejudice against Muslims as "illegal migrants" reduces—if not demolishes—char dwellers' socio-spatial mobility, but the possibility of flood and erosion is naturally higher in the areas where they live than on Assam's plains, and the government never resettles them after floods and land erosion even in normal cases. Thus, many refugee camp inhabitants have lost their land to flooding and are unable to imagine a home to return to. For many others, fear of militant attacks in their villages keeps them in the camps: many people told me that Bodos have now occupied their land and there is no option of going back. Finally, many inmates lost their land records, burned along with their houses during the violence. Some were living on government-owned land and now cannot legally reclaim their habitats (Figure 11.1).

The lack of proper documents led to further crisis when the state initiated the massive detention of "illegal migrants" in the form of the NRC's bureaucratic

Figure 11.1 Muslims who live in the Char areas of Assam; photo by Salah Punathil.

procedure. In my last visit to Assam, in December 2019, a few months after the NRC's final list was published, I found that it did not include many camp inhabitants: the required documents are not available to them or the documents they have shown have been deemed invalid. Many of them had great difficulty in providing all of the many necessary documents during the whole bureaucratic procedure of the NRC. The prejudice, arbitrariness, and contradictions in the bureaucratic process and state enactment of "migrant illegality" through the NRC in Assam are widely discussed. The NRC's procedural requirements often forced inmates who migrated for a better livelihood to return to their camps. Even before the NRC, Assam had created the category of D voters (doubtful voters), who live in fear of detention.[9] In addition to the previous misery of life in the relief camps, now there is the threat of being sent to "detention camps," which the Indian government is already constructing in Assam and across the country. In fact, there are already a few temporary detention centers housed in the jails of Assam where suspected migrants are detained for years.

Movement and Mobility in the Camps

Camps are not always static spaces, as we see in Agamben's formulation. Movement and mobility away from them are possible. Inmate narratives reveal that a few affluent people among those affected by violence left the camps long ago and settled in other places. Most camp dwellers work in construction in nearby areas, and some are migrant laborers who live elsewhere in Assam or in other states to meet their economic needs. A few have moved to India's southernmost states, like Kerala. Among them are manual laborers; some have even been able to move with their families, but they occasionally go back to visit the camp. Many people wish to retain their identity as camp dwellers, even if they can leave their camp, because they believe that someday the government will compensate the inmates with land or money. As Feldman (2015) illustrates, camps are also emotional spaces, and people have connections to the ones where they have stayed over a long period, even if they have found a new residence elsewhere.

When I revealed during my fieldwork that I am from Kerala of South India, a camp inhabitant phoned his younger brother, who had migrated to that state few years back, and made me talk to him; I was astonished that he spoke Malayalam, Kerala's regional language. This offers an interesting insight on how migration from a camp to elsewhere in the country, at least for a few, becomes a way to rid themselves of the suffering and humiliation they have experienced in Assam: their narratives reveal how this shift affords not only better economic prospects but also the opportunity to lead a dignified life. Even if the economic prospects are not so great, in cities and other places distant from Assam, they do not frequently encounter the label of "Bangladeshi" or other such everyday humiliations. While the segregated settlement of Bengali Muslims in some cities and fast-growing "Bangladeshi migration threat" propaganda across the country occasionally reproduce their experiences back in the camp, states like Kerala are still far better places for those migrants from the camps.

The Khagrabari Massacre of 2014 and New Camp

Khagrabari is a small locality in Assam's Baksa district, lying between the deep forest of Manas National Park and the Beki River. The river isolates this small site where Muslims live from the nearby villages. In the first week of May 2014, Bodo militants inflicted carnage on Kokrajhar, Baksa, Chirang, and other parts of Assam's BTAD, in a meticulously planned attack that killed forty-one people and left Khagrabari ablaze. Strikingly, most of the victims were women and children. Khagrabari, which is now officially the site of a camp, had all the features of a camp even before this violence. After losing their homes to flooding and erosion, a few Bengali-speaking Muslims moved into this place, which was then government land without any inhabitants. It is significant that such pushes into isolated spaces are a response to the suspicion and stereotyping of Muslims as "Bangladeshi illegal migrants." When the Beki River washed away their land and their livelihood of commercial agriculture, they ventured into an alternative means of subsistence, collecting both floating wood from the river and cotton scattered in the forest. This place is a perfect example of the camp-like spaces[10] where migrant Muslims in Assam live, plagued by poverty, health crises, illiteracy, and lack of proper shelter and completely excluded from state protection and welfare schemes for the poor. Some Muslim families here had experienced violence at the hands of Bodos in their home village and found refuge in this isolated place in their helpless situation (Figure 11.2).

The militant attack on May 2, 2014, made the camp-like space of Khagrabari become a real camp, protected by army security personnel. Some families lost more than one member in the massacre, bullets injured many people, and most of the houses were burned down. Now this camp has temporary shelters and day-to-day life goes on with help from the government's gracious relief and from

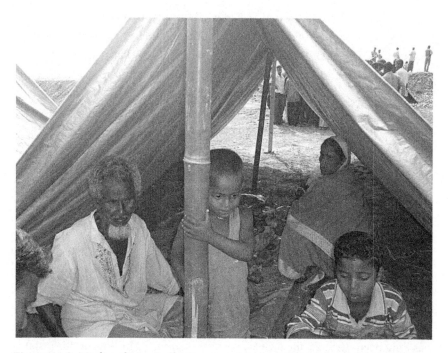

Figure 11.2 Muslims living in the temporary camp in Khagrabari after the violence in 2014; photo by Salah Punathil.

NGOs. While narrating this violent incident, camp dwellers told me that around forty people whose faces were covered with black cloths had entered the village and started firing at people and that the perpetrators included forest guards from the national park who are part of the Bodo community. The villagers said that these guards were known quite well to them and often used to interact with them in a friendly manner. They were shocked to see the forest guards joining with the militants and brutally attacking them in an afternoon. It was a special market day, and most of the men were not at home. Notably, among the thirty-eight dead, twenty were children. When the shooting started, villagers ran toward the river and jumped into it to save themselves from attack; however, they couldn't swim and were shot in the water instead. Asjiran Nercha, a woman survivor in the camp, recalled:

> When I was plucking leaves in front of my house, there was shooting from the forest. Then again, I heard shooting so near and wondered why it was happening so nearby. Then I went to the riverbank looking for my son. I saw from the riverbank that people were swimming across the river towards the other side and a few gunmen were standing and firing at the people who were swimming across the river.[11]

An elderly survivor told me that he had lived through Bodo attacks twice in two decades: "I was injured in the 1994 attack of Bodo militants," he said, indicating a mark on his shoulder. "While I lost my mother in the 1994 attack, I lost my sister in the Khagrabari Massacre."[12] The stories inside the camp reveal that women are the most traumatized of all. Many women whose children were killed right in front of them have a strong sense of guilt and remorse at having failed to save them. A sense of helplessness permeates their life today, as they are not able to find meaning in it.

Organizational Inventions among Muslims

Camp life in Khagrabari tells the story of how NGOs play an important role in helping inhabitants overcome the trauma of violence and get back to a normal life, offering facilities and immediate material support. Uddipana Goswami, in her work on internally displaced persons (IDPs) in Assam (2008), argues that NGOs often neglect Muslim camps for religious and political reasons. While this has long been the case, the NGO involvement among Muslims in this instance shows a shift in the situation. Unlike in the 1990s, in 2012 and 2014 many relief camps were closed within a few months of the attacks, as the post-violent condition of Muslims had clearly changed. This must be read in the context of a new political awareness and assertions being made within the population of Bengali-speaking Muslims in Assam. They pressured the state to rehabilitate the victims to their villages and played a key role in ensuring security and support for them.

In an interview, Abdul Razzak (pseudonym), member of a Guwahati-based NGO, explained the interventions that this organization, which works among Muslims in Assam, has made in the Khagrabari camp.[13] NGO associates offered special psychosocial support programs for children to overcome their trauma. Razzak said that many sports programs and games they led for the children of victims were crucial in bringing them back to normal life after the extremely shocking experience of violence. Similarly, NGOs and other organizations provided food and other basic amenities on the days when the attacks occurred. They also acted as mediators between state agencies and camp inhabitants in demanding and establishing relief facilities. But, perhaps more important, the Guwahati-based NGO's wing has helped the victims to follow court procedures to obtain justice. They pressured the administration and wrote letters urging Assam's chief minister not to delay the legal proceedings. They also offered guidance to victims before their court appearances to give testimony, as seen in the motto "Sach bolo, saaf bolo" (Speak truth, speak clearly), which the legal wing circulated among the victims. Ahmed (pseudonym), a lawyer and activist, claims that it was because of pressure from the Jhai Foundation that the National Investigation Agency filed a charge sheet on the ninth day of the incident and began a trial.[14] It was also lawyers and activists who brought eyewitnesses to Guwahati, Assam's largest city, where the trial took place. Interviews with these victims reveal the significance of such efforts. One woman victim, who lost her son, described her horrible experiences in the attack and then in court:

> My son was killed at close range. He had been hiding in the water, but for some reason he came back to the shore. One of the forest guards involved in the attack shot my son at close range. I saw my son pleading with the killer to spare him, as he was known to my son. The forest guard used to come to the village for tea or betel nuts. I was watching the incident from behind some bushes. I broke down in court while I was narrating the incident. At that moment, the lawyer who was defending the criminals accused me of lying. But I stayed firm and asked the lawyer whether he was present at the incident to be able to say that I was lying.[15]

Another woman described a similar experience of testifying in court about the violence she had endured:

> I jumped into the water with my baby to save myself. While one person kept shooting bullets towards me, I kept diving in the water and occasionally coming up to breathe. In the process, my baby died. The lawyer who defended the accused asked me a weird question about how many bullets were fired. I asked him whether I should have saved my life or counted the bullets.[16]

The Khagrabari case is still ongoing. Victims told me that they occasionally travel to the Guwahati High Court to participate in the process in order to obtain justice.

Although organizational interventions have had some impact on the lives of Muslims affected by violence, the case of Khagrabari shows that camps may persist as long as the state is reluctant to intervene in the crisis of violence-affected Muslims. When I first visited Khagrabari, in July 2016, security police were staying very close to the camp, in temporarily arranged tents and small cottages. But during my visit in December 2019, the government called these officers back, and only three or four police were seen staying there. Camp dwellers have said that this move by the state has only increased their fear and insecurity. In addition, I did not see any substantial changes in their living conditions. If the histories of older camps are any indication, there will not be any security police at this camp in the near future.

Conclusion

The experience of violence and camp life by Muslims in Assam cannot be comprehended adequately if we reduce the issue to a question of their identity as either Muslims or migrants. The notion that Bengali-speaking Muslims are predominantly "Bangladeshis" is a construction deeply embedded in both the long-term otherness of Muslims ingrained in India's religious nationalism (Van der Veer 2005) and the discourse of migrant "illegality" (De Genova 2002) in Assam. In most of the recent situations of ethnic assertion and attacks in which Muslims have been killed, the violent events were immediately framed as communal (religious) conflicts. Thus, it is impossible to decouple the Muslim identity of "migrants" from the "migrant" identity of Muslims when they become an experiment in violent political strategy to challenge the state and society. Camps represent the epitome of Muslims' experience of violence and marginalization. The history of Muslims' perpetual violent experiences and the reality of their being invariably marginalized after each attack make the camps in Assam important sites for analysis.

The empirical evidence in this chapter allows us a more nuanced understanding of the camp in the present than what Agamben proposed. The status of migrant Muslims in camps in India is paradoxical and complex. It is not the state that is directly responsible for the violence in Assam's history, as Agamben's formulation for the Western context proposes; rather, ethnic groups assume sovereign power to kill migrant populations, as posited by Mbembe (2003), and the state is complicit in the perpetuation of this violence. In this context, the government establishes camps as spaces of relief. However, they acquire the character of permanent sites of suffering as victims of violence continue to inhabit them for decades and are unable to lead normal lives. Camps also become easy targets of further violence by militant ethnic groups as the state refrains from protecting them. Symbolic violence thus permeates their life, as there is always the possibility of further physical attack: one ethnographic insight from the camps is the fear that seizes inhabitants whenever ethnic tensions and political crisis intensify in the region. Camps symbolize the space of "illegal migrants," and hence their inhabitants are subjected to everyday humiliation. Camps are also sites of structural violence: poverty, disease, illiteracy, unemployment, exclusion from state policies, and alienation from the mainstream expose the inmates to endless suffering. The biopolitics of camps—the governing of a violence-afflicted population by confining it to a space of relief—normalizes both structural and everyday violence and suffering. This suffering is reinforced through systematic exclusion, experienced in both lack of attention from the state and discriminatory practices. In other words, the distinction between thanatopolitics and biopolitics is blurred in this instance.

It is also clear that camps are not necessarily static spaces, nor reducible to mere biological life in a concentrated space under sovereign power, as in Agamben's (1998: 15, 87) formulation: his neat distinction between *zoë* (biological life) and *bios* (political life) is unsettled here, as the condition of migrants and other "unwanted" populations is more complex and confusing today (Fassin 2007; Feldman 2015). Fassin (2007) has challenged the static notion of the "bare life" of migrant populations in the contemporary world, demonstrating how some migrants acquire political recognition in changing sociopolitical circumstances and with new state policies and interventions. Ayse Parla's (2019) recent work has shown the potential of the idea of "hope" and social transformation even while analyzing precarious social conditions. Insights from camps in Assam reveal the socio-spatial mobility of individuals, as some have managed to move to metropolitan cities and places such as India's southernmost state, Kerala, for better livelihoods, and some have managed to leave camp life forever. In this context, life in camp is not completely enclosed and immobile, even if a large section of inhabitants continues to live in the same space. Similarly, camp dwellers have begun to articulate political rights over time, using different platforms. The involvement of various organizations, especially NGOs, in the recent past has brought some changes to the camp life of Muslims in Assam. Their new calls for justice show the community's emergent political voice and its conscious attempts to register resentment in the larger political sphere. While these are instances of hope and possibilities for positive changes in the lives of migrants, especially those in camps, a reverse scenario could also come true: migrants' political rights could also diminish in new political circumstances. For example, the recent publication of the NRC and passage of the Citizenship (Amendment) Act demands attention to an increasingly confusing and complex situation, in which Muslims are being pushed further to the margins of the nation-state. To sum up, camps are important sites of ethnographic analysis in the context of heightened migrant regime and a crisis of violence; it is such descriptive projects that will allow us to expand the horizon of the idea of a camp.

Acknowledgments

I thank Peter van der Veer and Birgit Meyer for their valuable comments, which helped me improve this chapter. I am also thankful to the Max Planck Institute for the Study of Religious Diversity in Gottingen, for providing all the resources I needed to carry out this work. The UPE project "Archiving Marginalities in North East India," University of Hyderabad and the ICSSR project "Popular Imaginaries and Discourses on Politics in India: Exploring Cultural Narratives as Alternative Sites of Knowledge Construction" facilitated to carry out the fieldwork in the initial phase of this research. I am also grateful to Abdul Kalam Azad and many other friends in Assam for their persistent support in carrying out the field work.

Accommodating Religious Diversity

Micro-Politics of Spatial Separation in German Refugee Accommodation Centers

Alexander-Kenneth Nagel

Introduction

In early 2017, the world held its breath as US president Donald Trump announced his infamous #muslimban, an executive order which denied immigration to (Muslim) refugees from Syria and citizens of six other predominantly Muslim countries. The year before, at the height of the so-called refugee crisis, several Eastern European countries, such as Slovakia and Hungary, had been deadly serious about not letting Muslim refugees in, pointing to both their own Christian heritage and the lack of preexisting religious infrastructure for Muslims. While this strategic rediscovery of Christian roots in some of the most secularized countries in Europe may appear somehow ironic—or even cynical—it forms part of a broader trend of reemphasizing religious boundaries as collective identity markers (Dahinden/Zittoun 2013). Likewise, the German discussion about refugee accommodation has extensively addressed the risk of interreligious conflicts in refugee camps. Some (of the more conservative) voices argued for a spatial separation along religious lines in order to protect religious minorities, whereas others strongly opposed this religious apartheid model and advocated that refugees had to be able to deal with the realities of a multireligious society from the very beginning. Regardless of the political preference for protection or conviviality, the examples underline the relevance of religious differences in public debates about refugees. At the same time, academic research on the significance and role of religion for refugees is still quite limited. In Germany, recent research endeavors were overshadowed by political discourses about the social and structural integration of refugees, which has translated into research projects on their participation in the educational system or the labor market (OECD 2017; Schroeder and Seukwa 2017). Other studies are exploring the attitudes and values of or vis-à-vis refugees, often driven by concerns of deviant behavior or radicalization (Feltes et al. 2018; Plener et al. 2017).

In this chapter, I will analyze the handling of religious diversity and practice in German accommodation centers from an institutionalist perspective and with particular emphasis on the material culture of these centers. In the following paragraphs, I will provide a brief overview of the religious patterns of recent refugee immigration to Germany and use the second section to outline my conceptual approach as well as the research design of the project I draw on. In the empirical part of the chapter, I will present results on the religious topographies of accommodation centers, temporary forms of religious space making, such as religious festivals, the micro-politics of separation as well as the memory culture and musealization of the camps themselves. In the fourth and final section, I will draw some conclusions, evaluate my conceptual approach, and explore avenues for further investigation.

Between the years 2014 and 2017, the Federal Office for Migration and Refugees registered 1,535,658 first-time applications for asylum. While the figure of 722,370 first-time applications in 2016 marks an annual all-time high in the history of postwar Germany, it must not be forgotten that there have been strong conjunctures of immigration before. After the Second World War, at least twelve million expellees from the former German territories in the East had to find a new home, and between the years 1991 and 1993, more than one million refugees from the Yugoslav Wars applied for asylum in Germany. Recent refugee immigration has also been strongly driven by violent conflicts as a glance at the countries of origin reveals: since 2014, Syria has taken a sad first place with 513,213 applicants, followed by Afghanistan (183,932), Iraq (153,175), Albania (76,523), and Eritrea (53,154). In all of these countries, Muslims form a religious majority (more so in Afghanistan where nine out of ten residents belong to a Sunni tradition and less so in Eritrea and Albania). Although the religious profile of countries of origin can by no means be used as an exact predictor of the religious affiliation of emigrants, the figures suggest that many of the recent refugees belong to some branch of Islam. Between the years 2010 and 2017, the German Federal Office for Migration and Refugees has published data on the religious affiliation of asylum seekers (see Figure 12.1).

Four points can be highlighted: First, ever since 2010, a clear majority of asylum seekers in Germany were Muslims, mainly from the Middle East

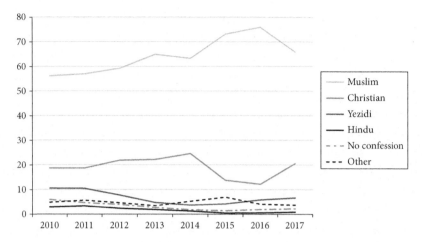

Figure 12.1 Religious affiliation of asylum applicants; created by Alexander K. Nagel.

and the Balkans. Second, from 2010 to 2016, the proportion of Muslims has increased from 57 to 73 percent. Third, the high proportion of Muslim immigrants marks a certain change in the religious immigration profile of Germany. Even though there is a history of recruitment contracts with Muslim countries, such as Turkey or Morocco, many of the labor migrants after the Second World War were Christian. Fourth, the relative decline of Christian and Yezidi asylum seekers is due to the high absolute numbers of Syrian applicants since 2014 and hence should not be interpreted as a general trend. The absolute numbers of Yezidi and Christian refugees have, in fact, roughly remained the same.

All in all, these figures point to a shift in the religious profile of refugee immigration to Germany: in a comprehensive study on the living conditions of accepted refugees who arrived between 2008 and 2012, Christians (mainly from Eritrea and Iran) still formed the majority of refugees (37 percent), followed by Yezidis from Iraq (28 percent) and Muslims from Syria and Afghanistan (17 percent). The study also indicated that Christian and Yezidi refugees rated their religiosity higher than Muslim refugees: while four out of five Christians and Yezidis classified their religious beliefs as "very strong" or "rather strong," the same applies only to one out of two Muslim respondents (Worbs et al. 2016: 209). These results may reflect the specific emigration history of Christians and Yezidis as restricted or even persecuted religious minorities who now make extensive use of their religious freedom. At the same time, they underline that Muslim refugees are not particularly religious as far as they were part of a religious majority in their countries of origin.

Nevertheless, refugee immigration is likely to contribute to a further pluralization of the German religious field and will most likely result in a slightly higher share of the Muslim population. By the end of 2016, the Federal Office for Migration published an estimation of about 4.5 million Muslims in Germany (roughly 5.5 percent of the overall population). Hence, the question comes up whether and how the refugee accommodation system in Germany is equipped to respond to the religious needs of Muslim (and other non-Christian) refugees. On the one hand, the corporatist nature of the German state is based on a benevolent understanding of religious neutrality. Unlike the laicist model in France or the disestablishment model in the United States, the German polity is based on the cooperation between state actors and religious communities as long as they meet certain organizational demands to form a corporation of public law. On the other hand, it is likely that the religious illiteracy of administrators and social service staff may result in a sense of uncertainty and thus translate into a more restrictive policy vis-à-vis non-Christian religious traditions. In the following section, I will further elaborate my research question and the conceptual approach of the chapter.

Religious Diversity and Practice in Refugee Accommodation Centers: Combining Institutionalist and Material Culture Approaches

As outlined earlier, there has been a close connection between religious conflict in refugee accommodation centers and measures of spatial separation. As a consequence, it seems reasonable to explore the spatial and other material aspects of the organization of refugee accommodation. To this aim, I will combine an institutionalist perspective on religious diversity in public institutions with a material culture approach accounting for the spatial and sensual nature of religious presence in refugee accommodation centers. So far, the sociology of organization has largely neglected the material shape of organizations and focused mainly on artifacts (such as letterheads) as an expression of their corporate identity (Froschauer 2009). Therefore, the chapter can also be read as a test case for the potentials of a material culture perspective for the interpretative study of organizations.

Institutionalist perspective: In recent years, there has been an emerging body of research on religious diversity in various kinds of organizations, such as hospitals, prisons, and the military (Griera and Martínez-Ariño 2014; Roy and Becci 2015). Earlier approaches envisaged these organizations mainly as a lens to analyze national regimes of religion at work (and hence aimed at a country-comparative perspective), whereas a newer strand of research has complemented this perspective with a focus on the idiosyncratic nature of complex, functional specific organizations, and their creative solutions in dealing with religious diversity. In this vein, scholars have taken an increasing interest in the qualifications and competences which are necessary for a professional perception and handling of religious needs often referred to as "religious literacy" (e.g., Dinham and Francis 2016). While it is not always clear whether religious literacy is restricted to the cognitive dimension of knowledge *about* religion(s) or also extends to informal habitual manners of dealing *with* religious practices or even a positive normative stance *toward* religion, many seem to agree that professionals in different branches of public administration are confronted with their own religious *il*literacy as the religious field becomes more complex. In some cases, this leads to an *intensified collaboration* with religious or interreligious communities (Griera/Forteza 2011; Koers/Nagel 2018). Another institutional response could be the *restriction* of religious practice and presence. It is likely that the securitization of some religious traditions, such as Islam, may reinforce such a restrictive handling of religion. In this chapter, I analyze the organizational behavior vis-à-vis religion by investigating the experiences and interpretations of the staff of refugee accommodation centers. As a consequence, I will rely on semi-structured interviews with administrators, social workers, and security staff, whereas I will not refer to the perspective of the residents themselves.

Material culture perspective: Political debates about refugees and religion were driven by a strong notion of exclusive spatiality. Nation-states as well as accommodation centers were broadly conceived of as territories which could only bear a limited number or particular kind of religions. Hence, the topic of religious diversity in refugee accommodation centers lends itself to a *spatial analysis* of the religious geographies in which the centers are embedded practices of religious space making as well as micro-politics of conviviality and separation. Drawing on Kim Knott (2008: 1109–10), I aim at understanding the "configuration" of accommodation centers in terms of their extension, that is, the "way in which 'stratified places' reveal the traces of earlier times and different ethnic and religious regimes" in a given space, simultaneity, that is, their "synchronic interconnections with other sites" as well as sites of power struggles. Another important facet of material analysis are the *aesthetic formations* of and within refugee accommodation centers. According to Birgit Meyer (2009: 7), the concept of aesthetic formation refers to "the formative impact of a shared aesthetics though [*sic*] which subjects are shaped by tuning their senses, inducing experiences, molding their bodies, and making sense, and which materializes in things." While the spatial approach sheds light on the religious topographies in which accommodation centers are situated as well as the micro-politics of separation, the aesthetic approach elucidates the role of sensorial practices and perceptions for religious space making, for example through religious festivals, and for processes of group-related religious or ethnic labeling.

In the following sections, I will make use of these conceptual tools and address the research question "how do refugee accommodation centers deal with religious diversity and practice?" in three operational dimensions: First, I will look at practices of musealization as a mode of reflection on and legitimation of accommodation centers in order to shed light on the temporal dimension of stratified places. Second, I will investigate—what I call—the religious topographies of accommodation centers, for example their spatial relation to sacred sites like churches or chapels, and examine processes of temporary space making in the course of religious festivals and the concerns of the staff to regulate religious "emissions." Third, I will address the aesthetic implications of labeling and conflict as well as the spatial micro-politics of separation within accommodation centers.

I will draw on empirical data which was gathered in a pilot project on "Religious Diversity and Practice in Refugee Accommodation Centers in Lower Saxony."[1] At this point, it is also important to note two restrictions in terms of data gathering: First, due to the institutionalist focus, we did not conduct interviews with refugees. As a consequence, we can only observe religious grounds of difference through the eyes of the staff. Second, we did not systematically gather data on material culture (e.g., through images or a thick description of sensual impressions in field notes), but included the spatial and aesthetic dimension as categories of content analysis.

Memory Culture and Musealization: The Border Transit Camp in Friedland

At a first glance, it may seem a bit odd to address the aspect of memory culture in a chapter on how refugee accommodation centers respond to religious diversity. Yet it is only consequential for an institutionalist perspective, which is sensitive to material culture, to treat sites and objects of memory culture as meaningful part of the organizational environment, which contributes to the legitimacy of an organization. Hence, in line with Kim Knott´s suggestions for spatial analysis I look at the memory sites attached to refugee accommodation centers as diachronically "'stratified places' (which) reveal the traces of earlier times and different ethnic and religious regimes" (Knott 2008: 1109). I argue that memory culture and musealization are vehicles to frame and administer the history and identity of refugee camps and to renegotiate the national self-understanding of Germany as an immigration country. In the following I will concentrate on the Border Transit Camp in Friedland and consider both objects of memory culture within the camp, a museum which is locally and topically directly attached to the camp and a huge monument (*"Heimkehrerdenkmal"*) as part of the memory culture of both the camp and the village as a whole (Baur 2014).

There are numerous objects and sites of memory culture on the camp territory or in its direct neighborhood: in the center of the camp, right in front of the dining hall, one of the original houses, a so-called Nissen hut, has been preserved. A small museum in itself, the hut contained some of the original furniture and was supposed to illustrate how life in the camp was like "back then." Other important sites of memory culture are the Lutheran Camp Chapel as well as the Friedland Bell (see Figures 12.2 and 12.3). The camp chapel has been an integral part of the camp since its inauguration in 1949 and is widely regarded as part of the "tradition" of the camp. At the same time, it is still in use and equipped with half a chaplain position. The "camp pastor" offers counseling which is not restricted to Protestants or even Christians and holds regular worship services. Furthermore, the chapel is used by Mennonite preachers and Brethren Congregations, who address the spiritual needs of many ethnic German immigrants from the former Soviet Union. Last, but not least, the Friedland Bell constitutes one of the most powerful objects of memory culture on the campground. The iron bell which weighs 700 kilograms was donated to the camp in 1949 by German expellees and was rung not only for services in the camp chapel but also to greet soldiers who were returning from war captivity between 1953 and 1956. The bell quickly turned into a central symbol for the camp and the German postwar history of expulsion and became an important focus of various practices of place making (Schießl 2016: 288–9). Not only was it sent on a journey throughout Germany to be rung at commemoration meetings of expellees, but its sound was broadcasted via radio and the organist of the camp chapel composed a song for the bell which called for the return of German war prisoners and settlers from the Soviet territories ("ruft die Friedlandglocke in die Welt hinaus / Laßt die deutschen Brüder heim ins Vaterhaus"; see Schießl 2016: 290).

Figure 12.2 Lutheran "Camp Chapel"; photo by Alexander K. Nagel.

As a matter of fact, the symbolic weight of the Friedland Bell is also palpable in the Museum Friedland, which was opened in 2016 and pays audiovisual homage to the bell in numerous pictures and video installations (see Figure 12.4)

According to its mission statement, the "Museum Friedland explores, secures, presents and conveys the past and present of Friedland Transit Camp. In addition, it focuses on the complex processes of farewell, arrival and new beginnings in general, as well as various aspects of migration policy, social participation, borders, identities and affiliations, consequences of war, human rights and asylum, both in the historical and contemporary perspective."[2]

The multilayered statement expresses the intention to expand the boundaries of memory culture in Friedland beyond the postwar history of expulsion and

Figure 12.3 Vista from Friedland Bell to St. Norbert Church; photo by Alexander K. Nagel.

resettlement and to reframe the camp as well as the village as landmarks of immigration and multiculturalism. The permanent exhibition starts with the postwar history of the camp in the first floor and traces the more recent stages of the German immigration history in the second floor (e.g., Vietnamese "boat people" and political refugees from Chile).[3] Given the strong connection to the Border Transit Camp which takes form in a "Museum Trail," a tour through the premises of the camp by a former resident, the museum has to perform a balancing act between embracing the powerful *spiritus loci* of the camp with its heavy and sometimes reactionary connotations of "liberation" and carefully redefining it based on tropes of a new beginning and the immigration society as an inclusive and participatory project.

Figure 12.4 Video installation of the Friedland Bell; photo by Alexander K. Nagel.

To make the memory cultural ensemble even more complex, the Association of Expellees (*Bund der Vertriebenen*) has erected a huge memorial site on an elevation close to the Border Transit Camp (see Figure 12.5). The memorial consists of four winglike concrete gates of 28 meters and can be seen from afar (e.g., the nearby highway) due to its monumentality and elevated location. In the interpretation of the Association of Expellees, the gates represent "gates to freedom" and thus tie in with the discourse of liberation which is connected to the postwar history of the camp. Attached to the gates there are twelve panels indicating the origin of the memorial ("In 1967 expellees established this memorial") and meticulously accounting for the (German) victims of the Second World War. In one gate, there is embedded a bell which resembles the original Friedland Bell (Schwelling 2008: 201).[4]

Figure 12.5 Memorial of expellees (Heimkehrerdenkmal); photo by Thorbjoern at German Wikipedia (CC BY-SA 3.0).

It is beyond the scope of this chapter to describe the memory cultural ensemble in more detail. Without doubt, the high density of memory cultural sites and approaches in Friedland is peculiar and corresponds to the "symbolic loading of the location of Friedland as 'emotional space,' 'area of security and comfort' and 'homeland myth'" (Schwelling 2008: 193, translation AKN). However, we can see similar attempts of musealizing and cultivating histories of immigration in other contexts, too, for example, an exhibition entitled "On the run" (*"Auf der Flucht"*) at the reception center in Braunschweig based on photographs by UNHCR staff and journalists,[5] or a memorial site at the former refugee reception center in Marienfelde.[6] In both cases, the "authentic location" is used as an argument to advertise the exhibition which underlines the complex nature of refugee accommodation centers as "stratified places" as indicated by Kim Knott and shows that "traces of earlier times" are not just present in a sense of archaeological sediments, but are carefully curated in order to craft actual discourses about immigration. Furthermore, the example of the Friedland Bell illustrates the prominence of aesthetic formations in the cultivation of national memories of immigration as visual, haptic, and auditive impressions are blended together to purport the myth of the Border Transit Camp.

Religious Topographies of Refugee Accommodation Centers

The spatial arrangements and context of accommodation centers are closely associated with their handling of religious diversity and practice. First of all, this refers to the *premises* of the centers themselves. Some of the centers in the sample were just larger single buildings with a limited area for communal use around them. In particular this holds true for smaller emergency shelters, which were established in school buildings or hotels, and municipal accommodation centers. In contrast, many of the state reception centers are designed to host more than 1,000 residents and therefore often consist of a number of different buildings. For example, the state reception center in Braunschweig encompasses six houses on 64,000 square meters and has a regular capacity of 973 beds. Likewise, the Border Transit Camp in Friedland has a regular capacity of 820 beds which are distributed over twelve houses (see below for an illustration). Both centers accommodate refugees in bedrooms with two to six beds. Despite their similarities, the centers differ significantly in their overall location and environment: while the first is located at the Northern rim of Braunschweig, a multicultural city with almost 250,000 residents, the latter is part of the village of Friedland with about 1,300 residents.

Apart from its edificial structure, the spatial *context* of an accommodation center strongly determines its religious geography. While Braunschweig has six (mainly Turkish) mosques which can be reached by bike in less than half an hour, residents in Friedland have to travel 14 kilometers to Göttingen in order to find a mosque. At the same time, the Border Transit Camp itself exhibits a variety of religious sites, as Figure 12.6 shows.

Figure 12.6 is an outtake of the official sitemap which shows the eastern part of the camp with quarters (blue), the dining hall (orange), and a couple of public buildings (green). Among the public buildings, there is—what I call—the *Spiritual Triangle*, which connects the three main religious sites of the camp, namely, the Roman Catholic St. Norbert Church (Figure 12.7), the Lutheran Camp Chapel (Figure 12.2), and the Friedland Bell (see Figure 12.3). As pointed out in the previous section, the bell is an integral part of the memory culture and musealization of the camp. Originally, it was part of the camp chapel and rung for the return of German postwar soldiers (*Heimkehrer*) in the early 1950s. Since 1970, the bell is attached to a steel frame which is marked by a prominent yellow cross. The Catholic Church is not situated at the campground, but in its direct neighborhood and supposed to cater the spiritual needs of villagers as well as camp residents. To reach out to the latter, the parish employs an

Figure 12.6 Sitemap of the Border Transit Camp, Friedland.

Arab-speaking deacon who has become an important contact person for many Syrian and Iraqi refugees, regardless of their faith. Last, but not least, the camp chapel is situated on the premises of the camp itself and exclusively directed to its residents.

Whereas the prominent Christian infrastructure in Friedland is a result of the specific history of the Border Transit Camp (see previous section), it is remarkable since almost all directors of state accommodation centers in our sample have emphasized a restrictive notion of religious neutrality as a basic principle of their work. In most cases, religious neutrality meant that collective and visible forms of religious practice (such as the Muslim Jumu'ah prayer) were not allowed on the public premises of the center (in contrast to private religious practice within the rooms). While most centers would not offer religious facilities

Figure 12.7 Roman Catholic Church St. Norbert; photo by Alexander K. Nagel.

like prayer rooms, the staff referred non-Christian (mostly Muslim and Yezidi) refugees to mosques or community houses in the neighborhood. Several social workers mentioned that they had a list with addresses of mosques and other (mostly religious) migrant self-organizations which they would share with residents upon request. In two cases, the staff mentioned that they had consulted with intelligence authorities (*Staatsschutz*) about which mosques to include in the list. This points to a high degree of uncertainty vis-à-vis Muslim actors and the prevalence of a discourse of securitization which responds to an increased public awareness for Islamic radicalization.

The spiritual triangle in Friedland is an obvious example that the restrictive notion of religious neutrality was not consistently applied. At the same time, the prominent Christian presence through churches, confessional welfare associations and Christian volunteers was to be found elsewhere, too. For example, some directors of emergency shelters were referring to a close exchange with neighboring churches and the state accommodation center in Oldenburg is situated in an old monastery. Social workers and church representatives underlined that Muslim refugees should feel invited to make use of the church or chapel for a moment of silent prayer or contemplation. In Friedland, it was reported that the Roman Catholic Sunday service was frequently attended by Muslim refugees as the deacon provided Arab translation. At the same time, one interview partner suggested that plans by local Muslims to build a small mosque or hold a public prayer in the village had faced severe and fundamental opposition. As a consequence, Muslim residents in Friedland were supposed to travel to nearby Göttingen in order to visit a mosque, although they had no money to purchase the train ticket.[7]

There are more examples to show how the restrictive understanding of religious neutrality was contested from many sides: First, some centers would register the religious affiliation of their residents even though it was not supposed to play a role for their accommodation. Second, all centers sought to provide "halal" food. Some externalized the responsibility by relying on the "halal" designation by external caterers and some just did not offer pork products. Third, many centers and emergency shelters collaborated closely with Christian parishes (both mainline and evangelical) to organize additional activities for the residents, such as sports, handicrafts, and preliminary German classes. Fourth, many of our respondents reported extensive missionary activism by Jehova's Witnesses, which they regarded as inappropriate and therefore sought to prevent as far as possible. Despite widespread concerns of the staff about Islamist indoctrination and intensive information and training campaigns on Islamism and political extremism, none of our interview partners had recognized any Muslim da´wa activities.

Another form of religious presence which undermines the restrictive notion of religious neutrality is the *celebration of religious festivals*, such as Ramadan and Christmas. Unlike worship sites, these festivals can be regarded as *temporary instances of religious space making* within the centers. It is remarkable that almost all accommodation centers and emergency shelters in the sample have celebrated Ramadan and Christmas in a collective and public fashion. Ramadan was mainly perceived as a challenge in terms of gastronomic logistics since food had to be supplied at unusual times. In many cases, the staff handed out food bags and thus turned the (otherwise inherently public) act of eating into a private matter. More significantly, some centers organized—

or allowed for—feasts for Iftar (breaking the fast) or Eid al-Fitr. Some staff members indicated that they enjoyed what they perceived as "reverse hospitality" which allowed the residents to "give something back." This notion elucidates the usual role division between active and powerful professionals and passive and receptive residents which is temporarily being inverted in an almost carnevalesque fashion.

In another case, nocturnal Iftar celebrations led to trouble with neighbors outside the center who complained to the local authorities about the nighttime disturbance. A staff member gladly reported the decision of the municipality: "They (the municipality, AKN) have backed us up. [. . .] We cannot deny that to anyone. It is their right (*'gutes Recht'*), it is in the constitution and this is how it is done" (translation AKN). Two things are interesting here: first, the juggling with personal pronouns, in relation to the municipality refugees and staff form a common entity ("*they* have backed *us* up"), whereas the residents as claimants of their constitutional right form a "they" which is distinct from this collective "we"; second, there is no doubt whatsoever that Iftar and Ramadan are protected by the basic right to religious freedom and Muslims must be allowed to exercise their religion.

This latter aspect is particularly relevant in comparison to Christmas celebrations in accommodation centers. Some of our interview partners talked about initial hesitations, as they did not want to overwhelm the (mostly non-Christian) residents with Christian symbols. Most of these considerations have started with a very practical question: (Where) should we put up a Christmas tree? To augur the result, trees were put up in almost all centers in the sample, based on three main justifications. Some argued that they had to put a tree because of external pressures, be it the spiritual desires of volunteers or the need to display the Christian profile of the welfare association which was running the center. Others held that they had talked to the residents about their hesitations "and they did not mind" since they were "guests in this country." The most interesting justification, however, was to redefine Christmas as an event which (unlike Ramadan) is rather "cultural" than "religious." Following this line of reasoning, putting up a tree and other Christmas activities can be perceived as vehicles of cultural transfer and integration ("*Kulturtransport*") rather than expressions of a distinct religion. Likewise, the main argument for the Lutheran chapel in the Border Transit Camp in Friedland was that it had become part of the "tradition" of the camp.

In order to understand the specific modes of Ramadan and Christmas as incidents of religious space making within the centers, it is helpful to take a look at the *aesthetic formations* associated with these events. Quite clearly, the aesthetic formation of Ramadan was connected to sensual experiences of *commensality* during Iftar. Eating together became a medium to alleviate the strict role division between residents and staff members. In a similar vein, the neighbors who were complaining to the municipality were apparently disturbed in a very sensual way by the (auditive and olfactory) emissions of the feast. Hence, in my working understanding, *religious emissions* are sensual expressions of religious objects or practices which impose themselves on actors to a certain degree. In this regard, Advent and Christmas practices in the centers also had a strong sensual impact. Apart from Christmas trees, they comprised leisure activities for children, such as baking, storytelling, and handicraft works. Many centers also distributed Christmas gifts which were donated by external partners from local companies or parishes. These activities add up to a dense, tangible, and multisensory presence of Christmas in many centers which created an atmosphere that is hard to elude. As a consequence, some staff members sought to prevent Christian overwhelming through what could be called practices of *religious emission control*, for example, a Christmas tree is removed from the foyer to the staff room and gifts are distributed deliberately without any narrative connection to Christmas. In the following section, I will further follow the trail of spatial politics and aesthetic formations and take a look at the perception, solution, and prevention of interreligious and intercultural conflicts in the centers.

Interreligious Conflict and the Micro-politics of Separation

As I mentioned earlier, interreligious conflicts used to be a major issue in the German media at the climax of the so-called refugee crisis between 2015 and 2016. Most of these reports focused on assaults by Muslim residents or security staff (e.g., guards within the centers employed by private security companies) on Christian and Yezidi refugees. In one case, a mass riot was supposed to have started over someone ripping pages out of a Quran.[8] The evangelical platform OpenDoors has published a number of reports on the "Lack of protection for religious minorities [. . .] in German refugee shelters."[9] The reports, which faced severe criticism for shortcomings in methodology and empirical analysis, drew on a sample of Christian (and some Yezidi) refugees who had made use of an emergency hotline for persecuted Christians, offered by the Council of Oriental Christians in Germany. They suggested that assaults on Christian and Yezidi refugees by Muslim refugees and security staff were frequent and substantial—and called for separate accommodation. In contrast, a position paper by the German Institute for Human Rights (mainly based on investigations by the Christian mainline churches) concluded that "there is no systematic discrimination for religious reasons to be determined in refugee accommodation centers, neither through security staff nor through refugees themselves" (DIM 2016: 2).

These accounts show that the issue of interreligious conflicts in accommodation centers is highly contested which makes empirical investigation on the matter very difficult. This being said, it does not come as a surprise that the staff members in our sample almost unanimously denied the prevalence of group-related interreligious tensions or conflicts. Instead, they pointed to the liminal and existential situation of the refugees which could trigger personal animosities as the following quotation by a social worker from a Christian welfare association illustrates:

> We did have conflicts, but this was really marginal. There is a lot of talk about minorities, Christians, persecution and mobbing of Christians and so on. It's actually not true. [. . .] We have had mobbing for completely other reasons. And once again: when you put 250 or 300 people in a small spot who have different opinions ("*Ansichten*") or so, then this will just lead to discussions, quarrel. (Translation by author)

The quotation indicates that staff members are well aware of the political discourse and do not want to nourish it any further.[10] Instead of (group-related) "conflicts," the respondent prefers to speak of (individual) "mobbing." Variations of this guiding motif could be found in almost all centers in the sample. The striking similarity between the statements suggests that they are not (only) meant to be answers to our question, but (also) a generalized apologetic response to an overarching discourse. It is perhaps not surprising that distinct incidents of conflict were mainly reported by the security staff. For instance, a policeman who was responsible for a big state reception center mentioned an assault by (Muslim) refugees from Northern Africa on (Christian) refugees from Eritrea:

> So, the Eritreans were easy to be recognized for all as they had the darkest skin, and evidently in the Arab World this is already a reason to say: "this one is below me, I am the better human being," this was my impression. And they took them to terms one by one, beat them and cut the cross from their neck and said: "next time I will cut your throat."

This example shows how racist and religious dimensions of conflict may be intertwined. According to the respondent, the perpetrators started the quarrel because they felt racially superior to the Eritreans, whereas the violent incidents around the cross point to a religious dimension. The quotation also indicates how cultural stereotypes may shape the definition of a situation by the staff and thus inform organizational behavior: the essentialist reference to "the Arab World" is part of a wider polemic pattern against refugees from Northern Africa whom the interview partner regards as "notorious criminals."

All in all, such polemics were rare in the sample; however, many of our respondents referred to *culturalist stereotypes*, mainly based on essentialist notions of nationality or ethnicity. As a matter of fact, normative evaluations by the staff are both relevant insights (as far as the "logic" of the organization is concerned) and a methodological challenge (as far as understanding the nature of conflicts is concerned). In this vein, the policemen noted that he had only become aware of intrareligious tensions between Sunni and Shi´a Muslims through an interpreter. On the one hand, this is an interesting example of how religious illiteracy works within the centers, and in some cases, such kind of ignorance can even be an advantage as it prevents certain conflicts from becoming salient. On the other hand, it underlines that in the actual research design we can only perceive conflicts through the eye of the professionals, including their blind spots and biases.

It is no wonder that the police officer quoted earlier draws a connection between the (alleged) visual recognizability of the Eritreans and their vulnerability. In many cases, conflicts (and their perception in terms of culturalist stereotypes) were closely associated with particular *aesthetic formations*. A speaking example for this can be found in the following vignette on tensions between Afghan and Pakistani refugees, which was told by social workers from a municipal accommodation center:

> In the beginning there was nothing but ignorance, they did not even greet each other when they passed by, but sought for as much distance as possible [. . .] in order not to touch each other. Cooking together did not work out at all, therefore separate kitchen containers were provided, one for the Afghans and one for the Pakistanis, since they even did not want to cook next to each other. And the main reason was that the Afghans said that the Pakistanis smelled bad. Because they use other spices than the Afghans and that is very . . . a very intensive smell. It did smell when you got into the compartments, that is: the sleeping compartments. That is different. And they also did not care for hygiene as much as the Afghans or like you know it from us Germans, but dishes were not cleaned and only put into the corner just to fill it with another portion of soup. And that they sat on the ground to eat, the Pakistanis, that is; the Afghans have started

to sit at the table, were interested: how do I eat with knife and fork? May I eat with my mouth full? Which is so important for us Europeans, a bit like Knigge (classical German etiquette guide, AKN), yes, they really found it interesting how we do this. But the Pakistanis did not care for that at all.

I present the quotation in full length because it elucidates paradigmatically how culturalist stereotypes are being formed based on aesthetic formations and translate into organizational behavior. In the first part of the sequence, the social worker reports about animosities between refugees from Afghanistan and Pakistan, which led them to provide separate kitchen containers (and bathrooms). In the second part, he elaborates on the "reasons" for these animosities and comes up with two explanations: first, he refers to the (emic) explanation that the Afghans claimed the Pakistanis smelled bad which is combined with an (etic) confirmation: they do indeed smell "intensive" as they use "other spices." Second, he infers from different notions of hygiene to a more general difference in mentality: whereas "the Afghans" are more European and show an eagerness to adopt German eating habits, "the Pakistanis" are portrayed as dirty and ignorant vis-à-vis the culture of the host society. While in the first part, both Afghans and Pakistanis are collectively referred to as "they" (in opposition to the German/European "we"), there is a strong paternalistic narrative emerging in the latter part which polemically contrasts the "Afghan" attempts to integrate (i.e., to do as the Germans do) with "Pakistani" ignorance. The example points to a number of relevant mechanisms of conflict perception and solution: first, incidents of uneasiness or conflict are perceived or reported; second, groups are being labeled based on their (alleged) olfactory emissions; and third, measures of spatial separation are applied in order to solve the conflict.

As a matter of fact, separation was the most important means to solve or prevent conflicts. For analytical reasons, three aspects of separation can be distinguished: First, the reception authority of Lower Saxony (*Landesaufnahmebehörde*) partly allocated refugees to different state accommodation centers based on their country of origin, but not on religious grounds. However, as a spokesperson of the reception authority highlighted, the basic idea was to "create heterogeneity." Second, there is what I call the *spatial micro-politics* within the reception centers. While there was hardly any separation reported on religious grounds, separate accommodation based on matters of not only personal vulnerability (e.g., women and children) but also ethnic or national criteria, turned out to be quite frequent. In some cases, separation was a reaction to incidents of conflict; in other cases, it was used as a preventive measure.

Decisions about separate accommodation have to maneuver between who should be separated from whom and the given physical conditions and restraints of "separatability." The most widespread spatial units of separation were chambers, floors, and houses, whereas frequently separated parties included Afghans and Pakistanis, refugees from Iraq and Iran, as well as Northern Africa and Eritrea. Third, there is what I call "separatory interventions," that is, situative practices of separation in order to solve a particular problem. For instance, emergency shelters sometimes solved personal (including marital) disputes by temporarily sending one party to another shelter. In another case, metal fences were put up to avoid quarrel in the food queue, a notorious site of trouble.

Conclusions

In this chapter, I combined institutionalist and material culture approaches in order to account for the management of religious diversity in German refugee accommodation centers. It soon became clear that material aspects of religion, such as religious geographies, processes of religious space making and aesthetic formations associated with religious celebrations or other public forms of religious practice correspond with organizational behavior in many different ways.

First, and quite obvious, as the separation of groups and individuals turned out to be an important measure of conflict resolution and prevention, the physical structure of the premises of a center opens up certain options of "*separatability*" and delimits other ones. In this sense, it does make a difference, if 800 refugees are situated in a former barracks building (one house, two floors) or in twenty separate huts. Furthermore, there was evidence that the (lack of) religious literacy of the staff turned out to be crucial for an interreligious reading of personal or group-related conflict. To put it into a nutshell: the organization can only address conflict lines which their staff is able to perceive. In this sense, religious illiteracy may be thought of as an advantage as far as it prevents interreligious conflicts from becoming salient. At the same time, however, it is highly problematic as far as it fosters a hegemonial understanding of religious neutrality.

Second, refugee accommodation centers exhibit and are embedded in religious geographies of their own kind. Despite the restrictive reading of a doctrine of religious neutrality which banned all forms of religious presence from the public and confined it to the "private" (as little privacy as there is), many accommodation facilities had a church or chapel at their doorstep or even on their grounds. The same applied to Christian welfare associations, such as Diakonie and Caritas (the two biggest faith-based welfare associations in Germany), which run a number of accommodation centers and maintain clothing counters and helpdesks in many others. This strong and institutionalized Christian presence suggests that the restrictive stance toward religious neutrality is hegemonial in the sense that it privileges Christian actors as part of the "tradition" of a center and purports a religious geography with Christianity in the center and other religious traditions (namely Islam) at the margins.

Third, the relationship between materiality and organizational behavior cannot be reduced to the simple formula "Being determines Consciousness." Instead, we see various forms of religious space making, often connected to particular aesthetic formations. Although the public practice of religious rituals was prohibited in all accommodation centers in the sample, festivals such as Christmas and Ramadan were widely celebrated. Visible symbols like Christmas trees, auditive signs like the sound of Christmas songs or the joyful noise of an Iftar feast, haptic experiences like in distributing and unwrapping a gift and olfactory stimuli like the smell of freshly baked biscuits or a barbeque after sunset, all amount to peculiar aesthetic formations which are closely connected to social dynamics of commensality and community. At the same time, it is a characteristic of these—what I call—"religious emissions" that they are hard to avoid and can manifest the presence of a religious "other," which may trigger conflict or at least complaints by the neighbors.

Fourth, apart from spatial figurations and religious space making through aesthetic formations, I have shown that accommodation centers are stratified spaces in which broader national debates on immigration, hospitality, and multiculturalism crystallize. As a matter of fact, the different strata of meaning do not speak for themselves but are subject to active reinterpretation and renegotiation through musealization and other memory culture practices. Thus, museums, exhibitions, memorials, and guided tours serve as vehicles of administering the "tradition" of accommodation centers and to break up—or purport—its hegemonic implications in terms of religion.

While the chapter sets out to advertise the capacity of institutionalist and material approaches to jointly offer new insights on religious diversity and practice in refugee accommodation centers, it points to a number of *gaps and avenues for future research*. First of all, it seems crucial to include the perspective of the refugees themselves and their perceptions of multireligious figurations within the material culture of the centers. Furthermore, it is desirable to implement some generically "material" approaches on the level of data collection of analysis, that is, a thick documentation of spatial and aesthetic dimensions of refugee accommodation.

Conversion through Destitution

Religion, Law, and Doubt in the UK Asylum System

William Wheeler

Introduction

"I slept beneath Jesus!" "Abdul," a young man from a war-torn country in the Middle East, told me, describing how, as a destitute refused asylum seeker, he slept in night shelters in churches—before adding, with his characteristic irreverent humor, "Hallelujah!"[1] Living in one particular church for several months, he gradually became a member of the church. It was through this experience— being supported by people whose faith inspired them to help the destitute—that he converted to Christianity in May 2014. The following year, he claimed asylum again, on the basis that he feared religious persecution in his country of origin.

In July 2016, I accompanied him and his minister, "Ben," to a First-Tier Tribunal (FTT) hearing for his appeal against the Home Office's latest refusal to grant him asylum. Although refused asylum, he had been granted humanitarian protection, for reasons unconnected to his religion. He now had five years' leave to remain in the UK, but he still hoped to win his asylum case. His solicitor, who had a bubbly but professional demeanor, declared in the prehearing consultation that we were unlucky: the immigration judge (IJ) who would hear this case had a reputation for always refusing conversion cases. Sure enough, the appeal was dismissed: the IJ (who was white and middle class, and gave no indication of his own religious belief or nonbelief) concluded that Abdul had been baptized for opportunistic reasons, to further his asylum case, rather than genuine belief. Although this decision was later set aside in the Upper Tribunal (UT) and remitted back to the FTT for a further hearing, Abdul at that point dropped his case.

In this chapter, I use Abdul's story to explore the relationship between asylum law and religious conversion. How do asylum decision makers and immigration courts assess whether the outward signs of conversion reflect inner belief? How do they judge whether a conversion is genuine and not opportunistic? Crucially, while it may seem that the law and religion are discrete spheres that only meet in the courtroom, the ethnographic account that follows suggests a much more sustained, intricate relationship. Abdul's legal status as a refused asylum seeker provided both the social context for his conversion (he was helped by a church when destitute) and a material motive (he could use conversion as the basis for a fresh asylum claim), but the two are not easily separable. This point, I argue, unsettles the binaries of sincere/fake, genuine/opportunistic on which the legal process rests.

Scholars of religious conversion, questioning the Protestant notion of conversion as an interior transformation of the individual, have long focused on the social relations and cultural context within which conversions take place (Buckser and Glazier 2003; Gooren 2010; Meyer 1999; Rambo 1993; Smilde 2007). Scholars have also attended to the political contexts that provide varying degrees of coercion or incentive for people to convert (Austin-Broos 2003; Kravel-Tovi 2014; Seeman 2003). The politics of migration is one such context: religious conversion can provide a basis for an asylum claim. As Susanne Stadlbauer (2019) describes, the widespread phenomenon of Iranian Christian converts claiming asylum in Germany has prompted suspicion, both in the media and among decision makers, that the conversion may not be genuine. Likewise, Don Seeman (2003) describes how, because a "return" to Judaism was the precondition of the Ethiopian Felashmura's immigration to Israel, they were deemed not to be converting for the "right" reasons. Similar dilemmas are discussed in Michal Kravel-Tovi's (2019) ethnography of conversion to Judaism in Israel: since conversion can carry tangible material benefits even for Israeli citizens, there is an anxiety that it cannot be freely chosen.

In such contexts, bureaucracies are tasked with assessing whether conversions are genuine. Hence the "faith test" in German assessments of Iranian converts discussed by Stadlbauer (2019). Hence too the complex processes of assessing Jewish converts in Israeli religious courts (Kravel-Tovi 2012). In such processes, as Kravel-Tovi (2012) shows, the subject's inner life becomes the object of bureaucratic knowledge, but this knowledge is necessarily incomplete, haltingly coproduced by converts, judges, and other actors. In what follows, I show how bureaucratic and legal knowledge about Abdul's conversion story is generated. If social life is irreducibly complex and thus inherently ambiguous, I show how decision makers "manage" doubt to make a clear ruling about his conversion (Good, Berti, and Tarabout 2015; Kelly 2015).

Such processes share the assumption that a "genuine" conversion is one made for spiritual rather than material rewards, that outward signs match inner belief. Seeman (2003: 36) writes of "the recalcitrance of social experience to the politically expedient 'pure hearts' discourse on which social bureaucracies rely." By juxtaposing Abdul's legal case, and similar case law, with his own accounts of his conversion story, I flesh out this "recalcitrance." The "pure hearts" discourse, I argue, assumes that religion is an interior sphere of belief abstracted from social and material worlds (Asad 1993; Keane 2002). This image does not match Abdul's religious experience, although, as we shall see, he has his own anxieties about the ambiguity of "using" religion for his asylum case.

Talal Asad (1993) has famously shown that the abstraction of religion from the social is historically contingent on the development of the western secular state. Thus, insofar as they are artifacts of the same historical process, there is a symmetry between religion and the law of the state: if the convert's outward signs are expected to transparently reflect their inner beliefs, legal determinations are expected to objectively represent reality; if religion is supposed to stand above the social as an abstract system of symbolic meaning, so too is the law expected to operate according to its own rational laws, autonomous of the social.

But legal ethnographies query these assumptions. Kravel-Tovi's (2012) description of the Israeli religious courts draws out how knowledge is generated through performance on the part of judges and converts. Indeed, Good et al. (2015: 15), comparing law and ritual, propose that legal decisions are "in part aesthetically and emotionally grounded rather than being arrived at by purely rational means." Ethnographies of asylum determination, in particular, stress the extrajudicial social and political pressures which formally weigh the process against the applicant, and informally shape decision makers' attitudes to the case (Campbell 2017; Gill and Good 2019; Good 2015; Thomas 2011). Building on this literature, the following material shows how, in Abdul's case, the law falls short of being the autonomous, objective field that it is set up to be. This matters because Abdul himself is acutely aware that the asylum process is opaque and highly politicized.

This chapter is based on events predating my current research position. I first got to know Abdul in 2014, while I was volunteering at an activist organization, and we became good friends. I first describe Abdul's conversion story as I understood it at that time, when it formed the basis of his asylum claim. This understanding was based on our extensive conversations; I am not religiously observant myself, and I have not witnessed him practicing his faith. I met Abdul regularly throughout the period when he submitted his claim, was refused and appealed. In the central parts of the chapter, I explore his Home Office refusal and his appeal to the immigration tribunal, contextualizing his case in the case law. Some months after the dismissal of the appeal, I mentioned the possibility of turning his story into an academic paper and possible publication. Abdul was enthusiastic about the idea and said he wanted to explain more. In the lengthy conversation that ensued, he offered me a fresh perspective on his conversion, directly confronting issues about sincerity and material reward. This conversation forms the basis of the final part of the chapter, where I show how it problematizes the categories the legal process was based on.

Although I hope that what follows will draw out some of the complexity of Abdul's social experience, it is not intended to be holistic. There is another dimension of his life which has also been, and continues to be, profoundly shaped by his immigration case. This aspect of his life is largely separate from his religious practice, but at certain moments it becomes relevant to the following story. However, I find this other dimension too sensitive to write about. So, at the moments in the story it becomes relevant, I hope the reader will forgive a certain vagueness.

Abdul's Conversion

Abdul came to the UK in 2006, when he was nineteen, fleeing his home country, where his father had been politically persecuted. Brought up Muslim, Abdul stopped practicing when he came to the UK. He claimed asylum, but received no decision on his case until he was refused in 2011, by which time the political situation in his country had changed, and the previous asylum claim was no longer relevant. Between claiming and being refused asylum, he had made British friends, studied English, and had been permitted to work. His life was now in the UK. Moreover, there was ongoing conflict in his country. He submitted two more applications for leave to remain, but these were refused, the second in February 2014: despite the deteriorating situation in his country of origin, it was deemed safe for him to return. After his 2011 refusal, things became much harder. Barred from formal employment, he engaged in exploitative "black work" in construction. Homeless, he spent some time living in a tent in the countryside, and some time in a homeless camp in Manchester. He lost his paperwork, and his efforts to retrieve it from the Home Office through freedom of information requests proved futile.

After the 2014 refusal, he was referred to a faith-based charity that provided accommodation for destitute asylum seekers and refugees in a network of night shelters in churches. He found it demeaning to be bussed out to a different church every evening, and to sleep on the church floor. However, in one of these night shelters he started talking with the volunteers about Christianity. Inspired by their motivation to help the destitute, he started attending this church, which carries out various community support activities, including with white British homeless. In May 2014, he decided to be baptized, with a full immersion baptism, a video of which was posted, with his consent, on YouTube. From then on, he attended the church every Sunday, and played an active role, particularly in helping cook for the shared meals (Abdul is an excellent, if eccentric, cook). He would join in improvised prayers in the services, and would introduce new people to the church. He attended church weekends away, bringing his irreverent sense of humor to the conviviality. He went to Bible study, but was less interested in reading than in doing: he describes himself as a "practical Christian," which he characterizes as helping other people out, particularly those in need.[2]

Abdul's legal status as a refused asylum seeker was the defining context of his conversion. As Sarah Willen (2007, 2014) has argued, migrant "illegality" is more than just a sociopolitical status: it structures people's experiential lifeworlds, setting severe constraints on their possibilities for social being. Abdul had become destitute and homeless as a direct result of his immigration status: he was forbidden to work, and, having "no recourse to public funds," he had no access to mainstream welfare benefits or Home Office support, or to social housing. Ashamed to tell his British friends about his status, he lost contact with many.

It was in these conditions that Abdul encountered the church, through the night shelter. Mark Rainey's (2017) ethnography of these night shelters explores the varying motivations of volunteers: while not all are religious, most perform a "social gospel," some with a more missional ethic, others with a sense of ethical commitment to the wider community. The church which became Abdul's home was not a strongly evangelizing church, and the interest in conversion came largely from him. Whatever the motivation, Rainey describes how volunteers perform often mundane, routinized practices of care—including shared meals, the focal point of social interaction. These shelters are no substitute for a long-term home; as Rainey (2017: 294) puts it, they are: "'spaces of asylum' that carry all the tensions this term entails. They are spaces of movement and fixity, dignity and indignity, of care, concern and welcome; but also of tiredness, restlessness, and anxiety."

For many, then, the night shelter is just a roof for the night; but for Abdul, this particular church became what Willen (2014) calls "an inhabitable space of welcome." It was a space where he could negotiate the constraints his immigration status put on his lifeworld. The conversation reported in the final section fleshes this point out. In the next sections, however, I examine how Abdul's conversion was disbelieved first by the Home Office and then by the IJ.

Home Office Refusal

In July 2015, Abdul submitted a fresh claim for asylum based on fear of religious persecution in his country of origin, where there is substantial evidence that apostates are persecuted. Abdul's fresh claim was submitted by a large, respected law firm. Various forms of evidence were submitted: a baptism certificate; a statement setting out the conversion story outlined earlier, composed through dialogue with the lawyer and the organization where I was volunteering; a statement from the minister, Ben; and other statements from church members. Once his claim was in, Abdul could access the Home Office's asylum support— housing in a town outside Manchester and financial support. In February 2016, he had his substantive interview (SEF) with a Home Office official. She was friendly, Abdul said, but he was scornful of the questions she posed. "They even asked me what Jesus ate!" he said with bitter humor. He was refused asylum in June 2016. However, he was granted humanitarian protection, giving him five years' leave to remain, because of the ongoing war in his country of origin.

Official Home Office guidance on asylum determination states that, in conversion cases, the claimant's own testimony is key, and the decision whether to grant the benefit of the doubt should be based on "the claimant's personal credibility" (Home Office 2015: 29). The Home Office follows the UNHCR's (2004) very broad definition of religion to encompass beliefs, identity and way of life, but the guidance places most emphasis on the applicant's interior state:

> What is being assessed is primarily whether the claimant has genuinely moved towards a firm decision to leave the faith of their upbringing and become a Christian. To be credible, something so potentially life-changing should not be perfunctory, vague, or ill-thought out. (Home Office 2015: 29)

However, decision makers, the guidance states, can ask about the claimant's level of understanding, although they are only qualified to assess answers to the most basic factual questions. In practice, interviewers go beyond their brief, asking a lot about trivial knowledge (APPG for Religious Freedom and AAG 2016). More broadly, treatment of conversion cases is typical of a "culture of disbelief" within the Home Office (e.g., Asylum Aid 1995, 1999; Griffiths 2012; Anderson et al. 2014). Decisions are primarily based on the substantive interview (SEF), which tends to be conducted in such a way as to catch the applicant out (Campbell 2017). While "credibility" is central to asylum determination, it is a vague term that can be interpreted to include a wide range of factors extraneous to the substance of the asylum claim, meaning that the benefit of the doubt is seldom granted (Good 2015).

All these points emerge in Abdul's Reasons for Refusal Letter. Following Marco Jacquemet (2009, 2011) and Massimiliano Spotti (2019), I approach this letter as the endpoint of an intricate process through which Abdul's conversion story is entextualized, a process shaped by the institutional position and cultural assumptions of the Home Office officials involved. During this process, the story is simplified so as to be comprehensible within bureaucratic categories. As is typical, this letter is printed in small print, itemized by paragraph, with extensive quoting of case law and confusing use of grammar and punctuation. All decisions on fresh asylum claims begin by quoting the findings of the IJ in the appeal against the initial asylum claim. In Abdul's case, the letter states that the IJ in 2011 had found him "not to be credible," and then proceeds to quote from his determination—but the quotations are confusing and do not suggest that the IJ found him to have fabricated his story. Nevertheless, as is standard, Abdul's lack of credibility is taken as "the starting point for any further consideration."

The substance of the letter focuses on Abdul's asylum interview. This encounter functions as the main source of bureaucratic knowledge about his story. One paragraph focuses on his account of going to the church when he was destitute, being supported there, and wanting to give something back. The letter then states that he had been asked if he attended more for community than faith. He had replied that it was more about community; he was a practical Christian, and did not read extensively. Abdul's conversion is thus entextualized through a leading question that asks him to oppose community and faith, an opposition that is then crystallized in the refusal letter. In the following paragraph, we hear that he had been asked if he had researched any other faiths before converting; he had not. The letter then addresses his responses about proselytizing: he had said that he talks about his faith but does not preach. The following paragraph itemizes his wrong answers, chiding him for his mistakes. For example, he "failed" to correct himself regarding a mistake about a biblical figure (whose name is, ironically, misspelled in the decision letter).

The next paragraph summarizes why his conversion is deemed not genuine. First, he "admitted" that he attended for the sense of community rather than religious reasons; secondly, he had only gone to the church because he was destitute and homeless; thirdly, his lack of knowledge; and, fourthly, his failure to proselytize.[3] The witness statements from the church and the baptism certificate are dealt with in less depth since the decision maker has already concluded that he did not attend for religious reasons. Abdul's own statement is ignored. As an object of bureaucratic knowledge, Abdul is known primarily through the Home Office interview. Several further paragraphs suggest, implausibly, that Christian converts are not really at risk in Abdul's country.

The production of knowledge about Abdul's religious experience rests on unspoken assumptions about what religion is. According to the version of his story entextualized through the interview, he attended church for community rather than faith, and he had not researched other faiths prior to his conversion. Religion figures as something the individual researches, shopping around for the religious beliefs that suit the individual; community is seen as an add-on, distinct from the inner core of belief. As noted earlier, scholars of conversion have long questioned this interior model of religious conversion. Indeed, it presupposes that religion is a sphere of belief completely abstracted from the social (cf. Asad 1993)—in stark contrast to my narration of Abdul's story earlier.

The letter does not simply communicate a decision. Its form is opaque, and the letter is imbued with a moralizing tone, from the initial finding of lack of credibility to Abdul's "failure" to correct himself about his mistakes. Abdul was not surprised by the decision: from his previous rejections, he felt intense distrust toward the Home Office, and his interview had exasperated and amused him in equal measure. The refusal letter only heightened this distrust (cf. Campbell 2017; Danstrøm and Whyte 2019; Griffiths 2012).

First-Tier Tribunal Hearing

Despite being granted humanitarian protection, Abdul appealed to the FTT. Although he now had the right to work and claim benefits, refugee status was preferable because it entitled him to an internationally recognized travel document, which he urgently needed for reasons connected to that other aspect of his life hinted at earlier.[4] He also wanted to prove his case in court. Before the hearing, his solicitor prepared a detailed statement, crafting a further entextualization of his journey of faith that responded to the points raised in the refusal letter. I traveled to the hearing with Abdul and Ben, the minister; amidst the banter between them, the minister described going to such a hearing before, when the IJ had treated him with undisguised hostility. Having felt unprepared for that hearing, he had prepared better this time. Unfortunately, it was the same IJ.

The hearing started in confusion, as it turned out that no one had read the 2011 appeal determination of Abdul's initial asylum claim—which the Home Office decision maker had taken as the starting point of their decision about his fresh claim. Abdul's lawyer had not seen it as Abdul had lost all his paperwork, and the Home Office Presenting Officer (HOPO) was unable to provide a copy. Accordingly, the substance of Abdul's initial asylum claim and its refusal was left in doubt. Most of the hearing involved the IJ questioning Ben. Though ostensibly courteous, he made little attempt to veil his skepticism about his branch of Christianity, expressing incredulity that people could ask to be baptized and then be baptized on the same day. Ben talked coherently about Abdul's journey of faith, and how he had developed through various stages of belief. Abdul himself, far from his usual humorously irreverent demeanor, responded briefly and succinctly to the questions put to him, showing deference to the IJ.

The HOPO was young, inexperienced, and nervous. The IJ, performing a separation between the executive and the judiciary, mocked her as she haltingly concluded, "These, your honour, are my humble submissions." Abdul's solicitor tried to raise a piece of case law which suggested that church attendance was sufficient evidence of faith, but this was brusquely dismissed by the IJ.

Kravel-Tovi (2012) describes an atmosphere of cooperation in Israeli religious courts, which shapes the knowledge that is produced about Jewish converts. By contrast, the atmosphere in Abdul's tribunal was hostile. In particular, the IJ's thinly veiled antagonism toward the minister shaped the sort of knowledge that was produced. Moreover, despite the appearance of symmetry—the HOPO on one side, Abdul's solicitor on the other, and the IJ on a slightly raised podium in the middle—the IJ did much of the cross-examination, filling in the gaps left by the inexperienced HOPO.[5]

The hearing matched other ethnographic accounts of UK asylum courts. Jessica Anderson et al. (2014: 9) see "the performance of law in this environment as being prone to confusion and scepticism, or 'disbelief.'" As John Campbell (2017: 96) highlights, many IJs, despite lacking comprehensive knowledge of asylum law, are characterized by "professional hubris." While HOPOs are not actually solicitors, and hence are treated with contempt by the appellants' advocates and the IJs, they nevertheless have an inbuilt advantage in that they spend the whole day with the same IJ. Moreover, they share access to parts of the building that are closed off to the appellants and their advocates (Hambly

2019; Campbell 2017, 2019). Crucially, many IJs, especially in FTTs, are swayed by extrajudicial factors: anti-migrant media discourses, and explicit government policy to create a "hostile environment" for irregular migrants (Hambly 2019). This IJ's hostility to conversion cases is symptomatic of the high level of judicial discretion and resultant arbitrariness in decisions (Anderson et al. 2014; Gill et al. 2015; Thomas 2011). In sum, the law is not the autonomous field that its authority rests on, especially in this highly politicized context.

The appeal was dismissed within a week. The IJ's statement of reasons sets out the background, the documents before the court, and describes the hearing, before setting out the IJ's findings. The findings begin by citing legislation and case law which establish that Abdul's credibility was adversely affected by his having remained in the UK without leave to remain since 2006. Recall the indeterminacy surrounding this point: given the absence of paperwork, the court knew nothing about the substance of Abdul's original asylum claim. So he was from the start not a credible witness—but no one knew why (cf. Good 2015).

In his statement of reasons, the IJ found that, based on the SEF interview, Abdul did in fact have a reasonable knowledge of Christianity; but he deemed the interview unhelpful, since knowledge is not the same as belief. The IJ then picked up on various inconsistencies in the evidence, which, he said, generated confusion about when the conversion took place. Abdul had, when questioned, said that he also approached mosques when he was destitute, so the IJ concluded that before April 2015, he must have been a practicing Muslim, which contradicted one of the witness statements. Several statements stressed Abdul's kindness and willingness to help others. The IJ argued that these could apply to any faith, and such behavior must be instrumental, in order to support Abdul's claim.

The IJ addressed only two aspects of Ben's evidence. First, because Ben had explained that the church provides shelter for anyone, regardless of their beliefs, the IJ concluded that Abdul had initially attended only for community and shelter, not for religion. Secondly, Ben had acknowledged the difficulty of assessing whether a conversion is genuine, but had said that he was convinced that Abdul's was. Though he had given a comprehensive explanation why he thought this in court, this was not recorded in the statement of reasons. Instead, the IJ declared that, in his view, the baptism was too quick—so it must have been opportunistic. Abdul's latest asylum claim had been refused in February 2014, so he must, the IJ reasoned, have seen a window of opportunity to advance his immigration status, hence the very rapid conversion in May 2014. In effect, he overruled Ben's authority to read the signs of Abdul's conversion, referring to legislation and case law which situate refused asylum seekers as not credible witnesses. This conflict of authority had been evident in the courtroom, and it was materialized in the statement of reasons.

Finally, the IJ asked whether Abdul had become a genuine Christian since his baptism. When Abdul was housed outside Manchester, he would walk every Sunday to and from church, a three-hour journey. Abdul had explained in the hearing that he preferred the community and friendship at his current church. A genuine Christian, the IJ argued, would have found a local church: he must have been going only for community.

Abdul's Case in Context

Abdul's lawyer appealed to the UT. Rather than hearing the evidence again, the UT immigration judge's role was to assess whether the FTT IJ had made an error of law in his decision. In August 2017, the UT found that he had done so, because he had not adequately evaluated Ben's evidence.[6] So the case was sent back to the FTT to be heard again before a different IJ. However, Abdul now dropped the case: work commitments had kept him from attending church for several months, Ben had left, and the new minister could not vouch for him in court.

The status of ministers' evidence is a key bone of contention in case law about asylum claims based on conversions in the UK. In the seminal case of *Ali Dorodian v SSHD* [2003] 01/TH/01537, the IJ declared that "no-one should be regarded as a committed Christian who is not vouched for as such by a minister of some church established in this country." Since then, the testimony, *in court*, of a minister, known as a "Dorodian witness," has been deemed crucial to the success of appeals. But interpretations vary. One interpretation sees the presence of a Dorodian witness as sufficient evidence of conversion. As a High Court judge, HHJ Gilbart, declared:

> It is a dangerous thing for anyone, and perhaps especially a judge, to peer into what some call a man or woman's soul to assess whether a professed faith is genuinely held, and especially not when it was and is agreed that she was and is a frequent participant in church services.[7]

In some decisions, then, the Dorodian case is interpreted to mean that church attendance—the outward sign of conversion—is sufficient evidence;[8] in others, judicial authority is effectively outsourced to the minister, whose role is to assess whether the conversion is genuine.[9]

But many IJs chafe at the idea that their authority can be outsourced in this way. As one IJ has remarked, the wording of the Dorodian judgment was that no one could be Christian *unless* vouched for, which does not mean that being vouched for is sufficient evidence that someone is Christian.[10] Such IJs suggest that ministers may sincerely believe that the asylum seeker is a genuine convert, but they are not qualified to judge because they do not know the full story. In such decisions, the IJs' negative assessment of the claimant's credibility casts doubt on evidence of other witnesses. As one IJ stated:

> the experience of the Tribunal, reflected in many decisions upheld on appeal in the higher courts, is that many who claim asylum on the basis of Christian conversion from Islam specifically engage as an active participant in a dishonest and calculated effort to falsely portray themselves as genuine converts.[11]

The IJ at Abdul's FTT hearing evidently belonged to the second camp, drawing on his own assessment of Abdul's credibility to dismiss Ben's testimony. However, when the appeal was taken to the UT, the higher IJ found that the Dorodian witness's evidence had not been properly evaluated. Remitted back to the FTT to a different IJ, the ruling may have been different—we will never know.

As Abdul's case makes clear, then, the struggle between these two approaches continues. A recent ruling of the Scottish Court of Session powerfully upheld the first approach: IJs should consider evidence "in the round," meaning that even if they find the convert's own evidence not credible, this should not be used to cast doubt on the evidence of other witnesses.[12] Since Dorodian witnesses are not just reporting what converts have told them, but on their observations of their religious practice, this evidence should be considered on its own merits.[13]

Problematizing Genuine/Opportunistic, Sincere/Fake

However, proponents of both approaches broadly agree on one key assumption: that a conversion is either genuine or not genuine, that the outward signs of a conversion may or may not reflect a transformation of inner belief. After all, when there are obvious material incentives for a conversion, this casts doubt on the sincerity of the convert and the transparency of the signs of their conversion. Where the different judicial approaches differ is in how they "manage" this doubt (Good, Berti, and Tarabout 2015). In Abdul's case, extrajudicial factors—the IJ's suspicion about conversion in general, and his hostility toward Ben's church—were evidently key to Abdul not being given the benefit of the doubt. But is the dichotomy between genuine and not genuine, sincere and insincere, as clear as it seems? Does material reward of a successful asylum application make the conversion fake? Grace Milton (2018) queries this assumption, arguing that it is based on a separation between the spiritual and the material which is alien to many religions, where salvation may be a "whole-life state." The ambiguity in Abdul's conversion takes us to the heart of how religion relates to the social, the spiritual to the material, sincerity to pragmatism. In his analysis of Venezuelan evangelical converts, David Smilde (2007: 14) argues that "there is no *natural* distinction between religious and nonreligious goals" [emphasis added]. Rather, the dualism between the religious and the material is contextually contingent: different religions, and even different adherents of the same religion, may draw the distinction in different ways.

In what follows, I report a discussion with Abdul about his conversion in July 2017, after the FTT hearing but before the UT hearing, which revealed a highly complex relationship between immigration status, destitution, a religious community of care, and conversion. When I proposed writing about Abdul's conversion for an academic paper, he was enthusiastic. Saying that he wanted to explain something, he confronted the issue of opportunism directly. He succinctly described what being a refused asylum seeker means: your case is closed. In order to put in a fresh claim, you need "a new story." He scornfully suggested that many conversions are not at all genuine. Following the changed political context in his country of origin, his reason for fleeing was no longer relevant. He couldn't go back, owing to the ongoing violence, but he did not have a *case*. While living in the church and participating actively in church life, he helped baptize a British person (Abdul could participate as a church member, despite not yet being baptized himself). This man, who knew a lot of asylum seekers, suggested he convert, in order to put in a fresh claim.

Abdul described his conversion as "60 percent for my case." But he also said, "I saw God." We tried to unpack this over the course of the conversation. The minister had told him that he would be reborn, that his sins would be cleansed, he said. He also explained that the church had helped him when he was destitute; he believed that some sort of divine providence had taken him there—as the minister told him, "God works in mysterious ways." But, despite being very articulate in English, Abdul struggled to convey what it was that made him convert—what that other 40 percent was about. A few times, he said, "It's hard . . ." (i.e., "hard to explain"). Perhaps the clearest explanation he gave was this: "I believe it. I was there, I was fed, I was cooking—I was cooking for 17 people. I was in charge, Ben left me there; I was part of something. He trusted me and I feel part of something." As an "inhabitable space of welcome" (Willen 2014), the church offered Abdul the chance to develop social relations and exert a sense of agency within the severe constraints set by his immigration status. This, then, is why he did not change church when he moved away: his faith was inseparable from the social relations within which it emerged—a point that had not been articulated in the courtroom.

Although the idea to convert was connected to his need for a fresh claim, he told me that he did not submit a fresh claim for over a year because, once converted, he did not want to use it for his case. He considered it "selfish." In Smilde's (2007) terms, the way Abdul drew the line between the spiritual and the material precluded using his conversion for his own benefit. The minister and others at the church disagreed: they drew the line between the spiritual and the material differently to Abdul. When he finally submitted the fresh claim, he explained, it was because he desperately needed to access asylum support from the Home Office (housing and £36.62 per week)—he stressed this immediate issue of destitution rather than the longer-term goal of getting refugee status. He expressed his anger at the "bastards" in the Home Office at the situation: "I feel they made me do it, made me do something selfish."

Despite the reassurances from the other church members, he told me that he continued to feel guilty about it. His discomfort arose from "using religion to get something out of it"; he compared imams who promised young men rewards in heaven, while enriching themselves on earth. If people intend to be good, he continued, they should be good for no reason. Later, he elaborated further: it would be like helping a homeless person and welcoming them into your home, and then demanding money. In Abdul's characterization, the material world of self-interest is distinct from the religious world of disinterested giving, mutual support, and shared meals.

Nevertheless, he did not regret using religion for his fresh claim. Although his asylum claim was unsuccessful, he felt that putting in the claim was key to getting humanitarian protection. Now permitted to work, in a library and as a cook, he said that he feels like he is someone; he feels that people know him, and he is paying bills: "Before, I was a ghost." As Willen (2014) argues, immigration status structures people's lifeworlds, setting constraints on the social relations they can enter—eloquently expressed in Abdul's memory of being "a ghost." Hence, he described the grant of humanitarian protection not in terms of individual advancement but in terms of the social relations it enables. While Abdul separated the spiritual and material motivations for converting, there is a homology between the two. Having been a "ghost" as a destitute refused asylum seeker, his participation in church life—cooking for others, helping out—mirrored the way he talked about having status. The benefits of having leave to remain were, on his own account, precisely that he could enter into social relations by engaging in labor with obvious social value, by being known, by paying into society. This would seem to question Abdul's sense that it was self-interested to "use" his religion for his case. Nevertheless, feeling forced into using the outward signs of his conversion pragmatically—to achieve a goal in the material world—he felt insincere, which left him with a strong sense of guilt (cf. Keane 2002).

Conclusion

Perhaps it is unsurprising that the courts struggle to perceive the irreducible complexity of social life. Abdul's reflections on his conversion suggest that different sorts of motivation interact: the more instrumental, and the more spiritual. As I have argued, there is no sharp dichotomy between the two, and, moreover, motivations oscillate with the ebb and flow of social life—it was when Abdul felt his destitution most acutely that he decided to "use" his conversion for his asylum claim, motivated by the pressing need for Home Office support. Outward signs of conversion such as church attendance can be transparent expressions of religious belief, but they can also be deployed pragmatically to "prove" the conversion. Such complexity exacerbates the uncertainty that is inherent in adjudicating such cases. But legal processes, as Good, Berti, and Tarabout (2015) argue, are about resolving doubt. If social life is characterized by uncertainty, the law must come down one way or the other, resolving doubt into narrow judicial truth. In this case, uncertainty is resolved by reducing the complexity of refused asylum seekers' conversions into a narrow binary of genuine/opportunistic. Fascinatingly, the Scottish Court of Session decision cited earlier questions this binary:

> It is also right to accept that asking the question in terms of whether a conversion is or is not genuine suggests a binary choice more appropriate to an instantaneous (or "Damascene") conversion whereas for many, perhaps most, the process of gaining a religious belief in adulthood may be more gradual, so that at any one point it may not be possible to say whether the "conversion" is complete, let alone "genuine."[14]

Here, then, is some judicial recognition that social life is complex and messy, and does not easily fit into the categories of the law. "But," the ruling continues, "these questions need not trouble us for present purposes." Even as complexity forces its way into the law, it is squeezed out again.

Legal judgments may cut through the uncertainty, but since they are not arrived at by solely rational means, Good, Berti, and Tarabout (2015: 1) propose that their legitimacy depends on "an authority that arises partly from the judges' displayed mastery of techniques of doubting, and of dispelling doubt, and partly from their social and political position." In Abdul's case, the IJ's cross-examination of the minister demonstrated his mastery of techniques of doubting, while also establishing his own authority. Without a reliable lawyer, Abdul's case would have been left there, this decision now set in stone. As it happened, a further judicial performance in a higher court resulted in this decision being set aside by a higher authority. We cannot know how the doubt would have been resolved— by the time his case was due to be heard again more than a year later, he no longer had the all-important Dorodian witness. Even had the case ultimately been resolved in his favor, the complexity of Abdul's social experience would surely *not* have entered the courtroom.

Earlier I noted the symmetry between secular understandings of religion as an abstract system of symbolic meaning, where words map directly onto belief devoid of social function, and the law as a transparent field that stands above the social (cf. Asad 1993; Keane 2002). The ethnographic account above unsettles both aspects of this symmetry. The IJ judged Abdul against a vision of religion as an abstract realm of belief; because his religious practice so obviously and pragmatically related to his social status as a refused asylum seeker, the IJ deemed it insincere. And yet, like any legal judgment, its authority depended on writing the social out of the courtroom. Rather than seeing the court's findings as coproduced by the various socially sited actors in the courtroom—with radically different degrees of power—the IJ presented them as objective findings, mapping directly onto reality and casting Abdul as an opportunist and fake.

Like many asylum seekers faced with illegible and highly politicized bureaucratic and legal structures, Abdul has intense distrust toward "the system" (cf. Campbell 2017; Danstrøm and Whyte 2019; Griffiths 2012). While he has his own anxieties that his own words and actions may not be wholly transparent, and that his religious life is not wholly independent of the material world, he is also all too aware that the law is neither autonomous nor transparent, even if its authority—an authority which has shaped his life story in the UK—rests on it being presented as such. It is unsurprising then that the net result of the entanglement of religious experience with legal processes should be anger and guilt: guilt at, in his view, exploiting his conversion pragmatically for material gain; and anger at the system that made him do it, but refused to believe him when he did. As Abdul is, at the time of writing, undergoing a personal crisis which—though not proximately related to the material discussed in this chapter—indirectly follows the refusal to grant him refugee status, it is hard not to share his anger.

Acknowledgments

I am grateful in the first instance to Abdul, for his warmth, humor, and friendship—and for all I have learned from him about religion, asylum, and what it means to live through destitution. I would like to thank also the editors for their constructive comments and the other participants at the Refugees and Religion conference. This chapter has further benefited from comments from Jeanette Edwards, Olga Ulturgasheva, Connie Smith, and Mark Rainey. Finally, my thanks to the Leverhulme Trust, which has funded the position through which I have written this material up.

Mobilizing Theory

Concluding Thoughts

Birgit Meyer

The contributions to this volume trace the itineraries of people on the move, fleeing from defunct states, religious persecution, war-torn environments, or poverty-stricken conditions and aspiring to enter Europe, with more or less success. Its focus is on people who not only traverse rough territories and borders and a host of institutions on the way but also move through different statuses—traveler, migrant, refugee, immigrant, citizen—that entail different rights and possibilities. Many flee from unbearable conditions, and the trajectory is long—with people getting stuck on the way—and once arrived in Europe, gaining asylum is a complicated legal-bureaucratic procedure. Religion plays a role throughout these trajectories, in multiple ways. While our title profiles the term "refugee," we do not use it to designate exclusively those who finally gain that legal status after a long trajectory, with lengthy periods of waiting in many places, including European refugee camps. We employ the term as a lens to investigate the complex itineraries of displaced people who seek to achieve that status, whether they eventually may be found to qualify for asylum or not. In so doing, we are careful to avoid framing refugees as "simply dispossessed, traumatized, and helpless victims" (Ninh; see also Horstmann and Jung 2015b: 2–5).

Throughout their itineraries, religion plays important but often overlooked roles, and one of the central aims of this volume is to explore these roles in ways that lead beyond well-trodden stereotypes about religion in modern, secular society. This neglect of religion in relation to the study of refugee issues is not simply an empirical problem, but also a conceptual one. It stems from the secularist approach in mainstream social and cultural science discourses, according to which religion, understood in terms of private belief, is marginal, as is also argued by three recent companion volumes on the theme of refugees and religion in the wake of the so-called refugee crisis that began in 2015 (Horstmann and Jung 2015b; Mavelli and Wilson 2017; Schmiedel and Smith 2018). By and large, our volume joins the conceptual critiques ventured by these works (with Mavelli and Wilson problematizing the secular-religious binary and Schmiedel and Smith identifying competing (political) theologies in relation to the arrival of refugees). Its distinct contribution lies in its anthropological approach to people on the move from Vietnam (Part II), from Africa (Part III), and to spaces of reception (Part IV).[1] It seeks to situate their arrival and accommodation in a historical perspective by retrieving from oblivion Europe's long history of accommodating refugees and migrants (Part I) and by exploring the conditions under which and ways in which refugees from Vietnam were received and settled in Europe during the Cold War. Each contribution offers specific, often dismaying insights into particular aspects of the huge phenomenon of people on the move to and within Europe and around the globe. Taken together, they help us chart the complex historical developments and global entanglements within which the current "refugee crisis" is occurring. Taking the refugees-and-religion nexus as a focal point reveals a lot about the legal, political, and symbolic operations through which nation-states, and the EU at large, seek to retain their boundaries and regulate the role and place of religion in society, in a world in motion. This concluding chapter addresses four themes: the problematic diagnostics implied in the term "crisis," state politics of religious plurality, religion as a boundary-transgressing force, and, by way of conclusion, the need to *mobilize* theory.

Beyond "Crisis"

The framing of the arrival of more than a million people at Europe's increasingly guarded borders in 2015 as a "refugee crisis"—or, to indicate that not all would be eligible to gain asylum: "migrant crisis"[2]—does not refer primarily to the critical situation of these people as such, but above all to the problem Europe has with their presence. It is a *European* "crisis" about refugees (see also Schmiedel and Smith 2018: 4)—a situation in which politicians and policymakers fail to offer refugees decent and fair treatment as required by international law and the UNHCR. As Morgenstern, Lynes, and Paul put it poignantly:

> the unspoken object of "crisis" in the formation "migrant crisis" was and always has been *Europe*, imagined as a site of right action and just governance, and never the migrant as such; (. . .) the legislative and geopolitical maneuvers taken under the auspices of "responding to the migrant crisis" since 2015 had been less about rescuing the migrant in peril, and more about rescuing the *idea of Europe*

from this same migrant, about restoring a vision of territorial governance and administrative right-headedness that had been imperiled *by* the arrival of the migrant to European shores. (2020: 28)

Zygmunt Bauman (2016) expressed his dismay that in Europe, with its tradition of Enlightenment, the Kantian principle of mutual hospitality, and the ideal of democracy and citizenship, there is a growing open hostility toward strangers in general and refugees in particular. The rise of identitarian xenophobic sentiments, which have long been dormant since the Second World War but gained momentum across Europe since 2015, makes it difficult for European national governments to live up to their stated commitment to the 1951 Geneva Convention that codified the rights of refugees and was made universally applicable by the 1967 protocol. Across Europe, citizens have stood up to push their governments to give shelter to refugees and to accommodate migrants. Engaging in all sorts of humanitarian aid (many grounded in Christian faith, see Barbato 2017; Carrière 2017; Valenta 2018), they criticize that the values that have long served as a marker of distinction for Europe's enlightened status and that legitimized its role as a vanguard of liberal democracy and human rights in the world are being jettisoned by depriving other human beings of their humanity. This is shown glaringly by the catastrophic situation in refugee camps in Greece, Turkey, and Libya and by the passage over the Mediterranean Sea— since 2014, more than 30,000 people have drowned.[3] In this sense, Europe—as the presumed embodiment of human rights—certainly is in a crisis.

While I recognize the gap between legal obligations toward refugees and their actual treatment, and while I share the sense of a crisis of humanitarianism and the imminent danger of squandering ethical values, as a scholar, I find it problematic to conceptualize the current situation as a crisis. Far from being neutral, the term "crisis" has been employed as a long-standing rhetorical figure to diagnose a particular situation as dangerous. As part of the "structural signature of modernity," the concept of crisis enshrines multiple, long-standing layers of meaning, including legal, medical, and theological ones (Koselleck 2006, orig. 1970). The framing of a particular situation as a crisis signals that the situation is at a critical turning point at which a legal-political decision must be taken or it is likened to a dangerous disease approaching its tipping point—life or death—or even that it is on the verge of the apocalypse that signals the end of the known world. Koselleck summarizes:

The legal, theological, and medical usage of "crisis" thus contains discipline-bound, specific meanings. Taken together, however, they could—in different ways—be incorporated into modern social and political language. At all times the concept is applied to life-deciding alternatives meant to answer questions about what is just or unjust, what contributes to salvation or damnation, what furthers health or brings death. (Koselleck 2006: 361)

Though Koselleck wrote his impressive history of the concept of crisis fifty years ago, his essay is still of great help in understanding how deeply this multidimensional concept of crisis shapes contemporary discourses about refugees. The political use of the term "crisis" connotes a view of Europe as a sick body that is threatened with invasion by strangers and even raises apocalyptic ideas about the pending downfall of the Occident. Having gained prominence through the political theologies of far-right populist groups like PEGIDA (e.g., Schmiedel 2018: 211–17; Polak 2018: 244), such views now resonate in broader society. The use of the term "crisis" involves a diagnostic act that may legitimate huge political consequences and evokes moods that are difficult to control. Heeding Koselleck's advice "for scholars to weigh the concept carefully before adopting it in their own terminology" (ibid.: 399), I think that the term "crisis" is of little analytical value for grasping the current stakes in the accommodation of refugees. I agree with Janet Roitman that "crisis is the unexamined point of departure for narration. It is a blind spot for the production of knowledge about what constitutes historical significance and about what constitutes social or historical meaning" (2014: 66).[4] Exactly for this reason, its use itself and the way it produces a particular past and future is to be analyzed. Needed is a critical exploration of the diagnostics and prognostics that accompany the use of the term "crisis" as a form of governance (see also Wilson and Mavelli 2017: 9).

Ironically, in March 2019, the European Commission declared the end of the "migration crisis of 2015," largely as a consequence of the "Turkey deal" in March 2016 (Morgenstern, Lynes and Paul 2020: 27), even though people are still dying in their attempts to cross the Mediterranean Sea, go through terrible hardships in fleeing from Syria, and are kept in deplorable camps at Europe's borders or in Libya. In the meantime, we find ourselves in the midst of the "Corona crisis." Public concerns have turned to the vulnerability of the separate nation-states within the EU, while the fact that the virus also hits people in overcrowded refugee camps is barely noted. There is a remarkable homology here between the framing of the arrival of refugees and migrants in 2015 and the current corona pandemic as crisis: in both cases, there is an image of Europe and its member states as potential patients that might be afflicted by outside intruders, with the states claiming the authority to protect and sanitize these endangered bodies of the nation. Both "crises" take recourse to the same mix of medical and political-theological vocabularies, through which political entities become naturalized and elevated to a higher purpose.[5] Clearly, the use of the concept of crisis as a frame provides a powerful narrative to insist on the need for immediate action—and even a state of emergency—in a situation of life and death, to cure or even save the body politic.[6]

This body politic is imagined to have retained its purity through the protection of its boundaries. As stressed by Peter van der Veer in the Introduction, Mary Douglas's *Purity and Danger* (1966) affords fundamental insights into the transfiguration of the imagined community of the nation into a naturalized entity. Her idea of the body as "a model which can stand for any bounded system" (1966: 115) and the associated notions of purity, dirt, and danger are indispensable for a critical deconstruction of the crisis framing and can help us grasp the mobilization of powerful narratives for the sake of closures and exclusions. While "purity and danger are the main elements of a symbolic repertoire that one finds in a wide range of ritual purifications at the individual and group level" (Van der Veer, Introduction), including in religious and ethnic minorities, it is clear that nation-states have the power to turn their symbolic repertoires into political realities and binding orders. While the focus of our volume is on contemporary European nation-states—especially Germany—that receive rather than produce refugees, we are certainly aware that the power of states to purify the nation has caused and still causes the displacement of huge numbers of people. Some of these refugees may eventually apply for asylum in the West, while many remain stuck in semipermanent regional camps, as the chapter by Salah Punathil on experiences of violence and persecution of Muslims in Assam, India, shows in an exemplary manner.

Another problem of the crisis framing, along with the rhetorical invocation of the body politic as threatened, is the sense of exceptionality and extraordinariness that accompanies it. This may condone historical amnesia, making it seem as if the refugee issue were a recent phenomenon in the wake of globalization. This volume, especially Part I, works against this forgetfulness. As Van der Veer points out, already in the aftermath of the Reformation, "The idea of purification by expulsion became a legitimate aspect of statecraft" and the religious refugee a mass phenomenon. But in the framework of the so-called refugee crisis, this history, which contains basic insights relevant for today's world, tends to be forgotten. Similarly, "far from being an exceptional crisis the 2015 moment of large groups of refugees into Germany is merely a moment in a long history of forced, partly forced, and relatively unforced movement of people in Europe and the rest of the world" (Van der Veer, Chapter 2; see also Nagel). In the aftermath of the Second World War, in 1950, there were twelve million refugees (the so-called *Heimatvertriebene*) from Eastern Europe in Germany (four million in the German Democratic Republic [GDR—communist East Germany], eight million in the Federal Republic of Germany [FRG—West Germany]). Having grown up in the FRG myself, I find it intriguing to note that the process of accommodating such huge numbers of refugees, though certainly difficult and painful for many of them (e.g., Krauss 2011; Hoffmann and Schwartz 1999), has received relatively little attention in the German national memory (at least in my experience, which echoes Kalsky 2007).

What this shows is that the acceptability and growing "invisibility" of former refugees depends on how they are classified. There is a big difference between people who can be "naturalized," by virtue of their "blood," as part of the German nation, and others who may not be qualified to belong, because of their ethnicity, race, or religion. Against this background, German chancellor Merkel's slogan *Wir schaffen das* seems to echo the post–Second World War effort to accommodate a huge number of refugees, bringing back to public memory an awareness of Germany as a country of immigration. This idea is also profiled by the musealization of certain parts of the Border Transit Camp in Friedland in 2016, which hosted mainly Christian refugees from Eastern Europe in the period after the Second World War and now accommodates new arrivals of (mainly Muslim) refugees, as shown by Alexander-Kenneth Nagel. Such reminders of Germany's welcoming stance toward refugees were commended by many, including the Protestant and Catholic churches. But the ongoing protests against this stance also show that hospitality is partial and not meant for every refugee. This confirms the power of national narratives to judge who belongs and who does not, as well as to determine the conditions under which refugees can be accommodated (often in terms of "integration" rather than multicultural plurality).

The framing of the arrival of the refugees in 2015 as a crisis also instills forgetfulness about relatively recent accommodations of refugees. Compared with the current upheaval about refugees and migrants coming into Europe, Vietnamese who fled communism were welcomed more easily than is currently the case with people from the Middle East and Africa. As Part II, *People on the Move from Vietnam*, shows, since the end of the First Indochina War in 1954 and even more so after the Fall of Saigon in 1975, huge numbers of Vietnamese settled in Europe, the United States, and other countries (for figures, see Ninh). At the height of the Cold War, they were taken as the refugees from communism who deserved support by states and mainstream churches. As Phi-Vân Nguyen points out, Catholic support for Vietnamese as well as Chinese and Korean "victims of Communist atrocities" was framed in terms of a battle between atheist communism and Christianity. The logic of the Cold War induced sympathy for people who were persecuted for their religion, be it Catholicism or Buddhism. Compared with the current situation, it is remarkable how relatively smooth the adoption of Vietnamese refugees—often circumscribed as "boat people"— from camps in Asia into "third countries" occurred. Remarkably, in the FRG, these refugees were received without having to submit individual asylum applications, but were accepted as part of a defined "contingent" of Vietnamese in need (*Kontingentflüchtlinge*) (Ngo and Mai). Similarly, Christians from Syria also received and still receive special treatment; being subject to persecution on religious grounds (in their case not by communism, but by Islam), they are more likely to be granted asylum than other refugees (Murre-van den Berg). This is not to suggest that the actual reception of Vietnamese Catholics, Buddhists, and adherents of indigenous religions and Middle Eastern Orthodox Christians in European host societies went smoothly; our volume discloses many structural similarities among the problems faced by refugees from Vietnam, the Middle East, and Africa in finding a place and gaining acceptance in their new host societies (see in the next section). The point is that the likelihood of being welcomed and granted asylum depends to a large extent on the place of refugees and their religion in geopolitical scenarios, such as the Cold War or the "Clash of Civilizations" (Huntington) that became dominant post-9/11.

In sum, our volume works against the lure of exceptionalism conveyed by the crisis framing, which arguably contributes to a muting of past experiences with refugees in European memory. One insight offered by our volume is that we must draw explicit links between ongoing research on recent migrations by people from the Global South and the history of refugees and religious plurality in Europe. The fact is that European states have produced *and* accommodated (religious) refugees throughout the past 500 years. This being so, we must regard Europe as religiously plural by default (see also Kippenberg, Rüpke, and Von Stuckrad 2009).

State Politics of Religious Plurality

"Thinking with history," Wayne te Brake invites us to detect recurrent patterns in the regulation of religion by states throughout European history and beyond. As he explains, in the aftermath of the Peace of Westphalia in 1648, the weak compromises that underpinned religious plurality were often derailed, yielding polarization and the (forced) dislocation of religious minorities. "Official religious intolerance" and the striving for "religious 'unity and purity'" by rulers and their privileged religious partners ended up classifying people with certain religious convictions as dissidents. Depending on the formal and legal structures of the state they were in, dissidents could face forced migration, tolerance for their expression of their religion, the need to adjust and adapt to the circumstances, or the need to go into hiding and dissimulate. The different national templates of regulating religion on the level of the state in various European countries and the UK that te Brake distinguishes still have repercussions in the accommodation of refugees in our time. While he emphasizes the power of political and religious authorities to regulate religion, he also calls on us to recognize the "powerful agency of religious 'dissenters,' 'outsiders' and 'newcomers'" and how this plays out in actual "patterns of coexistence"—a point that, of course, motivates the ethnographic approach to people on the move and fixed in institutions throughout this volume.

Te Brake's project of "thinking with" the insights gained through his earlier detailed historical research (2017) offers much welcome historical relief to theoretical work around secularity and secularism in religious studies and anthropology (e.g., Asad 2003; Casanova 2019b; Mahmood 2015; Wohlrab-Sahr and Burchardt 2011). Among scholars in these fields, there is broad agreement to reject the conventional secularization thesis that has long offered the dominant analytical frame in the study of religion in modern societies and still informs public debates. What comes in its place is the understanding that the category of the secular as deployed by modern states produces, facilitates, and regulates what we have come to define as religion (see Giumbelli 2013).[7] The question how to grasp the dynamics and plurality of contemporary religious environments in the context of secular formations in nation-states in the Global North and Global South is one of the greatest empirical and conceptual issues faced by the study of religion today. As Salah Punathil's contribution shows, in most of the world, nation-states are only recent inventions and national borders shift for all kinds of reasons, such as religious conflicts, while secularity is shaped in highly context-dependent ways that may offer much room for the public manifestation of (a certain) religion. Punathil demonstrates the fragility and porosity of borders between states in South Asia and between refugee camps and the rest of society. Both territorial sovereignty and local security are constantly contested in many societies.

Aiming to grasp the accommodation of refugees in particular nation-states, our volume speaks to these broader issues. For it is through the study of modalities of accommodation that it is possible to lay bare partly taken-for-granted state-religion arrangements, beyond the proverbial "separation of Church and State." Claims in favor of such a separation are enveloped in the long-standing policies deployed by nation-states in regulating religion that are grounded in specific national templates and patterns of coexistence (in the sense of te Brake). Accommodation systems for refugees reflect such national templates (see also Bowen, Bertossi, Duyvendak, and Krook 2013). As Alexander-Kenneth Nagel shows, German refugee accommodation centers are not well equipped to host refugees with a Muslim background. Analyzing the spatial layout of Friedland, he observes a mismatch between the strong insistence on religious neutrality and the framing of the camp as a secular space, on the one hand, and its prominent Christian infrastructure—with a church, a chapel, and an iconic bell on the campground and activities of Christian welfare initiatives—on the other. It is a microcosm that crystallizes how a formally secular space of reception is inflected with the mostly unquestioned presence of Christianity and a lingering tendency to privilege refugees with a Christian background. This raises issues for Muslim refugees as to the extent they are accommodated to live their religion (apart from receiving halal food) and may fuel interreligious tensions.

Such issues and tensions, of course, also play out in the public domain in general and shape our current plural religious environments at large. Clearly, existing national templates and long-standing pattern of coexistence do not entail that all religions are valued and treated equally. In Germany, which receives much attention in our volume, the "parity template" (te Brake) allowed for the peaceful coexistence of Catholics and Lutherans after the *Augsburger Religionsfriede* (1555) that was extended to Calvinists in 1648. Challenged during the nineteenth-century *Kulturkampf*, this template retained its resilience and is still in place. But as the contributions by Thien-Huong Ninh, Tam Ngo and Nga Mai, Abdoualye Sounaye, and Alexander-Kenneth Nagel highlight, religious newcomers—refugees and migrants—face difficulties in being recognized; they "may perceive religious parity as exclusionary privilege" (te Brake) that cements the status quo, but offers religious newcomers and minorities little room for religious expression.[8] This pertains particularly to the public expression of material religious forms, from clothes to building temples and mosques. While freedom of religion is granted quite easily on the level of belief and conviction, the material and corporeal manifestation of religions triggers societal tensions and debates.[9]

The limited possibilities for full material and corporeal manifestations of religion are not necessarily and exclusively due not only to legal barriers and state policies that do not allow them to live their religion but also to public opinion. Across Europe, the balance between the acknowledgment that refugees and migrants have certain, albeit limited legal rights to practice their religion, as backed by national constitutions, and the actual acceptance of them doing so in public opinion is shifting. This lack of acceptance is grounded in resilient patterns of the discrimination of minorities like the Jews and "gypsies" and racist stereotypes based in colonialism and its fantasies of the superiority of the white Europeans; in such situations, the presence of such others is often met with a sense of disgust, and they are rejected for being "dirty" and polluting the nation.[10] While these ideas and affects do not directly relate to policies that regulate religious coexistence, they nonetheless linger on and, as we see, are easily resuscitated by far-right populist movements. As Oscar Verkaaik and Pooyan Tamimi Arab (2016) note, there is a cleavage between constitutional and cultural secularism, in that certain rights, such as the freedom of religious expression, are challenged in the name of culturalized and exclusivist understandings of citizenship and belonging (see also Tonkens and Duyvendak 2016). While public opinion has come to be more secularist in orientation and has suspicions about the religiosity of refugees and migrants (van der Veer 2006; Schuh, Burchardt and Wohlrab-Sahr 2012), there is also a tendency to rediscover the Christian roots of national and European culture, in whose name refugees and migrants with a non-Christian—de facto usually Muslim—background are held to not belong (Nagel, Sounaye; see also Götz 2020; Marzouki, MacDonnell, and Roy 2016; Meyer 2019; Van den Hemel 2018). Such a mobilization of a "secular sacred" (Balkenhol, van den Hemel, and Stengs 2020) in the current politics of belonging arouses moods and emotions that tap into cosmologies and repertoires of a culturalized Christianity or Christendom. These repertoires are at the heart of the political theology of populism, as several contributors to the volume *Religion in the European Refugee Crisis* (Schmiedel and Smith 2018) argue compellingly.[11]

As Erin Wilson and Luca Mavelli point out in the Introduction to their volume *The Refugee Crisis and Religion* (2017), public discourse distinguishes between "good" and "bad" religion, the latter being strongly identified with Islam, understood as a religion that persecutes religious Others. The suspicions about Islam also entail a "'good Muslim, bad Muslim' narrative" (2017: 6) that construes Muslims either as potentially dangerous or as victims of their own religious tradition. In public discourse, there certainly is a hierarchy of valuation of religions, in which Christianity tends to be privileged (especially persecuted Christians from Vietnam or the Middle East, as noted earlier) and in which

Buddhism ranks higher than Islam. While it is important to analyze how such hierarchies underpin public debates and shape the readiness to prefer certain refugees to others, this is not the whole story. True to its ethnographic orientation, our volume shows how refugees and migrants on the ground grapple with their situation in societies that have long been dominated by Christianity and are now in a process of rapid de-churching. As Ninh observes, "even though religious diversity and freedom are fundamental rights in these Western countries [Germany and the US—BM], religion has become the proxy through which Vietnamese refugees are marginalized to the fringes of society as ethnic and racial minorities." Heleen Murre-van den Berg points out that Syriac Orthodox Christians, who are often mistaken for Muslims in their first encounters with native Dutch, navigate between affirming their acceptance of the secular state in the Netherlands and struggling to transmit their traditional ethical norms, which diverge from the secular Dutch majority and bring them closer to the Muslims from whom they insist they differ. And Abdoulaye Sounaye reports the struggles of West African Muslim refugees in Berlin to eschew marginalization and discrimination not by native Germans, but also by other Muslims. Their efforts to build their own mosque and thus a viable social and ritual place in Muslim Berlin are part of their attempts to gain space and status as black African Muslims. It is interesting to note that, while Vietnamese refugees were more welcome than current refugees from Africa and the Middle East, the experiences of both groups of refugees in deploying their religion in their new host societies are quite similar. They all remained religious, ethnic, and racialized Others. Granted certain rights, they are expected to reciprocate the "gift of freedom" by being "grateful for having been saved" (Hoskins; see also Ghorashi 2014; Nayeri 2019); they feel and are made to feel that they are not quite at home in a mainstream national or European culture that is increasingly closing down and looking back to its presumed roots and heritage.

While our volume concentrates on the accommodation of (former) refugees and their trajectory as migrants and citizens in Europe, the perspective on national templates of regulating religion is also useful with regard to states in the Global South, as shown by the intriguing case of Morocco, which many people on the move from sub-Saharan Africa pass through and where they may get stuck for some time or even decide to stay. Johara Berriane unpacks how Pentecostals from Congo and other African countries find niches in the existing regulation of religious coexistence in this majority Muslim country, in which Sunni Islam is the state religion, while Jews are recognized as a national minority and mainstream Christian churches are recognized as spaces for worship for foreigners (conversion to Christianity is forbidden). The enduring and often loud presence of house churches in Moroccan cities entails complex negotiations on the part of the state authorities to grant the religious rights of these Pentecostal newcomers, while also keeping them under control and preventing them from proselytizing.

So, this section highlights that national templates and long-standing patterns of coexistence form the conditions under which refugees are accommodated and in which they and other migrants have to position themselves. A focus on refugees and religion, as in this volume, offers privileged insights into such patterns as well as their gradual negotiation and transformation. This reveals a logic of closure and fixing through which people on the move are put in a certain state-run order that does not quite fit them. Taking such a perspective is of crucial importance to determine the space afforded to refugees and migrants and to apprehend how they respond and negotiate possibilities. But this perspective is partial. The next section will look at the refugees-and-religion nexus from the angle of movement.

Religion as a Boundary-Transgressing Force

Over the past two decades, much attention has been paid to transnational religion, in the sense of people moving between different locations, as travelers, pilgrims, migrants, or refugees. Rethinking religion from the vector of mobility was important to correct a scholarly bias toward the nation as the taken-for-granted habitat of religion and unit of scholarly analysis. As Peggy Levitt put it aptly in her conceptual roadmap for the study of "religion on the move": "We assume that religious practices and organizations obediently respect national boundaries. We take stasis and boundedness as the default categories for organizing religious life while, in fact, many religious ideas and practices are often and unabashedly in motion" (2013: 159). Endorsing Levitt's critique does not contradict the main idea conveyed in the previous section. The point is to fold both perspectives—of religion as being subject to the ordering structures and boundaries of nation-states *and* as a boundary-transgressing force—into each other (see also Hüwelmeier and Krause 2010: 1). The regulatory mechanisms in state and society do not fully capture and contain people in motion, so it is an important task for scholars to explore what exists in excess of the orders into which these people are accommodated. What are their own narratives about being on the move, and how do these narratives link up with theological ideas about mobility?

Of course, mobility is intrinsically engrained in religious traditions such as Judaism, Christianity, and Islam, which spread around the globe long before the current global order of nation-states emerged and which involve theologies of mobility, foregrounding experiences of diaspora and exile in the case of Judaism and missionizing activities and global networks in the case of Christianity and Islam. This huge and intriguing theme deserves an extensive comparative investigation. In our volume, the chapters by Phi-Vân Nguyen and Thien-Huong Ninh call attention to the transnationality of the Catholic Church. While the former looks at the flight of Catholic refugees from North Vietnam in the 1950s, from where the exodus of Catholics around the world started to unfold, the latter explores how contemporary Catholic ex-refugees reach back to Vietnam from Germany and the United States. Starting his chapter with the iconic image of a Vietnamese refugee holding a crucifix while deep asleep, Nguyen points to the political relevance of mediating the exodus of Vietnamese Catholics from North to South Vietnam as grounded in their deep faith. Such a faith is held to motivate people to move away from regimes that suppress their religion and seek refuge elsewhere. The idea of authentic faith as the genuine cause for people fleeing and applying for asylum is not only reiterated in Christian representations of the predicament of refugees but also taken as a crucial factor in court decision whether to grant or withhold asylum, as is the case with Muslims who converted to Christianity (Wheeler; see also Stadlbauer 2018; Reid 2018).[12]

Zooming in on the transnational ties between Catholics in Vietnam, the United States, and Germany, Ninh points out how the new iconography of a Vietnamese-looking *Our Lady of Lavang* serves former refugees as an emblem of a deterritorialized imagined community "beyond the territorial boundaries of their dead homeland (South Vietnam) and new host societies." Authorized by the Vatican and recognized in Vietnam, this Lady has become a new iconic figure that joins Vietnamese Catholics across the world, serving as a reminder of coerced displacement and dispersion. This case is very interesting because it reveals how communities of refugees that settled in new host countries deploy creative energies to craft new religious forms that circulate through transnational networks, setting Catholicism in motion by generating new cultic material forms. We find a similar dynamic at work among the Syriac Orthodox community in the Netherlands. As Heleen Murre-van den Berg points out, its leaders search for new materials and modalities to transmit the Orthodox literary heritage to subsequent generations to keep the tradition alive and ongoing. This suggests that refugees "in diaspora" may play a central role in fueling innovations that are, after all, the sine qua non for the reproduction of a religious tradition under new circumstances.

Similarly, Tam Ngo and Nga Mai draw attention to the amazing industriousness of Vietnamese Buddhists in building temples and pagodas. Differentiated between former contract laborers, successors of the "boat people," and newly arrived refugees, the Vietnamese population in Germany experiences many divisions and conflicts. Stating that "all these people have left Vietnam, but they have not left it behind," the authors offer intriguing insights into the ways past tensions and distinctions still play out among the former refugees in the host country, while at the same time the Vietnamese state seeks to use Buddhism to gain control over this diaspora. The chapter brings to mind the remarkable resilience of former refugees and migrants in the face of their experiences, long after they have settled and may even have received dual citizenship. They are on the move, but do not achieve a full rupture with their—for many, traumatic—past.

Tropes of journeys, flows, crossings, and dwellings abound in the repertoires of religious traditions (Tweed 2006). And yet, as Janet Hoskins points out, "the theological implications of migration and especially the forced displacement of refugees have rarely been explored. (. . .) Religious ritual and scripture can serve to provide a narrative that explains the reasons for this displacement."[13] Her chapter compares the theological narratives of Caodaism and Mother Goddess temples. Both are indigenous religious traditions that operate on a transnational scale and are popular among refugees and migrants outside of Vietnam. Both traditions emphasize movement, albeit in different ways, with the former endorsing "the idea of a sacred journey to 'the west'" and the latter engaging in "trance dances" through which spirits from Vietnam are conjured and made present in the diaspora. Hoskins's approach is compelling because it shows how vernacular theologies of mobility feed into migration narratives grounded in divergent experiences and underpin attitudes toward the host country and the original home.

The importance of theologies of mobility also comes to the fore in Alessandro Gusman's account of Congolese refugees stuck in Kampala. Invoking the narrative of the exodus of the people of Israel and their long crossing through the desert, Pentecostals inscribe their suffering and despair in this ancient epic frame, feeling "captive" and waiting to get to the "Promised Land." Interesting here is that this narrative of movement is mobilized in a moment when people are bound to wait in transit, offering them hope to get moving again. For them, faith is a guide that helps them endure and remain patient, while not losing hope in the possibility of (re)gaining social and spatial mobility. Similarly, failing to jump over the fences that separate Morocco from the enclaves of Ceuta and Melilla,[14] Congolese Pentecostals in Morocco feel stuck at the increasingly guarded borders of Europe. They attribute their forced immobility to the spell of curses that tie them, via their families, to ancestral powers that are understood as demons; they seek deliverance from these ancestral powers to get rid of "the spiritual blocks to their emigration." Biblical role models, including Job, are cited to help these Pentecostals make sense of and endure their precarious situation. These three chapters show in an exemplary manner that attention to the interface of (vernacular) theologies of mobility and migration narratives offers deep insights into the everyday struggles of people on the move. They also teach that the notion of "people on the move" needs to be qualified. Being on the move may de facto imply being bound to wait for a long time. Rather than being nothing, "waiting is a particular engagement in, and with, time" (Bandak and Janea 2018: 1), as our volume also shows.

Waiting is also the main "activity" for those who managed to reach their destination in Europe or UK and apply for asylum. In this limbo, many refugees depend on support from religious groups, including Christian churches and organizations, some of which actively proselytize among non-Christians. William Wheeler narrates the unsettling story of Abdul, whose conversion story from Islam to Christianity became the object of bureaucratic and legal inquiry and was eventually judged inauthentic by the Home Office, as is the case with large numbers of persons on the move who file for asylum in vain.

So, this section spotlights the importance of theologies of mobility and transmitted narratives in situations of displacement and migration, triggering departures, giving meaning to the experiences undergone, and making long holdups bearable. While regulated by nation-states in one way or another, religion potentially exceeds this regulation because it implies a principle of movement and mediation between here and there, immanent and transcendent, beginning and end (see Tweed 2006; for my own approach, see Meyer 2020a). This comes particularly to the fore when studying people on the move from the angle of their own religious views and narratives. Their stories challenge conceptualizations of religion as entirely bound within national templates, however real and taken for granted they may appear. Looking at religion as a boundary-transgressing force in a global order of nation-states, this volume points to the ongoing interplay of flows and closures in which not only refugees but also the societies from where they flee and those they reach out to, are entangled (see Meyer and Geschiere 1998).

Mobilizing Theory

Over the past decade, and even more so since the arrival of large numbers of refugees in Europe, I have noticed that the difference between my work as a scholar studying religion in Africa and my attempts to grasp the politics of religious plurality in the world I inhabit as a citizen (the Netherlands and Germany) is becoming increasingly blurred. The geographical, cultural, and political boundaries that separate Europe from Africa are proving to be highly permeable, echoing long-standing connections and entanglements (Friese 2014). While "Europe" has long been present in "Africa" and other regions of its imperial outreach, people from these regions are in Europe, or are trying to get in. As I argued recently (Meyer 2018), European societies have long become de facto postcolonial "frontier zones" (Chidester 1996) in which religious and other differences are articulated, encountered, negotiated, and governed. As the refugee issue shows so clearly, the enforcement and surveillance of boundaries as well as the regulation of religious plurality are a matter of politics that is geared to delineate and order a world that is de facto shaped by long-standing transregional connections and always in motion.

Requiring collaborations among scholars with expertise on societies in the Global South *and* Europe, a viable analysis of these dynamics demands a new transregional and pluralistic mindset, as well as new synergies between academic fields such as African and Asian anthropology, European history, law, religious studies, and migration studies (Meyer 2020b). This endeavor must mobilize theory. And I mean "mobilize" not simply in the sense of a call for theory to make sense of the trajectories of people on the move, but in the sense of "theory as a practice of travel and observation" that harks back to the Greek term *theorein*, as proposed by James Clifford (1989). Postcolonial thought has deployed the point he raised more than thirty years ago that the privileged position of the West as the natural place of theory is "increasingly contested, cut across, by other locations, claims, trajectories of knowledge articulating racial, gender, and cultural differences," yielding calls for theory from the South. And for the study of religion, along similar lines Thomas Tweed has launched a take on theory as itinerary. For him, theories are "proposals for a journey, representations of a journey, and the journey itself" (2006: 9). My idea of mobilizing theory builds on these insights, while at the same time the focus on the refugees-and-religion nexus offers a special twist. The contributions to our volume have each traced specific parts of the itineraries of refugees, and together they offer a dazzling picture of an entangled world with connections and relations, as well as borders and boundaries. Theory is to be rendered mobile to make sense of this entangled world from multiple locations and grounded in the practices and experiences of people on the move.

Though subject to long-standing criticism from postcolonial angles, a Eurocentric bias still lingers on in the social and cultural sciences. This is because the disciplines that comprise the social sciences and humanities traditionally entail a strong orientation toward the nation-state as the presumably natural social and political form. Even in the face of globalization, there is still not only a "methodological" but also an "epistemological" nationalism (Beck 2007) that preempts taking historical and current entanglements seriously as a ground for knowledge production and that is prepared to rethink Europe from its supposed margins (Mbembe 2017) and with people on the move, for a different view of the world.

It is easier to think in terms of bounded units than in terms of motion. This is at least the conventional mode of knowledge production in which scholars are trained. Deconstructed through genealogical research on the rise of modern epistemologies of power knowledge along lines set out by Foucault, this way of knowledge production is nonetheless resilient. It is deeply engrained in the sociological imagination, yet always haunted by the presence of Others who challenge conventional ordering principles. For those drawing and guarding political boundaries, movement "in the sense of disrespect of boundaries and borders, the transgression of imaginary lines or indeed concrete ones (in the form of walls and fences) between regions and categories of people claiming these regions as their territories, as their turf, which should not be invaded and polluted" (Verrips 2011: 209), is suspicious because it causes disorder. The political measures taken to prevent or at least channel movement are an important research topic. However, as this volume shows, such research cannot be done successfully from an epistemology grounded in a sedentary, bounded logic for which movement is itself a problem.

In his insightful study of Kant and his colleague philosopher and linguist Christian Jakob Kraus (1753–1807), who conducted research on "gypsies" ("Zigeuner") in Königsberg, Kurt Röttgers contrasts two forms of reason: settled ("sesshaft") and nomadic (1993; see also Verrips 2011: 205–7). Kant favored the settled, ordering, and measuring reason of the land surveyor, who was to chart the true order of the world, over the nomadic reason of skeptics and empiricists; his dislike of this type of reason was grounded in his disapproval of nomads who detest steady work on the soil. By contrast, Kraus, through his investigations among the "gypsies," encountered and valued such a nomadic or itinerant (*vagabundierend*) reason that, alas, he could only talk about (also with Kant), but not write about, due to his persistent writer's block. Röttgers sees this itinerant reason, which he traces through the few documents left by the more or less forgotten Kraus, as part of an alternative, nomadic Enlightenment. Existing in the shadow of pure, settled reason, nomadic reason is not interested in reaching fixed points, but seeks to extend lines, "to continue the route of the nomads adequately in theory; Deleuze/Guattari would say: making rhizomes" (1993: 107, translation BM).

Röttgers's exposé is intriguing because it offers a glimpse of a genealogy of modern knowledge production predicated on the role of the land surveyor who oversees, charts, and maps and is at loss with regard to people on the move. My point is not to reject this territorial form of knowledge production per se, but to keep in mind that itinerant or nomadic reason is an alternative possibility, if only to better understand the interfaces of flows and closures to which the study of people on the move, and refugees in particular, draws attention (see also Braidotti 2011). Nomadic reason is at the heart of the idea of mobilizing theory I have in mind. Of course, anthropology has long challenged the settled reason at the core of Eurocentric modes of knowledge production (Därmann 2005; Fabian 2000: 275–81). The by now dawning insight that Europe is a postcolonial frontier zone calls for a sustained effort in the social and cultural sciences to mobilize theory to be able to make critical sense of our open and at the same time closed, interconnected world. The research on the refugees-and-religion nexus presented in this volume underscores the pressing importance of this endeavor.

Acknowledgments

This concluding chapter was written in the context of the research program Religious Matters in an Entangled World* chaired by me and funded thanks to the Spinoza Prize awarded to me by the Netherlands Foundation of Scientific Research (NWO) and the Academy Professor Prize by the Royal Netherlands Academy of Arts and Sciences (KNAW). I am grateful to Jojada Verrips for his helpful, sharp, and stimulating comments on an earlier version of this chapter, and for thinking along all the way. Many thanks also to Peter Geschiere, Pooyan Tamimi Arab and Peter van der Veer, and Mitch Cohen for superb editing.

* www.religiousmatters.nl

Notes

Chapter 1

1 I use the term "mechanisms" to denote a delimited class of events or interactions that alter the relations among historical actors in identical or closely similar ways across a variety of situations; think of them as the "verbs" that connect the subjects and predicates of historical processes. "Processes," by extension, are clusters or concatenations of mechanisms that recurrently alter the relations of historical actors over longer periods of time and in a variety of situations with a limited range of variant outcomes.

2 Unless otherwise noted, what follows in this historical discussion derives from the research that I published in te Brake (2017).

3 For more background on the two principal examples—the Dutch Republic and Saxony—see Prak (2005) and Schunka (2006).

4 I should also note that the triumph of Reformed Protestantism in Dutch Republic banished Catholicism from public life and precipitated a significant Catholic emigration (Janssen 2014).

5 The "national" vignettes in this section are based on readily accessible online resources, bolstered by a series of broadly contextual reports on the contemporary patterns and politics of religious diversity from the Pew Research Center Project on Religion and Public Life; for access to the available publications, visit https://www.pewresearch.org/ and http://www.globalreligiousfutures.org/.

6 In what follows, I will use the terms I introduced earlier in Table 1.3 and Figure 1.2 to describe "national templates" or frameworks for the management of religious diversity, even though I introduced them, and generally use them, as descriptors of the relationships of specific communities of faith with their most proximate political authorities (local rulers). In this more general and comparative usage, the terms may be considered aspirational or prescriptive rather than reliable descriptors of "facts on the ground."

7 The (Christian) *privilege* template of the modern Kingdom of the Netherlands, which also descends from an early modern regime of (Reformed) privilege in the Dutch Republic, appears to offer refugees similar and equally confounding incentives to "conversion" to Christianity.

8 I explore both the historical and the contemporary experience of religious "outsiders" more specifically in an illustrative survey of the religious landscape of the city of Mainz, Germany, in te Brake (forthcoming).

9 I should note that while the rise of anti-Semitism and Islamophobia appears to be a general phenomenon, it affects religious "newcomers" differently, depending on the template that shapes the management of religious diversity.

10 This may be especially challenging for religiously devout refugees who originated in situations where their religious identities were dominant or in the majority—that is, easily taken for granted.

Chapter 2

1 https://www.sueddeutsche.de/politik/kirche-und-asyl-wers-glaubt-1.4067808?reduced=true

Chapter 4

1 Lavang is approximately 60 kilometers north of Hue (the former capital of Vietnam) in Central Vietnam.

2 This may be a surprise for many since not even the Vietnamese Catholic community in France has a national-level association. France plays an important and historic role within Vietnamese Catholicism and has a sizable Vietnamese Catholic population.

3 The federation's website is: www.ldcg.de

4 Popularly and collectively known as "Các Thánh Tử Đạo Việt Nam" (Vietnamese Catholic martyrs)

5 The Center closed on January 20, 2007, due to financial restraints and the justification that Vietnamese Catholics around the world have successfully adapted into their host societies. Father Dinh Dao (the last director of the Coordinating Office of the Apostolate for the Vietnamese in the Diaspora), email correspondence, April 25 to May 29, 2012.

6 Monsignor Philippe Tran Van Hoai was the ideal candidate to direct the newly established organization. Since 1969, he had been studying and working in Rome. At the end of the Vietnam War in 1975, Monsignor Tran was appointed as the director of the Vietnamese Refugee Office of Caritas Italiana to rescue and resettle Vietnamese "boat people" who were fleeing from communism. In 1992, he founded the Movement of the Vietnamese Laity in Diaspora.

7 Although scholars such as Penny Edwards (2002) have written about the construction of national costumes within imperial and colonial projects, including those related to configuring nation and race, the meanings ao dai promoted by members in the diaspora have different meanings and need further exploration.

8 In January 2011, this original statue was replaced by a newer model sculpted by a local Vietnamese artist (Father Than 2009).

9 After the installment of the Vietnamese-looking Our Lady of Lavang statue in the shrine, the European statue of the Virgin Mary was relocated and placed behind a large tree about 500 meters from the shrine, its original location.

10 The office was under the directorship of Monsignor Philippe Tran Van Hoai and his assistant, Monsignor Dinh Duc Dao.

Chapter 5

1 Pew-Templeton Global Religious Futures 2010, The Future of World Religions: Vietnam's Religious Demography. Research report available online at http://www .globalreligiousfutures.org/countries/vietnam#/?affiliations_religion_id=0&a ffiliations_year=2010&region_name=All%20Countries&restrictions_year=2016 (accessed July 31, 2019).

2 The full name is Đại Đạo Tam Kỳ Phổ Độ, which I translate as "The Great Way of the Third Era of Redemption," although many others prefer "the Third Era of Salvation." I have developed this translation to highlight continuties with other "redemptive societies" in the Sino-Vietnamese tradition (see also Hoskins 2015: 33–4, 51–2, 63–4).

3 The New Testament is also interpreted by Caodaists as having prophesied the emergence of their own religion. They refer in particular to these verses from Mathew referring to the worship of a single eye: "The light of the body is the eye. If, therefore, thine eye be *single*, thy whole body shall be full of light" (Matthew 6:22). The appearance of the Jade Emperor after midnight on Christmas Eve 1925 is seen as corresponding to the verse in Revelation 16:15, which said, "the day of the Lord will come like a thief in the night" (Thessalonians 5:2). See also Peter 3:10, and Revelation 22:7 ("Look, I am coming soon! Blessed is the one who keeps the words of the prophecy written").

4 Ten short videos of Đạo Mẫu trance dancers (both male and female, young and old) can be found at the teaching website: http://dornsife.usc.edu/transnational-religion. Seven of the most popular spirits are profiled on that website (the national hero, the fifth mandarin in blue, the sixth lady in green, the golden prince, the third princess in white, the ninth princess in pink, and the impish youngest prince), with clips from ceremonies where they are incarnated by various mediums, in both California and Vietnam.

5 In 2016, the US Census Bureau estimated that the total population of Vietnamese Americans was 2,067,527 (92.9 percent reporting one race, 6.5 percent reporting two races, 0.5 percent reporting three races, and 0.1 percent reporting four or more

races). California and Texas had the largest populations of Vietnamese Americans: 40 and 12 percent, respectively. About 41 percent of the Vietnamese immigrant population lives in five major metropolitan areas: in descending order, Los Angeles, San Jose, Houston, San Francisco, and Dallas-Fort Worth. There are Caodai temples in or adjacent to each of these metropolitan areas, and also others in New Orleans, Seattle, Wichita (Kansas), the suburbs of Washington, D.C., and Montreal, Canada (Hoskins 2015: xiv, 163).

6   More details are available in Broucek 2016.

7   Refugees and former workers came to the divided Germany at about the same time: 35,000 refugees arrived in West Germany starting in 1979, and about 70,000 contract workers began to arrive in East Germany in 1980. These two migration streams also correspond to regions of origin in Vietnam, with most refugees hailing from former South Vietnam and most contract workers from former North Vietnam. The most recent census figures I could find were from 2016, when an estimated 176,000 people of Vietnamese origin lived in Germany, and two-thirds were foreign-born migrants. A little less than half of them (85,000) still had a Vietnamese passport (Bosch and Su 2018: 15).

8   This refugee association, called *Danke Deutschland* ("Thank you Germany," after a famous song) in German and Hội Tri ân Nước Đức ("German Gratitude Society") or "Cảm ơn Nước Đức" in Vietnamese, sponsors cultural gatherings with food, dances, and entertainment in cities like Spandau (near Berlin). Here are some activities on their website: http://www.nguoiviet.de/hoi-doan/Cong-dong-nguoi-Viet-tai-Br andenburg-noi-loi-CAM-ON-NUOC-DUC-37629.html

9   It is an interesting question as to why West German refugees have expressed the "thank you for rescuing us" argument most strongly. Former refugees in France, while often proud of their associations with elite French schools and universities, almost all also profess to despise the oppressions of French colonialism. And for Vietnamese Americans, the United States is both the rescuer and the betrayer— betrayer because of the perception that the United States could have won a military victory, but chose not to, and rescuer because there was a willingness to receive refugees in the 1980s and former prisoners in Vietnamese reeducation camps and their families in the 1990s.

Chapter 6

1   Hüwelmeier (2011) has done similar work on Pentecostal churches in mitigating the political tensions between these two Vietnamese opponents.

2   Duy Dinh, "The Rivival of Bolero in Vietnam," *The Diplomat*, October 12, 2016. Available online: https://thediplomat.com/2016/10/the-revival-of-bolero-in-vie tnam/ (accessed March 16, 2020)

3   Ngô Đình Diệm was the first president of the South Vietnam serving from
    1955 until he was ousted and killed in a 1963 military coup. Ngô Đình Diệm was
    born to a Catholic family. Buddhists, under his rule, criticized and protested against
    his discriminated religious policies which favored Catholic Churches and oppression
    of religious freedom. Protests and social unrests, many led by Buddhist practitioners
    and supporters, against his religious policy, played an important role in the downfall
    of Ngô Đình Diệm's regime.

4   The information on the trip of Venerable Thích Đức Thiện was covered on the
    Nguoitviet.de, available online: http://nguoiviet.de/tam-linh/dai-le-phat-dan-va-du
    -an-xay-ngoi-chua-viet-tai-thu-do-berlin-duc-34883.html (accessed March 16,
    2020).

5   The term *Thượng Đế* in Vietnamese, or *Shangdi* in Chinese, refers to the highest
    figure who has founded the universe. The term is commonly known as the Heavenly
    Ruler or the Highest Deity to followers of folk religion. To lesser extent, through
    English-Vietnamese translation, *Thượng Đế* also means the God in Christianity, or
    Allah in Islam. However, *Thượng Đế* is an alien term to Buddhists. The arbitrary use
    between *Thượng Đế* and Buddha, sometimes both appear in the same sentences, has
    become one point of critique on Master Ruma's religious teaching.

6   Public Security online newspapers, the mouthpiece of the Public Security
    Departments in Vietnam, often reported on the practices of Light and Sound
    Meditation as well as the dissemination of this religious belief which are considered
    as criminal activities. Some examples of the media clippings: Public Security online
    newspaper of Dien Bien province http://cand.com.vn/Xa-hoi/Ta-dao-Phap-mon-Die
    u-am-xuat-hien-o-Dien-Bien-144214/, Hoang Phap Pagoda's website http://www
    .chuahoangphap.com.vn/tin-tuc/chi-tiet-su-tran-tam-co-phai-tu-si-dao-phat-2110/.

Chapter 7

1   http://data.unhcr.org/drc/country.php?id=229. A population of around 850,000
    Congolese currently lives abroad, the majority in other African countries. Uganda
    is by far the first country of refuge for people fleeing from the DRC, hosting
    almost 340,000 Congolese (data, June 2019: UNHCR, Operational Portal, Refugee
    situations, DRC situation, http://data.unhcr.org/drc/regional.php).

2   David Dodman, *Revealing the Hidden Refugees in African Cities*, https://www.iie
    d.org/revealing-hidden-refugees-african-cities

3   Until 2009, their presence was regulated by the *Control of the Alien Refugee Act*
    (1964), which formally forced refugees to live in the camps.

4   *Églises de Réveil* (Awakening Churches) are Pentecostal-like churches, originated in
    Congo and in other French-speaking countries, both as independent churches and
    as part of larger evangelical denominations. The growth of the Charismatic renewal

in Congo DRC took place in the second half of the 1990s. Pentecostalism is today in a dominant position within the Congolese diasporic religious field (Garbin 2014). Some congregations originated in the DRC and opened branches in other countries following the paths of the Congolese diaspora, whereas others were created in diasporic contexts and sometimes established branches in the DRC.

5   With reference to lived religion, David Hall (1997), who first introduced this idea in the debate, aimed at shifting the focus of religious studies from institutional settings to religious practices as they are enacted in people's everyday lives.

6   See the reference to prayer in the next section.

Chapter 8

1   This chapter has been supported by several institutions and funding agencies, notably through a scholarship from the German Historical Institute in Paris, which enabled me to conduct the necessary fieldwork. The completion of the final draft was made possible by the Centre Marc Bloch in Berlin. I thank Birgit Meyer for her comments and Sally Sutton for her help during the preparation of the manuscript.

2   The 2014 national census reports that approximately 0.2 percent of the total population of Morocco were foreigners (86,206 persons), of whom 40 percent were European citizens (Bel-Air, 2016). Even if we add the 50,000 migrants who became residents during the migrant regularization operation (of which 80 percent were nationals from non-Arabic-speaking African countries) and the estimated 15,000 undocumented African migrants living in the country (Sidiguitiebe 2016), the number of foreign citizens in Morocco remains at under 1 percent of the total population.

3   The notion of house churches also refers to "evangelizing congregations self-consciously separated from mainline churches" (Coleman 2000: 19). In the Moroccan case, house churches are so-called because of the privacy of these religious places.

4   I participated in several religious gatherings and held regular discussions and informal interviews with congregants. I also conducted in-depth interviews in French with twenty-two congregants, seventeen of whom were church leaders, and five congregants who were particularly involved with their churches.

5   Examples are Takadoum, Hay Nahda, J5, J3, Youssoufia, Bouitat, and Sidi Moussa in the neighboring town of Salé.

6   The mobile features of migrant house churches and the churches' integration in transnational religious spaces have been analyzed in more detail in Berriane 2020.

7   I met only one female church leader in Ivory Coast and was told of a female Liberian prophet who runs a church in Rabat. The pastors' wives (primarily in

Ivorian churches, less so in Congolese churches) were often also involved in services and sometimes gave the sermon.

8 This term will be explained in more detail later.

9 Such as the private house churches where Moroccan Christians worship.

10 Interview with the director of Caritas Maroc in Rabat (25.10.16) and the pastor of the EEAM parish in Rabat (21.06.16).

11 A language spoken by Congolese.

12 The national and international media's broadcast Moroccan and Spanish border agents' violent repression of migrants in 2005 made the issue of migration in Morocco more visible, and several informal associations were founded by African migrants to highlight the plight of sub-Saharan migrants in Morocco and elsewhere.

Chapter 9

1 One needs only to mention the "Refugees are Welcome" campaign embraced by many civil society organizations and religious institutions across Germany.

2 In most evocations of these categories, my interlocutors hardly escape that of the bad refugee.

3 The OPlatz movement, as it is also referred to, was active from 2012 through 2014, helping asylum seekers, mostly from Africa, pressure German authorities to reexamine their applications, most of which were rejected. It started with camping at Oranienplatz, involved hunger strike, and even touring Germany to raise awareness about the conditions of refugees and migrants.

4 For example, posting halal certification and nonalcoholic restaurants are parts of the Islamic mark on the city.

5 A Sufi group that emerged in Ethiopia and blossomed in Lebanon. Officially, they are the "founders" of the Omar Mosque in Berlin.

6 Devotional prayers.

7 One of the most dynamic mosques in the Kreuzberg neighborhood in Berlin. The mosque is actually a complex that hosts a mosque, a restaurant, and a travel agency catering to Muslims of many nationalities.

8 In her ethnographic account of *The Religious Identity of Young Muslim Women in Berlin*, Bendixsen (2013, 2–3) notes that securitization and politicization are having a lasting effect of how Islam in institutionalized and practiced in Berlin. This is in line with some of the views my interlocutors have expressed about attending specific mosques. Officials at both Omar mosque and the First African Mosque have mentioned German security forces seeking their collaboration to prevent violence and terrorism. Apparently, some mosques in Berlin were already under

surveillance as German authorities feared they would promote radicalization and jihadism in a post-9/11 context.

9 According to one of my interlocutors, the mosque has developed a refugee initiative, though with limited reach compared to that of Omar mosque.

10 Again, it is important to note the popularity of slogans such us "Refugees are Welcome" and "*Kein Mensch ist illegal*" (no person is illegal), which have become, in 2015 and 2016 in particular, the rallying claims of both refuges and migrants themselves, but most importantly of their supporters.

11 The Izala network in Europe hosts regularly leaders of its movement from West Africa. Abubakar Giro and Kabiru Gombe, the two most popular of the movements, toured Europe in 2017 and 2018, leading preaching in Hamburg, for example.

12 https://www.youtube.com/watch?v=Hsx99UuU1uI

13 Eid refers to the two main Muslim festivals, the first celebrating the end of a month of fasting (Ramadan) and the second one the end of the Hajj pilgrimage.

14 https://www.youtube.com/watch?v=21Mz96-INEQ

15 https://www.youtube.com/watch?v=Hsx99UuU1uI

16 A Jihadi Islamic organization also referred to as the Islamic State (IS) and which has been fighting the secular state in many parts of the world. It acquired influence in Libya and West Africa after the collapse of the Libyan state. Some of my interlocutors feared that they would be perceived as adherents of this organization, and sent on a mission in Europe.

17 This is in reference to several attacks in France for which ISIS claimed responsibility. Some of them involved young French men of African descent.

18 One of the most popular Sufi communities in West Africa.

19 In the sense of finding a place and making room for a specific practice.

20 Place here refers first to a physical space—a mosque, for example. Space refers primarily to how they make room for themselves in the society, whether through a mosque community or through a civil society organization.

21 To succeed or achieve a goal and become established, well to do. Let's note that this idea is particularly prevalent among my interlocutors regardless of their social, intellectual, economic, and political background.

22 In particular the Lampedusa Berlin group: https://www.facebook.com/LampedusaBerlin/.

Chapter 10

1 Most of this earlier work is comprised in Murre-van den Berg 2015a, where also extensive references to earlier research can be found. To support my argument in the following sections, I will mostly refer to this work, adding further references when crucial for the history of research or for the current argument.

2 Note that several publications are accompanied by audio files (cassettes, CDs, online), reflecting the limited literacy among the lay in both the classical and the modern languages, but also the ongoing importance of auditory traditions, from liturgical music to folk narratives.

3 AP 14: Qasha Shmuel Dawid, *Zmaryate d-ʿedta men leshana ʿattiqa pushqa b-leshana hadta* (Church Hymns from the Old Language Translated into the New), Chicago 1930s).

4 The percentages (here and in the following paragraphs) for the first two collections are based on the published manuscript catalogues, and for the two electronic collections it is based on a survey of the websites of November 2017 (available with the author).

5 Another reason for the relative decline is the fact that in the catalogues multiple manuscript copies of the same text are counted individually, whereas in the electronic bookshops every item is counted only once, despite the fact that, of course, multiple copies are produced and distributed.

6 Stichting Wereldtaal Houten 1993; The MEB version was published in Istanbul, probably in the early 2000s.

7 AP reprinted one the most important of these early Catholic catechisms, the Syriac translation of Robert Bellarmine's *Doctrinae Christianae*, first published in Rome in 1841.

8 This is different in the East Syriac realm, where a distinct form of modern Aramaic was standardized in the nineteenth century, and which therefore is well represented in the AP collection.

9 This dictionary by a Chaldean scholar and cleric (in a reprint of 1985, including its preface in the modern literary language of Urmia) one would have expected in the AP collection rather than in MEB; it thus points to the ongoing exchanges between the two literary traditions.

10 A German edition, published by Harrasowitz under the title *Geschichte der syrischen Wissenschaften und Literatur* (Leipzig, 2012), is also available via the MEB.

11 Sebastian P. Brock, David G. K. Taylor; with documentary produced by Giacomo Pezzali (Trans World Film 2001), available in German, English, and Dutch.

12 AP 58; *Tashʿita d-Atur*; it was written in the 1930s and survived in a manuscript copy of 1,290 pages. At the time, only a small part of it was published in a volume *Kursiya d-saliq w-psiqateʿal tashʿita d-Atur* (*Throne of Seleucia and notes on the History of Atur*) (AP 58; Chicago, 1931).

Chapter 11

1 The NRC is a list maintained by the Indian government with the names and other relevant information of all Indian citizens in India, beginning with those in Assam. It was implemented to help identify illegal migrants.

2   The first protest began in Assam and India's entire northeast on the very day the CAA was passed. The Assamese caste groups and tribal communities oppose this act because it provides citizenship status to Hindu migrants from Bangladesh. On the other hand, the protests in other parts of the country were largely against the exclusion of Muslims and the NRC's nationwide implementation.

3   Migrants to Assam from what is now Bangladesh have also included Hindus. However, there is considerable uncertainty over the identity of migrants. Many came during the colonial period and many more arrived between Indian independence and March 24, 1971, which was just before Bangladesh declared its independence and is now the citizenship cut-off date for people who live in Assam. Certain Assamese political organizations allege that a large number of Bengali Muslims came to India after 1971 and are thus illegal. If that is so, they may be refugees as well as migrants. However, these categories are partly distinctive and partly overlapping in this context.

4   The last instance was in 2014.

5   I have been visiting various Muslim settlements and camps in Assam for past three years as part of my research on violence and the citizenship crisis there.

6   Mbembe's view on sovereignty and violence is significant here for its distance from the dominant understanding of sovereignty located within the boundaries of the nation-state or within institutions empowered by the state.

7   The Koch Rajbongshis, a scheduled tribe in India, mostly live in Assam.

8   There were violent incidents in Western Assam in 2012 and 2014.

9   D voters are a class of disenfranchised people in Assam. Their citizenship is suspect because of an alleged lack of proper credentials. A few have already been sent to detention centers. Their stories are now part of the public discussion because of investigative reports by journalists and activists after the passage of the NRC and the CAA.

10 By "camp-like space" I mean the isolated places where Muslims are forced to live, exposed to greater vulnerability.

11 Asjiran Nercha, thirty-one, interviewed in Khagrabari on May 24, 2016.

12 Naseema Khatun, fifty-seven, interviewed in Khagrabari on May 27, 2016.

13 Abdul Razzaq, thirty-three, interviewed in Guwahati on December 27, 2017.

14 Ahmed, thirty-four, interviewed in Guwahati on December 29, 2017.

15 Amina Khatun, thirty-four, interviewed in Khagrabari on May 24, 2016.

16 Kamarunissa, twenty-eight, interviewed in Khagrabari on May 25, 2016.

Chapter 12

1   The project was conducted together with Veronika Rückamp and with support by Thorsten Wettich and Mehmet Kalender. In the course of this project, we

performed twenty-seven semi-structured interviews with members of the administrative, social work, and security staff of accommodation centers as well as with representatives of neighboring religious communities. The sample includes five state reception centers (*Landesaufnahmestellen*), four emergency shelters (*Notunterkünfte*), and three municipal reception centers. Particular emphasis was put on the so-called Border Transit Camp in Friedland (a small municipality, 14 kilometers from Göttingen), which is the oldest state reception center in Lower Saxony with a remarkable religious geography and an ambitious museum attached to it.

2 https://www.museum-friedland.de/de/about-us/mission-statement/.

3 In organizational terms, the museum is an administration unit of the Ministry for Internal Affairs of the state of Lower Saxony and formally directed by a ministerial representative (a former Theologian) in collaboration with an external exhibition agency ("*Die Exponauten*") and an academic advisory board. The museum is supposed to be only the first step of an ambitious plan, that is, to create a think tank and documentary center to address a wide range of issues connected to migration.

4 As historical studies show, the creation of the memorial site was complicated and not without frictions: the first initiative was taken by the German chancellor Konrad Adenauer, who sought for a memorial in order to document his efforts for the German war prisoners in the 1950s and assembled an advisory board including various associations of expellees, the Red Cross and representatives of the Protestant and the Roman Catholic Church. Originally, it was intended to erect a monumental statue of Jesus Christ, which should be visible across the border unto the Soviet-occupied zone. However, the idea was rejected, because it was regarded to be "too much Catholic." After the project had been pending for some years, it was finally taken over by the Association of Expellees, who raised more than half a million DM in donations and decided on the design of the memorial ((Schwelling 2008: 196–200).

5 https://www.lab.niedersachsen.de/standorte/standort_braunschweig/ausstellung-auf-der-flucht-162782.html.

6 https://www.notaufnahmelager-berlin.de/de/.

7 Our interviews with the spokespersons of both Turkish and Arabic mosques in Göttingen revealed that both were prepared to welcome refugees and also provided some support, but at the same time were concerned about the impact of the newcomers on the public image of established Muslim immigrants. Some of the (Arabic) communities considered themselves responsible for the moral education of refugees, that is, to acquaint them with the German way of life.

8 http://www.tagesspiegel.de/politik/fluechtlingsheim-in-suhl-streit-zwischen-fluechtlingen-ueber-koran-eskaliert/12211756.html.

9 https://www.opendoors.de/sites/default/files/2016_10_Lack_of_protection_for_reli gious_minorities_E4_2017_04.pdf.

10 This stance was widespread among social workers and administrators, whereas security personnel were more inclined to address group-related conflicts.

Chapter 13

1 To preserve anonymity, I have changed Abdul's name and other details, including dates. While I prefer not to name his country of origin, suffice it to say that asylum cases based on conversion among people from his country are rare.

2 His integration into the church community resembles the Muslim Syrian refugees in Lebanese evangelical churches described by Kraft (2017). While some convert, many attend the churches not only for the material support but also for the sake of community and holistic care provided.

3 Abdul's church does not encourage proselytizing. In Abdul's case, the issue is irrelevant, as evidence strongly suggests that merely practicing Christianity would put him at risk in his country.

4 With humanitarian protection, a travel document is much more expensive and, crucially, it is not recognized in many countries, including in the EU. Further, he would have needed to somehow renew his passport from his country of origin.

5 For Campbell (2017: 76), the spatial layout of these tribunals "reinforces the procedural rules defining who has the right to speak, the forms of speech recognized by the court, and the power of the IJ."

6 He also found the FTT IJ's final point, about not changing church when he moved house, "hard to follow."

7 *SA (Iran), R (on the application of) v SSHD* [2012] EWHC 2575 (Admin) [24].

8 For example, *MB (Iran) v SSHD* [2017] AA/00132/2016.

9 For example, *Naser v SSHD* [2017] PA/02202/2016. Some IJs also argue that the outward signs of conversion—even if not genuine—would be enough to endanger the applicant in their country of origin. However, this issue is particularly relevant to Iranian cases, and it was not raised in Abdul's case.

10 *Behzad Alami v SSHD* [2018] PA/13581/2016 [23].

11 *Ali Reza Rezayee v SSHD* [2017] PA/02782/2016 [7].

12 *TF and MA (Iran) v SSHD* [2018] CSIH 58.

13 The ruling also establishes that churchgoers other than ministers can provide expert evidence, which has been picked up in subsequent UT decisions, for example, *SP (Iran) v SSHD* [2019] PA/10885/2018 and *SA (Iran) v SSHD* [2019] PA/05745/2018.

14 *TF and MA (Iran) v SSHD* [2018] CSIH 58 [43].

Mobilizing Theory

1 Building on a conference hosted at the Max Planck Institute Göttingen, which was directed by Peter van der Veer, the volume by Horstmann and Jung, which focuses mainly on people from Asia, shares common ground with ours.

2 The claim that many of the presumed refugees are "mere" economic migrants betrays a wish to release the moral burden that comes with the failure to treat them well; instead, their arrival is seen as caused by human trafficking, which is criminalized rather than valued as border crossing help for people in need (Berg 2019).

3 http://www.unitedagainstracism.org/campaigns/refugee-campaign/working-with-the-list-of-deaths/

4 And so, as she puts it poignantly: "*The point is to take note of the effects of the claim to crisis, to be attentive to the effects of our very accession of that judgment.* Crisis engenders certain forms of critique which politicize interest groups. This is a politics of crisis" (2014: 12, italics in original).

5 The trope of the pandemic and the call for (racial) hygiene measures was present in nativist politics of closure throughout the twentieth century. The current "Corona crisis" brings this back to mind. Also, in far-right circles, strangers tend to be seen as harbingers of pandemics that have to be kept out to protect the body of the nation. At the same time, such circles downplay the threat of the literal virus and attribute the measures to control it, lockdowns and other strategies, to the striving of global elites to destroy homogenous nations in favor of cosmopolitanism.

6 Still, it is important to note that there are differences in the degrees to which states claim power and are prepared to limit the judiciary and the expression of critique and differences in how they treat refugees (as a comparison of, for example, Hungary and Poland with a country like Germany shows). For this reason, I think it is problematic to apply Giorgio Agamben's idea that the "state of exception" becomes normalized as a form of governance in all sorts of crises—be it related to refugees or the corona pandemic. Agamben's recent online intervention, in which he criticizes state measures to hamper the corona pandemic through the lens of this idea (https://www.journal-psychoanalysis.eu/coronavirus-and-philosophers/), reveals the shortcomings of such an undifferentiated attitude toward the modern state, as many critics have argued.

7 The point then is to study "the ways in which the state relates to 'religion,' in the sense of establishing a place for it in society by taking into account the role played by various social agents (including 'religious' ones) in the processes of shaping such relations" (Giumbelli 2013: 96).

8 Even on the Christian spectrum, churches frequented by people from Africa, Asia, or South America are still called migrant churches; the use of this term indicates

that they are still seen as foreign and marginal to what is taken as mainstream European Christianity (see Frederiks 2019).

9 The research program "Religious Matters in an Entangled World," which I chair at Utrecht University, focuses on matters of conflict and concern arising around material religious forms, such as buildings, objects, images, and food in plural societies (with particular emphasis on the Netherlands and Ghana): www.religiousmatters.nl.

10 For example, Jojada Verrips (2020) on recent references, smeared on containers in public space in Berlin, to "gypsies" and "Arabs" as "shit." This shows the resilience of long-standing patterns grounded in biblical tropes of "shit gods" that keep on being evoked to generate a sense of Others as abject.

11 Developed mainly by theologians, this volume offers very good analyses of theological issues arising from the refugee question, especially in Germany. Schmiedel, in particular, offers a compelling and insightful analysis of the political theology of PEGIDA, for whom Christianity is key to the identity of Europe. Rather than accepting the characterization of PEGIDA as "unchristian," he offers a thorough analysis of the "theological tropes for the demarcation of the 'people'" (2018: 212) and its claim that Christianity is under threat in its discourse. For Schmiedel, this is the condition for being able to speak back. Even though as a scholar I do not engage in such speaking back, I appreciate his effort and think that a lot can be learned from his theological analysis.

12 Susanne Stadlbauer and Annelise Reid both enriched the workshop on which this volume is based with their papers on suspicions raised about Muslims converting to Christianity. While Stadlbauer explored converts' negotiations of a new, modern sense of the self, Reid argued that conversion should be situated in a relational process of the "making of belief" that includes converts, proselytizing Churches, agencies testing the authenticity of asylum applications, and courts.

13 More generally on migrants, much work has been done on theologies of mobility in the context of migration (see Hüwelmeier and Krause 2010), especially on Pentecostalism as a religion that travels well, also due to the "portability" of the Holy Spirit (Csordas 2009; see also Hüwelmeier 2010 on Vietnamese Pentecostals), and with regard to indigenous spirits and their capacity to mediate between homelands and host countries (Lambek 2010). Of course, traditions like Candomblé, Winti, and Santeria also contain vernacular theologies around the capacity of spirits to evoke long-dead ancestors and mediate the memory of enslavement across the transatlantic world (see Balkenhol, Blanes, and Sarro 2020).

14 The film *Les sauteurs – Those who jump* (dir. Abou Bakar Sidibé, Moritz Siebert, Estphan Wagner, 2016) documents the attempts of young Africans stranded in Morocco to jump across the fence to Melilla: http://www.zalab.org/en/projects/les-sauteurs-those-who-jump/

Bibliography

Accoroni, D. (2011), "Islamic Integration and Social Wellbeing in Paris: The Soninke Foyer and the Mouride Brotherhood," *Social Anthropology and Ethnology*, London: University College.

Adogame, A. (1998), "A Home Away from Home: The Proliferation of the Celestial Church of Christ (CCC) in Diaspora-Europe," *Exchange* 27(2): 141–60.

Adogame, A., ed. (2005), "Religion in the Context of African Migration," *Bayreuth African Studies Series*, Eckersdorf: Thielmann and Breitinger.

Agamben, G. (1998), *Homo Sacer: Sovereign Power and Bare Life*, trans. Daniel Heller-Roazen, Stanford: Stanford University Press.

Agamben, G. (2005), *State of Exception*, trans. Kevin Attell, Chicago: University of Chicago Press.

Alioua, M. (2009), "Le 'passage au politique' des transmigrants subsahariens au Maroc," in A. Bensaad (ed.), *Le Maghreb à l'épreuve des migrations subsahariennes. Immigration sur émigration*, 279–304, Paris: Karthala.

All Party Parliamentary Group for International Freedom of Religion or Belief, and Asylum Advocacy Group (2016), "Fleeing Persecution: Asylum Claims in the UK on Religious Freedom Grounds." Available online: https://appgfreedomofreligionorbeli ef.org/media/Fleeing-Persecution-Asylum-Claims-in-the-UK-on-Religious-Freed om-Grounds.pdf (accessed July 7, 2019).

Ammerman, N. T. (2013), *Sacred Stories, Spiritual Tribes: Finding Religion in Everyday Life*, New York: Oxford University Press.

Anderson, B. (1983), *Imagined Communities: Reflections on the Origin and Spread of Nationalism*, London: Verso.

Anderson, J., J. Hollaus, A. Lindsay, and C. Williamson (2014), "The Culture of Disbelief: An Ethnographic Approach to Understanding an Under-Theorised Concept in the UK Asylum System." *RSC* Working Paper *Series*, July: 102. Available online: https://www.rsc.ox.ac.uk/publications/the-culture-of-disbelief-an-ethnograp hic-approach-to-understanding-an-under-theorised-concept-in-the-uk-asylum-s ystem (accessed July 9, 2019).

Arendt, H. (1958), *The Human Condition*, Chicago: University of Chicago Press.

Arendt, H. (2007), *Jewish Writings*, New York: Schocken.

Asad, T. (1993), *Genealogies of Religion: Discipline and Reasons of Power in Christianity and Islam*, Baltimore: Johns Hopkins University Press.

Asad, T. (2003), *Formations of the Secular: Christianity, Islam, Modernity*, Stanford: Stanford University Press.

Ashiwa, Y. and D. L. Wank (2009), *Making Religion, Making the State: The Politics of Religion in Modern China*, Stanford: Stanford University Press.

Asylum Aid (1999), "Still No Reason at All: Home Office Decisions on Asylum Claims; Report." Asylum Aid. Available online: https://www.asylumaid.org.uk/wp-content/uploads/2013/02/Still_No_Reason_At_All.pdf (accessed July 20, 2019).

Atour Publications (AP). www.lulu.com/spotlight/atourpub (accessed June 9, 2018).

Atto, N. (2011), "Hostages in the Homeland, Orphans in the Diaspora: Identity Discourses Among the Assyrian/Syriac Elites in the European Diaspora," Ph.D. Leiden University.

Austin-Broos, D. (2003), "The Anthropology of Religious Conversion: An Introduction," in A. Buckser and S. D. Glazier (eds.), *The Anthropology of Religious Conversion*, 1–12, Lanham and Oxford: Rowman and Littlefield.

Azad, A. K. (2015), *One Year of Khagrabari Massacre: Quest for Justice Continues*, Guwahati: Jhai Foundation. Available online: https://www.indiaresists.com/wp-content/uploads/2015/05/One-year-of-Khagrabari-Massacre_-Quest-for-Justice-Continues.pdf (accessed March 11, 2020).

Baida, J. and V. Féroldi (1995), *Présence chrétienne au Maroc*, Rabat: Editions et Impressions Bouregreg.

Baker, C. (2013), "The Contagion of the Sacred and the Right to the City: Modalities of Belonging, Becoming and Participation Amongst Diasporic Religious Communities, and the Growth of the Postsecular City," in J. Garnett and A. Harris (eds.), *Rescripting Religion in the City: Migration and Religious Identity in the Modern Metropolis*, 89–101, Burlington: Ashgate.

Bakker Kellogg, S. (2019), "Perforating Kinship: Syriac Christianity, Ethnicity, and Secular Legibility," *Current Anthropology* 60(4): 475–98.

Balkenhol, M., E. Van den Hemel, and I. Stengs, eds. (2020), *The Secular Sacred: Emotions of Belonging and the Perils of Nation and Religion*, London: Palgrave.

Balkenhol, M., R. L. Blanes, and R. Sarró, eds. (2020), *Atlantic Perspectives: Places, Spirits and Heritage*, Oxford and New York: Berghahn.

Bandak, A. and M. Janeja (2018), "Introduction: Worth the Wait," in M. K. Janeja and A. Bandak (eds.), *Ethnographies of Waiting: Doubt, Hope and Uncertainty*, 1–40, London and New York: Bloomsbury.

Barbato, M. (2017), "Pilgrim City or Belonging Beyond the State: St. Augustine, Pope Francis and the Refugee Crisis," in L. Mavelli and E. K. Wilson (eds.), *The Refugee Crisis and Religion: Secularism, Security and Hospitality in Question*, 131–44, London and New York: Rowman & Littlefield International.

Baruah, S. (2007), *Durable Disorder: Understanding the Politics of Northeast India*, New York: Oxford University Press.

Bass, L. E. (2014), "African Immigrant Families in Another France," *Migration, Diasporas and Citizenship*, Basingstoke: Palgrave Macmillan.

Bauman, Z. (2016), *Strangers at Our Door*, Cambridge and Malden: Polity Press.

Baumann, G. (2010), "Nation, Ethnicity and Community," in K. Knott and S. McLoughlin (eds.), *Diasporas: Concepts, Intersections, Identities*, 45–9, London and New York: The University of Chicago Press.

Baumann, M. (2000), *Migration, Religion, Integration. Buddhistische Vietnamesen und Hinduistische Tamilen in Deutschland*, Marburg: Diagonal-Verlag.

Baur, J. (2014), "Grenzdurchgangslager Friedland," in Bundesinstitut für Kultur und Geschichte der Deutschen im östlichen Europa (eds.), *Online-Lexikon zur Kultur und Geschichte der Deutschen im östlichen Europa*. Available online: ome-lexikon. uni-oldenburg.de/p36233 (accessed June 27, 2018).

Bava, S. (2016), "Migrations africaines et christianismes au Maroc. De la théologie des migrations à la théologie de la pluralité religieuse," *Les Cahiers d'Outre-Mer* 274(2): 259–88.

Bayly, S. (2007), *Asian Voices in a Postcolonial Age: Vietnam, India and Beyond*, Cambridge: Cambridge University Press.

Beauchemin, C., ed. (2018), *Migration between Africa and Europe*, Springer International Publishing.

Beck, U. (2007), "The Cosmopolitan Condition: Why Methodological Nationalism Fails," *Theory, Culture & Society* 24(7–8): 286–90.

Becker, A. (2015), *Revival and Awakening: Christian Mission, Orientalism, and the American Evangelical Roots of Assyrian Nationalism (1834–1906)*, Chicago: The University of Chicago Press.

Bedjan, P. (1890–97), *Šarbē d-sahdē wa-d-qaddīšē – Acta Martyrum et Sanctorum Syriace*, vols. 1–7, Paris: W. Drugulin.

Bendixsen, S. K. N. (2013), *The Religious Identity of Young Muslim Women in Berlin: An Ethnographic Study*, Leiden: Brill.

Benko, S. (2004), *Studies in the Pagan and Christian Roots of Mariology*, Leiden: Brill.

Benveniste, E. (1969), *European Language and Society*, 87–9, Miami: University of Miami Press.

Berg, J. (2019), "Fluchthilfe im Spannungsfeld zwischen Kriminalisierung und Anerkennung," Bachelor's thesis, Institute for Social and Cultural Anthropology, Freie Universität Berlin.

Bernstein, J. and M. C. Okello (2007), "To Be or Not To Be: Urban Refugees in Kampala," *Refuge: Canada's Journal on Refugees* 24(1): 46–56.

Berriane, J. (2016), *Ahmad al-Tijânî de Fès. Un sanctuaire soufi aux connexions transnationales*, Paris: l'Harmattan.

Berriane, J. (2018), "The Moroccan Moment and Communities of Itinerants: Mobility and Belonging in the Transnational Trajectories of Sub-Saharan Migrants," in O. Bakewell and L. Landau (eds.), *Forging African Communities: Mobility, Integration and Belonging*, 57–74, London: Palgrave Macmillan.

Berriane, J. (2020), "Religion in Spaces of Transit: African Christian Migrant Churches and Transnational Mobility in Morocco," *Journal of Intercultural Studies* 41(4): 424–41.

Berriane, J. (forthcoming), "Faith Papers. Transnational Mobility, Christian Networks, and Citizenship in Morocco and Senegal," in S. Awenengo Dalberto and R. Banégas (eds.), *Biometric Citizenship? The Social Life of IDs in Africa*, London: Routledge.

Bilger, B. (2016), "Where Germans Make Peace with Their Dead," *New Yorker*, September 12 Issue.

Bird, K., T. Saalfeld, and A. Wüst, eds. (2011), *The Political Representation of Immigrants and Minorities: Voters, Parties and Parliaments in Liberal Democracies*, London: Routledge.

Birol, S. (2016), "Syrisch-Orthodoxe Christen in Deutschland," in T. Bremer, A. Elias Kattan, and R. Thöle (eds.), *Orthodoxie in Deutschland*, 235–50, Münster: Aschendorff Verlag.

Blagov, S. (2001), *Caodaism: Vietnamese Traditionalism and Its Leap into Modernity*, New York: Nova Science Publishers.

Boddy, J. (1994), "Spirit Possession Revisited: Beyond Instrumentality," *Annual Review of Anthropology* 21: 407–34.

Bosch, F. and P. H. Su (2018), "Invisible, Successful and Divided: Vietnamese in Germany since the late 1970s," United Nations University World Institute for Development Economics Research, Working Paper 2018/15 February.

Bowen, J., C. Bertossi, J. W. Duyvendak, and M. L. Krook, eds. (2013), *European States and Their Muslim Citizens: The Impact of Institutions on Perceptions and Boundaries*, Cambridge: Cambridge University Press.

Braidotti, R. (2011), *Nomadic Theory: The Portable Rosi Braidotti*, New York: Columbia Universoty Press.

Bredeloup, S. (2013a), "Circumstancial Solidarities and the Transformation of Migratory Networks," *Journal of Intercultural Studies* 34(5): 517–32.

Bredeloup, S. (2013b), "The Figure of the Adventurer as an African Migrant," *Journal of African Cultural Studies* 25(2): 70–182.

Brock, S. (2006–7), "East Syriac Pilgrims to Jerusalem in the Early Ottoman Period," *Aram* 18–19: 189–201.

Broucek, S. (2016), *The Visible and Invisible Vietnamese in the Czech Republic*, Prague: Institute of Ethnology CAS 2016.

Broussole, B. and L. Provençal (2013), "L'Évacuation des catholiques du Tonkin en 1954–1955," *Bulletin de l'Association amicale santé navale et d'Outremer* 125: 24–30.

Brubaker, R. (2015), *Grounds for Difference*, Cambridge, MA: Harvard University Press.

Buckser, A. and S. D. Glazier (2003), *The Anthropology of Religious Conversion*, Lanham and Oxford: Rowman and Littlefield.

Bùi, V. L. (1959), "The Role of Friendly Nations," in R. W. Lindholm (ed.), *Vietnam: The First Five Years, an International Symposium*, 48–54, East Lansing: Michigan State University Press.

Buruma, I. (1994), *Wages of Guilt: Memories of War in Germany and Japan*, New York: Farrar, Strauss and Giroux.

Buturovic, A. (2006), "European Islam," *The Oxford Handbook of Global Religions*, October. Available online: https://doi.org/10.1093/oxfordhb/9780195137989.003.0043

Campbell, J. R. (2017), *Bureaucracy, Law and Dystopia in the United Kingdom's Asylum System. Law and Migration*, Abingdon, Oxon and New York: Routledge.

Campbell, J. R. (2019), "The World of Home Office Presenting Officers," in N. Gill and A. Good (eds.), *Asylum Determination in Europe: Ethnographic Perspectives*, 91–108, Palgrave Socio-Legal Studies, Cham: Springer International Publishing.

Cardinal Spellman Funds/S/B-10/To Card. Spellman Korea/Folder 8 (1951a), "Statement by the Permanent Representative of Korea to the United Nations, Genocide in Korea, 3 May 1951."

Cardinal Spellman Funds/S/B-10/To Card. Spellman Korea/Folder 8 (1951b), "Letter of B.c. Limb, Permanent Representative of Korea to the United Nations to Cardinal Spellman, 7 May 1951."

Cardinal Spellman Funds/S/B-10/To Card. Spellman Korea/Folder 8 (1952), "Letter from John T. Mao, Praefectura Apostolica Taipeihensis to Cardinal Spellman, 19 January 1952."

Cardinal Spellman Funds/S/B-10/To Card. Spellman, Pacific Visits (1948), "Letter, 10 June 1948."

Cardinal Spellman Funds/S/B-10/To Card. Spellman, T. F. E. (1956), "Letter from Cardinal Spellman to Mons. Fleming, 5 January 1956."

Cardinal Spellman Funds/S/C-34/To Card. Spellman CRS-NCWC/Folder 1 (1957), "Minutes, Meeting of the Board of Trustees, Catholic Relief Services - National Catholic Welfare Conference 12 November 1957."

Cardinal Spellman Funds/S/C-49/To Card. Spellman Vietnam/Folder 2 (1954a), "Copy, Translation, Letter of the President of the Government, State of Vietnam to Cardinal Spellman, 25 July 1954."

Cardinal Spellman Funds/S/C-49/To Card. Spellman/Folder 4 (1954b), "Ngo Dinh Diem to Cardinal Spellman."

Carling, J. (2002), "Migration in the Age of Involuntary Immobility: Theoretical Reflections and Cape Verdean Experiences," *Journal of Ethnic and Migration Studies* 28(1): 5–42.

Carrière, J.-M. (2017), "The Refugee Experience as Existential Exile: Hospitality as Spiritual and Political Response," in L. Mavelli and E. K. Wilson (eds.), *The Refugee Crisis and Religion: Secularism, Security and Hospitality in Question*, 145–56, London and New York: Rowman & Littlefield International.

Carroll, M. P. (1999), *Irish Pilgrimage: Holy Wells and Popular Catholic Devotion*, Baltimore: Johns Hopkins University Press.

Casanova, J. (2019a), "Asian Catholicism, Interreligious Encounters and Dynamics of Secularism in Asia," in K. Dean and P. van der Veer (eds.), *The Secular in South, East, and Southeast Asia*, 13–37, New York: Palgrave MacMillan.

Casanova, J. (2019b), "Global Religious and Secular Dynamics: The Modern System of Classification," Georgetown University Berkley Center for Religion, Peace, and

World Affairs. https://berkleycenter.georgetown.edu/publications/global-religiou s-and-secular-dynamics-the-modern-system-of-classification

Castañeda-Liles, M. D. (2018), *Our Lady of Everyday Life: La Virgen de Guadalupe and the Catholic Imagination of Mexican Women in America*, New York: Oxford University Press.

Catholic Relief Services - National Catholic Welfare Conference (1954), "N.C.W.C.- Participation in the United States Escapee Program (U.S.E.P.)," The International Catholic Migration Congress, Breda Netherlands, September 11–16, 1954,

Chadwick, O. (1993), *The Christian Church in the Cold War*, New York: Penguin Books.

Chattopadhyay, S. (2005), *Representing Calcutta: Modernity, Nationalism and the Colonial Uncanny*, New York: Routledge.

Chidester, D. (1996), *Savage Systems: Colonialism and Comparative Religion in Southern Africa*, Charlottesville: University Press of Virginia.

Choi, K.-Y. (2016), "Foreigners Who Loved Korea: Paul Yu Pin, the Roman Catholic Cardinal Who Supported the Korea Independence Movement," *Korea Herald*, December 6.

Choudhury, N. (2016), "State of Exception and Beyond: Introductory Remarks," *International Journal of Migration and Border Studies* 2(2): 95–8.

Chu, L. (2008), "Catholicism vs. Communism, Continued: The Catholic Church in Vietnam," *Journal of Vietnamese Studies* 3(1): 151–92.

Clark, A. C. R. (2017), "Adjustment and Advocacy: Charles Mccarthy, SJ, and the China's Jesuit Mission in Transition," in A. E. Clark (ed.), *China's Christianity: From Missionary to Indigenous Church*, 199–218, Leiden: Brill.

Clifford, J. (1989), "Notes on Travel and Theory," *Inscriptions* 5. https://culturalstudies.u csc.edu/inscriptions/volume-5/james-clifford/

Coleman, S. (2000), *The Globalization of Charismatic Christianity: Spreading the Gospel of Prosperity*, Cambridge: Cambridge University Press.

Collyer, M. (2007), "In-Between Places: Trans-Saharan Transit Migrants in Morocco and the Fragmented Journey to Europe," *Antipode: A Radical Journal of Geography* 39(4): 668–90.

Columban Fathers (2010), "Columban History in China." https://web.archive.org/w eb/20150203200524/http://columban.org/94/regions/china/china-updates/history- china/ (accessed July 17, 2019).

Columban Fathers (2017), *Those Who Journeyed with Us, 1918–2016*, Missionary Society of St. Columban.

Comaroff, J. and J. Comaroff (1999), "Occult Economies and the Violence of Abstraction: Notes from the South African Postcolony," *American Ethnologist* 26(2): 279–303.

Confederation of Bishops of Vietnam (2016), *Yearbook of the Catholic Church of Vietnam* (Niên Giám Giáo Hội Công Giáo Việt Nam), Hanoi: Hanoi Publishing House. Available online: http://thuvienconggiaovietnam.net/admintvcg/uploads/boo kFileTemp/090453_icon.pdf

Cottin, S. (2007), "La Tijâniyya lyonnaise. Une voie dans son temps," *Archives de sciences sociales des religions* 52(140): 69–89.

Cowan, D. (2004), "Legal Consciousness: Some Observations," *The Modern Law Review* 67(6): 928–58.

Coyault, B. (2014), "L'africanisation de l'Église évangélique au Maroc. Revitalisation d'une institution religieuse et dynamiques d'individualisation," *L'Année du Maghreb* 11: 81–103.

Csordas, T. J. (2009), *Transnational Transcendence: Essays on Religion and Globalization*, Berkeley: University of California Press.

Dahinden, J. and T. Zittoun (2013), "Religion in Meaning Making and Boundary Work: Theoretical Explorations," *Integrative Psychological and Behavioral Science* 47(2): 185–206.

Dang, T. T. V. (2005), "The Cultural Work of Anticommunism in the San Diego Vietnamese American Community," *Amerasia Journal* 31(2): 65–86.

Danstrøm, M. S. and Z. Whyte (2019), "Narrating Asylum in Camp and at Court," in N. Gill and A. Good (eds.), *Asylum Determination in Europe: Ethnographic Perspectives*, 175–94, Palgrave Socio-Legal Studies, Cham: Springer International Publishing.

Därmann, I. (2005), *Fremde Monde der Vernunft. Die ethnologische Provokation der Philosophie*, München: Fink.

Das, V. (2015), "What Does Ordinary Ethics Look Like?," in *Four Lectures on Ethics: Anthropological Perspectives*, 53–126, Chicago: Hau Books.

Dasgupta, K. and A. Guha (1985), "1983 Assembly Poll in Assam: An Analysis of Its Background and Implications," *Economic and Political Weekly* 19(2): 843–53.

Datta, A. (2016), "Rethinking Spaces of Exception: Notes from a Forced Migrant Camp in Jammu and Kashmir," *International Journal of Migration and Border Studies* 2(2): 162–75.

De Bel-Air, F. (2016), "Migration Profile: Morocco," *Policy Brief*, H. 05.

de Certeau, M. (1984), *The Practice of Everyday Life*, Berkeley: University of California Press.

De Genova, N. (2002), "Migrant 'Illegality' and Deportability in Everyday Life," *Annual Review of Anthropology* 31(4): 419–47.

De Genova, N. (2013), "Spectacles of Migrant 'Illegality': The Scene of Exclusion, the Obscene of Inclusion," *Ethnic and Racial Studies* 36(7): 1180–98.

De Genova, N., ed. (2017), *The Borders of "Europe": Autonomy of Migration, Tactics of Bordering*, Durham: Duke University Press.

de Jaegher, R. (1952), *The Enemy Within: An Eyewitness Account of the Communist Conquest of China*, New York: Doubleday.

de Jaegher, R. (1957), "World's Youngest Nation Faces Up to Old Menace," *Free Front*, December 12.

de Jaegher, R. (1958a), "Anti-Communist India," *Free Front*, February 20.

de Jaegher, R. (1958b), "Burma, the Golden Land," *Free Front*, January 17.

de Jaegher, R. (1958c), "Third Congress Against Soviet Intervention in Latin America," *Free Front*, March 4.

de Jaegher, R. (1958d), "True China or Red China, Will U.S. Recognition Change?," *Free Front*, September 12.

de Jaegher, R. (1959a), *Life of Archbishop Paul Yu Pin*, Saigon: Free Pacific Editions.

de Jaegher, R. (1959b), *Tiểu sử Đức giám mục Vu Bân, Linh hồn của phong trào Thái Bình Dương tự do*, Saigon: Free Pacific Editions.

de Jaegher, R. (1962), *The Growth of the Free Pacific Association in Vietnam*, Saigon: Free Pacific Association.

de Rochcau, G. (1954), "Le problème des réfugiés vietnamiens," in *The International Catholic Migration Congress, Breda Netherlands, 11–16 September 1954*, The Hague: Catholic Institute for Social Ecclesiastical Research.

De Witte, M. (2008), "Accra's Sounds and Sacred Spaces," *International Journal of Urban and Regional Research* 32(3): 690–709.

Deutsches Institut für Menschenrechte (DIM) (2016), "Religionsbezogene Gewalt in Flüchtlingsunterkünften. Standards etablieren und Gewaltschutzkonzepte erweitern." Available online: https://www.institut-fuer-menschenrechte.de/filead min/user_upload/Publikationen/POSITION/Position_5_Religionsbezogene_Ge walt_in_Fluechtlingunterkuenften.pdf (accessed June 27, 2018).

Dinham, A. and M. Francis (2016), "Religious Literacy: Contesting an Idea and Practice," in A. Dinham and M. Francis (eds.), *Religious Literacy in Policy and Practice*, 3–26, Bristol: Policy Press.

Donders, R. (1954), "The Forced Migration and the Refugee Problem of Hong Kong (1949–1954)," in *The International Catholic Migration Congress, Breda Netherlands, 11–16 September 1954*, The Hague: Catholic Institute for Social Ecclesiastical Research.

Donovan, J. T. (2004), "The American Catholic Press and the Cold War in Asia: The Case of Father Patrick O'Connor, S.S.C. (1899–1987)," *American Catholic Studies* 115(3): 23–49.

Dorais, L. J. (2005), "From Refugees to Transmigrants: The Vietnamese in Canada," in W. W. Anderson and R. G. Lee (eds.), *Displacements and Diasporas: Asians in the Americas*, 170–93, New Brunswick: Rutgers University Press.

Douglas, M. (1966), *Purity and Danger: An Analysis of Concepts of Pollution and Taboo*, London: Routledge and Kegan Paul.

Dror, O. (2005), *Cult, Culture and Authority: Princess Lieu Hanh in Vietnamese History*, Honolulu: University of Hawaii Press.

Dror, O. (2016), "Foundational Myths in the Republic of Vietnam (1955–1975): 'Harnessing' the Hung Kings against Ngô Đình Diệm, Communists, Cowboys, and Hippies for Unity, Peace, and Vietnameseness," *Journal of Social History* 49(4): 1–36.

"Đức giáo hoàng Pio XII gửi thông tri Sacro Vergente Anno cho dân tộc Nga," *Đạo Bình Đức Mẹ* (1952) 15/8/: 5.

Dutton, G. (2016), *A Vietnamese Moses: Philiphê Bình and the Geographies of Early Modern Catholicism*, Berkeley: University of California Press. Available online: https ://www.luminosoa.org/site/books/10.1525/luminos.22/

ECPAD/Fonds Indochine/NVN 54–166 (1955a), "Réfugiés catholiques au large de Phát Diệm."

ECPAD/Fonds Indochine/SC 55–2 (1955b), "Visite du Cardinal Francis Spellman."

Edwards, P. (2002), "Restyling Colonial Cambodia (1860–1954): French Dressing, Indigenous Custom and National Costume," in T. Chafer and A. Sackur (eds.), *Promoting the Colonial Idea: Propaganda and Visions of Empire in France*, 389–416, London: Palgrave MacMillan.

Eisfeld, A. (2004), *Die Aussiedlung der Deutschen aus der Wolgarepublik 1941-1957*, Mitteilungen Osteuropa Institut München, 50, Anhang 4.

Ély, P. (1964), *Mémoires. L'Indochine sans la tourmente, Tome I*, Paris: Plon.

Endres, K. (2008), "Fate, Memory and the Postcolonial Consciousness of the Self: A Vietnamese Spirit Medium," *Journal of Vietnamese Studies* 3(2): 34–65.

Endres, K. W. (2011), *Performing the Divine: Mediums, Markets and Modernity in Urban Vietnam*, Copenhagen: NIAS Press.

Englund, H. (2002), "Ethnography After Globalism: Migration And Emplacement In Malawi," *American Ethnologist* 29(2): 261–86. https://doi.org/10.1525/ae.2002.29.2.261

Erpenbeck, J. (2015), *Gehen, Ging, Gegangen*, München: Knaus.

Escoffier, C. (2008), *Transmigrant-e-s africain-e-s au Maghreb: Une question de vie ou de mort*, Paris: L'Harmattan.

Espiritu, Y. L. (2002), "'Viet Nam, Nuoc Toi' (Vietnam, My Country): Vietnamese Americans and Transnationalism," in P. Levitt and M. C. Waters (eds.), *The Changing Face of Home*, 367–98, New York: Russell Sage Foundation.

Espiritu, Y. L. (2014), *Body Counts: The Vietnam War and Militarized Refugees*, Berkeley: University of California Press.

Evans, R. (2012), "The Other Horror," *New Republic*, June 25, 2012.

Ewing, K. P. (2008), *Stolen Honor: Stigmatizing Muslim Men in Berlin*, Stanford: Stanford University Press.

Fabian, J. (2000), *Out of Our Minds: Reason and Madness in the Exploration of Central Africa*, Berkeley: University of California Press.

Farquhar, M. (2016), *Circuits of Faith: Migration, Education, and the Wahhabi Mission*, Stanford: Stanford Studies in Middle East.

Fassin, D. (2007), "Humanitarianism as a Politics of Life," *Public Culture* 19(3): 499–520.

Fassin, D. and C. Kobelinsky (2012), "Comment on juge l'asile," *Revue francaise de sociologie* 4(53): 688–757.

Feldman, I. (2015), "What Is a Camp? Legitimate Refugee Lives in Spaces of Long-Term Displacement," *Geoforum* 66: 244–52.

Feltes, T., K. List, and M. Bertamini (2018), "More Refugees, More Offenders, More Crime? Critical Comments with Data from Germany," in H. Kury and S. Redo (eds.), *Refugees and Migrants in Law and Policy*, 599–624, Cham: Springer.

Fernandez, E. (2003), "America from the Hearts of a Diasporized People," in F. Matsuoka and E. Fernandez (eds.), *Realizing the America of Our Hearts: Theological Voices of Asian Americans*, St. Louis: Chalice Press.

Fiddian-Qasmiyeh, E. (2011), "Introduction: Faith-Based Humanitarism in Contexts of Forced Displacement," *Journal of Refugee Studies* 24(3): 429–39.

Fjelstad, K. (1995), *Tu Phu Cong Dong: Vietnamese Women and Spirit Possession in the San Francisco Bay Area*, Ph.D. diss., Department of Anthropology, University of Hawaii.

Fjelstad, K. and H. T. Nguyen (2006), "Introduction," in K. Fjelstad and T. H. Nguyen, *Possessed by the Spirits: Mediumship in Contemporary Vietnamese Communities*, 7–18, Ithaca: Cornell University Press.

Fjelstad, K. and H. T. Nguyễn (2011), *Spirits Without Borders: Vietnamese Spirit Mediums in a Transnational Age*, New York: Palgrave.

Fontanari, E. (2018), *Lives in Transit: An Ethnographic Study of Refugees' Subjectivity Across European Borders*, London and New York: Taylor and Francis.

Foucault, M. (1990), *The History of Sexuality: An Introduction*, New York: Vintage Books.

Foucault, M. (1997), "Il faut défendre la societé," in *Cours au Collège de France*, Paris: Seuil.

Frank, B. and P. H. Su (2018), "Invisible, Successful and Divided: Vietnamese in Germany since the late 1970s," United Nations University World Institute for Development Economics Research, February: 1–22.

Frederiks, M. (2014), "Religion, Ethnicity and Transnational Migration - An Epilogue," in G. G. Smith and S. Grodź (eds.), *Religion, Ethnicity and Transnational Migration between West Africa and Europe*, 219–29, Leiden: Brill.

Frederiks, M. T. (2019), "'Microcosm' of the Global South: The Discursive Functionality of Migrant Christianity in World Christianity Discourses," *Exchange* 48(4): 313–33.

Freidingerova, T. (2019), *Precarious Journeys: Mapping Vulnerabilities of Victims of Trafficking from Vietnam to Europ*, Pacific Links Foundation: Anti-Slavery www. antislavery.org

Freud, S. (1918, 1964), "Mourning and Melancholia," in J. Stratchey (ed.), *The Standard Edition*, 243–51, London: The Hogarth Press.

Friese, H. (2014), *Grenzen der Gastfreundschaft: die Bootsflüchtlinge von Lampedusa und die europäische Frage*, Bielefeld: Transcript.

Froschauer, U. (2009), "Artefaktanalyse," in S. Kühl, P. Strodtholz, and A. Taffertshofer (eds.), *Handbuch Methoden der Organisationsforschung*, 326–47, Wiesbaden: VS Verlag für Sozialwissenschaften.

Fukuyama, F. (1992), *The End of History*, New York: The Free Press.

Furner, M. (1998), "The Repression and Survival of Anabaptism in the Emmental, Switzerland, 1659–1743," Ph.D. diss., Cambridge University.

Gaibazzi, P., D. Stephan, and A. Bellagamba (2017), *EurAfrican Borders and Migration Management: Political Cultures, Contested Spaces, and Ordinary Lives*, New York: Palgrave Macmillan.

Garbin, D. (2014), "Regrounding the Sacred: Transnational Religion, Place Making and the Politics of Diaspora Among the Congolese in London and Atlanta," *Global Networks* 14(3): 363–82.

Gatrell, P. (2019), *The Unsettling of Europe: How Migration Reshaped a Continent*, London: Allen Lane.

Ghorashi, H. (2014), "Racism and 'the Ungrateful Other' in the Netherlands," in P. Essed and I. Hoving (eds.), *Dutch Racism: Thamyris Intersecting Place, Sex and Race*, no. 27, 101–17, Amsterdam and New York: Rodopi.

Gifford, P. (1998), *African Christianity: Its Public Role*, Bloomington: Indiana University Press.

Gill, N. and A. Good, eds. (2019), *Asylum Determination in Europe: Ethnographic Perspectives*, Palgrave Socio-Legal Studies, Cham: Springer International Publishing. https://doi.org/10.1007/978-3-319-94749-5_1

Gill, N. R. Rotter, A. Burridge, M. Griffiths, and J. Allsopp (2015), "Inconsistency in Asylum Appeal Adjudication," *Forced Migration Review* 50: 52–4.

Gillet, P. (2012), "Les débuts difficiles de la Société des auxiliaires des missions (La SAM), Bruxelles," *Histoire des missions chrétiennes* 23: 97–128.

Giumbelli, E. (2013), "The Problem of Secularism and Religious Regulation. Anthropological Perspectives," *Religion and Society: Advances in Research* 4: 93–108.

Good, A. (2015), "'The Benefit of the Doubt' in British Asylum Claims and International Cricket," in D. Berti, A. Good, and G. Tarabout (eds.), *Of Doubt and Proof: Ritual and Legal Practices of Judgment*, 119–40, Juris Diversitas, Farnham: Ashgate Publishing.

Good, A., D. Berti, and G. Tarabout (2015), "Introduction: Technologies of Doubt in Law and Ritual," in D. Berti, A. Good, and G. Tarabout (eds.), *Of Doubt and Proof: Ritual and Legal Practices of Judgment*, 17–34, Juris Diversitas, Farnham: Ashgate Publishing.

Goodwin-Gill, G. (2008), "The Politics of Refugee Protection," *Refugee Survey Quarterly* 27(1): 8–23.

Gooren, H. P. P. (2010), *Religious Conversion and Disaffiliation: Tracing Patterns of Change in Faith Practices*, New York and Basingstoke: Palgrave Macmillan.

Goswami, U. (2008), "Nobody's People: Muslim IDPs of Western Assam," in Samir Kumar Das (ed.), *Blisters on Their Feet: Tales of Internally Displaced Persons in India's North East*, 176–93, New Delhi: Sage.

Götz, I. (2020), "'We' and 'The Others' as Constituents of Symbolic Politics: On the Populist Exploitation of Long-Lasting Nationalist Sentiments and Resentments Regarding Citizenship in Germany," in M. Balkenhol, E. van den Hemel, and I. Stengs (eds.), *The Secular Sacred: Emotions of Belonging and the Perils of Nation and Religion*, London: Palgrave.

Greene, G. (1955a), "Drama of Indochina – The Dilemma of the South," *The Sunday Times*, April 24: 8.

Greene, G. (1955b), "Last Drama of Indochina II – Refugees and Victors," *The Sunday Times*, May 1: 12.

Greene, G. (1955c), "Last Drama of Indochina III – The Man as Pure as Lucifer," *The Sunday Times*, May 8: 12.

Griera, M. del Mar and M. Forteza (2011), "New Actors in the Governance of Religious Diversity in European Cities: The Role of Interfaith Platforms," in J. Haynes and A. Hennig (eds.), *Religious Actors in the Public Sphere: Means, Objectives, and Effects*, 113–31, Milton Park, Abingdon, and New York: Taylor and Francis Ltd.

Griera, M. del Mar and J. Martínez-Ariño (2014), "The Accommodation of Religious Diversity in Prisons and Hospitals in Spain," *RECODE Working Papers* 28: 1–13.

Griffiths, M. (2012), "'Vile Liars and Truth Distorters;' Truth, Trust and the Asylum System," *Anthropology Today* 28(5): 8–12.

Grodź, S., G. Smith, and A. Adogame (2014), *Religion, Ethnicity and Transnational Migration between West Africa and Europe*, Leiden : Brill.

Guha, A. (2014), *Planter Raj to Swaraj: Freedom Struggle and Electoral Politics in Assam*, New Delhi: Tulika Books.

Guhain, H. N. (1985), *Assam: A Burning Question*, Guwahati: Spectrum.

Gupta, A. (2012), *Red Tape: Bureaucracy, Structural Violence, and Poverty in India*, Durham: Duke University Press.

Gusman, A. (2018), "Stuck in Kampala: Witchcraft Attacks, 'Blocages' and Immobility in the Experience of Born-Again Congolese Refugees in Uganda," *Cahiers d'études africaines* 231–2: 793–815.

Gusman, A. (2020), "'Here, Here Is a Place Where I Can Cry.' Religion in a Context of Displacement: Congolese Churches in Kampala," in H. Dilger, A. Bochow, M. Burchardt, and M. Wilhelm-Solomon (eds.), *Affective Trajectories: Religion and Emotion in African Cityscapes*, 222–42, Durham and London: Duke University Press.

Gutekunst, M., A. Hackl, S. Leoncini, J. S. Schwarz, and I. Götz, eds. (2016), *Bounded Mobilities: Ethnographic Perspectives on Social Hierarchies and Global Inequalities*, Bielefeld: Transcript-Verlag.

Haas, H. de (2008a), "The Myth of Invasion: The Inconvenient Realities of African Migration to Europe," *Third World Quarterly* 29(7): 1305–22.

Haas, H. de (2008b), *Irregular Migration from West Africa to the Maghreb and the European Union: An Overview of Recent Trends*, No. 32, Geneva: International Organization for Migration.

Hall, D., ed. (1997), *Lived Religion in America: Toward a History of Practice*, Princeton: Princeton University Press.

Hambly, J. (2019), "Interactions and Identities in UK Asylum Appeals: Lawyers and Law in a Quasi-Legal Setting," in N. Gill and A. Good (eds.), *Asylum Determination in Europe: Ethnographic Perspectives*, 195–218, Palgrave Socio-Legal Studies, Cham: Springer International Publishing.

Hammer, E. J. (1955), *The Struggle for Indochina, 1940–1955*, Palo Alto: Stanford University Press.

Hämmerli, M. and J.- F. Mayer, eds. (2014), *Orthodox Identities in Western Europe: Migration, Settlement and Innovation*, Farnham: Routledge.

Hansen, P. (2008), "The Virgin Heads South: Northern Catholic Refugees in South Vietnam, 1954–1964," PhD diss., Department of Theology.

Hansen, P. (2009a), "Bắc Di Cư: Catholic Refugees from the North of Vietnam, and Their Role in the Southern Republic, 1954–1959," *Journal of Vietnamese Studies* 4(3): 173–211.

Hansen, P. (2009b), "The Virgin Heads South: Northern Catholic Refugees and Their Clergy in South Vietnam, 1954–1964," in T. D. DuBois (ed.), *Casting Faiths, Imperialism and the Transformation of Religion in East and Southeast Asia*, 129–53, Basingstoke: Palgrave Macmillan.

Haynes, N. (2012), "Pentecostalism and the Morality of Money: Prosperity, Inequality, and Religious Sociality on the Zambian Copperbelt," *Journal of the Royal Anthropological Institute* 18(1): 123–39.

Heiss, J. P. (2015), *Musa: An Essay (or experiment) in the Anthropology of the Individual*, Berlin: Duncker & Humblot.

Highmore, B. (2010), *Ordinary Lives. Studies in the Everyday*, London: Routledge.

Hillmann, F. (2005), "Riders on the Storm: Vietnamese in Germany's Two Migration Systems," in F. Hillmann, A. L. van Naerssen, and E. Spaan (eds.), *Asian Migrants and European Labour Markets: Patterns and Processes of Immigrant Labour Market Insertion in Europe*, 80–100, London: Routledge.

Hoare, F. (2006), "The Influence of the Crusade Symbol and War Metaphor on the Motivation and Attitudes of the Maynooth Mission to China, 1918–1929," *U.S. Catholic Historian* 24(3): 55–74.

Hoffmann, D. and M. Schwartz, eds. (1999), *Geglückte Integration? Spezifika und Vergleichbarkeiten der Vertriebenen-Eingliederung in der SBZ/DDR*, Munich: R. Oldenburg Verlag.

"Hội thanh niên công giáo Triều Tiên," *Đạo Bình Đức Mẹ* (1952), August 15: 18.

Home Office (2015), "Assessing Credibility and Refugee Status." Available online: https://www.gov.uk/government/publications/considering-asylum-claims-and-assessing-credibility-instruction (accessed August 1, 2019).

Home Office (2018), "Vietnam: Ethnic and Religious Groups," June 28. Available online: https://assets.publishing.service.gov.uk/government/uploads/system/uploads/attachment_data/file/695864/Vietnam_-_Ethnic_and_Religious_groups_-_CPIN_v2.0_ex.pdf

Horsfall, S. (2000), "The Experience of Marian Apparitions and the Mary Cult," *Social Science Journal* 37(3): 375–84.

Horstmann, A. (2018), "Helping the Wounded as Religious Experience. The Free Burma Rangers in Karen State, Myanmar," in B. Yeoh and B. Brown (eds.), *Asian Immigrants and Religious Experience: Transnational Religious Experience*, 201–20, New Mobility in Asia Series, Amsterdam: Amsterdam University Press.

Horstmann, A. and J. H. Jung (2015a), "Introduction," in A. Horstmann and J. H. Jung (eds.), *Building Noah's Ark for Migrants, Refugees, and Religious Communities*, 1–20, London: Palgrave MacMillan.

Horstmann, A. and J. H. Jung, eds. (2015b), *Building Noah's Ark for Migrants, Refugees, and Religious Communities*, London: Palgrave MacMillan.

Hoskins, J. A. (2006), "Caodai Exile and Redemption: A New Vietnamese Religion's Struggle for Identity," in P. Hondagneu-Sotelo (ed.), *Religion and Social Justice for Immigrants*, 191–209, Rutgers: Rutgers University Press. Available online: https://epdf.pub/religion-and-social-justice-for-immigrants.html

Hoskins, J. A. (2011), "Diaspora as Religious Doctrine: 'An Apostle of Vietnamese Nationalism' Comes to California," *Journal of Vietnamese Studies* 4(1): 45–86.

Hoskins, J. A. (2012), "God's Chosen People: Race, Religion and Anti-Colonial Resistance in French Indochina," *The Asia Research Institute Working Paper Series* No. 189, September 2012, National University of Singapore.

Hoskins, J. A. (2015), *The Divine Eye and the Diaspora: Vietnamese Caodaism Becomes Transpacific Caodaism*, Honolulu: University of Hawaii Press.

Hoskins, J. A and H. T. Nguyen (2020), "Vietnamese Transnational Religions: The Cold War Polarities of Temples in Little Hanois and Little Saigons," in P. Clart and A. Jones (eds.), *Transnational Religious Spaces: Religious Organizations and Their Interaction in Africa, East Asia, and Beyond*, Berlin: De Gruyter.

Huntington, S. (1996), *The Clash of Civilizations*, New York: Simon and Schuster.

Hussain, M. (1993), *The Assam Movement: Class, Ideology and Identity*, Delhi: Manak.

Hussain, M. (2000), "State, Identity Movements and Internal Displacement in the North-East," *Economic and Political Weekly* 35(51): 4519–23.

Hüwelmeier, G. (2010), "Moving East: Transnational Ties of Vietnamese Pentecostals," in H. Hüwelmeier and K. Krause (eds.), *Traveling Spirits: Migrants, Markets and Mobilities*, 133–44, New York: Routledge.

Hüwelmeier, G. (2011), "Socialist Cosmopolitanism Meets Global Pentecostalism: Charismatic Christianity among Vietnamese Migrants after the Fall of the Berlin Wall," *Ethnic and Racial Studies* 34(3): 436–53.

Hüwelmeier, G. (2014), "Transnational Vietnamese - Germany and Beyond," in S. Hahn and S. Nadel (eds.), *Asian Migrants in Europe: Transcultural Connections*, 225–40, Göttingen: Vandenhoeck & Ruprecht.

Hüwelmeier, G. (2015), "From 'Jarmark Europa' to 'Commodity City.' New Marketplaces, Post-Socialist Migrations, and Cultural Diversity in Central and Eastern Europe," *Central and Eastern European Migration Review* 4(1): 27–39.

Hüwelmeier, G. (2016), "Enhancing Spiritual Security in Berlin's Asian Bazaars," *New Diversities* 18(1): 9–21.

Hüwelmeier, G. (2017a), "Socialist Cosmopolitans in Postsocialist Europe: Transnational Ties among Vietnamese in the Cold War Period and Thereafter," *Journal of Vietnamese Studies* 22(1): 130–58.

Hüwelmeier, G. (2017b), "From Contract Workers to Entrepreneurs: Gender and Work among Transnational Vietnamese in East and Reunited Germany," in J. M. Cho and

D. T. McGetchin (eds.), *Gendered Encounters between Germany and Asia*, 275–90, Palgrave Series in Asian German Studies, Cham: Palgrave Macmillan.

Hüwelmeier, G. and K. Krause, eds. (2010), *Traveling Spirits: Migrants, Markets and Mobilities*, New York: Routledge.

Huynh, N. and C. Nguyen (2009), *Memory Is Another Country: Women of the Vietnamese Diaspora*, Santa Barbara: ABC-CLIO.

Jacobs, S. (2004), *America's Miracle Man in Vietnam: Ngo Dinh Diem, Religion, Race and U.S. Intervention in Southeast Asia, 1950–1957*, Durham: Duke University Press.

Jacquemet, M. (2009), "Transcribing Refugees: The Entextualization of Asylum Seekers. Hearings in a Transidiomatic Environment," *Text & Talk* 29(5): 525–46.

Jacquemet, M. (2011), "Crosstalk 2.0: Asylum and Communicative Breakdowns," *Text & Talk* 31(4). Available online: https://doi.org/10.1515/text.2011.023

Jammes, J. (2014), *Les oracles du Cao Đài: Étude d'un mouvement religieux vietnamien et de sesréseaux*, Paris: Les Indes Savantes.

Janssen, G. H. (2014), *The Dutch Revolt and Catholic Exile in Reformation Europe*, Cambridge: Cambridge University Press.

Jellema, K. (2007), "Returning Home: Ancestor Veneration and the Nationalism of Đổi Mới Vietnam," in P. Taylor (ed.), *Modernity and Re-enchantment: Religion in Post-revolutionary Vietnam*, Singapore: ISEAS Publishing.

Kaag, M. (2008), "Mouride Transnational Livelihoods at the Margins of a European Society: The Case of Residence Prealpino, Brescia, Italy," *Journal of Ethnic and Migration Studies* 34(2): 271–85.

Kalsky, M. (2007), ". . . want jullie zijn zelf vreemdelingen geweest in Egypte," in *De vreemdeling en de Bijbel*, 108–21, Amsterdam: Amsterdam University Press.

Kalu, O. U., ed. (2007), *African Christianity: An African Story*, (1), Trenton: Africa World Press, Inc.

Kaplan, B. J. (2002), "Fictions of Privacy: House Chapels and the Spatial Accommodation of Religious Dissent in Early Modern Europe," *American Historical Review* 107: 1031–64.

Kaplan, B. J. (2007), *Divided by Faith: Religious Conflict and the Practice of Toleration in Early Modern Europe*, Cambridge, MA: Harvard University Press.

Kauffman, C. J. (2005), "Politics, Programs, and Protests: Catholic Relief Services in Vietnam, 1954–1975," *The Catholic Historical Review* XCI (2): 223–50.

Keane, W. (2002), "Sincerity, 'Modernity,' and the Protestants," *Cultural Anthropology* 17(1): 65–92.

Keane, W. (2014), "Freedom, Reflexivity, and the Sheer Everydayness of Ethics," *HAU: Journal of Ethnographic Theory* 4(1): 443–57.

Keith, C. (2012), *Catholic Vietnam: A Church from Empire to Nation*, Berkeley: University of California Press.

Kelly, T. (2015), "Afterword," in D. Berti, A. Good, and G. Tarabout (eds.), *Of Doubt and Proof: Ritual and Legal Practices of Judgment*, 183–91, Juris Diversitas, Farnham: Ashgate Publishing.

Kent, P. C. (2002), *The Lonely Cold War of Pope Pius XII: The Roman Catholic Church and the Division of Europe, 1943–1950*, Montreal: McGill-Queen's University Press.

Kettani, M. and M. Péraldi (2011), "Les mondes du travail. Segmentations et informalités," in M. Péraldi (ed.), *D'une Afrique à l'autre. Migrations subsahariennes au Maroc*, Paris: Karthala.

Khalili, L. (2004), "Grass-Roots Commemorations: Remembering the Land in the Camps of Lebanon," *Journal of Palestine Studies* 34(1): 6–22.

Kimura, M. (2008), "Conflict and Displacement: A Case Study of the Election Violence in 1983," in S. K. Das (ed.), *Blisters on Their Feet: Tales of Internally Displaced Persons in India's North East*, 150–63, New Delhi: Sage.

Kimura, M. (2013), *The Nellie Massacre of 1983: Agency of Rioters*, New Delhi: Sage.

Kippenberg, H. G., J. Rüpke, and K. von Stuckrad, eds. (2009), *Europäische Religionsgeschichte: ein mehrfacher Pluralismus*, Göttingen: Vandenhoeck & Ruprecht.

Kirchschläger, R., and A. Stirnemann (1991–9), *The Vienna Dialogue: Five Pro Oriente Consultations with Oriental Orthodoxy*, Stiftungsfonds Pro Oriente, Wien: F. Berger and Söhne.

Kleinschmidt, J. (2013), "Die Aufnahme der ersten 'boat people' in die Bundesrepublik," *Deutschland Archiv Online*, November 26. Available online: https://www.bpb.de/geschichte/zeitgeschichte/deutschlandarchiv/170611/die-aufnahme-der-ersten-boat-people-in-die-bundesrepublik (accessed March 14, 2020).

Klempner, L. J. (2016), "Blessed Is Egypt My People: Recontextualizing Coptic Identity outside of Egypt," Ph.D. thesis VU Amsterdam.

Klinken, A. S. van (2013), *Transforming Masculinities in African Christianity: Gender Controversies in Times of AIDS*, Farnham: Ashgate.

Knott, K. (2008), "Spatial Theory and the Study of Religion," *Religion Compass* 2(6): 1102–16.

Knott, K. and S. McLoughlin, eds. (2010), *Diasporas: Concepts, Intersections, Identities*, London and New York: The University of Chicago Press.

Körs, A. and A.-K. Nagel (2018), "Local 'Formulas of Peace:' Religious Diversity and State-Interfaith Governance in Germany," *Social Compass* 65(3): 346–62. 0037768618787240.

Koselleck, R. (2006), "Crisis," *Journal of the History of Ideas* 67(2): 357–400.

Kossert, A. (2008), *Kalte Heimat. Die Geschichte der deutschen Vertriebenen nach 1945*, München: Siedler.

Kösters, F., ed. (2005), *Die Geschichte des kirchlichen Suchdienstes*, München: Gebr. Geiselberger.

Krauss, M., ed. (2011), *Integrationen. Vertriebene in den deutschen Ländern nach 1945*, Göttingen: Vandenhoeck & Ruprecht.

Kravel-Tovi, M. (2012), "Rite of Passing: Bureaucratic Encounters, Dramaturgy, and Jewish Conversion in Israel," *American Ethnologist* 39(2): 371–88.

Kravel-Tovi, M. (2014), "Bureaucratic Gifts: Religious Conversion, Change, and Exchange in Israel," *American Ethnologist* 41(4): 714–27.

Kravel-Tovi, M. (2019), "Jews by Choice? Orthodox Conversion, the Problem of Choice, and Jewish Religiopolitics in the Israeli State," *Ethnography* 20(1): 47–67.

Kreibaum, M. (2016), "Their Suffering, Our Burden? How Congolese Refugees Affect the Ugandan Population," *World Development* 78: 262–87.

Kwon, H. (2008), *Ghosts of War in Vietnam*, Cambridge: Cambridge University Press.

Lambek, M., ed. (2010), *Ordinary Ethics: Anthropology, Language, and Action*, New York: Fordham University Press.

Lambek, M. (2012), "Religion and Morality," in D. Fassin (ed.), *A Companion to Moral Anthropology*, 341–58, Malden: Wiley-Blackwell.

Larkin, B. (2014), "Techniques of Inattention: The Mediality of Loudspeakers in Nigeria," *Anthropological Quarterly* 87(4): 989–1015.

"La situation religieuse dans le monde," *L'actualité religieuse dans le monde* (1955): 15–23.

Lauser, A. (2018), *Staging the Spirits: LênĐồng - Cult – Culture - Spectacle. Performative Contexts of a Vietnamese Ritual from Controlled Possession to Staged Performance.* GISCA Occasional Papers, No. 20, Göttingen: Institute for Social and Cultural Anthropology.

Lauterbach, K. (2014), "Religion and Displacement in Africa: Compassion and Sacrifice in Congolese Churches in Kampala, Uganda," *Religion and Theology* 21(3–4): 290–308.

Lê, Đ. T. P. (2009), *Chứng từ của một giám mục, Những câu chuyện về một thời*, San Diego: Nguyệt san Diễn đàn giáo dân.

Lefebvre, H. (1991), *The Production of Space*, Malden: Wiley-Blackwell.

Lehmann, H. (2007), *Transformationen der Religionen in der Neuzeit*, Göttingen: Vandenhoeck & Ruprecht.

Leustean, L., ed. (2014), *Eastern Christianity and Politics in the Twenty-First Century*, Oxford: Routledge.

Levitt, P. (2012), "Religion on the Move: Mapping Global Cultural Production and Consumption," in C. Bender, W. Cadge, P. Levitt, and D. Smilde (eds.), *Religion on the Edge: De-centering and Re-centering the Sociology of Religion*, 159–78, Oxford: Oxford University Press.

Luis, H. A. (2018), *Governing Muslims and Islam in Contemporary Germany*, Leiden, Boston: Brill.

Lüthi, L. (2020), *Cold Wars, Asia, the Middle East, Europe*, Cambridge: Cambridge University Press.

Lyytinen, E. (2017), "Informal Places of Protection: Congolese Refugees' Communities of Trust in Kampala, Uganda," *Journal of Ethnic and Migration Studies* 43(6): 991–1008.

Madrisotti, F. (2018), *L'étape marocaine des self-made-migrants. La recherche d'une émancipation économique et sociale par la mobilité*, PhD thesis.

Mahmood, S. (2015), *Religious Difference in the Secular Age: A Minority Report*, Princeton: Princeton University Press.

Malkki, L. H. (1996), "Speechless Emissaries: Refugees, Humanitarianism, and Dehistoricization," *Cultural Anthropology* 11(3): 377–404.

Mandel, R. (1996), "A Place of Their Own," in B. Metcalf (eds.), *Making Muslim Space in North America and Europe*, 147–66. Berkeley: University of California Press.

Manhattan, A. (1984), *Vietnam, Why Did We Go? The Shocking Story of the Catholic 'Church's' Role in Starting the Vietnam War*, Ontario: Chick Publications.

Marabello, S. and B. Riccio (2018), "West African Migrations to Italy: An Anthropological Analysis of Ghanaian and Senegalese Politics of Mobility in Emilia Romagna," *Revue Européenne Des Migrations Internationales* 34(1): 127–49.

Marfleet, P. (2011), "Understanding 'Sanctuary': Faith and Traditions of Asylum," *Journal of Refugee Studies* 24(3): 440–55.

Mariani, P. (2011), *Church Militant: Bishop Kung and Catholic Resistance in Communist Shanghai*, Cambridge, MA: Harvard University Press.

Marshall, R. (2016), "Destroying Arguments and Captivating Thoughts: Spiritual Warfare Prayer as Global Praxis," *Journal of Religious and Political Practice* 2(1): 92–113.

Marzouki, N., D. McDonnell, and O. Roy, eds. (2016), *Saving the People: How Populists Hijack Religion*, London: Hurst.

Mattingly, C. (2013), "Moral Selves and Moral Scenes: Narrative Experiments in Everyday Life," *Ethnos* 78(3): 301–27.

Mauss, M. (1990), *The Gift: The Form and Reason for Exchange in Archaic Societies*, trans. W. D. Halls, London: Routledge.

Mavelli, L. and E. K. Wilson eds. (2016), *The Refugee Crisis and Religion: Secularism, Security and Hospitality in Question*, Oxford: Rowman and Littlefield International.

Mbembe, A. (2003), "Necropolitics," trans. Libby Meintjes, *Public Culture* 15: 11–40.

Mbembe, A. (2017), *Critique of Black Reason*, Durham: Duke University Press.

Mengozzi, A. (2011), *Religious Poetry in Vernacular Syriac from Northern Iraq (17th–20th Centuries): An Anthology, Introduction and Translation* (CSCO 627-628 / Scr. Syr. 240–241), Louvain: Peeters.

Mengozzi, Alessandro (2020), "The digital afterlife of Yazdandukht and Mar Qardagh: From the Persian martyr acts in Syriac to Sureth poetry on YouTube, via a historical novel in Arabic', *Kervan: International Journal of Afro-Asiatic Studies*," 24/2, 199–229.

Metcalf, B. D., ed. (1996), *Making Muslim Space in North America and Europe*, Berkeley: University of California Press.

Meyer, B. (1998), "'Make a Complete Break with the Past.' Memory and Post-Colonial Modernity in Ghanaian Pentecostalist Discourse," *Journal of Religion in Africa* 28(3): 316–40.

Meyer, B. (1999), *Translating the Devil: Religion and Modernity among the Ewe in Ghana*, International African Library 21, Edinburgh and London: University Press for the International African Institute.

Meyer, B. (2009), "From Imagined Communities to Aesthetic Formations: Religious Mediations, Sensational Forms, and Styles of Binding," in B. Meyer (ed.), *Aesthetic Formations: Media, Religion, and the Senses*, 1–28, New York: Palgrave Macmillan.

Meyer, B. (2010), "'There Is a Spirit in That Image': Mass-Produced Jesus Pictures and Protestant-Pentecostal Animation in Ghana," *Comparative Studies in Society and History* 52(1): 100–30.

Meyer, B. (2018), "Frontier Zones and the Study of Religion," *Journal for the Study of Religion* 31(2): 57–78.

Meyer, B. (2019), "Recycling the Christian Past: The Heritagization of Christianity and National Identity in the Netherlands," in R. Buikema, A. Buyse, and A. Robben (eds.), *Culture, Citizenship and Human Rights*, 64–88, London and New York: Routledge.

Meyer, B. (2020a), "Religion as Mediation," *Entangled Religions* 11(3). https://doi.org/10.13154/er.11.2020.8444

Meyer, B. (2020b), "Remapping Our Mindset: Towards a Transregional and Pluralistic Outlook," *Religion*, Special Issue on "The Future of the Study of religion/s," ed. by Steven Engler and Michael Stausberg, 50(1): 113–21.

Meyer, B. and A. Moors, eds. (2006), *Religion, Media, and the Public Sphere*, Bloomington and Indianapolis: Indiana University Press.

Meyer, B. and D. Houtman (2012), "Introduction: Material Religion – How Things Matter," in D. Houtman and B. Meyer (eds.), *Things: Religion and the Question of Materiality*, 1–26, New York: Fordham University Press.

Meyer, B. and P. Geschiere, eds. (1998), *Globalization and Identity: Dialectics of Flow and Closure*, Oxford: Blackwell.

Miller, E. (2013), *Misalliance, Ngo Dinh Diem, the United States and the Fate of South Vietnam*, Cambridge, MA: Harvard University Press.

Milton, G. (2018), "Asylum Seeker Conversions: Misconceptions Inherent in the Public Response," *The Cadbury Centre Blog on Religion in Politics and Public Life*. Available online: https://blog.bham.ac.uk/cpur/2018/02/09/asylum-seeker-conversions-misconceptions-inherent-in-the-public-response/

Mitscherlich, A. (1967), *Die Unfähigkeit zu trauern. Grundlagen kollektiven Verhaltens*, München: Piper.

Monforte, P. (2014), *Europeanizing Contention: The Protest Against "Fortress Europe" in France and Germany*, New York: Berghahn.

Monteil, V. (1964), *Islam noir*, Paris: Seuil.

Morephrem Bookshop (MEB). http://morephrem.com/bookshop/index.php (accessed June 9, 2018).

Morgan, J. (2019), "Exploring Fictive Kinship among Unaccompanied Refugee Minors in the Church of Sweden," *Svensk Teologisk Kvartalskrift* 95(3): 165–78.

Morgan, J. G. (1997), *The Vietnam Lobby: The American Friends of Vietnam, 1955–1975*, Chapel Hill: University of North Carolina Press.

Morgenstern, T., K. G. Lynes, and I. A. Paul (2020), "In and Against Crisis," in K. Lynes, T. Morgenstern, and I. A. Paul (eds.), *Moving Images Mediating Migration as Crisis*, 27–47, Bielefeld: Transcript.

Morris, L. (2000), "Rights and Controls in the Management of Migration: The Case of Germany," *Sociological Review* 48(2): 224–40.

Mourji, F., J.-N. Ferrié, S. Radi, and M. Alioua (2016), *Les Migrants subsahariens au Maroc. Enjeux d'une migration de résidence*, Rabat: KAS.

Mudu, P. and S. Chattopadhyay (2018), *Migration, Squatting and Radical Autonomy*, New York: Routledge.

Mueller, B. (2019), "39 Vietnamese Died in a U.K. Truck, 18,000 More Endure This Perilous Trip," *The New York Times*, November 1, 2019.

Mungello, D. E. (2015), *The Catholic Invasion of China: Remaking Chinese Christianity*, Lanham: Rowman and Littlefield.

Münz, R. and R. Ohliger (2003), *Diasporas and Ethnic Migrants*, London: Frank Cass.

Murray, D. (2018), *The Strange Death of Europe: Immigration, Identity, Islam*, Oxford: Bloomsbury Continuum.

Murre-van den Berg, H. L. (1999), *From a Spoken to a Written Language: The Introduction and Development of Literary Urmia Aramaic in the Nineteenth Century*, Leiden: De GoeieStichting.

Murre-van den Berg, H. L. (2007), "Syriac Christianity," in K. Parry (ed.), *The Blackwell Companion to Eastern Christianity*, 249–68, Malden, Oxford, and Victoria: Blackwell Publishing.

Murre-van den Berg, H. L. (2013), "A Center of Transnational Syriac Orthodoxy: St. Mark's Convent in Jerusalem," *Journal of Levantine Studies* 3(1): 61–83.

Murre-van den Berg, H. L. (2015a), *Scribes and Scriptures: The Church of the East in the Eastern Ottoman Provinces (1500–1850)*, Eastern Christian Studies 21, Louvain: Peeters.

Murre-van den Berg, H. L. (2015b), "Classical Syriac and the Syriac Churches: A Twentieth-Century History," in M. Doerfler, E. Fiano, and K. Smith (eds.), *Syriac Encounters: Papers from the Sixth North American Syriac Symposium*, Duke University, June 26–29, 2011 (Eastern Christian Studies 20; Louvain: Peeters), 119–48.

Naïdenoff, G. (1955a), "Vainqueurs aux mains nues, les réfugiés viêt-namiens demandent justice à l'opinion," *Missi* 5: 157–77.

Naïdenoff, G. (1955b), "La Campagne de solidarité vietnamienne ne fait que commencer," *Missi* 5: 189.

Naïdenoff, G. (1956a), "La Campagne de solidarité vietnamienne continue sans répit," *Missi* 2: 71.

Naïdenoff, G. (1956b), "La Triple Chrétienté du Viêt-Nam dans les conjonctures présentes," *Missi* 2: 39–46.

Nayeri, D. (2019), *The Ungrateful Refugee: What Immigrants Never Tell You*, Edinburgh: Canongate Books.

Ngô, Đ. T. (2010), *Đạo Mẫu Việt Nam*, Hanoi: NhàXuấtBảnTônGiáo.

Ngo, T. T. T. (2016), *The New Way: Protestantism and the Hmong in Vietnam*, Seattle: University of Washington Press.

Nguyen, L.-H. T. (1995), "The Double Diaspora of Vietnam's Catholics," *Orbis: Journal of World Affairs* 39(4): 491–501.

Nguyen, M. (2012), *The Gift of Freedom: War, Debt and Other Refugee Passages*, Durham: Duke University Press.

Nguyen, P. T. (2017), *Becoming Refugee American: The Politics of Rescue in Little Saigon*, Urbana: University of Illinois Press.

Nguyen, P.-V. (2016), "Fighting the First Indochina War Again? Catholic Refugees in South Vietnam, 1954–1959," *SOJOURN* 31(1): 207–46.

Nguyễn, T. H. (2015), "Integration, Changes, Tradition and Cultural Identities of the Vietnamese Diasporic Community," The Case Study at Silicon Valley, California, Tạpchí *Vănhóahọc* (*Journal of Cultural Studies*) 5: 15–32.

Nguyễn, T. H. (2016), *The Religion of Four Palaces: Mediumship and Therapy in Viet Culture*, Hanoi: The Gioi Publishing House.

Nguyen, V. T. (2012), "Refugee Memories and Asian American Critique," *Positions: Asia Critique* 20(3): 911–42.

Nguyen, V. T. (2015), *The Sympathizer*, New York: Grove Press.

Nguyen, V. T. (2016), *Nothing Ever Dies: Vietnam and the Memory of War*, Cambridge, MA: Harvard University Press.

Nguyen, Y. T. (2018), "(Re)making the South Vietnamese Past in America," *Journal of Asian American Studies* 21(1): 65–103.

Nguyen-Vo, T. H. (2005), "Forking Paths: How Shall We Mourn the Dead?" *Amerasia Journal* 31: 157–75.

Nielsen, J. (1999), *Towards a European Islam*, New York: Palgrave Macmillan.

Nieswand, B. (2010), "Enacted Destiny: West African Charismatic Christians in Berlin and the Immanence of God," *Journal of Religion in Africa* 40(1): 33–59.

Ninh, T. H. (2013), "The Caodai Mother Goddess in a Globalizing World: Mediation Between Religious Universalism and Homeland Orientation among Vietnamese Caodaists in the United States," *Asian Anthropology* 12(1): 53–67.

Ninh, T. H. (2017), *Race, Gender, and Religion in the Vietnamese Diaspora: The New Chosen People*, Cham: Palgrave.

Nirenberg, D. (2014), *Neighboring Faiths*, Chicago: University of Chicago Press.

Norton, B. (2003), "'Hot-Tempered' Women and 'Effeminate' Men: The Performance of Music and Gender in Vietnamese Mediumship," in K. Fjelstad and T. H. Nguyen (eds.), *Possessed by the Spirits*, Ithaca: Cornell University Press

Norton, B. (2009), *Songs for the Spirits: Music and Mediums in Modern Vietnam*, Urbana: University of Illinois Press.

OECD (2017), *Finding Their Way. Labour Market Integration of Refugees in Germany*, Paris: OECD Publishing. Available online: http://www.oecd.org/els/m

ig/Labour-Market-Integration-Refugees-Germany-2017-de.pdf (accessed June 27, 2018).

Olupona, J. and R. Gemignani (2007), *African Immigrant Religions in America*, New York: New York University Press.

Omata, N. (2012), "Refugee Livelihoods and the Private Sector: Ugandan Case Study," Working Paper Series no. 86, Refugee Studies Centre, University of Oxford.

Orsi, R. (2003), "Is the Study of Lived Religion Irrelevant to the World We Live In?" *Journal for the Scientific Study of Religion* 42(2): 169–74.

Orsi, R. (2010), *The Madonna of 115th Street: Faith and Community in Italian Harlem, 1880–1950*, New Haven: Yale University Press.

Ortner, S. (2016), "Dark Anthropology and Its Others: Theory since the Eighties," *HAU: Journal of Ethnographic Theory* 6(1): 47–73.

Osborne, M. (1980), "The Indochinese Refugees: Cause and Effects," *International Affairs* (Royal Institute of International Affairs *1944-*) 56(1): 37–53.

Østebø, T. (2015), "African Salafism: Religious Purity and the Politicization of Purity," *Islamic Africa* 6(1–2): 1–29.

Özyürek, E. (2014), *Being German, Becoming Muslim: Race, Religion, and Conversion in the New Europe*, Princeton: Princeton University Press.

Paramore, K. (2009), *Ideology and Christianity in Japan*, London: Routledge.

Parla, A. (2019), *Precarious Hope: Migration and the Limits of Belonging in Turkey*, Stanford: Stanford University Press.

Perrin, D. (2009), "Immigration et création juridique au Maghreb. La fragmentation des mondes et des droits," in A. Bensaad (ed.), *Le Maghreb à l'épreuve des migrations subsahariennes. Immigration sur émigration*, 245–66, Paris: Karthala.

Peteet, J. (2005), *Landscape of Hope and Despair: Palestinian Refugee Camps*, Philadelphia: University of Pennsylvania Press.

Pew Research Center (November 8, 2017), "Orthodox Christianity in the 21st Century." http://www.pewforum.org/2017/11/08/orthodox-christianity-in-the-21st-century/

Pew-Templeton Global Religious Futures (2010), "The Future of World Religions: Vietnam's Religious Demography." Research report available online at http://www .globalreligiousfutures.org/countries/vietnam#/?affiliations_religion_id=0&a ffiliations_year=2010&region_name=All%20Countries&restrictions_year=2016 (accessed July 31, 2019).

Phạm Ngọc Chi Committee of Aid for Resettlement of the Refugees from North Vietnam (1955), *Refugees of North Vietnam, the Refugees Fled for the Sake of Their Faith*, Saigon.

Phạm, B. H. (2007), *Người Nam Bộ và Tôn Giáo Bản Địa [The People of the Southern Region and Indigenous Religions]*, Hà Nội: Nhà Xuất Bản Tôn Giáo.

Phan, P. C. (1991), "Aspects of Vietnamese Culture and Roman Catholicism: Background Information for Educators of Vietnamese Seminarians," *Seminaries in Dialogue* 23: 2–8.

Phan, P. C. (2003), *Christianity with an Asian Face: Asian American Theology in the Making*, Maryknoll: Orbis Books.

Phan, P. C. (2005), "Mary in Vietnamese Piety and Theology: A Contemporary Perspective," *Ephemerides Mariologicae* 51: 457–72.

Phan, P. C. (2006), "Christianity in Indochina," in S. Gilley and B. Stanley (eds.), *World Christianities, c. 1815-c.1914*, 513–27, Cambridge: Cambridge University Press.

Phạm, P. Q. (2009), *Hero and Deity: Tran Hung Dao and the Revival of Popular Religion in Vietnam*, Thailand: Mekong Press.

Picard, J. A. (2016), "'Fertile Lands Await' the Promise and Pitfalls of Directed Resettlement, 1954–1959," *Journal of Vietnamese Studies* 11(3–4): 58–102.

Piketty, T. and others (2018), "We Need a Paradigm Shift in the Way We Think About Migration," *The Guardian*, June 28.

Plener, P. L., R. C. Groschwitz, E. Brähler, T. Sukaleand, and Jörg M. Fegert (2017), "Unaccompanied Refugee Minors in Germany: Attitudes of the General Population Towards a Vulnerable Group," *European Child & Adolescent Psychiatry* 26(6): 733–42.

Polak, R. (2018), "Turning a Curse into a Blessing? Theological Contributions to a Resource-Oriented Narrative on Migration in Europe," in U. Schmiedel and G. Smith (eds.), *Religion in the European Refugee Crisis*, 243–64, London: Palgrave Macmillan.

Potulicki, M. (1954), "The Emigration of Refugees," in *The International Catholic Migration Congress, Breda Netherlands, 11–16 September 1954*, The Hague: Catholic Institute for Social Ecclesiastical Research.

Power, T. P. and K. Whelan, eds. (1990), *Endurance and Emergence: Catholics in Ireland in the Eighteenth Century*, Dublin: Irish Academic Press.

Prados, J. (2009), *Vietnam: The History of an Unwinnable War*, Lawrence: University Press of Kansas.

Prak, M. (2005), *The Dutch Republic in the Seventeenth Century: The Golden Age*, trans. Diane Webb, Cambridge and New York: Cambridge University Press.

Pries, L. (2018), *Refugees, Civil Society and the State: European Experiences and Global Challenges*, Cheltenham: Edward Elgar Publishing.

Raendchen, O. (2000), *Vietnamesen in der DDR. Ein Rückblick*, Berlin: Seacom.

Rainey, M. (2017), "Time in the Shelter, Time on the Street: Refused Asylum Seekers and the Tragedy of the Border," PhD diss., Goldsmiths, University of London. Available online: https://doi.org/10.25602/GOLD.00020474 (accessed June 1, 2019).

Rakodi, C. (2014), "Religion and Social Life in African Cities," in E. Pieterse and S. Parnell (eds.), *Africa's Urban Revolution*, 82–109, London and New York: Zed Books.

Rambo, L. R. (1993), *Understanding Religious Conversion*, New Haven and London: Yale University Press.

Rawls, J. (1971), *A Theory of Justice*, Cambridge, MA: Harvard University Press.

Read, C. J. (2012), "A Place in the City: Narratives of 'Emplacement' in a Delhi Resettlement Neighbourhood," *Ethnography* 13(1): 87–101. https://doi.org/10.1177/1466138111432034

Reid, A. (2018), "The Making of Belief in Secular Times: Negotiating Inclusion within the Dutch Asylum Context," Paper Presented at the Conference Refugees and Religion, Utrecht University, September 27–28, 2018.

Riccio, B. and S. degli Uberti (2013), "Senegalese Migrants in Italy: Beyond the Assimilation/Transnationalism Divide," *Urban Anthropology and Studies of Cultural Systems and World Economic Development* 42(3/4): 207–54.

Robbins, J. (2004), "The Globalization of Pentecostal and Charismatic Christianity," *Annual Review of Anthropology* 33(1): 117–43.

Robbins, J. (2016), "What Is the Matter with Transcendence? On the Place of Religion in the New Anthropology of Ethics," *Journal of the Royal Anthropological Institute* 22(4): 767–81.

Robinson, W. C. (1998), *Terms of Refuge: The Indochinese Exodus and the International Response*, London and New York: Zed Books.

Roitman, J. (2014), *Anti-Crisis*, Durham and London: Duke University Press.

Romeny, R. B. ter Haar, N. Atto, J. J. van Ginkel, M. Immerzeel, and B. Snelderseds (2009), "The Formation of a Communal Identity among West Syrian Christians: Results and Conclusions of the Leiden Project," *CHRC* 89(1–3): 1–52.

Rosales, G. and C. G. Arévalo (1997), *For All the Peoples of Asia: FABC Documents from 1970–1991*, Manila: Claretian.

Rosander, E. and D. Westerlund (1997), *African Islam and Islam in Africa: Encounters between Sufis and Islamists*, London: Hurst.

Ross, K. R., M. Tadros, and T. M. Johnson, eds. (2018), *Christianity in North Africa and West Asia*, Edinburgh: Edinburgh University Press.

Röttgers, K. (1993), *Kants Kollege und seine ungeschriebene Schrift über die Zigeuner*, Heidelberg: Manutius.

Roudometof, V. (2014), *Globalization and Orthodox Christianity: The Transformations of a Religious Tradition*, New York and London: Routledge.

Roy, O. and I. Becci (2015), *Religious Diversity in European Prisons: Challenges and Implications for Rehabilitation*, Cham: Springer.

Rücker, A. (1931), "Mitteilungen: Ein alter Handschriftenkatalog des ehemaligen Nestorianischen Klosters in Jerusalem," *Oriens Christianus* 28: 90–6.

Russell, A. (2011), "Home, Music and Memory for the Congolese in Kampala," *Journal of Eastern African Studies* 5(2): 294–312.

Sacks, M. S. (2013), *Before Harlem: The Black Experience in New York City Before World War I*, Philadelphia: University of Pennsylvania Press.

Said, E. (1984), "Reflections of Exile," *Granta* 13: 159–72.

Salemink, O. (2007), "Spirits of Consumption and the Capitalist Ethic in Vietnam," in P. Kitiarsa (ed.), *Religious Commodifications in Asia: Marketing Gods*, 147–68, London and New York: Routledge.

Salemink, O. (2013), "Appropriating Culture: The Politics of Intangible Cultural Heritage in Vietnam," in H.-T. Ho Tai and M. Sidel (eds.), *State, Society and the*

Market in Contemporary Vietnam: Property, Power and Values, New York and London: Routledge.

Salemink, O. (2015), "Spirit Worship and Possession in Vietnam and Beyond," in B. S. Turner and O. Salemink (eds.), *Routledge Handbook of Religions in Asia*, 231–46, London: Routledge.

Salemink, O. (2018), "Described, Inscribed, Written Off: Heritagisation as (Dis) connection," in P. Taylor (ed.), *Connected and Disconnected in Vietnam: Remaking Social Relations in a Post-Socialist Nation*, 311–46, Canberra: Australian National University Press.

Samaddar, R. (2016), "Forced Migration Situations as Exceptions in History?," *International Journal of Migration and Border Studies* 2(2): 99–118.

Santoro, N. J. (2011), *Mary in Our Life: Atlas of the Names and Titles of Mary, the Mother of Jesus and Their Place in Marian Devotion*, Bloomington: iUniverse, Inc.

Sanyal, R. (2010), "Squatting in Camps: Building and Insurgency in Spaces of Refuge," *Urban Studies* 48(5): 877–90.

Sarau, O. (1898), *Catalogue of the Syriac Manuscripts the Library of the Museum Associations of Oroomiah College (Qodiqos d-ktābē suryāyē d-gāu beblīytiqī d-Collījīyā d-Urmī)*, Persia: Oroomiah.

Sarrazin, T. (2012), *Deutschland schafft sich ab: Wie wir unser Land aufs Spiel setzen*, München: Deutsche Verlagsanstalt.

Sarrazin, T. (2018), *Feindliche Übernahme: Wie der Islam den Fortschritt behindert und die Gesellschaft bedroht*, München: Finanzbuch Verlag.

Schader, M. (2017), *Religion as a Political Resource: Migrants from Sub-Saharan Africa in Berlin and Paris*, London: Springer.

Schendel, W. van and I. Abraham, eds. (2005), *Illicit Flows and Criminal Things: States, Borders, and the Other Side of Globalization*, Bloomington: Indiana University Press.

Schielke, S. (2010), "Second Thoughts about the Anthropology of Islam, or How to Make Sense of Grand Schemes in Everyday Life," *ZMO Working Papers*, 2.

Schielke, S. and L. Debevec, eds. (2012), *Ordinary Lives and Grand Schemes: An Anthropology of Everyday Religion*, New York: Berghahn Books.

Schießl, S. (2016), *Das Tor zur Freiheit. Kriegsfolgen, Erinnerungspolitik und humanitärer Anspruch im Lager Friedland (1945–1970)*, Göttingen: Wallstein.

Schiller, N. G. and A. Caglar (2010), *Locating Migration: Rescaling Cities and Migrants*, Ithaca: Cornell University Press.

Schinkel, W. (2017), *Imagined Societies: A Critique of Immigrant Integration in Western Europe*, Cambridge: Cambridge University Press.

Schmiedel, U. (2018), "'We Can Do This!' Tackling the Political Theology of Populism," in U. Schmiedel and G. Smith (eds.), *Religion in the European Refugee Crisis*, 205–24, London: Palgrave Macmillan.

Schmiedel, U. and G. Smith, eds. (2018), *Religion in the European Refugee Crisis*, 1–12, London: Palgrave Macmillan.

Schmoller, A., ed. (2018), *Middle Eastern Christians and Europe: Historical Legacies and Present Challenges*, Wien: LitVerlag.

Schroeder, J. and L. H. Seukwa (2017), "Access to Education in Germany," in A. Korntheuer, P. Pritchard, and D. B. Maehler (eds.), *Structural Context of Refugee Integration in Canada and Germany*, 53–61, Köln: GESIS-Schriftenreihe 15.

Schuh, C., M. Burchardt, and M. Wohlrab-Sahr (2012), "Contested Secularities: Religious Minorities and Secular Progressivism in the Netherlands," *Journal of Religion in Europe* 5(3): 349–83.

Schunka, A. (2006), *Gäste, die bleiben: Zuwanderer in Kursachsen und der Oberlausitz im 17. und frühen 18. Jahrhundert*, Münster: LIT.

Schwartz, S. B. (2008), *All Can Be Saved: Religious Tolerance and Salvation in the Iberian Atlantic World*, New Haven: Yale University Press.

Schwelling, B. (2008), "Gedenken im Nachkrieg. Die 'Friedland-Gedächtnisstätte,'" *Zeithistorische Forschungen* 5(2): 189–210.

Schwenkel, C. (2015), "Socialist Mobilities: Crossing New Terrains in Vietnamese Migration Histories," *Central and Eastern European Migration Review* 4(1): 13–25.

Seeman, D. (2003), "Agency, Bureaucracy, and Religious Conversion: Ethiopian 'Felashmura' Immigrants in Israel," in A. Buckser and S. D. Glazier (eds.), *The Anthropology of Religious Conversion*, 29–42, Lanham and Oxford: Rowman and Littlefield.

Service historique de l'armée de terre (SHAT)/10H (1955a), "Lettre N.3483/CMC du général de brigade Brebisson, Chef de la Mission française de liaison au général d'armée, Commissaire général de France et commandant-en-chef de l'Indochine, 16 Mars 1955."

Shachar, A. (2009), *The Birthright Lottery*, Cambridge, MA: Harvard University Press.

Shapendonk, J. (2012), "Turbulent Trajectories: African Migrants on Their Way to the European Union," *Societies* 2: 27–41.

Sheringham, O. and A. Wilkins (2018), "Transnational Religion and Everyday Lives: Spaces of Spirituality Among Brazilian and Vietnamese Migrants in London," in N. Bartolini, S. MacKian, and S. Pile (eds.), *Spaces of Spirituality*, 168–83, London: Routledge.

Sidiguitiebe, C. (2016), "Maroc. Campagne de régularisation des migrants: ce qu'il faut savoir." URL: http://telquel.ma/2016/12/13/campagne-regularisation-migrants-ce-quil-faut-savoir_1527188

Smilde, D. (2007), *Reason to Believe: Cultural Agency in Latin American Evangelicalism*, Anthropology of Christianity 3, Berkeley and London: University of California Press.

Smith, A. (1759), *The Theory of Moral Sentiments*, London: G. Bohn.

Smith, M. P. (2005), "Transnational Urbanism Revisited," *Journal of Ethnic and Migration Studies* 31(2): 235–44. https://doi.org/10.1080/1369183042000339909

Smith, S. (2019), *The Scramble for Europe: Young Africa on Its Way to the Old Continent*, Medford: Polity.

Snyder, T. (2010), *Bloodlands*, New York: Basic Books.

Solibakke, K. I. (2012), "Muslim Migration to Germany: A Response to Thilo Sarrazin's Deutschland schafft sich ab," in B. Becker-Cantarino (ed.), *Migration and Religion: Christian Transatlantic Missions, Islamic Migration to Germany*, 219–35, Chloe, Leiden: Brill.

Sommers, M. (2001), "Young, Male and Pentecostal: Urban Refugees in Dar es Salaam, Tanzania," *Journal of Refugee Studies* 14(4): 347–70.

Soucy, A. (2012), *The Buddha Side: Gender, Power, and Buddhist Practice in Vietnam*, Honolunu: University of Hawai'i Press.

Spotti, M. (2019), "'It's All About Naming Things Right:' The Paradox of Web Truths in the Belgian Asylum-Seeking Procedure," in N. Gill and A. Good (eds.), *Asylum Determination in Europe: Ethnographic Perspectives*, 69–90, Palgrave Socio-Legal Studies, Cham: Springer International Publishing.

Stadlbauer, S. (2018), "Secrecy, Secrets, and Emergent Religious Identities: Conversion to Christianity among Refugees in Germany," Paper Presented at the Conference Refugees and Religion, Utrecht University, September 27–28, 2018.

Stadlbauer, S. (2019), "Between Secrecy and Transparency: Conversions to Protestantism Among Iranian Refugees in Germany," *Entangled Religions* 8. Available online: https://doi.org/10.13154/er.8.2019.8322 (accessed July 14, 2019).

Stein, B. (1979), "The Geneva Conferences and the Indochinese Refugee Crisis," *The International Migration Review* 13(4): 716–23.

Streib, H., A. Dinter, and K. Söderblom, eds. (2008), *Lived Religion: Conceptual, Empirical and Practical-Theological Approaches*, Leiden: Brill.

Strong, D. (2018), *A Call to Mission – A History of the Jesuits in China 1842–1954*, Adelaide: ATF.

Su, P. H. (2017), "'There's No Solidarity': Nationalism and Belonging among Vietnamese Refugees and Immigrants in Berlin," *Journal of Vietnamese Studies* 12(1): 73–100.

Suslov, M., ed. (2016), *Digital Orthodoxy in the Post-Soviet World: The Russian Orthodox Church and Web 2.0*, Columbia: Columbia University Press.

Swiffen, A. and J. Nichols (2017), *Legal Violence and the Limits of the Law: Cruel and Unusual*, New York: Routledge.

Szymanska-Matusiewicz, G. (2015), "The Two Tết Festivals: Transnational Connections and Internal Diversity of the Vietnamese Community in Poland," *Central and Eastern European Migration Review* 4(1): 53–65.

Szymanska-Matusiewicz, G. (2017), "Remaking the State or Creating Civil Society? Vietnamese Migrant Associations in Poland," *Journal of Vietnamese Studies* 12(1): 44–74.

Tai, H. T. (2001), *The Country of Memory: Remaking the Past in Late Socialist Vietnam*, Berkeley: University of California Press.

Tan, M. (2019), "Spiritual Fraternities: The Transnational Networks of Ngô Đình Diệm's Personalist Revolution and South Vietnam's First Republic, 1955–1963," *Journal of Vietnamese Studies* 14(2): 1–67.

Taylor, P. (2001), *Fragments of the Present: Searching for Modernity in Vietnam's South*, Honolulu: University of Hawaii Press.

Taylor, P. (2004), *Goddess on the Rise: Pilgrimage and Popular Religion in Vietnam*, Honolulu: University of Hawai'i Press.

Taylor, P. (2007), *Modernity and Re-enchantment: Religion in Post-Revolutionary Vietnam*, Singapore: Institute of Southeast Asian Studies.

Te Brake, W. P. (2017), *Religious War and Religious Peace in Early Modern Europe*, Cambridge Studies in Contentious Politics, Cambridge: Cambridge University Press.

Te Brake, W. P. (forthcoming), *Religious Peace: Historical Reflections on a Moral Imperative*.

Terpstra, N. (2015), *Religious Refugees in the Early Modern World: An Alternative History of the Reformation*, New York: Cambridge University Press.

Teule, H. and A. Brüning, eds. (2018), *Handboek Oosters Christendom*, Leuven: Peeters.

The Christian Century Editors (1958), "Proselyting with Relief Goods," *The Christian Century June* 18: 707–8.

The International Catholic Migration Commission and T. C. C. E. Foundation (1954), International Catholic Migration Congress, The Hague: Catholic Institute for Social Ecclesiastical Research.

"The Korean Dead," *The Korean Information Bulletin* (1951) 2(5): 1–2.

Thomas, R. (2011), *Administrative Justice and Asylum Appeals: A Study of Tribunal Adjudication*, Oxford: Hart.

Ticktin, M. (2011), *Casualties of Care: Immigration and the Politics of Humanitarianism in France*, Berkeley: University of California Press.

Timéra, M. (2009), "Aventuriers ou orphelins de la migration internationale. Nouveaux et anciens migrants 'subsahariens' au Maroc," *Politique Africaine* 3: 175–95.

Timm, U. (2003), *Am Beispiel meines Bruders*, Köln: Kiepenheuer.

"Tình hình công giáo Trung Hoa," *Đạo Bình Đức Mẹ* (1952), March 1: 4–5.

"Tình hình giáo hội Cao Ly," *Đạo Bình Đức Mẹ* (1952), May 31: 6–7.

Tololyan, K. (1996), "Rethinking Diaspora(s): Stateless Power in the Transnational Moment," *Diaspora* 5: 3–36.

Tổng giáo phận Hà Nội (2019), "Thánh lễ kỷ niệm 65 năm thành lập Legio Mariae tổng giáo phận Hà Nội, 10 Tháng 8."

Tonkens, E. and J. Duyvendak (2016), "Introduction: The Culturalization of Citizenship," in J. W. Duyvendak, P. Geschiere, and E. Tonkens (eds.), *The Culturalization of Citizenship: Belonging and Polarization in a Globalizing World*, 1–20, London: Palgrave.

Trần A. D. (1996), *Hàng giáo phẩm công giáo Việt Nam (1960–1995)*, Paris: Mission catholique vietnamienne.

Trần N. A. (2013), "Contested Identities: Nationalism in the Republic of Vietnam (1954–1963)," PhD diss., University of California Berkeley.

Trần T. L. C. (1996), "Les Catholiques vietnamiens pendant la guerre d'indépendance (1945–1954) entre la reconquête coloniale et la résistance communiste," PhD diss., Institut d'études politiques.

Tran, Q. C. (2009), *Trung Tâm Thánh Mẫu Toàn Quốc La Vang* (The National Marian Center of Lavang). Tổng Giáo Phận Huế (The Archdiocese of Hue], June 24, 2013.

Available online. http://tonggiaophanhue.net/home/index.php?option=com_content&view=article&id=38:phn-1-s-tich-c-m-la-vang&catid=14:duc-me-lavang&Itemid=99

Truitt, A. (2017), "Quán Thế Âm of the Transpacific," *Journal of Vietnamese Studies* 12(2): 83–107.

Trung Tâm Lưu Trữ II (TTLT2)/Phủ thư tướng/An Ninh (1955), "Hồ sơ về chuyến thăm trại sinh viên và đồng bào di cư Bắc Việt của ông Joseph Buttinger nam 1954 37tr."

Tweed, T. (1997), *Our Lady of the Exile: Diasporic Religion at a Cuban Shrine in Miami*, New York: Oxford University Press.

Tweed, T. (2006), *Crossing and Dwelling. A Theory of Religion*, Harvard: Harvard University Press.

United Nations High Commissioner for Refugees (2004), "Guidelines on International Protection No. 6: Religion-Based Refugee Claims under Article 1A (2) of the 1951 Convention and/or the 1967 Protocol Relating to the Status of Refugees (HCR/GIP/04/06)," UNHCR. Available online: https://www.unhcr.org/publications/legal/40d8427a4/guidelines-international-protection-6-religion-based-refugee-claims-under.html (accessed July 9, 2019).

United Nations Human Rights Report (2014), "Press Statement on the Visit to the Socialist Republic of Viet Nam by the Special Rapporteur on Freedom of Religion or Belief," Hanoi, July 31, archived online, at http://www.ohchr.org/EN/NewsEvents/Pages/DisplayNews.aspx?NewsID=14914&LangID=E

Vacchiano, F. (2013), "Fencing in the South: The Strait of Gibraltar as a Paradigm of the New Border Regime in the Mediterranean," *Journal of Mediterranean Studies* 22(2): 337–64.

Vajpeyi, A. (2007), *Prolegomena to the Study of People and Places in Violent India*, New Delhi: WISCOMP.

Valenta, M. (2018), "Naked in the Sanctuary: The Religious Resistance," Paper presented at the Conference Refugees and Religion, Utrecht University, September 27–28, 2018.

Van den Hemel, E. (2018), "Post-Secular Nationalism. The Dutch Turn to the Right & Cultural-Religious Reframing of Secularity," in H. Alma and G. Vanheeswijk (eds.), *Social Imaginaries in a Globalizing World: On the Contemporary Dynamics Between the Religious, the Non-Religious and the Secular*, 247–64, Boston: De Gruyter.

Van der Veer, P. (1995), *Nation and Migration: The Politics of Space in the South Asian Diaspora*, Philadelphia: University of Pennsylvania Press.

Van der Veer, P. (2002), "Transnational Religion: Hindu and Muslim Movements," *Global Networks* 2(2): 95–111.

Van der Veer, P. (2005), "Writing Violence," in D. Ludden (ed.), *Making India Hindu: Religion Community and the Politics of Democracy in India*, 250–69, Oxford: Oxford University Press.

Van der Veer, P. (2006), "Pim Fortuyn, Theo van Gogh, and the Politics of Tolerance in the Netherlands," *Public Culture* 18(1): 111–24.

Van der Veer, P. and H. Lehmann (1999), *Nation and Religion: Perspectives on Europe and Asia*, Princeton: Princeton University Press.

Van Dijk, R. (2002), "The Soul Is the Stranger: Ghanaian Pentecostalism and the Diasporic Contestation of 'Flow' and 'Individuality,'" *Culture and Religion* 1(3): 49–65.

Van Dijk, R. (2009), "Social Catapulting and the Spirit of Entrepreneurialism. Migrants, Private Initiative, and the Pentecostal Ethic in Botswana," in G. Hüwelmeier and K. Krause (eds.), *Traveling Spirits: Migrants, Markers, and Mobilities*, 101–17, New York and London: Routledge.

Van Hoorn, H. (2003), "Zwischen allen Stühlen. Die schwierige Stellung sudetendeutscher Antifa-Umsiedler in den ersten Jahren der SBZ/DDR," in J. C. Behrends, T. Lindenberger, and P. G. Poutrus (eds.), *Fremde und Fremd-Sein in der DDR. Zu historischen Ursachen der Fremdenfeindlichkeit in Ostdeutschland*, 159–78, Berlin: Metropol Verlag.

Vásquez, M. and J. Dewind (2014), "Introduction to the Religious Lives of Migrant Minorities: A Transnational and Multi-sited Perspective," *Global Networks* 14(3): 251–72.

Vásquez, M. and K. Knott (2014), "Three Dimensions of Religious Place Making in Diaspora," *Global Networks* 14(3): 326–47.

Vecchio, F. (2016), "The Economy of Seeking Asylum in the Global City," *International Migration* 54(1): 19–31.

Verkaaik, O. and P. T. Arab (2016), "Managing Mosques in the Netherlands: Constitutional versus Culturalist Secularism," *Journal of Muslims in Europe* 5: 251–68.

Verrips, J. (2011), "Some Notes on (New) Savages and Savagery," *Etnofoor* 23(1): 205–12.

Verrips, J. (2020), "Disgust and Difference. Conflicting Sensations of the Sacred," in M. Balkenhol, E. van den Hemel, and I. Stengs (eds.), *The Secular Sacred: Emotions of Belonging and the Perils of Nation and Religion*, 237–61, London: Palgrave.

Vertovec, S. (2000), "Religion and Diaspora," University of Oxford, April 1, 2013. Available online: http://www.transcomm.ox.ac.uk/working%20papers/Vertovec 01.PDF

Vertovec, S. (1999), "Three Meanings of 'Diaspora,' Exemplified among South Asian Religions," *Diaspora* 7: 277–300.

Von Holdt, K. (2013), "The Violence of Order, Orders of Violence: Between Fanon and Bourdieu," *Current Sociology* 61(2): 226–43.

Walzer, M. (1983), *Spheres of Justice*, New York: Basic Books.

Waters, M. C. and T. R. Jimenez (2005), "Assessing Immigrant Assimilation: New Empirical and Theoretical Challenges," *Annual Review of Sociology* 31: 105–25.

Weiner, M. (1983), "The Political Demography of Assam's Anti-immigrant Movement," *Population and Development Review* 9(2): 279–92.

Weiss, K. (2005), "Nach der Weende: Vietnamesische Vertragsarbeiter und Vertragsarbeiterinnen in Ostdeutschland heute," in K. Weiss and M. Dennis (eds.),

Erfolg in der Nische. Die Vietnamesen in der DDR und in Ostdeutschland, 77–96, Münster: LIT.

Werner, J. (1981), *Peasant Politics and Religious Sectarianism: Peasant and Priest in the Cao Đài in Vietnam,* New Haven: Yale University Southeast Asia Studies.

Wiest, J.-P. (1999), "The Legacy of Vincent Lebbe," *International Bulletin of Mission Research* 23(1): 33–7.

Wilhite, D. E. (2017), *Ancient African Christianity,* London and New York: Routledge.

Willen, S. S. (2007), "Toward a Critical Phenomenology of 'Illegality': State Power, Criminalization, and Abjectivity among Undocumented Migrant Workers in Tel Aviv, Israel," *International Migration* 45(3): 8–38.

Willen, S. S. (2014), "Plotting a Moral Trajectory, Sans Papiers: Outlaw Motherhood as Inhabitable Space of Welcome." *Ethos* 42(1): 84–100.

Wilson, E. K. and L. Mavelli (2016), "The Refugee Crisis and Religion: Beyond Conceptual and Physical Boundaries," in L. Mavelli and E. K. Wilson (eds.), *The Refugee Crisis and Religion: Secularism, Security and Hospitality in Question,* 1–22, London and New York: Rowman & Littlefield International.

Wohlrab-Sahr, M. and M. Burchardt (2011), "Vielfätige Säkularitäten: Vorschlag zu einer vergleichenden Analyse religiös-säkularer Grenzziehungen," *Denkströme: Journal der Sächsischen Akademie der Wissenschaften zu Leipzig* 7: 53–71.

Wolf, B. (2007), *Die vietnamesische Diaspora in Deutschland: Struktur und Kooperationspotenzial mit Schwerpunkt auf Berlin und Hessen,* Eschborn: Deutsche Gesellschaft für Technische Zusammenarbeit (GTZ) GmbH.

Worbs, S., E. Bund, and A. Böhm (2016), "Asyl-und dann? Die Lebenssituation von Asylberechtigten und anerkannten Flüchtlingen in Deutschland: BAMF-Flüchtlingsstudie 2014," Bundesamt für Migration und Flüchtlinge.

Wunn, I. and H. Mohaghegh (2007), *Muslimische Gruppierungen in Deutschland: ein Handbuch,* Stuttgart: W. Kohlhammer Verlag.

Young, E. P. (2013), *Ecclesiastical Colony: China's Catholic Church and the French Religious Protectorate,* New York: Oxford University Press.

Yuval-Davis, N. (2006), "Belonging and the Politics of Belonging," *Patterns of Prejudice* 40(3): 197–214. https://doi.org/10.1080/00313220600769331

Zeghal, M. (2005), *Les islamistes marocains. Le défi à la monarchie,* Casablanca: Le Fennec.

Contributors

Johara Berriane (PhD in Islamic Studies) is researcher at the Centre Marc Bloch in Berlin. Her main research interests are the nexus of mobility and religion (Islam and Christianity) in African cities. She holds a PhD from the Freie Universität Berlin and was research fellow in Oxford, Rabat, Paris, and Dakar. In her current research, she studies the role of the Catholic Church in the governance of intra-African migrations in North and West Africa. She is the author of *Ahmad al-Tijânî de Fès: un sanctuaire soufi aux connexions transnationales* (2016).

Wayne P. te Brake (PhD in History, 1977) is Professor Emeritus of History at Purchase College, State University of New York. His broadly comparative work on social, political, and religious history includes *Shaping History: Ordinary People in European Politics, 1500-1700* (1998) and *Religious War and Religious Peace in Early Modern Europe* (2017). He is currently completing a manuscript entitled *Religious Peace: Historical Reflections on a Moral Imperative*.

Alessandro Gusman (PhD in Anthropology, 2009) is Assistant Professor of Anthropology at the University of Turin, Italy. His research focuses on the presence of Pentecostalism in Uganda and, more recently, on Congolese churches in Kampala and on end-of-life care in the Italian context. He is the author of the books *Pentecôtistes en Ouganda. Sida, moralité et conflit générationnel* (2018) and *Antropologia dell'olfatto* (Anthropology of Smell, 2004), and coeditor of *Strings Attached: Aids and the Rise of Transnational Connections in Africa* (2014). His work has appeared in several national and international journals.

Janet Alison Hoskins is Professor of Anthropology and Religion at the University of Southern California, Los Angeles. Her books include *The Divine Eye and the Diaspora: Vietnamese Syncretism Becomes Transpacific Caodaism* (2015), *The Play of Time: Kodi Perspectives on Calendars, History and Exchange* (1993), and *Biographical Objects: How Things Tell the Stories of People's Lives* (1998). She is the contributing editor of four books: *Transpacific Studies: Framing an Emerging Field* (with Viet Thanh Nguyen, University of Hawaii, 2014), *Headhunting and* *the Social Imagination in Southeast Asia* (1996), *A Space Between Oneself and Oneself: Anthropology as a Search for the Subject* (1999) and *Fragments from Forests and Libraries* (2001).

Nga T. Mai is a doctoral candidate at the University of Amsterdam, the Netherlands, and a researcher at Max Planck Institute for the Study of Religious and Ethnic Diversity in Göttingen, Germany. She is interested in Vietnamese immigration in Germany. Her current project examines how migrants' intimate relationships and self-perception are mediated by the question of migration legality and legalization processes.

Birgit Meyer (PhD in Anthropology, 1995) is Professor of Religious Studies at Utrecht University, the Netherlands. Trained as a cultural anthropologist, she studies religion from a material and postcolonial angle, seeking to synthesize grounded fieldwork and theoretical reflection in a multidisciplinary setting. Recent publications include *Sensational Movies: Video, Vision and Christianity in Ghana* (2015), *Creativity in Transition: Politics and Aesthetics of Cultural Production across the Globe* (2016, coedited with Maruška Svašek), *Taking Offense: Religion, Art and Visual Culture in Plural Settings* (2018, coedited with Christiane Kruse and Anne-Marie Korte), *Sense and Essence: Heritage and the Cultural Construction of the Real* (2018, coedited with Mattijs van de Port), and *Figuration and Sensations of the Unseen in Judaism, Christianity and Islam: Contested Desires* (2019, coedited with Terje Stordalen). She directs the research program *Religious Matters in an Entangled World* (religiousmatters.nl).

Heleen Murre-van den Berg (PhD, Leiden, 1995) is Professor of Global Christianity, Director of the Institute of Eastern Christian Studies, and Vice Dean of the Faculty of Philosophy, Theology, and Religious Studies at Radboud University, Nijmegen. Recent publications include *Scribes and Scriptures: The Church of the East in the Eastern Ottoman Provinces (1500-1850)* (2015) and the edited volume (with Tijmen Baarda and Karène Sanchez), *Arabic and its Alternatives: Religious Minorities and their Languages in the Emerging Nation States of the Middle East (1920-1950)* (2020). Currently, she directs an ERC-funded project, "Rewriting Global Orthodoxy: Oriental Christians in Europe (1970–2020)."

Alexander-Kenneth Nagel (PhD in Sociology, 2008) is Professor for the Social Scientific Study of Religion at the University of Göttingen, Germany. His research has focused on migration and religious pluralization, faith-based welfare production, and contemporary apocalypticism. Recent publications include a special issue of *Social Compass on Interreligious Relations and Governance of Religion in Europe* (2018, coedited with Mar Griera), an edited volume on the *Civic Potentials of Religious Immigrant Communities* (2015), and several articles and reports on the religious backgrounds of refugee reception in Germany.

Phi-Vân Nguyen is an assistant professor of History at the Université de Saint-Boniface. She was trained in Geneva and London, before receiving her PhD from the Université du Québec à Montréal in 2015. Her research interests focus on war, migration, religion, and politics in Vietnam. Her work has been published in *The Journal of Asian Studies, French Colonial History* and *SOJOURN*. She is currently creating a website on a conference held in July 1979 on the Southeast Asian refugee crisis. She is also preparing a book manuscript tentatively entitled *Voting with their Feet, How the 1954 Vietnamese Migrants Became Cold War Refugees, 1954–1995*.

Thien-Huong Ninh is Professor in the Sociology Department at Cosumnes River College. She studies religious transnationalism and globalization, focusing on the cases of Vietnamese Catholic and Caodai refugees and East Asian new religious movements (Caodaism and Daesoon Jinrihoe). Her recent publications include *Race, Religion, and Gender in the Vietnamese Diaspora: The Chosen People* (2017) and "Global Chain of Marianism: Diasporic Formation among Vietnamese Catholics in the U.S. and Cambodia," which appeared in the *Journal of Vietnamese Studies* special issue on "Globalizing Vietnamese Religions" that she coedited with Janet Hoskins.

Tam T. T. Ngo (PhD in Social Anthropology, 2011) is a senior researcher at the NIOD Institute for War, Holocaust and Genocide Studies (Amsterdam, the Netherlands) and the Max Planck Institute for the Study of Religious and Ethnic Diversity (Göttingen, Germany). Her research interests are religious changes, the dialogues between spiritualism and sciences, and memory politics in postwar late socialist Vietnam and among the Vietnamese diasporas in Germany using anthropological methods and discourse analysis. At the NIOD, she is leading a research project, "Bones of Contention: Technologies of Identification and Politics of Reconciliation in Vietnam," which investigates the use of spiritual and DNA forensics to find and identify war dead in Vietnam and its implication for the country's reconciliation politics. She is the author of *The New Way: Protestantism and the Hmong in Vietnam* (2016).

Salah Punathil (PhD in Sociology) is Assistant Professor at the Centre for Regional Studies, University of Hyderabad, India. Between July 2018 and June 2020, he was a postdoctoral fellow at the Max Planck Institute for the Study of Religious and Ethnic Diversity, Göttingen, Germany. His research interests include ethnic violence, migration, citizenship, Muslims in South Asia, and the intersection of archives and ethnography. His book *Interrogating Communalism: Violence, Citizenship and Minorities in South India* was published in 2019. Salah is the recipient of M. N. Srinivas Award for Young Indian Sociologist, 2015. Salah's current research focuses on the migration of Muslims from the present-day Bangladesh region to the North East India and the crisis of citizenship and ethnic violence in contemporary time. While historicizing the migration question in South Asia, his work aims to explore how national and ethnic boundaries affect the everyday lives of migrant communities.

Abdoulaye Sounaye is a senior research fellow and leads the Contested Religion unit at the Leibniz Zentrum Moderner Orient of Berlin, Germany. His current project ("Remoboko: Religion, Morality and Boko in West Africa: Students Training for a Good Life") examines religiosity on university campuses in Niger and Nigeria, focusing on Salafism and Pentecostalism. His academic interests lie in the critical examination of the contemporary dynamics and articulations of the complex religion, state, and society. He has published extensively on Salafism in Niger. His most recent book, *Islam et Modernité: Contribution à l'Analyse de la Ré-Islamisation au Niger*, éditions l'Harmattan, was published in 2016.

Peter van der Veer is Director at the Max Planck Institute for the Study of Religious and Ethnic Diversity in Göttingen, Germany, and University Professor Emeritus at Utrecht University. He is a fellow of the Royal Netherlands Academy of Arts and Sciences. He works on the comparative study of religion and nationalism. Among his major recent publications are *The Modern Spirit of Asia* (2014) and *The Value of Comparison* (2016).

William Wheeler holds a PhD from the Anthropology Department, Goldsmiths College, University of London, and is now a Leverhulme Early Career Fellow in Social Anthropology at the University of Manchester. His current research project examines how asylum seekers in the UK seek to move forward with their lives while negotiating protracted legal struggles and extended periods of destitution.

Index

Printed in Great Britain
by Amazon

53667499R00192